# Writer's Choice

## COMPOSITION AND GRAMMAR

# Case Studies: Writers at Work

**Keith Webb,
Maisha Maurant,
Nunzio Lupo**
Detroit Free
Press *Team*
*Pages 42-47*

**T. Ernesto Bethancourt**
*Novelist*
*Pages 142-147*

**Ella Jenkins**
*Songwriter*
*Pages 4-9*

**Judy Rand**
*Science Editor*
*Pages 188-193*

**Dr. Benjamin
S. Carson**
*Public Speaker*
*Pages 250-255*

**Zilpha
Keatley
Snyder**
*Fantasy Writer*
*Pages 100-105*

## Student Advisory Board

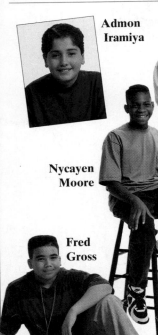

**Admon
Iramiya**

**Phildonna
Ratliff**

**Amanda
Mason**

**Arti
Patel**

**Monica
Vera**

**Nycayen
Moore**

**Maria
Concepción**

**Fred
Gross**

**Alina
Braica**

**Trina
Chu**

**Seema
Panjwani**

**Jeffery
Johnson**

# Writer's Choice

## COMPOSITION AND GRAMMAR

Paul Gauguin, *The Meal*, 1891

*Consulting Author for Composition*
**Jacqueline Jones Royster**

*Grammar Specialist*
**Mark Lester**

*Visual-Verbal Learning Specialists*
**Ligature, Inc.**

*GLENCOE*

Macmillan/McGraw-Hill

New York, New York     Columbus, Ohio     Mission Hills, California     Peoria, Illinois

Copyright © 1994 by the Glencoe Division of Macmillan/McGraw-Hill School Publishing Company. All rights reserved. Except as permitted under the United States Copyright Act, no part of this publication may be reproduced or distributed in any form or by any means, or stored in a database or retrieval system, without prior written permission from the publisher.

Printed in the United States of America.

Send all inquires to:
Glencoe/McGraw-Hill
15319 Chatsworth Street
P.O. Box 9609
Mission Hills, CA
91346-9609

ISBN 0-02-635735-6
(Student's Edition)
(ISBN 0-02-635736-4
Teacher's Wraparound
Edition)

3  4  5  6  7  8  9  10   VHJ
99  98  97  96  95  94

## Consulting Author for Composition

**Jacqueline Jones Royster** is Associate Professor of English and Director of the University Writing Center at The Ohio State University. She is also on the faculty at the Bread Loaf School of English, Middlebury, Vermont. Dr. Royster's professional interests, besides improving the teaching of writing, include literacy studies and black feminist literature.

As Consulting Author, Dr. Royster guided the development of focused, modular lessons to engage middle school students in the writing process. She contributed to the articulation of the contents and objectives across all three levels, 6–8. Dr. Royster also prepared extensive critiques of lessons and features from initial outlines through all stages of development. In addition, Dr. Royster advised on elements of the accompanying teaching material, with special attention to assessment.

## Grammar Specialist

**Mark Lester** is Professor of English at Eastern Washington University. He formerly served as Chair of the Department of English as a Second Language, University of Hawaii. He is the author of *Grammar in the Classroom* (Macmillan, 1990) and of numerous professional books and articles.

As Grammar Specialist, Dr. Lester reviewed student's edition material from Part 2: Grammar, Usage, and Mechanics. He wrote the Grammar Hints that appear throughout this section. In addition, Dr. Lester contributed extensively to the *Teacher's Wraparound Edition* for Part 2.

## Composition Advisers

**Philip M. Anderson** is Associate Professor in the Department of Secondary Education and Youth Services at Queens College, City University of New York, where he is also Director of the English Education program.

**Beverly Ann Chin** is Professor of English at the University of Montana, where she is Director of Freshman Composition and Co-director of English Teacher Education. She is also Director of the Montana Writing Project.

**Charleen Silva Delfino** is District English Coordinator for the East Side Union High School District in San Jose, California. She is also Director of the Writing Project at San Jose University.

The advisers helped develop the tables of contents and determine pacing, emphasis, and activities appropriate for middle school students. They reviewed and commented on the manuscript for complete units.

## Acknowledgments

Grateful acknowledgment is given authors, publishers, photographers, museums, and agents for permission to reprint the following copyrighted material. Every effort has been made to determine copyright owners. In case of omissions, the Publisher will make acknowledgments in future editions.
*Continued on page 679*

## Humanities Consultant

**Ronne Hartfield** is Executive Director of Museum Education at the Art Institute of Chicago. Dr. Hartfield consults widely and is a nationally known expert in the areas of urban arts and multicultural education.

As Humanities Consultant, Dr. Hartfield suggested and critiqued works of fine art and folk art, pointing out esthetic matters (mentioned in the *Teacher's Wraparound Edition*) and suggesting activities for engaging the student's attention.

## Visual-Verbal Learning Specialists

**Ligature, Inc.**, is an educational research and development company with offices in Chicago and Boston. Ligature is committed to developing educational materials that bring visual-verbal learning to the tradition of the written word.

As visual-verbal and curriculum specialists, Ligature collaborated on conceiving and implementing the pedagogy of *Writer's Choice*.

## Educational Reviewers

The reviewers read and commented upon manuscripts during the writing process. They also critiqued early drafts of graphic organizers and page layouts.

Toni Elaine Allison
Meridian Middle School
Meridian, Idaho

Amy Burton
Sterling Middle School
Fairfax, Virginia

Mary Ann Evans-Patrick
University of Wisconsin, Oshkosh
Oshkosh, Wisconsin

Marie Hammerle
Oak Creek Elementary School
Cornville, Arizona

Randy Hanson
Mapplewood Middle School
Menasha, Wisconsin

Geraldine Jackson
Mountain Gap Middle School
Huntsville, Alabama

Jeanne Kruger
Blair Middle School
Norfolk, Virginia

Diana McNeil
Pillans Middle School
Mobile, Alabama

Linda Miller
Lake Travis Middle School
Austin, Texas

Nadine Mouser
St. Thomas More School
Houston, Texas

Roslyn Newman
Woodland Middle School
East Meadow, New York

Evelyn Niles
Boys and Girls High School
Booklyn, New York

Janet E. Ring
Dundee School District 300
Carpentersville, Illinois

Kathleen Oldfield
Main Street School
Waterloo, New York

## Student Advisory Board

The Student Advisory Board was formed in an effort to ensure student involvement in the development of *Writer's Choice*. The editors wish to thank members of the board for their enthusiasm and dedication to the project.

The editors also wish to thank the many student writers whose models appear in this book.

Thanks are also due to *Merlyn's Pen* and *Cricket* for cooperation in providing student models.

# Writer's Choice
## COMPOSITION AND GRAMMAR

*Writer's Choice was written for you, the student writer. You're the writer in the title, and real students like you contributed to the materials you'll study. The book is organized into three main parts: (1) Composition; (2) Grammar, Usage, and Mechanics; and (3) Resources and Skills.*

## Part 1   Composition

*The lessons in Composition are designed to give you help with specific writing tasks. You can use the units and lessons in order from beginning to end or select just the ones that help with your own writing needs.*

# Part 2   Grammar, Usage, and Mechanics

*In the unique Troubleshooter you'll learn to identify and correct the most common student writing problems. In later units you'll find plenty of practice to reinforce what you learn. A special unit, entitled Grammar Through Sentence Combining, will help you see the relationship between grammar and your writing.*

# Part 3   Resources and Skills

*You can use these resources and skills not just in English class but wherever you need to communicate effectively. The tone and approach are user-friendly, with many opportunities to practice and apply the skills you learn.*

# Contents

# CONTENTS

# CONTENTS

# Part 2  Grammar, Usage, and Mechanics

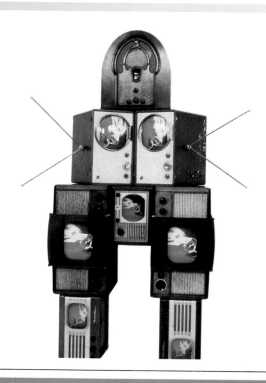

# CONTENTS

xiii

# CONTENTS

# Part 3  Resources and Skills

# Literature

Each literature selection is an extended example of the mode of writing taught in the unit.

# Literature Models

Excerpts from outstanding works of fiction and nonfiction exemplify specific writing skills.

# Workshop Literature

Each workshop uses an excerpt from a novel or long work of nonfiction to link grammar, usage, or mechanics to literature.

# Case Studies

Each case study focuses on a real writer working on a real-life writing project. Come on backstage!

# Fine Art

Fine art—paintings, drawings, photos, and sculpture—is used to teach as well as to inspire.

# Writer's Choice

## COMPOSITION AND GRAMMAR

**W**elcome to Writer's Choice! *Your writing and your choices are what this book is all about. This book allows you to choose quickly the lesson that will help you with a writing problem or task. You can use any lesson at any time—even if you haven't read earlier lessons. Now, take a few minutes to get to know each of the main parts of the book, which are illustrated on the upcoming pages.*

# Part 1 Composition

*Unit Opener*

*Case Study*

# Part 2 Grammar, Usage, and Mechanics

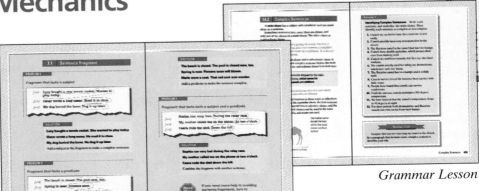

*Troubleshooter*

*Grammar Lesson*

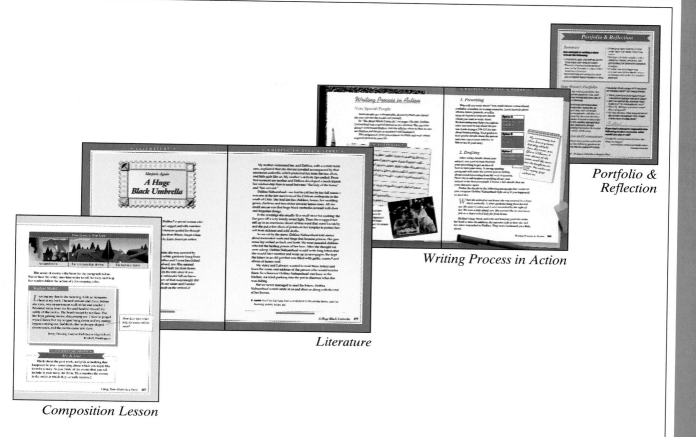

Portfolio &
Reflection

Writing Process in Action

Literature

Composition Lesson

# Part 3   Resources and Skills

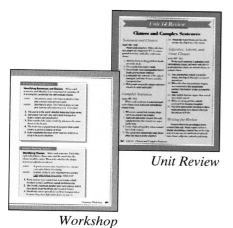

Unit Review

Workshop

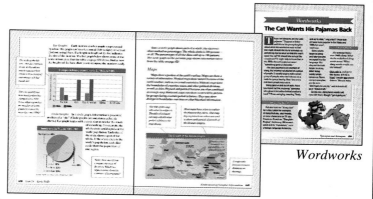

Wordworks

Resources and Skills Lesson

# Inside Composition

The basic building block of the Composition units is the four-page lesson. Each lesson clearly focuses on a specific writing problem or task. You will always find clear and specific instruction, models of effective writing, and a variety of writing activities.

**Writing Process Tips** help you connect the skills you're learning to other stages of the writing process.

### And Then . . .

Certain words and phrases, called transitions, can help readers keep track of the order of events in your writing. Some examples of transitions include *before, after, until then, next, first,* and *finally.*

Read the story below. Then reread it, paying attention to the highlighted words. What do the transitions add to the story?

**Grammar**
**Editing Tip**

When you edit, be sure that story events don't jump unnecessarily from past to present tense. See pages 366–367 to review verb tenses.

What does the transition phrase "until then" tell the reader?

**Literature Model**

When John Cowles and his wife and baby moved to Wisconsin in 1843, they built a one-room cabin to live in. All the cabin needed was a front door. That was due to arrive before the weather turned cold. Until then they had hung a heavy quilt over the doorway.

John Cowles was a doctor. One night before supper, a messenger came for him. Someone was sick on a farm about twelve miles away. "I'll be home tonight or tomorrow morning," he told his wife. He quickly packed his things and rode off into the darkness.

His wife left a pot of beans simmering on the hearth in case he was hungry when he got home. Then she got into bed with her baby and went to sleep.

Sometime during the night, Mrs. Cowles awakened. She sensed that someone was in the cabin with her, probably her husband. But when she opened her

**Literature Models** help you learn from the pros. You'll see how published authors have met the writing challenges you face.

Personal Journal

## 4.3  Using Time Order in a Story

### Which Came First?

"Which came first, the chicken or the egg?" As you probably know, there is no right or wrong answer to this riddle. You may have a good answer for why the egg came first. Someone else may have an equally good answer for why the chicken came before the egg.

Just as there is no one right answer to this question, there is no one right way to tell a story. As a writer, you decide which event in your story comes first. It could be when the character wakes up, when she rushes out of her apartment, when she reaches the train station, or when she realizes her wallet is missing. However, you do want to tell events in an order that will make sense to your readers.

### First . . .

A good way to help your readers follow your story is to use time order, the order in which events occur. Making a list of story events in time order will also help you plan your story. Look at the illustration at the top of the next page. It shows a series of events arranged in time order.

**W**riter's Choice Pages give you a choice of writing activities to help you apply what you have learned. You'll also find fine art or a special feature on using computers in writing.

• WRITER'S CHOICE •

## Activities

Here are some activities to help you apply what you have learned.

**1. Guided Assignment**

You are a mystery writer. You are using the painting on this page to come up with ideas for your next story. What happened before this scene? What's happening at the moment? What might happen after? Brainstorm plot and character ideas based on this painting. Then draft your story. Be sure to use transition words to indicate time relationships.

PURPOSE  To write a mystery story
AUDIENCE  Mystery story readers
LENGTH  1–2 pages

**2. Open Assignment**

Look in your journal at the entry for the activity on

**3. Science**

Suppose that your science class has started a tutoring program for third-grade students. Part of the program involves teaching through stories. You have been asked to write a story about a lesson on a science topic of your choice. For example, you might write a story to teach students how a plant grows.

Write a one- or two-page story that will be engaging for younger students. Remember to use characters, plot, and setting to create your story. Be sure you use time order and transition words to relate events.

Alex Colville, *Taxi*, 1985

**S**pecial Illustrations combine words with images to help you *see* ideas and master the skills of writing. We call these illustrations visual/verbals.

Story Events in Time Order

Fox sees the fire.  Fox runs away from the fire.  Fox reaches a ravine.

*a Story*  **159**

This series of events is the basis for the paragraph below. Notice how the writer uses time order to tell the story and help er readers follow the action of a fox escaping a fire.

**Student Model**

*L*eaving my den in the morning, I felt an immense heat at my back. I turned around and there, before my eyes, was an enormous wall of fire and smoke! I bounded away from the fire and headed toward the safety of the ravine. The brush swept by my face. The fire kept gaining on me, threatening me. I tried to propel myself faster, but my tongue hung down and my energy began running out. Suddenly, the landscape sloped downwards, and the ravine came into view.

*How does time order help the writer tell the story?*

Jenny DeLong, Canyon Park Junior High School, Botthell, Washington

**S**tudent Models present writing by students like you to help you achieve your own writing goals.

• JOURNAL ACTIVITY •

## Try It Out

Think about the past week, and pick something that happened to you---something about which you might like to write a story. As you think of the events that you will include in your story, list them. Then number the events in the order in which they actually occurred.

**J**ournal Activity, at the bottom of the second page of every lesson, gives you a chance to reflect and respond to the lesson material.

*Using Time Order in a Story*  **157**

# Inside Grammar

**T**his grammar handbook works for you, not the other way around. You'll learn how to find and fix errors in your writing. Two special sections—the Troubleshooter and the Workshops—help you expand your grammar skills.

**T**he Troubleshooter presents in one place the solutions to the nine errors most frequently made by student writers. Your teacher may refer you to the Troubleshooter by marking errors in your writing with the abbreviations shown down the far left side of the page.

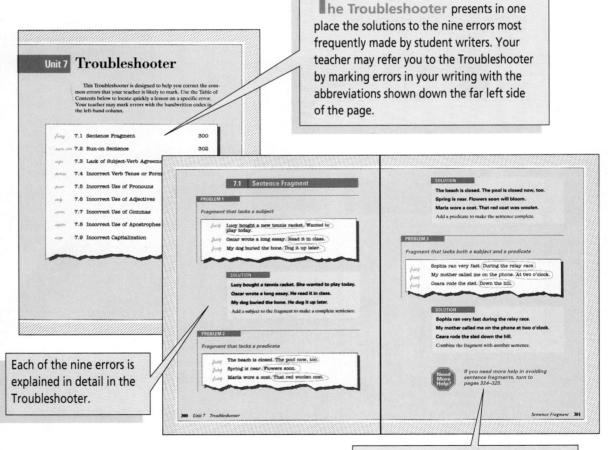

Each of the nine errors is explained in detail in the Troubleshooter.

For each common error, the Troubleshooter shows you the solution. If you need more help, the Troubleshooter also refers you to the appropriate lesson.

**G**rammar Lessons present instructions on the left-hand page and practical exercises on the right-hand page.

**V**isuals such as computer-generated art and photographs work for you, showing important grammar concepts visually and verbally.

**T**he Workshop at the end of each unit presents exercises based on a selection from a novel or other work of literature.

---

### 14.2 Complex Sentences

A **main clause** has a subject and a predicate and can stand alone as a sentence.

Sometimes sentences have more than one clause, and only one of the clauses is a main clause. The other clause is a subordinate clause.

A **subordinate clause** is a group of words that has a subject and a predicate but does not express a complete thought and cannot stand alone as a sentence. It is always combined with a main clause.

A sentence with a main clause and a subordinate clause is a complex sentence. In each complex sentence below, the main clause is in light type, and the subordinate clause is in dark type.

> When the sun set, the caravans stopped for the night.
> The dromedary has one hump, **which stores fat.**
> Most people know **that camels are stubborn.**

A **complex sentence** is a sentence that has one main clause and one or more subordinate clauses.

Subordinate clauses can function in three ways: as adjectives, as adverbs, or as nouns. In the examples above, the first sentence has an adverb clause, the second has an adjective clause, and the third has a noun clause. Such clauses can be used in the same ways that adjectives, adverbs, and nouns are used.

The mother camel carried the load, while the baby camel walked behind.

MAIN CLAUSE          SUBORDINATE CLAUSE

450  Unit 14  Clauses and Complex Sentences

---

**Exercise 3**

**Identifying Complex Sentences**  Write each sentence, and underline the main clause. Then identify each sentence as *complex* or *not complex.*

1. Camels are useful because they cross the desert easily.
2. Camels provide necessary transportation in the desert.
3. The Bactrian camel is the camel that has two humps.
4. Camels have double eyelashes, which protect their eyes from blowing sand.
5. Camels are stubborn animals, but they are also hard workers.
6. The camels usually used for riding are dromedaries, which have only one hump.
7. The Bactrian camel has two humps and is solidly built.
8. Camels survive desert life because they can live with little water.
9. People have found that camels can survive sandstorms.
10. Until the sun sets, camels maintain a 105-degree temperature.
11. We have learned that the camel's temperature drops to 93 degrees at night.
12. For short periods both dromedaries and Bactrian camels can exist on fat from their humps.

*Writing Link*

Imagine that you are traveling by camel in the desert. In a paragraph that includes some complex sentences, describe your trip.

*Complex Sentences*  451

---

### *Grammar* Workshop

### Prepositions, Conjunctions, and Interjections

This Chinese-American folk tale tells the story of a painted horse that comes to life. The passage has been annotated to show some of the parts of speech covered in this unit.

*Literature Model*

from THE MAGICAL HORSE

*by Laurence Yep*

As the boy sat with his body aching from the hard work and eating his cold rice, he gazed up at the painting. His father had caught the horse as if it were suspended upon one hoof. And as he watched, the horse's sides seemed to heave in the moonlight—as if it were breathing in the incense. On a whim, Sunny set out feed for his painted horse just as he did for the other animals.

He slept among the beasts for warmth, so he was not surprised when he felt an animal's warm breath blow on him. When a nose nudged him, he sat up irritated, intending to shove the creature away, but his hand paused in the air.

By the light of the moon, he saw a silvery horse standing over him. He looked over at the wall where the painting had been and saw that the canvas was empty. The next thing he knew, he was on the back of the horse, his hands clinging to the flying mane, the horse's hooves booming rhythmically along a road that gleamed like a silver ribbon winding up into the sky.

Prepositional phrase (adverb phrase)

Pronoun as subject of the preposition *on*

Prepositional phrase (adjective phrase)

Coordinating conjunction

442   Unit 13  Grammar Workshop

---

**Grammar Workshop Exercise 1**

**Using Prepositions**  The following sentences are based on the passage from "The Magical Horse." Rewrite each sentence, inserting the correct prepositional phrase in parentheses.

1. The horse (on the canvas, with the canvas) seemed to be breathing.
2. Sunny set out food (for he, for him).
3. The boy lay down and slept (among the animals, between the animals).
4. When he woke up, the empty canvas stood (in the wall, against the wall).
5. The horse and the boy galloped (down the road, through the road).

**Grammar Workshop Exercise 2**

**Using Conjunctions**  Rewrite each sentence, inserting the most appropriate conjunction (word or word pair) in the blank or blanks provided.

SAMPLE    The father wanted to create a perfect horse, _____ he painted without resting.

ANSWER    The father wanted to create a perfect horse, and so he painted without resting.

1. When the painting was finished, _____ Sunny _____ his father admired the magnificent horse.
2. _____ Sunny _____ his father knew that the horse would come to life.
3. The father was old _____ tired from hard work.
4. The painter died, _____ his spirit entered into the horse in the painting.
5. Sunny _____ buried his father, _____ _____ earned the money for the funeral.

*Prepositions, Conjunctions, and Interjections*  443

---

# Inside Resources

The lessons in this unit give you the skills necessary to prepare and deliver an oral report, take a test, use a dictionary, and find books in the library. Each lesson is complete, concise, and easy to use.

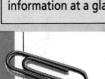

**G**raphics help you understand complex information at a glance.

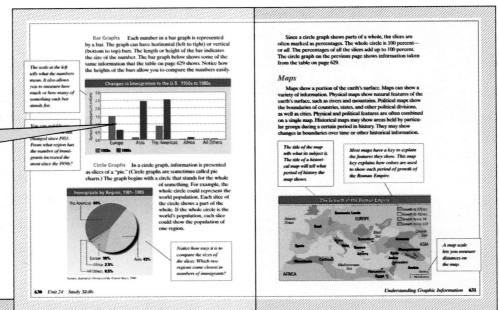

**W**ordworks pages like this one provide a light-hearted look at the origins of the English language as well as some of the quirks. These features appear in the vocabulary and spelling unit and will help you master the concepts taught there.

# Part 1
# Composition

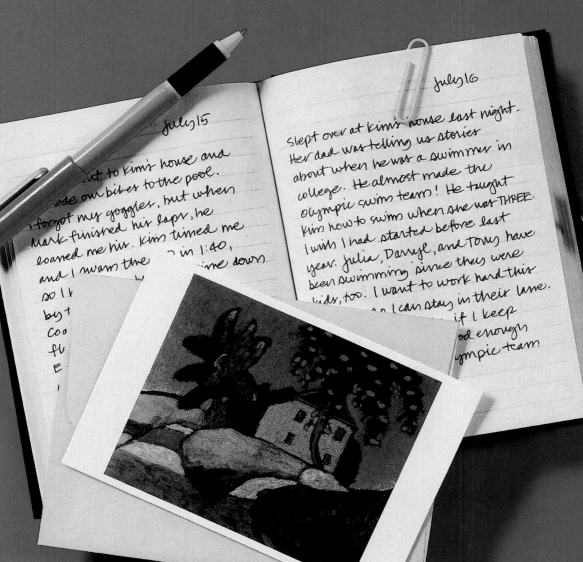

# Part 1 Composition

# Personal Writing

# Celebrate Yourself

Simone Bouyer, *Peace Posse*, 1990

# JENKINS CELEBRATES LIFE

> *"Personal writing should be something you do on a regular basis because that improves your skill and puts you in tune with yourself. Pretty soon you won't have just letters and words on the page but something very warm and alive—something that can bounce off to someone else."*
>
> Ella Jenkins

I n the Bahamas, singer and songwriter Ella Jenkins found a magical scene. Men played calypso, people danced, and children played. "Amidst all the things that were happening, the ocean had the loudest roar." She wrote about those ocean sounds in *Come Dance by the Ocean,* a record album with a message about planet Earth. Like other albums Jenkins has produced over the past thirty-five years, this one celebrates the islands, cultures, living things, and oceans of our world.

**Writing a Song**

1. Seeing Other Lands    2. Gathering Ideas    3. Writing to Celebrate

### FOCUS

Celebrating wonderful moments and important ideas—that's one joy of personal writing.

## 1 Seeing Other Lands

In writing the album *Come Dance by the Ocean,* Jenkins expressed her feelings about many things she loves. She wrote about the excitement of traveling by plane, the wonder of seeing different lands and animals, and the joy of encountering the world's amazing variety of people and cultures.

Music has been a natural part of Jenkins's life for as long as she can remember. "As a child I tried to add melodies to rhymes I heard," she said.

Jenkins's interests broadened as she went through school. In high school she studied Spanish, her first step into another culture. "I loved the way it sounds," she said.

In college Cuban musicians taught Jenkins to play conga drums and maracas. At the same time she read about other cultures and listened to songs from Africa, India, Egypt, and other lands. By her mid-thirties, Jenkins was carrying her

▼ *As a student, Jenkins learned to play musical instruments from other lands.*

5

message to young people through music. "You have to respect that other people come from other places," she said. "They're trying to learn about you, and you want to learn about them."

**INTERFACE** *Make a list of joyous experiences—dancing, singing, camping, walking in new snow, winning a race. What made the experience joyous for you? Which one would you like to write about?*

## 2 Gathering Ideas

▼ *For Ella Jenkins keeping personal notes in her "Random Thoughts" notebooks is a key part of her writing process.*

When Jenkins began creating *Come Dance by the Ocean,* she looked for ideas in a collection of personal notebooks. She said, "I keep notebooks when I travel called 'Random Thoughts.' I use them to jot down notes about things that strike me."

When Jenkins wanted to gather her ideas, the notes from "Random Thoughts" helped. Her notes also provided material for the poem "A Winter Plane Ride."

Jenkins wrote the notes that inspired this poem on a flight from Portland, Oregon, to Chicago. "It was so exciting to see the differences between one part of the country and another," she said. "I could have written a lot of little things that I was seeing, but all of a sudden I heard this voice, the pleasant voice of the pilot telling

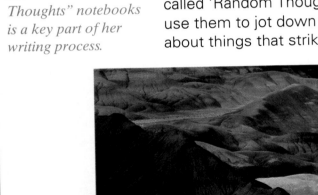

Some people
Never smile at all
Some people
Always frown
Some people
Never bounce a ball
Some people
Are always down

PARIS - 7-9-65
by Ella Jenkins

"Come Dance by the Ocean"

Early this morning when I looked out,
I saw some dolphins playing about.
One chased two, then two chased one.
I'd say that all three had an ocean of fun.
Come on, come dance by the ocean.
Come on, come dance by the sea.
Come on, come dance by the ocean.
Come on, come dance with me.

us about the sights. You'd have thought I was in class because I wrote down everything he said," she recalled.

Later these notes helped Jenkins capture the moment.

"Things grab you in life," she said. "No one experienced that plane ride as I did. Each person on that plane had a different experience, so no one could write about it as I did."

▲ *The ocean was the inspiration for Jenkins's song "Come Dance by the Ocean."*

## 3 Writing to Celebrate

Now Jenkins knew what ideas and feelings she was going to put in her album. The next step was figuring out the words and melodies for each song. The title song, "Come Dance by the Ocean," was easy. "I was remembering the music by the ocean, the steel drums," she said. "I loved the way they sounded

and how the head of the group invited us to come on and enjoy ourselves. And I thought, 'come on' is a good way of beckoning people."

Jenkins also had a melody in her head. So she hummed it into a tape recorder and then began putting words to the music. "First, I got my main ideas—all the things people were doing by the ocean. Then I tried fitting different words into the melody." Finally, Jenkins settled on an opening verse. With this playful song, she invited listeners to celebrate all the things we have in common—nature, music, new places, and people.

For her poem "A Winter Plane Ride" Jenkins used a free and informal style. In the poem Jenkins described her flight over snowy mountains and colorful canyons. She wrote:

*I see light blankets of snow*
*Lying gently upon the*
*mountaintops*
*Now the canyons are*
*coming—*
*Rippled ridges wrapped*
*around colors, cleverly*
*shouting*
*Yet not making a sound.*

With her song and her poem, Jenkins began her message: look around you, listen, and enjoy.

**INTERFACE** *Choose one experience from your list of joyous experiences. Write a few notes describing what happens and how you feel. If you were to turn these notes into a finished piece of writing, would it be a song? A poem? Why?*

▼ *Ella Jenkins travels the world sharing her love of music.*

ELLA · JENKINS
Come Dance By The Ocean

# ON ASSIGNMENT

## 1. Creative Writing

**Describe an important, joyous moment in your life.**

- Review the notes you made for the Interface on page 8. Then write a sentence summing up why you found the moment memorable.

- Choose a form in which to write a finished piece. It can be a story, a poem, a song—whatever you wish.

## 2. About Literature

**Explore the personal writing of a person you admire.**

- In the library look for books of letters, memoirs, poems, songs, or other personal writing by a person you admire.

- Read a few pages of the individual's personal writing.

- Keep notes of your responses to the personal writing you read.

## 3. Cooperative Learning

**Create an anthology of personal writing by you and your classmates.**

- Meet with a small group of students to talk about the personal writing each of you wrote for On Assignment 1. What subjects did you discuss?

- Exchange pieces, and offer suggestions for improvement.

- Revise your writing.

- As a group, meet to plan an introduction for your anthology. Decide on someone (or perhaps two people) to write the introduction. Also, have people type or print the pieces, find illustrations or photographs, lay out the pages, and create a cover.

- Meet as a group when you have a draft of the introduction and materials for the book. Review the introduction, and offer editing suggestions.

- When all the material is ready, assemble your book. Present it to the class.

*What Is Important to You?*

Jot down an answer to the question at the top of the page. Maybe your answer is like that of a student in the picture; maybe it's different. Whatever you write, it's about what matters to you.

Your conversations with friends are a way to explore what is important to you. Personal writing can do the same thing. Notes and lists you keep in a class journal help you make plans and think about assignments. Perhaps you keep a private journal as well. You decide if anyone else will read this kind of personal writing. You may also write letters and post cards to your friends and family. Maybe you write poetry or stories. These are usually meant to be shared, but they often begin as personal writing, too.

## Free to Be Me

The personal writing that you do for yourself gives you a way to express and explore your thoughts and feelings. When something incredible or upsetting occurs, put your reactions on paper. Write down ideas. Writing about your thoughts and feelings helps make them clearer to you.

While some kinds of personal writing are just for you, other kinds are meant to be shared. A letter to a friend, for example, is personal writing in which you share your thoughts and feelings with another person. The examples at the right and below show both kinds of personal writing.

Dear Lynn,

I wish we had never moved! It was so awful today. I got on the bus and didn't know anyone! All day long kids were staring at me. I felt like hiding in my locker or wearing a paper bag over my head.

I miss talking to you. I miss eating lunch with you. I even miss your jokes! Please write soon and tell me what's happening.

Your best friend,
Kara

July 12

Something happened tonight that I'll never forget. Everyone else was asleep. I walked a few yards from our camp and turned on my flashlight. Wherever I pointed the light, pairs of yellow eyes looked back. I never knew so many small animals lived in the woods right by our cabin. ... were really close and very ... ut

### • JOURNAL ACTIVITY •
### *Think It Through*

You have probably had many ideas and experiences today. In your journal list as many of these as you can recall. You can use some of these ideas for personal writing.

# In Your Own Words

The personal writing you do is like talking on paper. You can write informally, as you would talk. You can experiment by using words in an unexpected way or by expressing an unusual idea. You can even make up words.

One thought will lead to another. Follow thoughts wherever they may lead. Any subject might be worth writing about. You might even try a poem, story, or a letter you will never send.

Personal writing can be informal, and it can be fun. When you write for yourself, you don't have to worry about punctuation, spelling, or grammar—just ideas. The goal of personal writing is to use your own words and style to write about what is important to you. Read the model below to see how one student expressed herself.

## Student Model

*The writer uses everyday language to write about a personal subject: herself.*

*Do you think most people Nancy's age share her concerns?*

I am Nancy Young,
I remained at the age of twelve for too long,
I cannot wait until I reach the mere age of thirteen,
Drive a car,
Go to college,
Go to the prom,
And finally,
Own my own life. . . .
I just want feelings that I can express on paper. . . .
All I want is paper,
Pen and ink,
To bear down on,
Make an impression,
Of me.

Nancy McLaurin Young,
Savannah Country Day School,
Savannah, Georgia

# *Activities*

Here are some activities to help you apply what you have learned.

## 1. Guided Assignment

Study the sculpture on this page. A repository is a place to keep important items. In your journal write what you think about the sculpture. The questions below might help you with your writing:

- Do any items in the repository mean anything to you?
- What would you include in a repository of your own? Why?

PURPOSE   To tell about what is important to you and why

AUDIENCE   Yourself

LENGTH   1 page

## 2. Open Assignment

Imagine, ten years from now, opening a letter and finding a message you wrote to yourself when you were younger. Write a message to the person you will be in ten years. Include three things that are important to you now. The list you made for the Journal Activity may help you.

## 3. Music

Listen to a tape or CD of music you have never heard before. In a one-page message to a friend, tell what you think of the music and why you think your friend would or would not like it. These questions in the next column may help you explain your response:

- What does the music remind you of?
- Does the music suggest a mood? What is it?

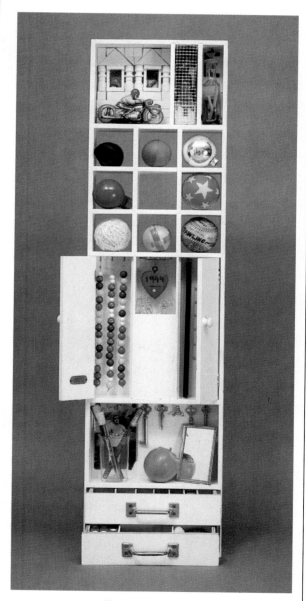

George Brecht, *Repository*, 1961

*Keeping Track*

**\*\*** Due Wednesday for Social Studies
Write letter to historic figure
from Inca civilization
—must be a real person
—ask figure about self
beliefs, accomplishments

**\*** Don't forget band practice again!

Think about it—Mom wants answer soon.
• Summer at home and work in the store?
• Summer with Uncle James?
• Summer computer classes at the high school?
May 17
May 18

Things to do:
1. Write story for English
2. Study for Math Test
3. Call Jason
4. Mow Yard, trim hedge
5. Buy new cleats

flute, director tapping on stand, laughing kids
hard chairs, pinched finger from music stand
Sounds
Touch
Band Practice
Smells
Sights
Tastes
peanut butter somebody ate at lunch
tubas, big drums
cold water, reed for my oboe

This notebook holds a few examples of a kind of writing that may never be seen by anyone except the writer. A quick look will help you understand how common and useful such writing is. Think about the content of each of the examples. Consider the purpose the writer might have had for writing. Look at the form the writer decided to use in each case. What other forms of writing can people use when they write just for themselves?

# Day by Day

The French word for *day* is *jour.* A word that comes from *jour* is *journal.* Your journal is a place for daily writing. It is your space for exploring ideas and keeping track of information. You may record the events of your day and your reactions to them. The writer of the computer journal below used her journal to express how she feels about something she thought of one day. You may also list writing ideas that come to you. Reread your journal often. Think about what you have written. Try out some of your writing ideas.

## Journal Writing Tips

1. Try to write in your journal every day.

2. Date journal entries for future reference.

3. Write whatever comes to mind.

4. Use any form that feels comfortable.

April 3

Sometimes I'm kind of scared about growing up. I haven't the slightest idea what I want to be. Dad says not to worry about it. He says some grown-ups don't know what they want to be when they grow up either.

**HELP**

## • JOURNAL ACTIVITY •
### Try It Out

Write in your journal for at least five minutes a day for a week. At the end of the week, read your entries. In your journal make one observation about any entry that seems interesting.

## *Facts and Questions*

When you want to discover more about something you've covered in a class, you may use your journal as a learning log. A learning log is a place to write comments on what you are studying and to jot down questions you want to ask. You can use your journal for this purpose or keep a separate notebook as a log. Study the page below on which one student listed information about an early civilization. Observe that the notes are informal and personal. Think about how you can use a log to respond to what you are learning.

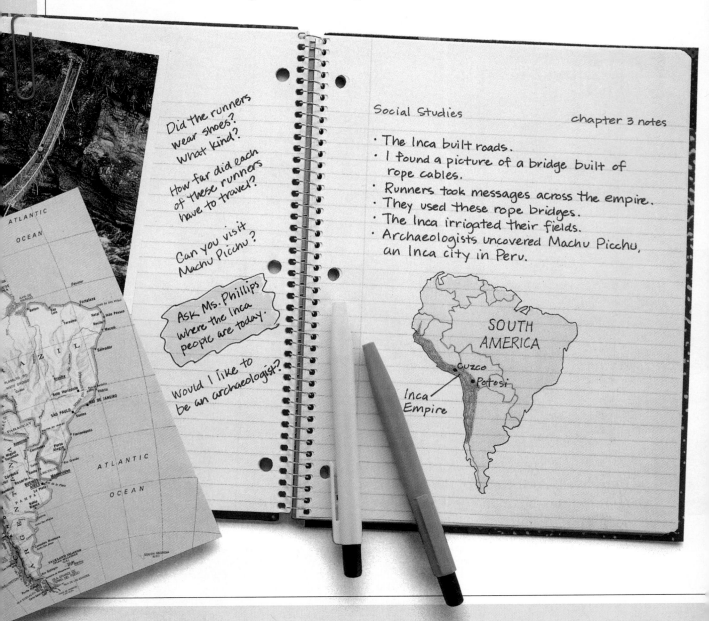

Did the runners wear shoes? What kind?

How far did each of these runners have to travel?

Can you visit Machu Picchu?

Ask Ms. Phillips where the Inca people are today.

Would I like to be an archaeologist?

Social Studies                                    chapter 3 notes

- The Inca built roads.
- I found a picture of a bridge built of rope cables.
- Runners took messages across the empire.
- They used these rope bridges.
- The Inca irrigated their fields.
- Archaeologists uncovered Machu Picchu, an Inca city in Peru.

SOUTH AMERICA

Cuzco
Potosi
Inca Empire

# Activities

Here are some activities to help you apply what you have learned.

### 1. Guided Assignment

Make a list of all the things you like about yourself, such as your ability to make friends or the soft spot you have in your heart for animals. Remember that no one has to see this list but you. Be honest with yourself. Make it a long list, and include examples.

Use your list to help write a journal entry one to two pages long. Call it "Why I Like Myself." Write freely, putting down whatever comes to mind. Remember you can check spelling, punctuation, and grammar later. Now is the time to think and write.

PURPOSE    To get to know yourself
AUDIENCE   Yourself
LENGTH     1 to 2 pages

### COMPUTER OPTION

If you decide to use a computer as an electronic journal, you can create separate files for different types of writing. For example, one file can be a record of daily activities. You can decide to store writing ideas in a second file. In another file you can explore private thoughts and feelings. If you are concerned about privacy, you can create your files on disk and keep it in a safe place.

### 2. Open Assignment

Write something that you think is important and meaningful about yourself. Your writing may be in the form of a letter, a journal entry, or a poem. Choose an audience for what you write. You may write for a real person, such as a friend, teacher, or parent. Or you can write for an imaginary person, a historical figure, or a fictional character. Use one of the following ideas, or create one of your own.

- The best thing I ever did . . .
- I'd rather be . . .
- The truth is . . .
- I'm good at . . .
- I admire . . .

### 3. Cooperative Learning

Work with a small group of your classmates to learn more about a specific topic. List possible topics of interest, such as horses or skyscrapers, on the board. Choose the one topic that all of you would like to find out more about. Make a list of questions about the topic. Let each person contribute a question he or she would like to have answered. Write your question in your learning log, find the answer, and write a paragraph or two to answer the question. Share your answers to allow everyone to take notes in their learning logs.

## You're Invited!

Dear Alan,
Get out your baseball cap. We're
going to a game to celebrate
my birthday. Meet at my house
at 11:30 Saturday, May 12th.
A barbecue will follow.
                 Hope to see you there!
                       Jih-Sheng
   R.S.V.P.

Nearly everybody likes to celebrate, and birthdays are one occasion for a party. Greeting card companies sell convenient, fill-in-the-blank invitations for a variety of occasions. However, if you want that personal touch, you can write your own. A handwritten invitation to a celebration is a familiar type of personal writing. Read the invitation Alan received from Jih-Sheng. It is handwritten and includes all the information Alan needs to know about the birthday celebration.

Think of the special occasions that you and your family enjoy celebrating. Which ones might call for invitations?

# Good News and Good Times

The notes and cards on the bulletin board below are important to the person who saved them. Some of them will remind her of special times she spent with friends and family members. Others will remind her of special events to come. All are examples of what can lead people to use personal writing to share good news and good times. Special announcements tell of certain events, such as weddings and graduations. Other kinds of writing can help celebrate holidays and important occasions, such as birthdays, recitals, good report cards, and vacations.

## • JOURNAL ACTIVITY •
### *Try It Out*

Think of something that you would like to celebrate with others. Then, in your journal, design and write an invitation to your celebration. Supply all of the important information: who is giving the party, the purpose and form of the celebration, and the date, time, and location.

## Person to Person

When you write a personal letter you choose the person you are going to write to. Your relationship with that person helps you decide what to say and how to say it. Your choice of stationery and the photographs, drawings, or news clippings you include are important to the person who receives your letter.

Read the letter from Eddie to his older brother. What does the letter tell about the relationship between them? What might be different about a letter from Eddie to a friend?

Dear Reggie,

What's happening? Is college life as cool as you thought it would be? Are the classes hard? Who's your roommate? Do you get to go to all the games for free?

It is weird around here without you. Mom really misses you. She's always saying, "I wonder how Reggie is doing." If you don't write or call soon, she may just show up at your dorm!

Thanks for letting me have your old room. It was awful sharing a room with Ray. He was always getting into my stuff and bothering me. Don't worry, though. I'll let you have your room back at Thanksgiving.

Your bro,

Eddie

# Activities

Here are some activities to help you apply what you have learned.

## 1. Guided Assignment

Once you have accepted an invitation and enjoyed the occasion, you will probably want to write a thank-you letter to the person who invited you. Read the letter Alan wrote after Jih-Sheng's party.

June 3

Dear Jih-Sheng,

Mom told me to stop telling her about the game and write you a thank-you letter. She isn't very interested in baseball.

That was a great game, though. Remember that homer in the eighth? Mark was so excited I thought he was going to leap over the rail.

The barbecue was fun, too. I didn't tell Mom how much I ate!

Thanks for inviting me.

Your friend,
Alan

Write a letter thanking someone for a gift or a good time. Tell why you appreciate what was done for you. Use language that feels and sounds natural.

PURPOSE  To express thanks in writing
AUDIENCE  A friend or relative
LENGTH  1 to 2 pages

## 2. Open Assignment

Design and write your own greeting card. Match an occasion with a receiver in the lists below, or choose an occasion and receiver of your own.

| Occasion | Receiver |
|---|---|
| Congratulations | Best friend |
| Birthday | Parent |
| Announcement | New pen pal |

### COMPUTER OPTION

You can produce a greeting card on a computer. First, write your message. Then, if you have drawing software, use it to illustrate your card. Otherwise, paint or draw the design.

## 3. Cooperative Learning

In a small group brainstorm a list of one-on-one relationships, such as parent/child, sister/brother, teacher/student. Divide into pairs to role play the relationships through personal letters. Suppose you and your partner are role playing a parent/child relationship. If you choose the parent's role, you will write a letter to your child and your child will write to you. Then you will each respond to a letter you received.

Share your letters with your group. Discuss how the relationships made the letters different.

## See for Yourself

Another kind of personal writing is about personal experiences. What the writer tells depends on how he or she felt about what happened. For example, suppose you visit a skating rink for the first time. The fast pace of the skaters speeding around the rink surprises you and makes you nervous about falling. Your account of the experience will probably reflect your nervousness.

In the excerpt below, Farley Mowat, a writer and naturalist, describes a personal experience. He comes face to face with one of the wolves he traveled to the Arctic to study.

### Literature Model

*Notice the writer's use of the word "quarry." The reader knows Mowat was looking for the wolf.*

*Which details express the writer's feelings about this experience?*

My head came slowly over the crest—and there was my quarry. He was lying down, evidently resting after his mournful singsong, and his nose was about six feet from mine. We stared at one another in silence. I do not know what went on in his massive skull, but my head was full of the most disturbing thoughts. I was peering straight into the amber gaze of a fully grown arctic wolf, who probably weighed more than I did, and who was certainly a lot better versed in close-combat techniques than I would ever be.

Farley Mowat, *Never Cry Wolf*

## Recalling Your Experiences

The writing in the literature model is more formal than the writing in journals, notes, and letters because it is intended to reach a larger audience. It is still personal, however, because it tells how one writer reacted to an experience.

When you plan to write about a personal experience, begin by thinking about important or interesting events in your life. Concentrate on experiences that caused strong feelings or that made you think about something in a different way. The picture shows one student who is recalling some experiences that may lead to personal writing.

Trying out for the play scared me.

I can't believe I was elected class president.

Being a big brother for the first time is OK.

### • JOURNAL ACTIVITY •
### *Think It Through*

Recall three or four experiences you have had in the last month. List them in your journal, mark one to share, and name an audience for whom you would write.

# Selecting a Writing Idea

Consider an experience you would like to share with readers. Focus on how you felt about that experience. Think about the details that will help you explain your thoughts and feelings. One writer listed "I stepped on a snake" as one of her experiences. Then she listed feelings about that experience to use in her writing. Look at the cluster, and read the model below to see how Simone Tucker shared her meeting with a snake.

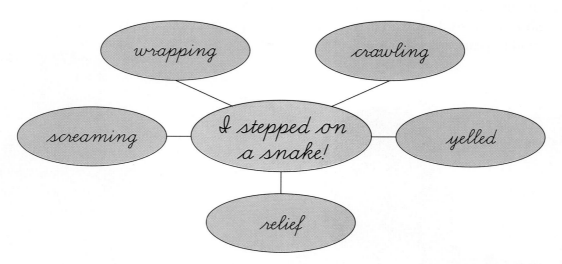

## Student Model

*Notice the words Simone uses in the first paragraph to focus on her fear.*

One day last summer my cousin and I went downstairs to iron our clothes. We entered the washroom and I stepped on something. It felt long, slimy, and as if it was crawling up and down my leg while wrapping around my foot. I screamed. My cousin immediately reached for the lights and turned them on, only to discover I was standing on a snake! We both yelled, "Snake!" Jumping and screaming, we ran upstairs.

*How does Simone let the reader know that her reaction to the snake changes?*

Several hours later, we found the snake, captured it in a bottle, and let it go. What a relief!

Simone Tucker, Kirby Junior High, St. Louis, Missouri

# Activities

Here are some activities to help you apply what you have learned.

## 1. Guided Assignment

Choose an experience from the list you made in the Journal Activity on page 23. Focus on your feelings about the experience. Was it frightening, or was it a good experience? Were other people involved? Where did it happen? Make a cluster like the one on the previous page. Then write about your experience in a short piece of personal writing to share with your class.

| | |
|---|---|
| **PURPOSE** | To express your feelings about a personal experience |
| **AUDIENCE** | Your teacher and classmates |
| **LENGTH** | ½–1 page |

## 2. Open Assignment

Say to yourself, "I remember a time when . . . ," and decide how to finish the sentence. Make a list of the reactions and feelings you had at that time. Write one or two pages about the experience. Choose one of the following feelings to help you get started, or think of a feeling of your own:

- I was really surprised.
- Something scared me.
- I was proud of myself.

## 3. Art

Another word for *carousel* is *merry-go-round*. Think about the meaning of the word *merry*. Look at the picture and list all of the colors you see. Is one color used more often than others? Do you think the colors fit the word *merry*?

Recall an amusement park ride you have taken or any experience you think would make an interesting painting. List the details you would use if you were creating the painting. Would you use bright colors as the artist did for the carousel? In one or two pages of personal writing, describe the picture you would create.

Torquato S. Pessoa, *Carousel*, 1960

### Writing About Literature
## Responding to a Character

## *What a Character!*

Characters bring a story to life. They can remind you of yourself or of people you know. Such personal responses help you remember characters.

In this excerpt Louise Bradshaw tells how she feels about her twin sister, Caroline. They live on an island in Chesapeake Bay in Maryland.

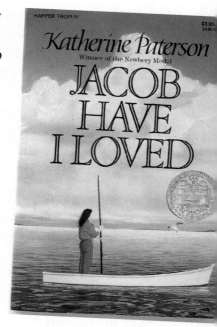

I would come in from a day of progging [poking, searching] for crab, sweating and filthy. Caroline would remark mildly that my fingernails were dirty. How could they be anything else but dirty? But instead of simply acknowledging the fact, I would fly into a wounded rage. How dare she call me dirty? How dare she try to make me feel inferior to her own pure, clear beauty? It wasn't my fingernails she was concerned with, that I was sure of. She was using my fingernails to indict my soul. Wasn't she content to be golden perfection without cutting away at me? Was she to allow me no virtue—no shard of pride or decency?

By now I was screaming. Wasn't it I who brought in the extra money that paid for her trips to Salisbury [a town where Caroline studied music]? She ought to be on her knees thanking me for all I did for her. How dare she criticize? How dare she?

Katherine Paterson, *Jacob Have I Loved*

# Listen to Me

Perhaps you have read a story with a character you would like to talk to. Maybe you thought it would be interesting to stop reading and say, "Wait! That's not such a good idea!" or "I know just how you feel." Using personal writing to respond to a character can help you better understand the character and the story. Look at the examples below. One reader wrote a lesson in progging for Caroline. The other reader sympathized with Louise.

Progging Directions for Caroline

1. Get a bucket, a boat, and a pole.

2. In your boat go to the place your sister finds crabs.

3. Poke in the mud until you find a crab.

4. Pick up the crab, and put it into the bucket.

5. Are your fingernails clean?

Dear Louise,
I have an older sister like Caroline. Sometimes I think I don't really like her much. Then I feel like I must be horrible to think about my own sister that way. It made me feel better to know someone else felt the same way I do.
Sincerely,
Julie

• JOURNAL ACTIVITY •
## Try It Out

In your journal make a list of ideas you would like to share with either Caroline or Louise. Show how you feel about the relationship between the sisters.

# Meeting New People

Sometimes a fictional character proves to be an important influence in a reader's life. Jean Little wrote a book about her childhood. In it she told about things that influenced the way she felt and thought. When she was very small, she met a character in a book her mother read aloud. The character was Mary Lennox from *The Secret Garden*. If you have read *The Secret Garden*, think about your own response to Mary. If you haven't read the book, try to imagine what kind of person Mary is as you read Little's reaction in the passage below.

## Literature Model

*What is the effect of the sentence "I laid down my spoon"?*

*An old poem says that a child born on Sunday will have a happy personality. What does this reference tell a reader?*

*Why do you suppose Little included the last paragraph?*

Mother opened the book and began. *When Mary Lennox was sent to Misselthwaite Manor to live with her uncle, everybody said she was the most disagreeable looking child ever seen. It was true, too.*

I laid down my spoon. From the first sentence, *The Secret Garden* seemed especially mine. I did not wonder what Mary Lennox looked like. I knew. She looked exactly like me.

Mary had clearly not been born on a Sunday, either. She, too, was selfish and bad-tempered and lazy. She even tried to get Martha to put her shoes on for her. I wasn't the only one who had done such a reprehensible thing.

Yet little by little, she grew into somebody quite different. And the way it happened made perfect sense. I knew that I, too, would be different if I could find a hidden garden and friends like Dickon and Colin and the robin.

Jean Little, *Little by Little*

# Activities

Here are some activities to help you apply what you have learned.

## 1. Guided Assignment

Père Tanguy, a friend of the artist, sold art supplies. Think about his clothes, his expression, and his work. Write to Père Tanguy. Ask him questions, or tell him what you think of his portrait. These questions may help you:

- Does he know many great artists? Why did he allow Van Gogh to paint his portrait?
- Is he an artist, too? If not, would he like to be?
- Whose pictures are on the wall? Why are they in his portrait?

**PURPOSE** To explore your thoughts and feelings about a character

**AUDIENCE** The art supplier

**LENGTH** 1- or 2-page letter

## 2. Open Assignment

Write a letter to a character listed below, to Caroline or Louise, or to a character you choose. Explain how you feel about the character and why.

- Tom Sawyer or Huck Finn from *The Adventures of Tom Sawyer* by Mark Twain

Vincent van Gogh, *Portrait of Père Tanguy*, 1887

- Cassie, Stacey, or T. J. from *Roll of Thunder, Hear My Cry* by Mildred Taylor

## 3. Social Studies

Think about a person you have studied in social studies. In your journal tell what the person did that is important and how this person's life affected the world. Then write your personal response to him or her.

*Writing About Literature: Responding to a Character* **29**

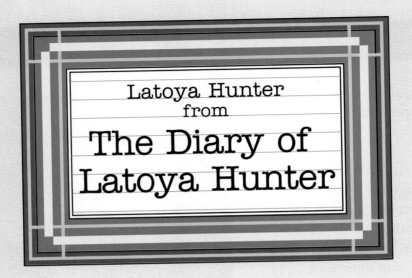

Latoya Hunter
from
# The Diary of Latoya Hunter

*A diary is usually a very personal written record, but a book
editor asked Latoya Hunter to keep a diary for everybody to see.
While Latoya's story is unusual because her writing was published,
her book reflects the thoughts and feelings of a typical teen-ager.
As you read these entries, notice how Latoya uses writing to discover
changes within herself. Notice as well how she considers the
ways that she is connected to other people.*

September 11, 1990

Dear Diary,

I never thought I'd get desperate enough to say this but I
envy you. You don't have to live in this troubled world; all
you do is hear about it. You don't have to go to J.H. and
watch the clock, praying for dismissal time to come. You also
don't have to go through a situation like sitting in a cafeteria
watching others laughing and talking and you don't know anyone. To sit there and eat the food that is just terrible because
there's nothing else to do.

You don't do any of those things. All you do is listen to pathetic[1] twelve-year-olds like me tell you about it.

I guess you can tell how my day went. Diary, what am I going to do? My best friend left to go to another school. I wish she could be with me. We had so much fun together. She moved right before summer started. She doesn't live anywhere close so it would be much easier if she stayed at the school closest to her. That's the only part of it that's easy. The hardest part is not being together.

September 30, 1990

Dear Diary,

I think I need a name for you. You've become like a best friend to me, you're someone I can talk to without being argued with. I think I know just the name for you. I'll call you Janice after my best friend from Jamaica. We were like sisters before I left. Over the years we've grown apart though, the letters have stopped but that friendship is still going on within me!

So today I christen[2] you diary, Janice Page.

October 2, 1990

Dear Janice,

It's hard to believe but people change as rapidly as the world does. If I had kept you as a diary two years ago, you would have heard about Jimmy. He was the first guy who I was close to and who was a real friend to me. I liked him because other boys always seemed to be in a popularity contest, and he didn't care about that stuff. He was handsome and everything but he never let it get to his head. Well lately he's been going to the other side. He has a new walk, new talk, new look—the works! He ignores me, I guess I'm not popular enough for him! He just isn't the same.

---

1 **pathetic** (pə thet′ik) causing pity or sorrow
2 **christen** (kris′ən) to give a name to a person or thing

October 7, 1990

Dear Janice,

This weekend was spent at home, at my brother's house and at church. My brothers just moved out recently. They don't live very far though, about 15 minutes away from the house. Their new house is nice. I like it there. They're both so funny. One is Dave and the other is Courtney. They're like twins except they look nothing alike and are a couple years apart. Dave is 23 and Courtney is 25. We don't communicate much anymore—they've got girlfriends and they're making new lives for themselves. It's impossible now to have a close relationship with either of them.

After church today I felt the urge to do something indepen-dent. I started walking and found myself heading home. Church and home aren't too close together so when I did get home I got in trouble with both parents—it's usually only my mom, but my father didn't approve either. That's really embarrassing that they got upset for that! I thought I was more grown than that. I know I am, but they don't. This whole entry is embarrassing. I'm not a baby, I can't believe they think that way of me. I only wanted to prove I could do something by myself. Even that is a crime these days in the parents law book. I can't do anything right these days.

October 8, 1990

Dear Janice,

Today I saw my old teacher, I was talking about the other day. I thought this should be the day I tell you about him. His name is Robert Pelka. He's a heavy man but that only means there's more of him to love. There's just something about him that makes him impossible not to like. He's warm, caring, loving and everything else that comes with a great human being. He didn't only teach me academic things like math, English and so on. He taught me how to be open-minded to all kinds of people. He did that by making us empathize with other people, in other words, put ourselves in their place and write about it. I went from being a sister of a retarded boy named Victor to being a

Jewish girl whose family was taken away from me back in the Hitler days.

Mr. Pelka made things we'd normally learn about from history books sort of come alive, it's like you're there. Those are just some of the things he introduced me to. The things he changed about me are innumerable. The world should know this man. He probably won't go down in any major history books but if this diary counts as a book of history, he just did.

November 18, 1990

Dear Janice,

I didn't go to church today. I got dressed up and everything but my cousins who I usually go with weren't going so I came back home. I didn't do much back here. I just circulated around this house. The old me would have went straight outside to my friend's house. I find I've lost interest in going outside. I was usually like a magnet drawn to steel when it came to going outside. Now, I could spend a whole week without stepping past the doorstep. Except for going to school of course. I think I've matured somewhat. I always was concerned about what I was missing outside. I never wanted to be left out on anything happening with my friends who are always doing something or going somewhere. In the way I've matured I've come to the sudden realization that there are many more things to life like being close to my family, before it's too late.

Pierre Bonnard, *The Window*, 1925

Bernice Cross, *In the Room*, c. 1950

Pretty soon I'll be off to college, then married with kids. I might be rushing things a bit, but these years go by very fast.

I'm my own person. I like to think that I'm not just my cousin's cousin or my friend's friend. I like to think I'm the individual Latoya Hunter.

## For Discussion

1. What feelings described by Latoya do you think many teenagers have? What do you think Latoya discovered about herself through writing?

2. Latoya always had "Janice" when she needed someone to talk to. If you knew Latoya what do you think you would talk about with her?

# Readers Respond

What I liked best about *The Diary of Latoya Hunter* is that this girl was expressing her feelings to her diary because that was the only friend she had.

Latoya kind of reminded me of myself.

I would recommend this selection to my friend because Latoya tells about friendship.

**Phildonna Ratliff**

Latoya Hunter at first thinks her life is falling apart. Her best friend "Janice" is her diary. Later on she thinks that she matured and wants to be "the individual Latoya Hunter."

Latoya is a typical girl who faces problems most twelve-year-olds face. That makes the story more realistic. The part I remember most clearly is when she named her diary Janice.

I would recommend this literature to my friends because it would help them understand life a little better.

**Nycayen Moore**

## Do You Agree?

1. Do you agree that it's a sign of maturity to realize that you don't have to be always "doing something or going somewhere," as Latoya wrote?

2. Why do you think Latoya gave her diary a name? Think of a name that seems suitable for your journal or diary. Use it to write four or five journal entries. Does the name feel right to you? Can you tell why?

*The Diary of Latoya Hunter* **35**

# *Writing Process in Action*

## A Day That Mattered

Important moments in your life often pass by unnoticed because you're too busy living them to think about their impact. Later on, however, you may take time to reflect on some of these events and sort out your feelings about them.

In *The Diary of Latoya Hunter* on pages 30–34, the writer explores her thoughts and feelings in personal writing about special days in her life. The following assignment gives you the chance to do something similar.

### • Assignment •

| | |
|---|---|
| *Context* | *You're writing for a student publication called A Day That Mattered. You'll recall things you did and felt during a special day. It may have been an important day, a happy day, or a day of change.* |
| *Purpose* | *To communicate the importance of one special day through personal writing* |
| *Audience* | *Student readers of A Day That Mattered* |
| *Length* | *2 or more pages* |

The next few pages offer suggestions for each stage in the writing process. You don't have to remember all of these tips. Just refer to them when you need help as you're writing.

# 1. Prewriting

First, you'll want to zero in on a special day that you'd like to write about. As you read the selection, did it remind you of anything similar from your past? What about the day a best friend moved away? Or the day you won a long-deserved prize?

Now you're ready to explore several options to develop your idea. Try making a cluster diagram to help you focus on the thoughts and feelings you have about the day you're considering.

Once you've chosen and explored your topic, think about how you will order your ideas. Usually, the best way to tell a story is in the order in which events occurred, such as Hunter did.

**Option A**

Review your journal.

**Option B**

Look at photos and souvenirs.

**Option C**

List memorable events.

First dance
 performance
First week of jr. high
Youth group camp
Grandpa's visit
Backpacking in
 Yosemite
Work at child-care
 center
Week Smoky was
 lost

# 2. Drafting

Now it's time to expand your ideas and notes into sentences and paragraphs. No matter how much prewriting you have done, you may have difficulty getting started with your first draft. Sometimes it helps to pretend that you are writing or talking to a close friend. Your friend would want to know what happened and how you thought and felt about it. Notice how Hunter focuses on her feelings in the following excerpt:

*A*fter church today I felt the urge to do something independent. I started walking and found myself heading home. . . . I got in trouble with both parents. . . . That's really embarrassing that they got upset for that! I thought I was more grown than that. I know I am, but they don't.

Hunter uses an event—getting in trouble for walking home from church—to express her frustration that her parents treated her like a child.

As you write, refer to your prewriting notes to keep your writing on track. Remember to focus on what it is that makes this day special. Don't worry about including too many or too few details at this point. Just get your ideas down on paper. You can add, delete, or reorder details during revision.

## 3. Revising

If possible, lay your draft aside for awhile before you begin to revise it. Then try to read through your draft as though you were seeing it for the first time. Look for ways that you can make your writing clearer and more meaningful to your readers. Asking yourself questions like those below can help you evaluate your draft.

After considering these questions, you might discover that you need clearer or stronger details. Try doing some additional prewriting, such as listing details about the event. Remember, you can always return to the prewriting and drafting stages while revising.

**Question A**

Have I explained why this event was special?

**Question B**

Is the order of events clear?

**Question C**

Have I carefully used important details?

> It was the first Sunday in October. The many-colored fallen leaves swirled across our path as we drove to the airport. The drive to the airport seemed to take forever. I'm not a very patient person and riding in a car really bores me. I hadn't seen my grandfather (for almost three years,) so I was really excited. (When we got to the gate,) I could see my grandfather walking toward us. He waved his hat in the air. I jumped up and down. I must have looked pretty silly, but I didn't care.

## 4. *Editing*

The editing stage is your opportunity to clean up any errors in grammar, spelling, and punctuation. Be especially on the lookout for mistakes you may have made in past writing assignments. Do you have a tendency to use double negatives or sentence fragments? Watch for these problems.

The checklist at the right will help you edit your personal writing. Read through your revised draft several times, looking for only one or two kinds of errors at a time. Careful editing can make your writing as special as the event that inspired it.

*Checklist*

1. *Have I spelled everything correctly?*
2. *Have I used standard grammar and punctuation?*
3. *Have I used a variety of sentence structures?*
4. *Are my verb tenses correct?*
5. *Are my details vivid?*

## 5. *Presenting*

Although your writing is very personal, you may wish to share it with others. Through the process of sharing, you may come to understand something new about other people's experiences and, in turn, something about yourself.

You might want to exchange your writing with another student's and ask for feedback. Finally, consider enhancing your presentation by including a memento, such as a photo or souvenir, of that special time.

### Reflecting

Looking back on a memorable experience can help you see yourself in a new way. How did writing about a special day change your feelings about the events that took place? What details did you remember that brought the day into focus for you? What did you learn about yourself?

# Portfolio & Reflection

## Summary

**Key concepts in personal writing include the following:**

- Personal writing is a way of discovering what is important to you.
- Some personal writing is just for you; some is to be shared.
- A journal is a place for daily personal writing, for making notes about your thoughts and feelings. Often these notes can be a source of writing ideas.
- Personal writing is informal.
- A journal also may serve as a learning log in which you record questions and comments about information that interests you.
- You can share personal experiences and responses through writing.

## Your Writer's Portfolio

Look over the writing you did for this unit. Choose two pieces for your portfolio. Look for writing that does one or more of the following:

- records an idea or experience important to you
- can serve as a source for future personal writing
- expresses thoughts and ideas you would like to share

## Reflection and Commentary

Think about what you have learned in this unit. Answer the following questions as you look over the two pieces of writing you chose. Write a page of "Comments on Personal Writing" for your portfolio.

1. How does this piece of writing reveal something important to you?
2. How did the the journal activities help you develop this personal writing?
3. In what way did personal experience lead to this piece of writing?
4. What have you learned, through your writing, about your response to fictional characters?
5. What personal writing would you like to develop for other people to read?
6. What goals will you or have you set for your personal writing?

## Feedback

**If you had a chance to respond to the following student comment, what would you say or ask?**

*I discovered that I can invoke many wonderful memories just by looking at an object from the time of those memories.*

Tsoni Peled, Julian School,
Oak Park, Illinois

# The Writing Process

## Cultivating Ideas

C. T. Chew, *Ralph Doid's Dilemma*, 1983

FEATURING **The Freep**

*"Feature sections are not separate animals full of nice stories that come out of thin air. They need to be as topical and to-the-moment as any other section of the paper. We try to seize upon the news and be current and hot."*

Nunzio Lupo

What topics are on the minds of today's young people? Who are the hottest new music groups? What does it take to be deemed smart and cool? These are some of the questions addressed in "The Freep," a weekly feature page in the *Detroit Free Press.* The page generally contains a personality profile, a "Hot Box" on current trends, and a student-opinion column. A lead article focuses on a topic important to the

**Creating a Feature Page**

**1.** Planning the Page

**2.** Drafting the Words

**3.** Revising for Press Time

### FOCUS

A strong feature page addresses a specific audience with a lively discussion of current topics and issues.

young readers of "The Freep." Each issue mixes the serious, the fun, and the funny with eye-catching graphics that say, "Read me, read me."

Like most sections of a newspaper, "The Freep" reflects the collaboration of several people. Leading this effort is assistant features editor Nunzio Lupo. Working with him on "The Freep" is designer Keith Webb. The rest of the staff changes frequently, although a few writers are featured regularly. One of these is Maisha Maurant, who was responsible for the article "Smart, Cool and on the Air," which appeared recently in "The Freep."

## 1 Planning the Page

Lupo begins planning each issue three to four weeks before publication. Ideas come from many sources, often from other sections of the *Detroit Free Press*. Lupo also reads many youth-culture magazines, such as *Spin* and *Sassy*.

Another source of ideas is the letters to the editor in the *Detroit Free Press* and other newspapers. One such letter caught Lupo's attention. It was about two high school friends, disc jockeys who were smart *and* cool. Lupo gave the letter to Maurant and asked her to explore the topic of smart and cool friends for a "Freep" feature article.

Still in the prewriting stage, Lupo will brainstorm ideas for the graphics with Webb. For Lupo and Webb, the graphics are just as important as the words. Webb says, "Graphics should help tell the story, not just decorate it." From their brainstorming session, Lupo and Webb pull together an idea for a particular "Freep" feature.

## 2 Drafting the Words

Maurant usually has a week to write a feature. When she sits down to draft a manuscript, she's already gathered her notes on the subject. For the "Smart, Cool and on the Air" article, note-taking meant interviewing by telephone the two student disc jockeys. Maurant was also interested in facts such as the subjects' grade-point averages and their activities in and out of school.

Maurant starts her draft by writing the lead, the opening that establishes the direction the feature will take. She explains, "I'm impatient. I like to get a lead down to give me a feel for where I want to go."

Working at home, she outlines and drafts the article in longhand. Once in the office, Maurant transfers her notes, outline, and draft into the computer.

Maurant is a fast writer who can often complete a draft in a few hours. She never makes changes until she's written it all down once. As she explains, "It gives me something to go back and compare to." After Maurant has covered the facts, she'll return to her notes "to fill in things that make the story tighter."

Maurant keeps her young "Freep" audience in mind as she writes. "I try to use the most vivid words and images. My audience wants to be able to 'see' it."

Before she submits her article to Lupo, and if her deadline allows, Maurant likes to set the manuscript aside for a day. She feels that a fresh mind helps in the final reading. As she reads the article once again, Maurant looks for unanswered questions and unclear information.

▲ *After conducting an interview, Maurant likes to ask herself, "What is the most vivid element about this person or issue?" With that question as a guide, she begins writing her draft.*

## 3 Revising for Press Time

Maurant's copy is due to Lupo the Friday before publication, which is press time. On that day, she sends the copy to Lupo's computer electronically. After he reads it, Maurant and Lupo review it together at his computer.

Sometimes a feature sounds flat. When Lupo and the writer know that something's missing, they try to identify what's needed. Perhaps a stronger lead will help, or additional facts and quotations. Lupo and the writer will toss solutions back and forth. Lupo says, "Sometimes a reporter will think an idea is obvious when, in fact, only he or she can see it. I can point out that their view isn't getting through."

After the copy is revised, Lupo meets again with the designer. For "Smart, Cool and on the Air," Webb designed a graphic of a human brain. Lupo then wrote captions that described the smart and cool thoughts of this brain.

In the final step before publication, Lupo reviews the proofs. Copy editors have been working on the page, correcting spelling and grammar. With Lupo's sign-off, the page makes its way to press.

**INTERFACE** *The editor for your school newspaper has asked you to write an article. The topic is access for the handicapped at your school. How will you focus the subject?*

# ON ASSIGNMENT

## 1. Feature Writing

**Write a brief lead for a feature article about an issue affecting your community.**

- Choose an issue you are familiar with and interested in.

- What point is most compelling about this issue? Is there an image or detail that might help your audience understand this point?

- Consider your audience. How much do they know about the issue? What facts do they need to know?

## 2. About Literature

**Write a brief response to a personal-profile feature from a newspaper or magazine.**

- What details about the subject did the writer emphasize? What nouns and adjectives did the writer use to highlight these details?

- What assumptions do you think the writer brought to the subject? How might you have focused the feature differently?

## 3. Cooperative Learning

**Assemble a feature page for an audience of your choice.**

- With a small group of students, form an editorial team, and brainstorm ideas for the page. You may want to scan newspapers for ideas. List possible articles for your first publication.

- Each group member can choose one article to pursue. Conduct interviews, and research your topic. From your notes prepare a short paragraph to present to your editorial team for discussion.

- Together, assemble a mock-up of the completed page. Use brief paragraphs in place of finished articles. Write a title, and add graphics to help tell the story. Share your page with the rest of the class.

# Using the Writing Process

## *You Can Get There from Here*

Suppose that you're walking down a street lined with neat apartment buildings and nicely kept storefronts. Suddenly you come to a vacant lot covered with weeds and trash. What could you do to get rid of this eyesore? Transforming an empty lot into a bright spot in the community isn't impossible. If you plan well and follow through, you can be successful.

Like any project, achieving a finished piece of writing requires careful planning and following through. The paragraph below is the result of Tai-Tang-Tran's thinking and planning. He began with an idea and worked through various stages of the writing process to describe Chinese New Year traditions.

### Student Model

**M**any Chinese New Year traditions are about luck. One tradition that my family celebrates is the giving of lucky money. Parents give children money in a red envelope. The envelope symbolizes luck. Putting the money in the envelope means that the parent is sharing luck with a child. Both giving and receiving the red envelope bring luck.

Tai-Tang-Tran, Emerson Junior High School, Oak Park, Illinois

*Having read this passage, what do you suppose Tai's complete piece is about?*

## A Personal Process

Before Tai finished his essay, the longer piece of writing from which this passage came, he went through a process. First, he listed his ideas about traditions. Then he organized them into paragraphs, or groups of sentences related to the same idea. These earlier stages of Tai's writing appear on the right. He later rearranged and polished his writing until it was finished. Every writer works in his or her own way, but most writers take their writing through several stages before they finish.

## From Start to Finish

Many writers use the following stages of the writing process. Not every writer follows them in strict order, however. Many writers go back to certain stages before they finish a piece of writing.

**Prewriting**   In this stage you find and explore ideas and then decide on a topic to write about. Several techniques introduced in the next few lessons can help you during this stage. At this time you also decide on your audience, the people who will read or hear your writing. And you decide on the overall purpose of your writing.

**Drafting**   Transforming thoughts, words, and phrases into sentences and paragraphs is called drafting. You can rearrange and revise your writing more easily once your ideas are in draft form.

Chinese New Year traditions:
lucky red money
spiri...
dra...
luc...

Around Chinese New Year adults and children feel lucky. Parents always give children lucky money. Both the parents and the children get luck when giving or receiving the lucky money. The red envelope symbolizes luck, and the money inside means the adult giving the money is taking some of the adult's luck and sharing it with the children.

### • JOURNAL ACTIVITY •
### Think It Through

Think about the last time you wrote something. What challenges or rewards did that writing project present? Write your thoughts in your journal.

**Revising**    In the revising stage you look at your writing to be sure it's clear and organized. You can guide your revisions with questions such as, Does what I've written make sense? Have I presented my ideas in a sensible order? Have I kept my audience in mind?

Some pieces of writing need little revision. Others need revising two, four, even a dozen times before they satisfy their authors.

**Editing**    The editing stage differs from the revising stage, because it focuses on the mechanics of your writing. When you edit, you make sure you've spelled and punctuated your writing properly. You also want to correct any grammatical errors. If you or someone else has typed or printed out your work, you'll want to double-check to make sure no errors have crept in.

**Presenting**    In the last stage of writing, you present your work to your audience. You present some pieces of writing by handing them in to your teacher. You present other pieces more publicly. For example, you might read a research paper aloud before the class, mail a letter to a local newspaper, or publish a review in a school newspaper. You might even deliver a speech to members of a club or a community group or act in a skit for children.

This diagram shows the stages of the writing process. Remember it's up to you to decide how you move through the different stages.

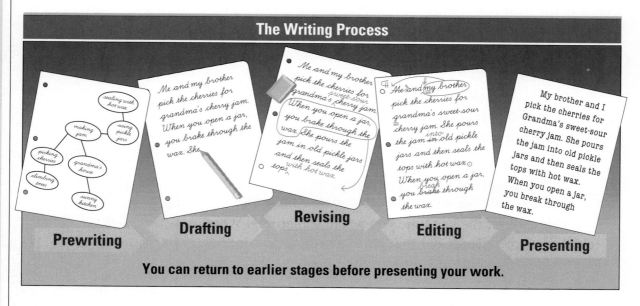

**The Writing Process**

Prewriting          Drafting          Revising          Editing          Presenting

You can return to earlier stages before presenting your work.

# *Activities*

Here are some activities to help you apply what you have learned.

## 1. Guided Assignment

Think about how you write. Do you go through a different process for different kinds of writing? For example, you may spend more time writing a report than writing a letter to a school newspaper. Consider how you adapt your writing process for different kinds of writing. To help you think about your writing process, you might look back at your writing for the Journal Activity on page 49. Then write a description of your writing process.

PURPOSE  To understand your writing process

AUDIENCE  Yourself

LENGTH  ½–1 page

### COMPUTER OPTION

If you sometimes use a computer in your writing, think about how using it affects your writing process. Take a look at writing you have done on the computer—notes, first and later drafts, and other stages. You might consider setting up different files for different stages. For example, set up separate files for prewriting notes, drafts, and so on.

## 2. Open Assignment

Write about the way you perform one of the processes below or another process with which you are familiar. In other words, break down the overall process into a few stages. Then discuss the ways in which using this process is similar to or different from using the writing process. Remember to consider each stage of the writing process when you make your comparison.

- learning a new sport or skill
- mastering an unfamiliar concept in math or science
- creating a piece of art
- preparing for a musical recital

## 3. Cooperative Learning

In a small group discuss the challenges that writing projects have presented. Give each member of the group a few minutes to describe his or her writing experiences. Then take turns suggesting ways to approach the challenges the other members have described. Take notes when it is your turn to receive suggestions from the others.

Write a couple of paragraphs that describe any writing problems you may have and the solutions suggested by others. Underline the solutions you think you will try.

# Prewriting: Finding and Exploring a Topic

## *I Have an Idea!*

What do you do first when you write? Probably you find something to write about. The students pictured here—Henry, Keshia, and Mike—are trying to think of ways to fill an empty lot. Similarly, you need to think of ways to fill an empty sheet of paper.

Some writers get writing ideas easily. They aren't even aware of having to think them up. Other writers have their own special methods for getting ideas. Some take a walk; others take a shower. Some listen to music; others listen to friends. The number of writing ideas you can think up is infinite. To help you find or generate them, you sometimes may need to try a few basic techniques.

## Where Do Good Ideas Come From?

You can find a writing idea almost anywhere. What catches your attention when you walk down a street or a school hallway? What makes you happy? What makes you angry? What ideas does your journal or today's newspaper suggest? Try carrying a small notebook with you. Whenever an idea comes to you, write it down. For example, Mike jotted down some ideas on the notecards shown here.

But what if no ideas come to you? Then you might want to brainstorm. When you brainstorm, you try to come up with as many ideas as you can. You don't worry about whether they're good or bad, practical or silly. The point is to get your thoughts flowing. Eventually you'll hit on an idea you can use. Keshia, Mike, and Henry generated the list of ideas on the right during their brainstorming session.

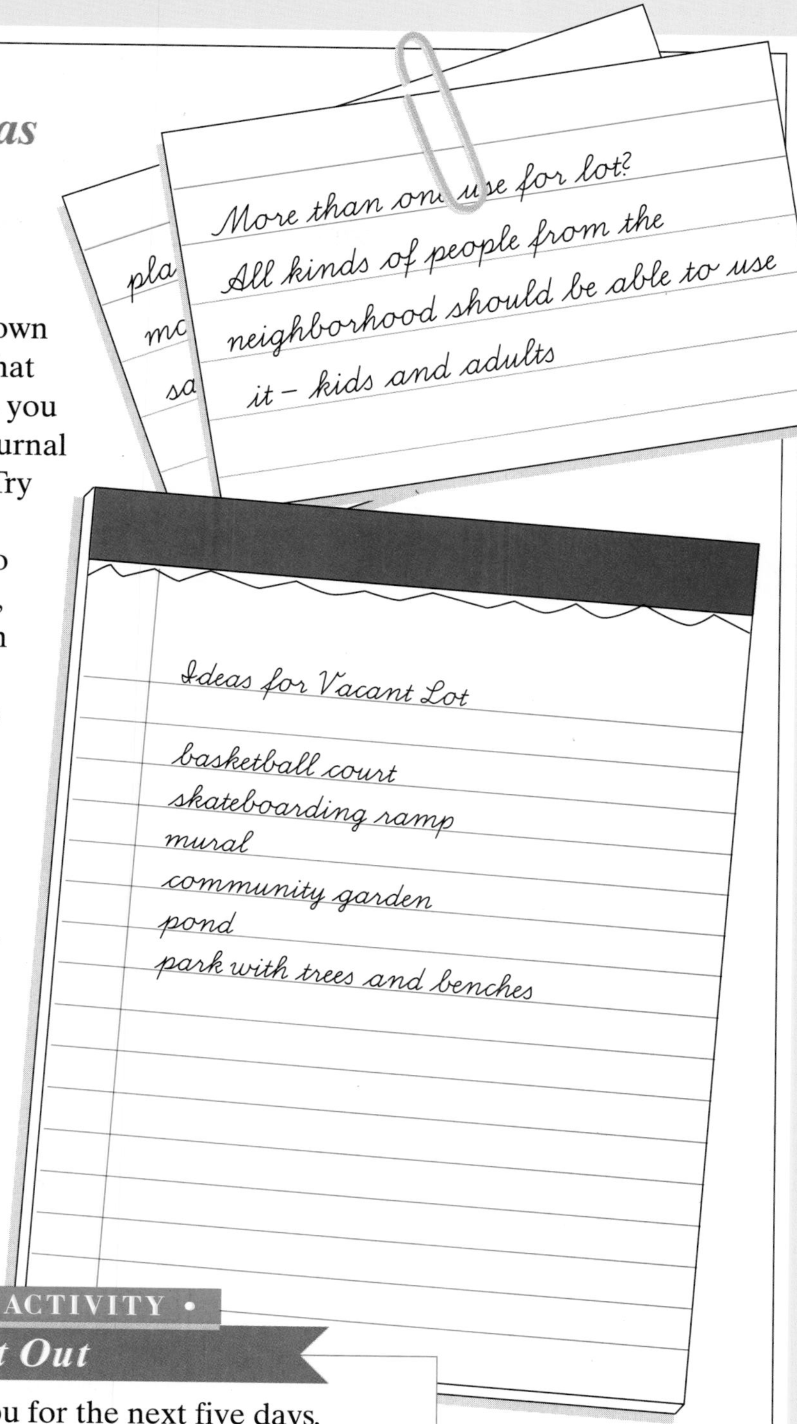

*More than one use for lot?*
*All kinds of people from the neighborhood should be able to use it – kids and adults*

*Ideas for Vacant Lot*

*basketball court*
*skateboarding ramp*
*mural*
*community garden*
*pond*
*park with trees and benches*

### • JOURNAL ACTIVITY •
### Try It Out

Carry a notebook with you for the next five days. Write down ideas whenever they occur to you. At some point, take ten minutes to brainstorm ideas. After five days write in your journal which worked better—letting ideas come naturally or brainstorming them.

# *Branching Out*

By brainstorming, you uncover many different ideas. You then can choose one idea that might make a good writing topic. But how do you know if you know enough to write about that topic? You must explore your topic, look at it more thoroughly. One way you can explore your topic is through clustering.

To cluster, write your topic in the middle of a piece of paper. Then, as you think about that topic, write down everything that comes to mind. Each time you write something down, draw a circle around it. Then draw lines to connect the ideas that seem related to each other. Using a cluster, you can show ideas branching out from your topic. For some examples, look at the clusters for *garden* and *play lot* shown below.

Clustering can help you decide which part of a topic to write about. You can't write about every idea that you generate through clustering. But you might discover a surprising connection between your topic and something else it calls to mind. Clustering can also help you organize your writing by showing you which ideas about a topic are broader or narrower than other ideas.

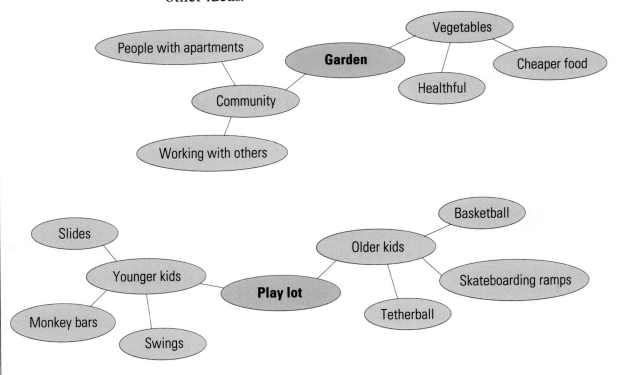

# Activities

Here are some activities to help you apply what you have learned.

## 1. Guided Assignment

Look at the painting on this page. Take five minutes to brainstorm topics it suggests. For example, it may remind you of a family reunion or of your favorite outdoor activity. Choose one topic from your list, and explore it by clustering. Spend five to ten minutes on your cluster. Finally, use items from your cluster to write about the painting.

Pat Thomas, *Picnic in Washington Park*, 1975

| | |
|---|---|
| PURPOSE | To discover how prewriting can help you with your writing |
| AUDIENCE | Yourself |
| LENGTH | 1–2 pages |

## 2. Open Assignment

Use one of the phrases in the next column or one of your own as the starting point for a ten-minute clustering session. Come up with as many branches for your cluster as you can. Use the idea or ideas you like best in a two-page piece of writing.

- a surprise party
- a phone ringing in a phone booth
- a ball game canceled due to rain
- a last-minute change of plans

## 3. Music

With your eyes closed, listen for five minutes to some instrumental music. Repeat this step at least once. When you feel familiar with the music, open your eyes, and play the recording again. This time, list the images the music brings to mind. Then create a cluster around one of these images. Use your favorite items from the cluster to write a poem.

## *Attention! Attention!*

Look at the notice below. What could be the purpose, or reason, for this piece of writing? Who's supposed to read it? Take a few minutes to write your answers to these questions.

You need to think about questions like these in the prewriting stage. Before you even begin drafting, you need to decide whose attention you're trying to get and why. Every successful piece of writing, whether it's a newspaper editorial or a cartoon, has a particular purpose and audience.

Fabulous Rummage Sale!

CLOTHES! TOYS!
Household Goods!
Saturday & Sunday
August 15–16
1500 block of Elm Street
9:00 A.M. to 4:00 P.M.

# What's the Purpose?

Most of your writing will have one of four purposes. Telling a story is one purpose for writing. Describing something is another. Sometimes you write to inform someone or to explain something. You can also write to persuade your readers to believe something or to take some action. Below are examples of writing for three of these purposes.

*These sentences describe the way the lot looks now.*

*In the last two years several businesses have come and gone in the building next to the lot.*

*This sentence explains how the empty lot affects businesses in the neighborhood.*

*The lot is overgrown with weeds and covered with trash. Glass from broken bottles is scattered over the ground.*

*If our community developed the lot, people in the neighborhood would have a place to meet and spend time together.*

*This sentence tries to persuade readers to develop the lot for the benefit of the neighborhood.*

Your purpose will help you decide what form your writing will take—essay, story, poem, or report. The same piece of writing can have several purposes. For example, all of the sentences shown above form part of a longer proposal for developing the empty lot.

## • JOURNAL ACTIVITY •
### Try It Out

Look for writing topics in your journal. When you spot a possible topic, list the purpose or purposes you might have in writing about it.

# *Who's Reading?*

Sometimes you choose your audience, as when you write a letter to a newspaper. Other times you get a writing assignment, and the audience—your teacher or class—is not up to you. Whether or not you choose your audience, it affects the way you write about a topic.

Think about who will eventually read your writing. How much does that audience know about the topic? What vocabulary is appropriate? Think about when and where your audience will read your writing.

The newspaper article and billboard below aim at audiences with different needs and interests. The newspaper article aims at readers with time to read a whole article. It informs the community about what's involved in developing the lot. People reading the billboard will probably pass by the sign quickly. The writing should jump out at them, and it should be easy to read. It aims to persuade readers to volunteer their help.

# Activities

Here are some activities to help you apply what you have learned.

## 1. Guided Assignment

Identify an improvement you would like to see in your neighborhood or community. The improvement could be physical, such as renovating an old building. It could also be a service, like adding a new bus route. To generate more details, create a cluster for your topic. Then write a letter about your idea to a neighborhood committee, a town council, or another governing group.

PURPOSE   To gain support for a community improvement

AUDIENCE   Mayor, town council, or other governing group

LENGTH   1 page

### COMPUTER OPTION

Before mailing your letter, you will want to check your writing for spelling errors. The spelling checker in your word-processing software can help. Keep in mind, however, that your computer's dictionary may not recognize proper nouns, such as the name of your town or your mayor.

## 2. Open Assignment

Suppose that, because of school budget cuts, one of your favorite programs will be eliminated next year. Write a letter about the situation for one of the audiences below. Decide whether your overall purpose will be to persuade, to inform, to describe, or to tell a story.

- your school board
- a friend whose family is thinking of moving into your school district
- a favorite coach or teacher who will be leaving because of the cuts

## 3. Cooperative Learning

In a small group brainstorm ideas to raise money for a local charity or project. Once the group chooses the idea they like best, have each person explore it in his or her own cluster diagram. As a group discuss the ideas everyone generated, and agree on how to carry out one idea. For example, decide on the date, location, time, and cost of admission. Then have each group member write an article, flyer, or letter to persuade one of the following groups to participate as described:

- fellow students to volunteer time and labor
- community members to attend the event
- businesses to donate or discount products needed for the event
- your school principal to allow the use of school property for the event or school sponsorship of the event

*Prewriting: Determining Purpose and Audience* **59**

# *Sketching It Out*

Should the monkey bars go next to the swings or the slide? How many plots should there be in the garden? Where do the benches go? After Mike, Keshia, and Henry decided which items to include in their plan for the lot, they sketched out possible combinations. The sketches on this page show different ways they can arrange the items.

Once you determine your writing topic, purpose, and audience, you might want to sketch out what you're going to say. You may have plenty of ideas, but which one will you begin with? What will you say next? How will you end? Answering these questions will help you organize your ideas. Your goal is to find an order that will help the reader follow your thinking.

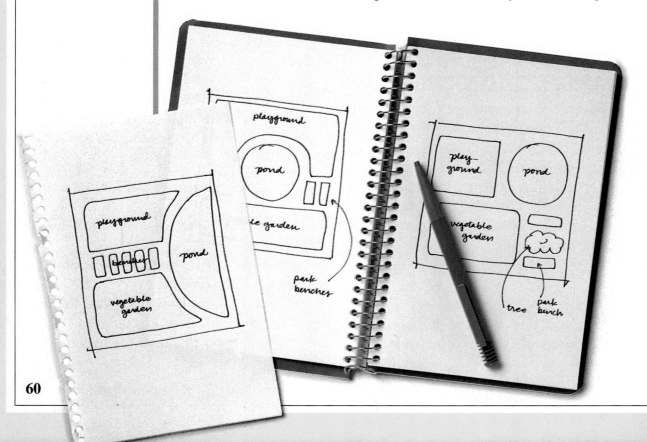

# Know Where You're Going

As a first step in ordering your thoughts, figure out the main ideas. You may have only one main idea, or you may have several. Remember your purpose for writing. What ideas will help you meet your goal?

Henry is reading a list of the main ideas he and the others will include in their proposal. They want to persuade a community improvement group to develop a neighborhood lot. Each main idea is a point meant to help persuade the community group to put the plan into action.

MAIN IDEAS FOR PROPOSAL

The empty lot is bad for the neighborhood.

Developing the lot will be good for the community.

We have suggestions for how our plan can work.

• JOURNAL ACTIVITY •

*Think It Through*

Select a piece of writing you created earlier for this unit. Read the piece to identify one or more main ideas. Underline each main idea you find.

## *Find an Order That Works*

Each main idea needs details, such as examples, facts, or reasons, to support it. The illustration on this page shows how a main idea and supporting details work together.

Brainstorm, or use prewriting notes to make a list of details. Once you have the details, you can put them in order. Your purpose will influence the order you choose. For example, to persuade your reader, you might list details in order of importance.

You can list the most important detail either first or last, depending on which order you think will be more convincing. If your purpose is to describe something, you might list the details in the order an observer would notice them. If your purpose is to explain something, you might work from the simplest details to the most difficult ones.

The page below lists the details that support one of the group's main ideas. Notice that the group listed details first and ordered them later.

The empty lot is bad for the neigborhood

②businesses near the lot suffer

①it's unsafe   *most important, mention first*

~~people think the lot makes our neighborhood the~~
~~ugliest in the city~~   *just an opinion, doesn't*
*really fit here*

# Activities

Here are some activities to help you apply what you have learned.

## 1. Guided Assignment

As a curator at an art museum, you keep track of the art works in the museum's collection. Write a description of the painting on this page for the museum's visitors.

Take five minutes to list details about the painting. Then select the most important details, and determine a sensible order for presenting them. Finally, write your description.

**PURPOSE** To experiment with ordering details to describe a painting

**AUDIENCE** Museum visitors

**LENGTH** ½–1 page

## 2. Open Assignment

Select one of the topics below or a topic of your own. Decide what your purpose is and who your audience will be. List two or three main ideas about the topic. Add supporting details. Put the ideas and details in a sensible order. Then write one page about your topic.

- a trip you would like to take
- an unusual house or building
- ways to save for something you want

Henri Matisse, *The Bowl with Goldfish*, 1914

## 3. Science

Think about a science topic you have studied recently. List the main idea or ideas and the important supporting details. Then order these ideas and details for a one-page paper about your topic.

## *Let Your Notes Be Your Guide*

You're ready to write a first draft of your essay, story, or report. How should you begin? You may feel that getting from your prewriting notes to a complete draft is a mysterious process, but it isn't. You have everything you need to write your draft. By drafting, you turn your lists, clusters, and other prewriting into sentences and paragraphs. The draft shown below didn't just write itself. The writer, Keshia, used her group's prewriting notes to guide her writing.

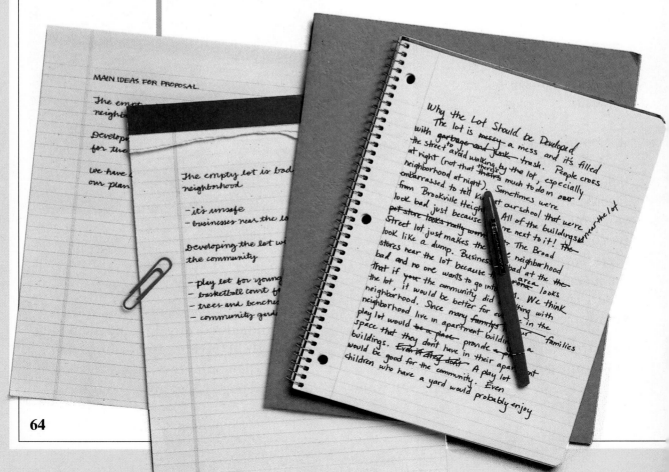

# Anything Goes

Sometimes stories and reports seem easy to write. Other times your first page stays blank no matter how long you look at it. Even experienced writers can have trouble getting started. You might already have a way to begin drafting. If you don't, or if you'd like to try another way, you might experiment with one of the following suggestions. They can help you put your ideas into a rough form, like the sketch shown here.

1. **Pretend you're writing to a friend.** Write as if you're talking about your idea with a friend who always listens and understands.

2. **Start on the easiest part.** You don't have to start at the beginning. Even a difficult piece may have some easier sections. Start by writing those, and the other parts will probably seem easier to write.

3. **Speak your ideas into a tape recorder.** Say what you're thinking on tape, and you'll have an instant first draft.

4. **Set reasonable goals.** Facing an entire essay, report, or story can be scary. Decide that you are going to write just one paragraph or even one sentence at a time.

## • JOURNAL ACTIVITY •
### Think It Through

Think about the techniques listed above or about one you have developed yourself. Then explain in your journal how these suggestions might help you with your drafting.

## Writing On

Once you've begun writing, the challenge is to continue writing. Keep your prewriting notes handy. You may find it helpful to look back at them when you reach a stopping point in your writing. Writers often must stop to review their notes to keep their ideas flowing in the right direction.

Completing your first draft is more important than perfecting every sentence. Later you can rearrange your sentences or improve the way they're stated. You can also leave grammar, spelling, and punctuation to a later stage.

Some writers like to draft on a computer. Others prefer to draft by hand. Do whatever works best for you. If you find yourself stuck, however, the illustration below offers some suggestions for getting your writing back on track.

# *Activities*

Here are some activities to help you apply what you have learned.

## 1. Guided Assignment

Suppose that you are a travel writer. The painting at the right will illustrate your next article. Use the painting to generate ideas about the city life you experienced on a recent trip. Use a prewriting technique to explore one idea. Then list and order details. Finally, draft a one-page article.

| | |
|---|---|
| **PURPOSE** | To experiment with generating a draft |
| **AUDIENCE** | Readers of a travel magazine |
| **LENGTH** | 1 page |

## 2. Open Assignment

Choose one of the topics listed below or one of your own. Create a cluster diagram to explore ideas. Then draft a one- to two-page paper on your topic.

- an important lesson I learned
- a person I admire
- a risk I took

## 3. Health and Safety

Since ancient times many people have valued the ideal of a sound mind in a sound body. What links can you find between health and school performance? List ideas about this topic. Explore your ideas through clustering, and decide how to order them. Then draft a one-page paper on this topic.

Charles Goeller, *Third Avenue*, 1933–1934

## *Get the Picture?*

Henry, Mike, and Keshia turned their ideas for the lot's layout into a rough sketch. When they looked at the sketch, however, they discovered that some parts didn't make sense together. As much as they liked the pond, they realized it didn't fit in with the other elements. They made a note to redraw the sketch without the pond. By looking at the whole picture rather than just at its parts, the group kept their proposal on track.

This approach—looking at a draft as a whole—will also work for you when you begin to revise. Step back from your writing, and look at the whole piece. Then decide whether it works.

## Making Sense

Putting some distance between yourself and your writing helps you see it better. Set your draft aside for a while before you read it again. When you return to the draft, you'll want to evaluate it for clarity, to decide whether it makes sense. Answering the questions on this checklist will help you decide how to revise your draft for clarity.

*Do I stick to my topic?*

*Do I accomplish my purpose?*

*Do I keep my audience in mind?*

*Does my main idea come across clearly?*

*Do I give enough details? Too many?*

## A Second Opinion

One of the best ways to evaluate a draft is to have a peer reviewer examine it. Getting another opinion helps you gain distance from your writing. The remainder of this lesson explains how to be a peer reviewer and what to do with a peer reviewer's advice.

**Reading It Over**   As a peer reviewer, you try to answer these questions: What's the main idea of this paper? Do the details in the paper support that idea? Keep these questions in mind as you read through the draft for the first time. Your goal isn't to label the writing good or bad. Instead, you want to tell the writer what you understand to be the paper's main idea and purpose. And you want to tell how you think the draft is working. This outside opinion helps the writer decide what, if any, revisions to make.

### • JOURNAL ACTIVITY •
### *Think It Through*

Think about the role of a peer reviewer. As you do, consider what kinds of advice you would like from a peer reviewer. What should your reviewer look for? How would you like your reviewer to evaluate your writing? Write your thoughts in your journal.

**Giving and Receiving Feedback**  After reviewing your classmate's writing, read it again, and make more detailed comments. To make comments, you might find it helpful to fill out a peer-review form. If your teacher has such a form, use that. If not, make a form of your own, including questions like those below.

When you receive a review of your work, discuss the comments with your peer reviewer. If your reviewer has criticisms, remember that your writing is being evaluated, not you. Finally, remember that you're the writer. You decide which changes you'll make to your writing.

*The peer reviewer understood the purpose of the paper and for whom it was written. The draft forms a good foundation for the paper.*

*Why does the peer reviewer suggest leaving out these comments?*

Why the Lot Sh
The lot is a n
trash. People c
avoid walking
that there's m
night). Somet
our school
All of the
because the
makes the
look like

PEER REVIEW

1. What is the main idea of this paper? *The Broad Street lot should be developed into a park, a play lot, and a community garden.*

2. What is the writer's purpose? *To convince people to fix up the lot*

3. Who would be the intended audience for this paper? *Brookville Heights Community Improvement Group*

4. Which parts of the paper stand out for you? Name or describe them, and explain why they seem important. *The plans for developing the lot were great. I felt excited as I read about them. They convinced me that the proposal was a good idea.*

5. Identify any parts of the paper that seem puzzling or out of place. *Some comments, like ones about nothing to do in the neighborhood and being embarrassed to say where they're from, should have been left out.*

# Activities

Here are some activities to help you apply what you have learned.

## 1. Guided Assignment

Select a piece of writing you have written recently. Exchange your paper with a classmate. Read your classmate's paper, and answer the questions shown on the peer-review form on the opposite page.

After you answer these questions, look back at the writing you did for the Journal Activity on page 69. Make sure you have given your classmate the kind of advice you would find helpful. Then exchange and discuss your comments with one another.

**PURPOSE**  To develop skill in offering and receiving peer-review comments
**AUDIENCE**  A peer writer
**LENGTH**  1 page of comments

## 2. Open Assignment

Write a page about one of the topics from the following list or a topic of your own. Set your writing aside for at least two days.

Then reread your work. Use the checklist on page 69 to evaluate your writing.

- the responsibilities of a citizen
- how to work with others
- team sports versus individual sports

## 3. Social Studies

You are an archaeologist who has just unearthed the painting below. Write a description of it. When you finish, have a fellow archaeologist (another student) review your writing for clarity.

Egyptian tomb painting, *The Garden Pool*, c. 1400 B.C.

*Revising: Evaluating a Draft*

## 2.7 Revising: Making Paragraphs Effective

# The Best-laid Plans

Just as a garden consists of plant beds, a piece of writing consists of paragraphs. Like a plant bed, each paragraph must have unity—that is, all sentences must work together. All the sentences in the following paragraph work together to support the main idea, about a childhood memory.

### Literature Model

S ome of my earliest memories are of the storms, the hot rain lashing down and lightning running on the sky—and the storm cellar into which my mother and I descended so many times when I was very young. For me that little room in the earth is an unforgettable place. Across the years I see my mother reading there on the low, narrow bench, the lamplight flickering on her face and on the earthen walls; I smell the dank odor of that room; and I hear the great weather raging at the door. I have never been in a place that was like it exactly; only now and then I have been reminded of it suddenly when I have gone into a cave, or when I have just caught the scent of fresh, open earth steaming in the rain.

N. Scott Momaday, *The Names*

*Notice that all the sentences in the paragraph support the idea in the first sentence.*

# Look for the Main Ideas

As you review your draft, look for paragraphs lurking among your sentences. To recognize them, just look for the main ideas. A main idea is like a magnet pulling sentences toward it to form a paragraph. Notice how the sentences in the literature model are related to the main idea of the paragraph.

Many paragraphs have a topic sentence that states the main idea. Sometimes a topic sentence is the first sentence in a paragraph. A topic sentence can also come at the end of a paragraph. Not all paragraphs need topic sentences, however. Many well-written paragraphs consist of sentences that support the main idea without directly stating it.

Although topic sentences are used in all types of writing, they're more common in paragraphs written to explain or persuade. Paragraphs that tell a story or describe something often don't have a topic sentence. Notice the way this draft has been broken into paragraphs. Does each paragraph have a topic sentence? If so, what is it?

Since many families in our neighborhood live in apartments, a play lot would provide space that they don't have in their apartment buildings. *Topic sentence* A play lot would be good for the community. Even children who have a yard would enjoy a playground where there would be other children to play with. *New paragraph* For younger children the play lot would include a sturdy swing-and-slide set, a climbing frame, a sandbox, and a merry-go-round. Older kids could use two basketball hoops and backboards and a tetherball pole. *This idea doesn't fit in.* Regular exercise might improve school performance, as well. These features would give children and teen-agers something to do besides going to the mall or watching television.

• JOURNAL ACTIVITY •

## Think It Through

Select paragraphs from three different types of writing. For example, you might choose paragraphs from a novel, a textbook, and an instruction manual. Is the main idea of each paragraph stated in a topic sentence? If so, copy the sentence into your journal. If not, write the main idea in your own words.

## Link Thoughts Sensibly

A well-constructed paragraph is more than just several sentences about a single idea. Those sentences must connect in some sensible manner by means of transitions. Transitions are words and phrases that help connect thoughts between sentences. They provide the links between ideas in a paragraph. *Also* and *as a result* are examples of these types of transitions.

Transitions such as *in front of* and *until then* help express a relationship in space or time. Other common transitions appear in the chart on this page. Notice how the revisions to the draft below use transitions to link thoughts within the paragraph and to show relationships.

| Common Transitions | | | |
|---|---|---|---|
| after | before | because | although |
| now | therefore | however | for example |
| here | then | like | next to |

This sentence was moved to the beginning because it provides a concrete example out of which the other sentences grow.

Why did the writer add the transition "It might also mean that"?

We don't think any store can be successful next in that location to the lot. Businesses nearby *also* suffer because of the lot's condition. *In the last two years* Several businesses have come and gone in the building next to the lot. We know that developing the lot would make our neighborhood feel safer and look better. *It might also mean that* People would shop closer to home.

# *Activities*

Here are some activities to help you apply what you have learned.

## 1. Guided Assignment

As an editor for a science magazine, you need to revise the following passage. Look for main ideas. For each main idea, mark where a new paragraph should begin, signaling a change from one point to another. You may move sentences around and add transitions.

Grafting allowed Luther Burbank to develop many new plants. Burbank was known throughout the world as the Plant Wizard. He began his work with plants as a young boy, when he noticed that no two plants were exactly alike. He figured out how to graft plants together, or to connect them so that they would grow into one plant. Sometimes he repeated an experiment thousands of times before he was happy with the results. One of his most unusual experiments was to graft a potato plant and a tomato plant together.

PURPOSE To gain skill in recognizing how sentences and main ideas work together

AUDIENCE Readers of a science magazine

LENGTH 1 page

## 2. Open Assignment

Select a first draft you wrote for an earlier lesson in this unit or for another class. Examine each paragraph in your draft. Think about the following questions as you read. Then make any necessary revisions to your draft.

- What are the main ideas?
- Should any of my main ideas be stated in topic sentences?
- Do the sentences of each paragraph support the paragraph's main idea?
- Is each paragraph arranged in a sensible order?
- Would transition words help readers follow my thoughts?

## 3. Cooperative Learning

In a small group prepare a report about important people in the field of education, health care, world peace, or equal rights. Ask a teacher or librarian to help you identify these people.

Each member should research a different person and share information with the group. Two volunteers should draft a report four to six paragraphs long. Each member should read and comment on the report. Another group member should volunteer to revise the paragraphs. If you like, present the report to the class.

### COMPUTER OPTION

If your group presents its report, you might want to design it on the computer. If you have access to desktop publishing software, use it to customize the look of your report.

## *Plots and Patterns*

As Keshia, Mike, and Henry continued to revise their sketch, they looked more closely at the details of their plan. It occurred to them that maybe the lot should have more than one kind of garden. Vegetables *and* flowers might make the garden more interesting.

Just as a variety of plants makes a garden more attractive, a variety of sentences can make your writing more appealing. You've already made sure that your main ideas are clearly stated in well-organized paragraphs. Now you can think about the sentences within your paragraphs and the way you use them. Using a variety of sentences helps create a sound and rhythm in your writing that will hold your readers' interest.

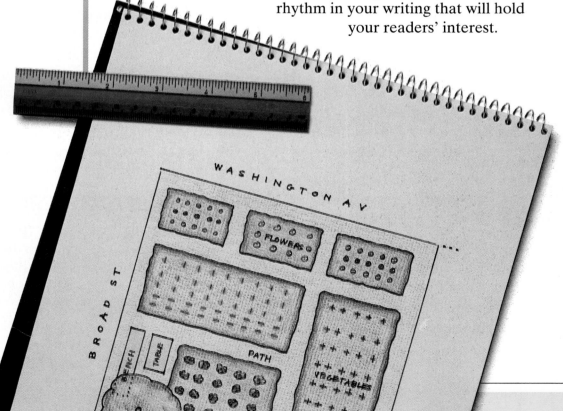

# The Long and the Short of It

Take a look at the length of your sentences. Too many short sentences make writing sound choppy. Some of these short sentences might be sentence fragments, or incomplete sentences. Change these sentences so that they express complete thoughts. Too many long sentences will make your thoughts difficult to follow. Some long sentences are run-on sentences. Breaking them into two or three sentences will make them easier to understand.

*We know that it will take money to develop the lot and we are willing to do our part to help raise the money. We could plan several fund-raising events Such as a car wash, a raffle, and a rummage sale. Also, Many teen-agers and grown-ups from the neighborhood have offered to help us also.*

Varying the order of words or phrases can also add life to your writing. For example, you can write "The bat hit the ball with a loud crack," or "With a loud crack, the bat hit the ball." Notice how revisions affect the rhythm of the paragraph shown above.

## • JOURNAL ACTIVITY •
### *Try It Out*

Select a passage of five to ten sentences from your journal. Experiment with ways to vary the length and word order of the sentences.

## Get It Together

You can also create variety by combining sentences that express similar ideas. Two or more sentences can be combined into one. For example, look at the following sentences and how they can be combined:

Wait until after the first frost to plant tomatoes. Wait until after the first frost to plant cucumbers, too.

Wait until after the first frost to plant tomatoes and cucumbers.

In both sentences, "Wait until after the first frost" expresses the same idea. "Tomatoes" and "cucumbers" are different nouns in those sentences. Consider combining sentences that express similar ideas but have different nouns, adjectives, or verbs.

When you combine sentences, certain words and phrases can help express relationships between ideas. For example, the sentence "Return that overdue book when you go to the library" uses the word *when* to express a relationship between two activities. Notice in the following paragraph how the writer combined similar thoughts and expressed relationships between activities.

Another way that neighborhood people can help is by volunteering their time to work in the lot. Volunteers can pick up trash, and They can clear out weeds. They can also plant grass, trees, and flowers. This can happen once the work gets started.

# Activities

Here are some activities to help you apply what you have learned.

## 1. Guided Assignment

The following passage will appear in a book about artist Josef Albers, who created the work shown below. Revise the sentences to create an effective sound and rhythm.

> Josef Albers was born in Germany. Albers left Germany for the United States. Albers arrived in the United States in 1933. Albers made pictures out of pieces of colored glass. Albers used primary colors (red, blue, and yellow), white, and black. Albers did not base his art on emotion. Albers based his art on intellect. Albers created abstract pictures by repeating straight lines.

| | |
|---|---|
| **PURPOSE** | To experiment with sentence variety and rhythm |
| **AUDIENCE** | Readers of an art book |
| **LENGTH** | 1 paragraph |

## 2. Open Assignment

Write a paragraph about one of the topics below or a topic of your own. Then try varying your sentences to make your writing flow easily.

- moving to another town or state
- your favorite movie
- how you imagine yourself as an adult

## 3. Mathematics

Select a math problem from a recent math assignment. Write one or two paragraphs, detailing your process for solving the problem. Then revise your sentences to create variety.

Josef Albers, *Latticework*, c. 1926

# Make a List, and Check It Twice

After all their hard work, Keshia, Mike, and Henry are almost finished. They're getting their proposal ready to present to their community improvement group. Before they present it, however, they want to make sure that everything looks good and reads as smoothly as possible.

Keshia goes over the group's checklist to be sure that they've covered every point they want to make. Mike examines the sketch, checking that every element of the plan is in place. Henry reads over the written proposal and checks all grammar, usage, and mechanics. You too will want to check your work carefully before you present it to its intended audience.

## Check It Out

Once you've made all the revisions you want, you need to edit your work. Editing means checking your spelling, punctuation, grammar, and usage. The editing stage is not the time to reorganize paragraphs or insert new ideas into your work.

When you edit, you go over your writing line by line, word by word. If you're uncertain of a spelling, consult a dictionary. Make sure you know the meanings of the words you use and that you've chosen the right words. See that you've used a singular verb with a singular subject and a plural verb with a plural subject. Check that you have used verb tenses appropriately. Examine your use of periods, commas, quotation marks, and semicolons.

- [ ] Have used all verbs properly?
- [ ] Do my subjects and verbs agree?
- [ ] Have used all pronouns properly?
- [ ] Have selected the right words for what I mean?
- [ ] Are my words spelled correctly?

You might ask a peer reviewer to help you edit. A peer reviewer can often spot errors in grammar, usage, and mechanics that you might overlook in your own work.

### • JOURNAL ACTIVITY •
### Try It Out

Look in your journal at writing that you have done recently. Choose a passage you think is in good enough shape to be published or handed in to your teacher. Use the checklist above, a dictionary, and the Grammar, Usage, and Mechanics section of this book to edit the passage.

## Mark Your Copy

Proofreading symbols, like those shown below, make editing easier. An editor uses these symbols to show a typist which changes to make. Even if you do your own typing or word processing, use proofreading symbols as you edit. Marking your copy clearly will help you catch and correct errors as you prepare the final version of your writing.

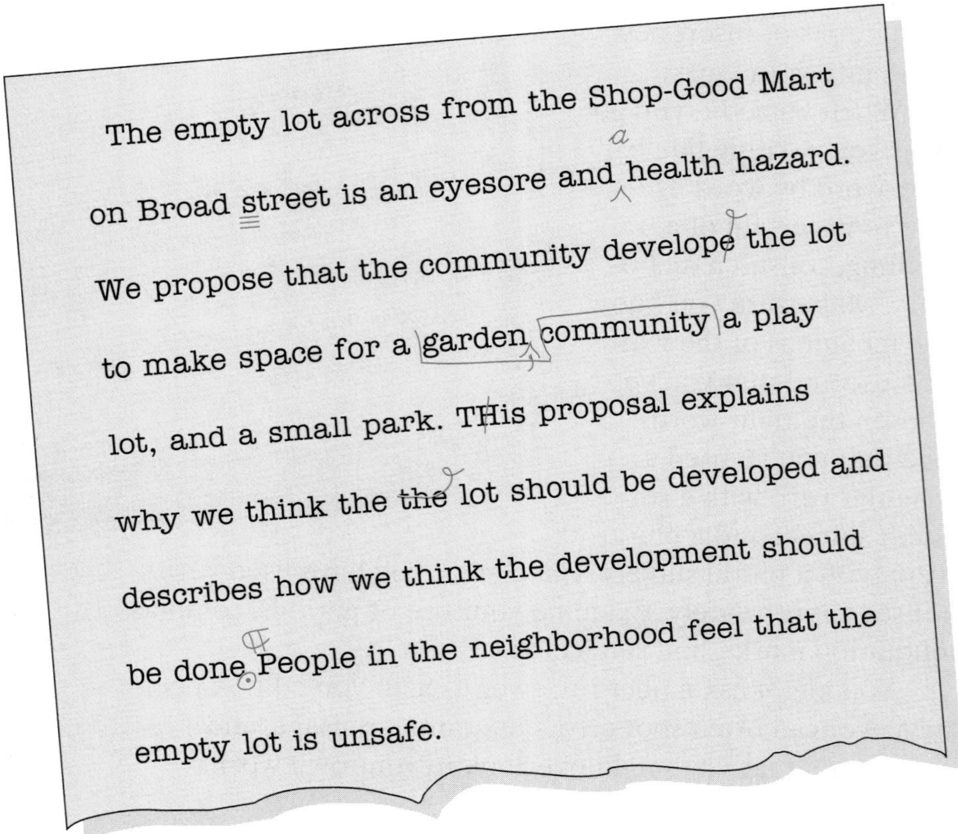

The empty lot across from the Shop-Good Mart on Broad street is an eyesore and a health hazard. We propose that the community develope the lot to make space for a garden community a play lot, and a small park. THis proposal explains why we think the the lot should be developed and describes how we think the development should be done. People in the neighborhood feel that the empty lot is unsafe.

| Proofreading Symbols | | | |
|---|---|---|---|
| ∧  Insert | ℘  Delete | ⌐  Reverse | ¶  New paragraph |
| ⊙  Period | ⋀  Comma | =  Capital letter | /  Lower-case letter |

# *Activities*

Here are some activities to help you apply what you have learned.

## 1. Guided Assignment

Proofread and edit the following passage for grammar, usage, and mechanics errors. Refer to the checklist on page 81 as you edit. Write out a copy of the passage with your changes incorporated. Give your corrected copy to your teacher.

> Birds have many of the same characteristics as human beings. The difference is that they had been adapted for flight. A birds body like a human body, has a head and torso. A bird has legs. but instead of arms, a bird has wings. A bird also has bones, but a bird's bones are hllow.
>
> The hollow bones are lighter than solid bones and it contains air sacs. Flying requires a large amount of Oxygen, Air sacks increase the amount of air a bird can take in with each breathe.

PURPOSE  To sharpen your editing and proofreading skills

AUDIENCE  Your teacher

LENGTH  2 paragraphs

## 2. Open Assignment

Select a revised piece of your writing to edit. As you edit, refer to the checklist on page 81. Use proofreaders' symbols to mark corrections on your paper. If you wish, have a classmate review your editing to make sure you have caught all your errors.

### COMPUTER OPTION

If your writing for the Open Assignment is on a computer, use a spelling-checker program to find any spelling errors. Be aware, however, that a spelling checker matches the words you type with words in its dictionary. If you make a typing error that results in another word, the spelling checker will not catch the error. For example, suppose that you mean to type the word *they* but type *the* instead. The spelling checker will recognize *the* as a word even though it is not the word you intended to type.

## 3. Cooperative Learning

Write a half-page summary of what you have learned about the writing process in this unit. Then join two classmates to form a group, and pass your papers around to one another. Each student will edit for spelling errors in the first paper he or she receives, for punctuation errors in the second, and for grammar or usage errors in the third. When everyone is finished, discuss whether it was easier or harder to divide the editing into three separate steps.

*Editing: Making Final Adjustments*  **83**

# *Take a Bow*

Mike, Henry, and Keshia feel an incredible sense of accomplishment. The sketch of the lot layout is complete, and the final version of the proposal is neatly typed. You also should feel proud when you look at your final version. All your hard work has come together in a clean, neat, and impressive piece of writing. You know that you've said everything you wanted to say in the best way possible. Now you can present your writing to its intended audience.

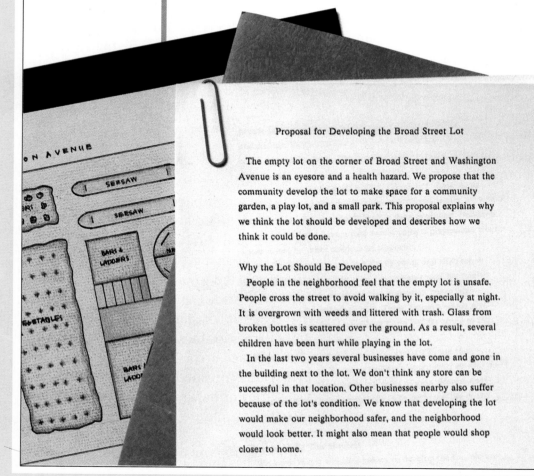

**Proposal for Developing the Broad Street Lot**

The empty lot on the corner of Broad Street and Washington Avenue is an eyesore and a health hazard. We propose that the community develop the lot to make space for a community garden, a play lot, and a small park. This proposal explains why we think the lot should be developed and describes how we think it could be done.

Why the Lot Should Be Developed

People in the neighborhood feel that the empty lot is unsafe. People cross the street to avoid walking by it, especially at night. It is overgrown with weeds and littered with trash. Glass from broken bottles is scattered over the ground. As a result, several children have been hurt while playing in the lot.

In the last two years several businesses have come and gone in the building next to the lot. We don't think any store can be successful in that location. Other businesses nearby also suffer because of the lot's condition. We know that developing the lot would make our neighborhood safer, and the neighborhood would look better. It might also mean that people would shop closer to home.

# Looking Good

A serious job candidate dresses appropriately to make a positive impression in an interview. If you're serious about your writing, you'll make sure to present it appropriately to make the best impression on your audience.

The way you present your work can vary. Sometimes you may write it out by hand, to give it a personal touch. Other times you'll want to use a typewriter or word processor. You might enclose your writing in a clear folder or binder to give it a more professional look. As in every other writing stage, your audience and purpose will influence your method of presentation.

For example, you might want to handwrite a letter of congratulations to a close friend. You need to type a formal paper for a class or a letter to a newspaper editor. You should probably prepare a formal proposal, like the one Henry, Mike, and Keshia present to their community groups, on a typewriter or word processor.

---

• JOURNAL ACTIVITY •
## Think It Through

Think about a piece of writing you have completed recently. Then think of two ways that you might prepare the writing for presentation. In your journal write a comparison of the two forms of presentation. Why did you choose these two forms? What difference would a change in presentation make?

## On Display

Naturally, when you've finished your writing, you want to share it with the audience you've had in mind all along. How you reach an audience depends partly on who the audience is.

The illustration below shows different ways of presenting your work to different audiences. Other forms of presentation include a speech, a letter, a submission to a school literary magazine, a written invitation, a press release, a dramatic reading, or a banner. Notice that some of these presentations are oral rather than written. Others might include illustrations or other types of images. You had a specific audience in mind as you wrote. How can you present your writing to reach this audience?

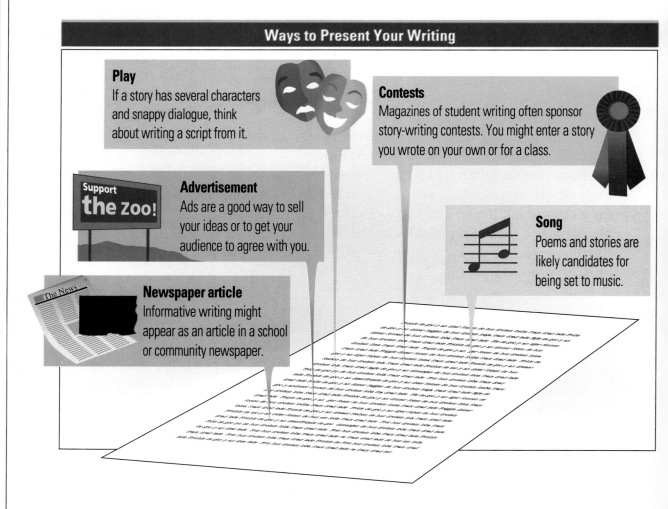

### Ways to Present Your Writing

**Play**
If a story has several characters and snappy dialogue, think about writing a script from it.

**Contests**
Magazines of student writing often sponsor story-writing contests. You might enter a story you wrote on your own or for a class.

**Advertisement**
Ads are a good way to sell your ideas or to get your audience to agree with you.

Support the zoo!

**Song**
Poems and stories are likely candidates for being set to music.

**Newspaper article**
Informative writing might appear as an article in a school or community newspaper.

The News

# Activities

Here are some activities to help you apply what you have learned.

## 1. Guided Assignment

Write three separate paragraphs about a sport, hobby, or other activity you enjoy. Write each paragraph for a different audience. For example, if you enjoy bicycling, you might write one paragraph to tell teen-agers what to consider when shopping for a bike. Your second paragraph might offer suggestions for family bike trips in your area, and a third could persuade working people to use bicycles instead of cars.

Think about how you could present each paragraph to its intended audience. Write your idea about the presentation after the paragraph.

PURPOSE   To explore ways to reach different audiences
AUDIENCE  Yourself
LENGTH    3 paragraphs

### COMPUTER OPTION

If one of your presentations for the Guided Assignment includes a poster, flyer, or other public notice, you might experiment with highlighting text by using different typefaces. Try printing several versions of the same notice, using different combinations of type sizes and styles. Then compare the effects of the different versions.

## 2. Open Assignment

Write a letter to the editor of a magazine or a newspaper, responding to an article you have read in that publication. Think about what kind of response you want to write. Before you begin writing, study the publication to get a sense for who reads it. These readers will be your audience. Think about them when you are writing.

Be sure you state your main idea and order your supporting details so that your writing is clear. Then mail your letter to the address provided in the publication. Watch future issues to see if your letter is printed.

## 3. Cooperative Learning

A political campaign involves reaching different groups of voters through different types of presentations. In a small group consider the forms of presentation that a U.S. presidential candidate might use in a campaign. These would include such things as posters, speeches, TV ads, and interviews.

Agree on a candidate your group would like to support. The candidate might be somebody you know personally or somebody famous. Working in pairs or as individuals, plan four different presentations that could form part of a campaign. Share your plans in the full group. Carry out at least one of the plans, and share it with the class.

**MINFONG HO**
*from*

# THE CLAY MARBLE

*In 1980, after North Vietnamese troops invaded Cambodia, writer Minfong Ho helped set up food programs for Cambodian children who had fled to Thailand's border. Despite starvation and sickness, many of these children, like Jantu and Dara in* The Clay Marble, *enjoyed making toys and marbles from clay. With that same creative spirit, Cambodians rebuilt their lives. Ho's writing shows how the strength gained from people working together can help to overcome the horrors of war.*

After that marble, Jantu was interested only in playing with clay. She would spend the long afternoons crouched by the mud puddle by the stone beam, scooping up handfuls of moist clay to shape little figures.

For some reason, the massive stone beam attracted Jantu. She loved playing there. "It's so old, so solid," she said. "I like being near it. It makes me feel like a cicada[1] molting under some big rain tree."

1 **cicada** (si kā′ də) a large, winged, flylike insect

At one end of the stone beam she had propped some fantail palm fronds,**2** to make a thatched shelter so that we could play in the shade. When we crouched under it, it was like being in a leafy cave.

We spent most of our spare time in there. I would sit on the stone beam, bouncing her baby brother in my lap, as Jantu sculpted her dainty clay figures.

"I wish we could always be together like this," I said one afternoon. "Don't you wish things would stay just the same?"

Jantu glanced up from the clay buffalo she was shaping and smiled at me. "But how can we always stay the same, Dara?" she asked. "We're not made of stone. You wouldn't want to lie half-buried in the fields for hundreds of years, anyway, would you?"

"No, I meant . . . I just meant that nothing nice ever lasts." I struggled to find words for what I wanted to say. "What we're doing now, just playing here together—I wish we could hang on to it, that's all."

Jantu put down the half-formed clay buffalo. "I know what you mean," she said slowly. "You try to hang on to older people—parents, uncles, grandmothers—and they disappear. You make friends, and they go off in different directions, never to be seen again. Everything crumbles so easily." Absentmindedly she picked up a dirt clod and crushed it in her fist, letting the crumbs of dirt dribble out. "We don't even have real families anymore," she said. "Just bits and pieces of one."

I stole a glance at my friend. I knew Jantu had lost both her parents and an older brother during the long war years, but she never talked about it.

"What do you mean?" I asked carefully.

"What I have, and what you have," she said, "are leftovers of families. Like fragments**3** from a broken bowl that nobody wants. We're not a real family."

**2 fronds** (frondz) leaves
**3 fragments** (frag′ mənts) parts broken off

"What's a real family, then?"

"A real family," Jantu said, "grows. It gets bigger. People get added to it. Husbands, mothers-in-law, babies."

I thought about this. It was true. My own family had been getting smaller, shrinking rather than growing. Was it just the fragment of a family now? "I'd like to be part of a real family again," I said wistfully.

"You could be," Jantu said. "And so could I."

"How?"

"You'll see. Watch," Jantu said. She started molding her clay buffalo again. With small twisting movements, her hands teased[4] out four legs, then shaped a pair of horns. Deftly[5] she smoothed and rounded the shape until it had become a miniature water buffalo.

Then, with a flourish, she lifted up a layer of straw in a corner of our shelter. Nestled in the straw was a group of other clay figures. Carefully she set the miniature buffalo next to them. "There," she said. "They're finished—the whole set of them."

"What are they?" I asked. "Can I see?"

Jantu smiled at me mysteriously. "I didn't want to show you until they were all ready."

"And are they ready?"

"They are!" Ceremoniously,

Pierre Bonnard, *The Lesson*, 1926

4 **teased** (tēzd) pulled apart
5 **deftly** (deft′ lē) skillfully

Jantu took a clay doll and set it on the stone beam. Just then a few drops of rain started to fall.

Jantu parted a section of the palm frond and scanned the sky anxiously. Thick gray clouds had drifted across to block out the sun. In the distance, a clap of thunder sounded.

The wind picked up and was sweeping up eddies[6] of dust into the air. Then the rain started in earnest, one of those sudden thunderstorms hinting of the monsoons[7] due to come soon. Jantu stretched her sarong[8] protectively over the pile of straw where her clay figures were. Hunched over them like that, she looked like a scruffy hen trying to hatch her precious eggs.

I huddled close to Jantu and listened to the rain drumming on the leaves. Raindrops pierced through the cracks of the palm fronds and felt light and cool on my bare arms. I thought of the long rainy afternoons I had spent on the porch at home when I was very young. As light and cool as the rain, my grandmother's fingers would massage my scalp while I rested my head in her lap. Nearby, the murmur of my family surrounded me, like a soft blanket.

I closed my eyes now and tried to imagine them all sitting around me: Grandmother stroking me, Father and Sarun whittling on the steps, Mother stoking the embers of the cooking fire. It wasn't just the thick thatched roof that had sheltered me, I realized now. It was the feeling I had had then, of being part of a family as a gently pulsing whole, so natural it was like the breathing of a sleeping baby.

When I opened my eyes, I saw that Jantu had a lost, faraway look in her eyes, and I knew that she was remembering, too, what it was like when her own family was whole and complete.

6 **eddies** (ed′ēz) currents of air moving in a circular motion against the main current
7 **monsoons** (mon soonz′) southwesterly winds of southern Asia that bring heavy rains
8 **sarong** (sə rông′) a long strip of cloth, often brightly colored and printed, worn around the lower part of the body like a skirt

Hung Liu, *Tale of Two Women*, 1991

As the rain died down, Jantu turned to me and smiled. "You still want to play with my family of dolls?" she asked.

I'd rather have my own family back, I thought, but dolls were better than nothing. "Sure," I said.

---

### For Discussion

1. How can a family of dolls like the one Jantu made lift the spirits of someone who is sad and lonely?

2. Life is constantly changing. What are some things in your life you wish would stay the same?

---

## Readers Respond

The scene I remember most clearly is when Jantu shows Dara the clay figures she has made. When the thunderstorm started, I felt anxious about what was going to happen to the girls and to Jantu's dolls. The writer definitely kept my attention.

**Monica Vera**

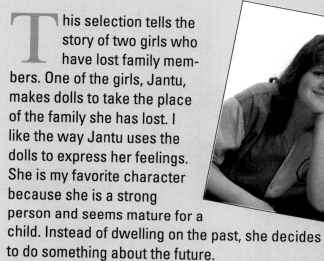

This selection tells the story of two girls who have lost family members. One of the girls, Jantu, makes dolls to take the place of the family she has lost. I like the way Jantu uses the dolls to express her feelings. She is my favorite character because she is a strong person and seems mature for a child. Instead of dwelling on the past, she decides to do something about the future.

I would recommend this selection to my friends. It tells a story about how these children cope with losing family members, and it is written from a kid's point of view. My friends could probably relate to the feelings this story expresses because many of them have lost a mother, father, or grandparent.

**Amanda Mason**

### Did You Notice?

1. Did you notice the thought process that Dara goes through during this piece? How does her thinking change from the beginning to the end?

2. What things or people in your life comfort or support you? In your journal write your feelings about these things or people and their importance to you.

# Writing Process in Action

## Many Kinds of Courage

In *The Clay Marble* by Minfong Ho, two young people, Jantu and Dara, have lost most of their family and friends in a war. They have not given up, though. They find comfort in each other's company and in the clay dolls they make.

Has someone you admire survived against great odds? Have you discovered in yourself courage you didn't know you had? The assignment that follows invites you to share a story of bravery.

### • Assignment •

| | |
|---|---|
| *Context* | A new student publication called <u>People Who Dared</u> prints stories, articles, and interviews about the bravery and endurance of young people. |
| *Purpose* | To share your admiration of someone who overcame difficulty through bravery |
| *Audience* | Student readers of <u>People Who Dared</u> |
| *Length* | 2 or more pages |

The following pages offer step-by-step advice on how to approach this assignment. Read through the pages before you begin. Then return to each step as needed while you work on your assignment.

# 1. Prewriting

What's your definition of courage? Is it facing danger to save a life? Is it making a difficult decision? Or is it simply surviving in a situation that would make many people give up?

Choose one of the ideas at the right or an idea of your own. Begin looking for examples of courageous people. Decide on one you'd like to write about. Then explore your topic by brainstorming, clustering, or listing. See pages 60–63 for suggestions on listing to explore a meaningful topic that fits the assignment.

**Option A**

Talk to friends, teachers, or relatives.

**Option B**

Look through magazines or newspapers.

**Option C**

Read a biography.

*courageous people—*
*Helen Keller*
*from small town*
*in Alabama*
*became deaf and*
*blind in infancy*
*learned to speak at*
*age ten*
*entered Radcliffe*
*College at age*
*nineteen*

# 2. Drafting

Look over your list, cluster diagram, or other prewriting notes. What problems did your subject face? Why do you think this person's act of bravery or courage is significant? Use your answers to these questions as foundations for sentences and paragraphs.

Remember that courage doesn't always come in a big, dramatic package. What kind of courage does Jantu show in the excerpt below?

With small twisting movements, [Jantu's] hands teased out four legs, then shaped a pair of horns. Deftly she smoothed and rounded the shape until it had become a miniature water buffalo.

Then, with a flourish, she lifted up a layer of straw in a corner of our shelter. Nestled in the straw was a group of other clay figures. Carefully she set the miniature buffalo next to them. "There," she said, "They're finished—the whole set of them."

As you write your draft, think about specific actions that will explain your admiration for the person you're writing about. Instead of saying that Jantu is brave, Minfong Ho showed her constructing a new "family" out of clay.

Remember, in the drafting stage you need to express your ideas in sentences and paragraphs. You can make changes later.

## 3. Revising

Look back at page 94 when you are ready to revise. Does what you've written fulfill the assignment? Make sure you haven't strayed from your topic. Sometimes it's a good idea to set your writing aside for a day or two before you make revisions. Then try to read your work as if you were seeing it for the first time. The questions below can help you think about the changes to make in your draft.

**Question A**

Have I explained why this person is courageous?

**Question B**

Does each paragraph add details to the picture?

**Question C**

Have I varied my sentences?

Most people would say it takes courage to ~~go~~ leave home in Alabama to attend a famous New England college. ~~to one of the most famous colleges in the country. Just leaving your home to go to another region takes courage.~~ How about if you ~~are a girl, going to college~~ For a girl to do this at a time when very few women ~~graduated from college? But~~ attended college takes even more courage. ~~imagine doing all this~~ if you were deaf and blind. ∧ as well. So imagine yourself as a girl from Alabama leaving home to attend Radcliffe College in Massachusetts in the early twentieth century. Now

## 4. Editing

You've worked hard to determine what you want to say and how to say it well. As you prepare your article to send to *People Who Dared*, make sure to get rid of any distracting errors. Readers can then better appreciate your writing.

This checklist will help you catch errors you might otherwise overlook. You'll want your article to reflect your hard work, so read and reread your work with care. Use a dictionary and the Grammar, Usage, and Mechanics part of this book to help you edit.

*Checklist*

1. Have I used any sentence fragments or run-on sentences?
2. Is every word spelled and used correctly?
3. Have I used pronouns correctly?
4. Do my subjects and verbs agree?

## 5. Presenting

Make sure your account of courage is neatly written or typed on clean white paper before you submit it to *People Who Dared*. If possible, include a picture—a photograph or a drawing—of your subject so that readers will connect the actual person with what you've written.

As an alternative way of presenting your writing, you and others in your class might present your account as a play or a dramatic reading.

### Reflecting

Consider what you've learned about courage from writing this account. Ordinary people sometimes have to defend those they love, stand up for something they believe in, or accomplish difficult goals. What do you think leads some people to be courageous? Would you like to be more courageous in certain ways? What can you do to develop your own courage?

# Portfolio & Reflection

## Summary

**Key concepts in the writing process include the following:**

- The writing process is made up of five stages. Writers use these stages in ways that work best for them.
- Prewriting, such as brainstorming and clustering, helps a writer find and explore possible writing topics.
- Drafting means turning prewriting into sentences and paragraphs.
- Revising means evaluating a draft for sense. Peer reviewing is one helpful way to revise a draft.
- Editing means checking a piece of writing for errors in grammar, usage, and mechanics.
- Presenting means sharing writing with its intended audience.

## Your Writer's Portfolio

Look over the writing you did for this unit. Choose two pieces for your portfolio. Look for writing that does one or more of the following:

- grows out of your prewriting ideas
- has ideas arranged in a sensible order
- states the main idea in a topic sentence
- reflects revising for sound and rhythm in sentences
- appeals to a particular audience
- has a clear purpose in mind
- reflects editing to fix any errors in grammar, usage, or mechanics
- shows the effects of helpful revisions suggested by a peer reviewer

## Reflection and Commentary

Think about what you learned in this unit. Answer the following questions as you look over the two pieces of writing you chose. Write a page of "Comments on the Writing Process" for your portfolio.

1. What techniques helped you most in finding or exploring writing topics?
2. What effect did your purpose and audience have on your writing?
3. Which stages of the writing process did you find yourself returning to?
4. What forms might you choose to present your writing?

## Feedback

**If you had a chance to respond to the following student comment, what would you say or ask?**

*One way I come up with writing topics is to write down sentences on pieces of paper and put them in a basket. Then I pull one out, and start writing about it.*
Barton Burkhart, Oak Creek Junior High School, Cornville, Arizona

# Writing to Describe

# Flights of Fancy

Franz Marc, *The Bewitched Mill*, 1913

# Fantasy

## SNYDER DESCRIBES GARGOYLES

*"For me the whole joy of writing is the chance to let my imagination freewheel. I like to balance a story between reality and fantasy. Then I can use descriptive language to give exciting and delicious hints in both directions."*

Zilpha Keatley Snyder

It's no surprise that Zilpha Keatley Snyder grew up to be a writer of imaginative fiction. As a young child, she began making imaginative journeys through the eyes of characters. Snyder recalls "spending several months walking to school as an Egyptian queen."

Snyder has written twenty-eight books, mostly for young adults. Her recent book *Song of the Gargoyle* is set in the Middle Ages, a favorite period of Snyder's since childhood. She explains, "I wanted to create a fairy tale." At the center of the tale is a young boy, Tymmon, who is searching for his kidnapped father. As he travels in search of his father, Tymmon faces the challenge of survival. He also meets a gargoyle named Troff. Ordinarily, a gargoyle is a monsterlike ornament made of stone. But Troff's no ordinary gargoyle: he's alive.

**Writing a Fantasy**

**1.** Describing the Setting          **2.** Filling the Scenes          **3.** Strengthening the Picture

### FOCUS

In descriptive writing, precise nouns and modifiers create an overall impression, or mood.

## 1 Describing the Setting

After Snyder has the basic idea of creating a fairy tale set in the Middle Ages, she begins describing the setting. To do this, she sketches some of the story's settings. For *Song of the Gargoyle*, she drew floor plans of castles. Photographs of real castles also helped Snyder visualize details about her story's castle.

After sketching ideas for a setting, Snyder describes the story's main characters from the inside out. She "writes down everything" she knows about the characters. How does she learn about them? "By trying to live in their shoes and react as they would," she says. With the character Tymmon, for example, Snyder played what she calls the what-if game. What if Tymmon meets Troff? How will he react? What if Tymmon

is frightened by Troff's appearance? What if Tymmon isn't sure whether Troff is a gargoyle or a dog with batlike ears?

What words and descriptions would communicate such reactions to the reader? Snyder decided that Tymmon's first reaction would be fear, caused by Troff's ugliness. She then wrote down descriptive details such as "bulging eyes" and "jagged bat-wing ears" that height-ened Troff's scary features.

Snyder thinks even her characters' names can work as descriptive details. The name Troff, for example, "sounded a bit like a dog's bark," Snyder says.

When picturing the story, Snyder's final step is to write what she calls the plot page. Here Snyder tries "to know the main thrust of the story and what the climax will be."

## 2 Filling the Scenes

Every morning Snyder sits down at her computer to write. When she's drafting a scene, she first establishes two sets of goals. Snyder explains, "On the left-hand side is action—the events I want to happen. On the right-hand side is exposition. There I highlight the information I need to get across to the reader."

Snyder then tries to put herself into a scene. "I try to see it as vividly as possible. Then I tell about what I see," she says. *Song of the Gargoyle,* for example, is told through the eyes of Tymmon. This means that Snyder describes the gargoyle from Tymmon's point of view. The order in which she reveals

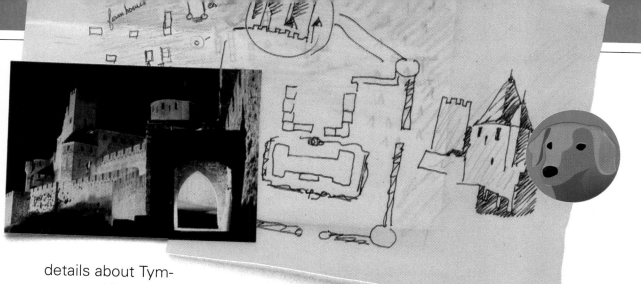

details about Tymmon and Troff contributes importantly to the suspense of the story. Short descriptive phrases, such as "not stone," "a monster certainly," "a living gargoyle," "hungry," reveal Tymmon's hesitation as he tries to make sense of the creature before him.

Snyder wrote a complete physical description of Troff to use later in the scene. Why later? Because "Tymmon was too frightened at first to notice details such as 'snub-snouted' or 'fisheyed.'"

**INTERFACE** *Write a description of a favorite pet or an imaginary creature from your childhood. Think of details, such as its eyes or paws. If it could talk, what might it say?*

▼ *In the following excerpt from* Song of the Gargoyle, *which details seem most descriptive? Why?*

T he bulging eyes blinked, the grin disappeared, and the tongue flapped up to lick the sagging jowls. Not stone. Not of stone and, he belatedly realized, certainly not where gargoyles were usually to be found–on the eaves of church or castle. But what then? A monster certainly. A monster so ugly that the mere sight of it might well, like the evil Medusa, turn the viewer to stone.

Tymmon's hand crept up to test his cheek for evidence of hardening. Still soft and warm. He swallowed hard. Swallowed again and tried to speak.

"What–what are you? What do you want of me?"

The monster cocked its head, its jagged batwing ears flopping. It certainly looked very like a gargoyle. A new thought occurred. Perhaps it was. Perhaps a magical gargoyle conjured into life by some powerful enchantment.

### 3 Strengthening the Picture

Snyder revises each day's work the next morning. She works to improve word choice and clarity. "I try to see if what I've written really calls forth my vision," she explains. This means making sure her descriptive details suggest the two possible interpretations of Troff. Is he a gargoyle? Or is he a dog?

Snyder also uses her computer's thesaurus function. She looks for what she calls "more flamboyant adjectives and adverbs." She seeks precise nouns and verbs.

When she's satisfied with the revised draft, Snyder shares it with a group of fellow writers. She says, "When you read aloud to other people, you hear things that you miss when reading alone." Snyder wants to be certain her readers see the picture she's described. In descriptive writing, that means creating an overall impression with carefully chosen words.

Zilpha Keatley Snyder
Song of the Gargoyle

SONG OF THE GARGOYLE
Zilpha Keatley Snyder

# ON ASSIGNMENT

## 1. Creative Writing

**Write a brief character description.**

- Choose an imaginary character, or write about one of the characters in the image on the right.

- Decide on an overall descriptive goal. Is there a reaction you want readers to have? What questions do you want readers to ask about this character?

- What details will help readers see your character? Consider the order in which you reveal these.

- Choose for the character a name that strengthens its description.

## 2. About Literature

**Write a brief response to a description of a legendary figure.**

- Consider the descriptions of King Arthur or Merlin found in *The Story of King Arthur and His Knight,* by Howard Pyle, and *The Once and Future King,* by T. H. White. Or visit the library, and choose another description that interests you.

- What overall impression does the writer give of the legendary figure?

- What descriptive details does the writer use to support that impression?

## 3. Cooperative Learning

**Describe an imaginary setting.**

- In a small group brainstorm for an imaginary setting, and choose one.

- Together, make a list of items you want to place in the setting. Does your setting have trees? Animals? An ocean or a sea?

- To each person assign one item to describe.

- When everyone has written a description, meet again as a group and read the descriptions out loud.

- As a group, write one description that places all your items in the setting.

*Case Study: Fantasy*  **105**

# Writing to Show, Not Tell

## *What in the World Is That?*

If you think the brightly colored creature in the picture on this page looks like a flower, you are actually pretty close. They are animals called sea anemones. They got their name because they resemble a flower called an anemone. People often use words for familiar things to label or describe something new.

In the novel *Journey Outside* a boy named Dilar has grown up on an underground river. When he discovers life on Earth's surface, he finds himself surrounded by new sights and sounds. In the passage below he describes one unfamiliar creature.

### Literature Model

*To what does Dilar compare the strange sights and sounds he encounters?*

H e cried out abruptly. Something was coming toward him in the air, a little fish gliding through the air, helping itself along with great fins that stuck out from its sides and then folded tight against them. A wonder, a wonder! The fish stopped suddenly in the top of one of the little trees, put out little legs to hold itself up, threw back its head, and opening its mouth made such sounds as Dilar had never heard before. No water murmured so joyously or so sweetly or so triumphantly; nothing, nothing had ever rung upon his ears like that or made his heart feel it must burst open with that song's wild delight. Even when it had ceased it echoed in his head.

Mary Q. Steele, *Journey Outside*

# Make It Come to Life!

Descriptions can make a person, place, or thing come to life. Think of a fictional character—one you remember because the author used effective descriptive details. Perhaps there is a place you now want to visit because a writer described it so clearly. When you write, select details so carefully that your reader can see, hear, smell, taste, and feel what you describe. In the passage below, Bethany Bentley does not merely tell the reader a storm passed through her town. She uses descriptive details that show the storm.

## Student Model

I looked outside from the beaten-up restaurant and saw the vivid purple sky flashing with lightning, while the willow across the street swayed in the wind.

The lights from the neighboring store reflected on the window and blurred my view of the storm. The rain crashed down on the roof and pelted the windows, also contributing to my blurry view.

I could see pieces of bark flying off of the willow tree. Litter flew high into the evening sky.

The lightning struck again. I shuddered as a cold draft drifted through the cracked window nearby.

Bethany Bentley, Oak Creek School, Cornville, Arizona

*Notice how the writer describes the movement of objects to show the violence of the storm.*

*How does the writer make this scene seem real?*

## • JOURNAL ACTIVITY •
### Try It Out

In your journal write several statements without any descriptive details, such as *The picnic was fun.* Then choose one of your sentences, and list five or six details that will help readers see, hear, smell, taste, or feel what you are describing.

# On Almost Every Page

Descriptive words and phrases are important in nearly all kinds of writing. A menu can make an ordinary sandwich sound so good you can taste it. A travel brochure takes you to places where you feel warm breezes, hear crashing waves, or smell the volcanic ash. A clear description of a lost pet leads to its return to the owner. A story fascinates you by its descriptions of a place or a person. Descriptions catch a reader's interest and stay in the reader's memory.

**Come to the 87th Annual Fourth-of-July Summerfest!**

**6:00** Enjoy our crispy fried chicken, maple-glazed baked beans, buttered sweet corn, flaky biscuits, fresh-squeezed lemonade, and ice-cold watermelon.

**7:30** Sit on a grassy river bank and listen to patriotic marches played by our high school band.

**9:00** Ooh! and Aah! with the crowd as fireworks boom, pop, and crackle into bouquets of color.

**UTAH**

Ski on snow-capped mountains. Breathe in the fresh scent of pine. Swim or water-ski in the cool, clear water of Echo Lake. It's all waiting for you in Utah.

**Victory Follows Free Throw in Final Game**

The last minute of the game was the stuff movies are made of. At the high school gym, ablaze with fluorescent lights, two thousand pairs of eyes concentrated on number 12 as they waited for the most important free throw of the season. The sweat poured down his face and dripped into his eyes. In the strained silence the snap of a fan's bubble gum cracked like the starting gun at a race.

Willa Cather
*My Ántonia*

**Descriptions of Birds in Dunes State Park**

She was so thin you could count her bones. Her skin was dead white. Fine, dark brown hair was scraped back so tightly that you could see the pulse throbbing at her temples. But Cora's black eyes snapped with anger. Once you looked into them, you knew Cora's spirit was strong.

**LOST**

Lost near Clark and California. Female cat named Whiteout. White with black nose. Wearing red collar with name spelled out in rhinestones. Declawed. Please help! Reward! 55-1234

108

# Activities

Here are some activities to help you apply what you have learned.

## 1. Guided Assignment

Some writers, such as restaurant reviewers, make a career of writing about food. Write a review of a meal you have eaten. Include descriptive words and phrases about how the food looks, tastes, smells, feels, and sounds. Choose details that will make readers feel as if they can hardly wait to eat a meal like the one you describe.

**PURPOSE** To write a description of a meal in a way that will make readers share your impressions

**AUDIENCE** A newspaper or magazine reader

**LENGTH** 1–2 pages

Mike Kabotie, *Shalako and Aholas*, 1970

## 2. Open Assignment

Write a description of a familiar object as if you were seeing it for the first time. Pretend you do not understand what the object is or what it does. Ask yourself questions about it. Is it like something you already know? Does it move? What are its shape and its size? Describe one of the following objects or choose your own:

- saxophone
- boom box
- backpack
- hang glider

## 3. Art

Study the painting on this page, and list words and phrases that can help you describe one of the figures. Include details of what the figure looks like. Include other details describing the sounds, smells, or tastes you imagine as you think about the figure. Then write a description of the figure for someone who has not seen the painting.

# Combining Observation and Imagination in a Description

## *Take a Good Look*

Martin Charlot, *Fruit of the Spirit,* 1983

Martin Charlot used his powers of observation and his imagination to create the fantasy world of this painting. In his world are things both real and imaginary. Imagine that you are flying in this special place. Use your five senses. Look around. Notice the color, movement, and life. Close your eyes, and concentrate on sounds and scents. Touch the plants, the water, the fish, the fruit. Now you, too, are combining the real and the imaginary.

# Sharing a World

Artists use images, colors, and shapes to draw you into their worlds. Writers do the same thing with sensory language— language that describes how something looks, sounds, feels, tastes, or smells. Their worlds may be fantasy worlds, like that shown in *Fruit of the Spirit* or in famous books such as *The Wonderful Wizard of Oz* or *The Hobbit*. In the passage below, Willa Cather uses sensory details to draw you into a world that is not fantasy but was once very real to her. From her memory she draws sensory images that allow readers to share her experiences of a place and a time in her past.

## Grammar
### Editing Tip

When editing, check for periods and other end marks after each sentence. For more information see pages 526–527.

### Literature Model

While the train flashed through never-ending miles of ripe wheat, by country towns and bright-flowered pastures and oak groves wilting in the sun, we sat in the observation car, where the woodwork was hot to the touch and red dust lay deep over everything. The dust and heat, the burning wind, reminded us of many things. We were talking about what it is like to spend one's childhood in little towns like these, buried in wheat and corn, under stimulating extremes of climate: burning when one is fairly stifled in vegetation, in the colour and smell of strong weeds and heavy harvests; blustery winters with little snow, when the country is stripped bare and grey as sheet-iron.

Willa Cather, Introduction to *My Ántonia*

To which senses does Willa Cather's language appeal? Give examples.

## • JOURNAL ACTIVITY •
### Try It Out

Think of a sound you like to hear—maybe a song or the crack of a bat or someone's voice. List eight or ten words that describe the sound.

# Use Your Imagination!

You are able to describe people, places, things, and situations because you first perceive the details through your senses. You see that your friend has curly hair. You smell new tar on the street. You can take those details from your own experience and use them in descriptive writing. Nikki Housholder uses this technique in the poem below. She combines ordinary details to create images her readers can share.

## Student Model

Waving trees,
Dark, lonely days
Sagging clouds over cold, crawling water,
Whispering leaves of short, furry bushes,
Surrounded by falling moonlight above,
With twinkling eyes spying from the dense darkness,
Opening the door to freedom.

Nikki Housholder, Oak Creek School,
Cornville, Arizona

*How is the sensory language in the fourth line different from that in the other lines?*

You can also use your senses to help you describe imaginary things. As you examine the fantasy image on this page, you will recognize details from animals in the real world. Think about how the illustrator created a new image by combining real details in unusual ways. The Scarecrow of Oz and the Hobbits are fantasy characters with details that could describe real people.

# *Activities*

Here are some activities to help you apply what you have learned.

## 1. Guided Assignment

Imagine that you are taking part in a student-exchange program with schools on another planet. On the first day in your new home, you shop for groceries with your sponsor family. Write to your Earth family. Describe four or five foods. Tell how the food looks, smells, feels, and tastes. Include words and images your family is already familiar with to describe these new and unfamiliar foods.

PURPOSE    To use sensory language to describe unfamiliar food

AUDIENCE    Your family

LENGTH    1–2 pages

## 2. Open Assignment

Write a description. Use your imagination to identify details that appeal to several senses but not the obvious one. For example, think of ways to describe rain without saying it is wet: rain runs, changes shape, makes puddles, helps grass grow, and brings out umbrellas. For your description choose one of the following topics, or make up your own:

- Describe a sunset without naming colors.
- Describe your favorite meal without using taste words.
- Describe a conversation without mentioning words.

## 3. Cooperative Learning

In a small group take turns describing the imaginary world pictured in the painting on page 110. Each individual should use only one sense in the description. For example, if the first person describes details relating to sight, the second person will focus on the sense of hearing, and so on.

Take turns reading your descriptions while other group members take notes. Then work as a group. Use your notes to help you choose details you agree work well. Decide how to put the details together to create a description that includes all five senses. Decide on the order that will make your description effective. When your writing is complete, share your description with the class.

### COMPUTER OPTION

If you have access to a computer lab at school, complete the Cooperative Learning assignment on a computer network. Group members can record notes on their computers and access one another's files to write descriptions. Use the Multiple Windows feature and the Cut and Paste options in your word-processing program to combine selected portions of each description into a single, final description. Then share your writing with your group.

*Combining Observation and Imagination in a Description*    **113**

## I've Got a Feeling

Caves are interesting and unusual places, but not everybody enjoys exploring them. The thought of being in a cave may scare you. On the other hand, it may excite your curiosity. Imagine entering the cave in the picture, and think about how it feels to be there. List a few details you would use to describe the picture so others can share your feelings.

As you read the literature model, consider how the writer uses descriptive details to help readers share Barney's feelings about the cave in the cliff called Kenmare Head.

### Literature Model

*Why is the sound of Barney's whispered greeting an effective detail?*

Hallo," Barney said tentatively into the darkness. His voice whispered back at him in a sinister, eerie way: not booming and reverberating round as it had in the narrow tunnel-like cave they had come through, but muttering far away, high in the air. Barney swung round in a circle, vainly peering into the dark. The space round him must be as big as a house—and yet he was in the depths of Kenmare Head.

Susan Cooper, *Over Sea, Under Stone*

## Creating a Mood

The details included in the photograph and the literature model do more than help describe a scene. They also create a mood, or feeling. The cave, which you experience through Barney's senses, seems eerie and sinister. The writer wants you to understand how Barney feels. He is frightened and a little desperate.

A writer can select different details to create different moods. For example, the writer tells us that Barney's voice "whispered back at him in a sinister, eerie way." Barney is also "vainly peering into the dark." These two details help the writer set the mood for the story.

If Barney were exploring this cave for fun, he would probably have different feelings about it. The writer would select different details to show a different mood. Look at the notes below. What would the mood of the passage on page 114 be if the writer had used details such as these?

### Grammar
### Editing Tip

Adjectives help make a description more effective. Adjectives modify nouns. For more information, see pages 404–405.

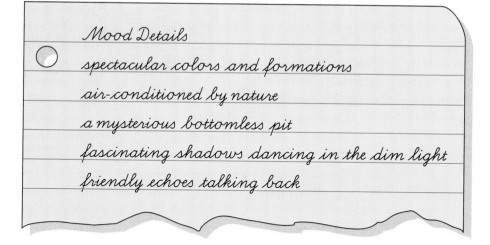

*Mood Details*

○ *spectacular colors and formations*

*air-conditioned by nature*

*a mysterious bottomless pit*

*fascinating shadows dancing in the dim light*

*friendly echoes talking back*

---

### • JOURNAL ACTIVITY •
### *Think It Through*

Think of a place you have been that inspires a mood. In your journal make a list of mood details like the list above. Then write a brief description that creates the mood suggested by the details you wrote.

## Choosing Your Words

When you describe a scene, the details you choose set the mood and bring the scene to life for your reader. Try it out. Suppose you are describing a cold winter day. Select one of the mood photos shown below. Find details in the list that help create a mood that matches the scene you chose. Then read Bryce Stoker's description of a personal experience. Notice his use of striking, specific words that bring details to life and create a mood.

| |
|---|
| **crisp, powdery snow** |
| **frostbitten ears** |
| **slushy, slippery sidewalks** |
| **biting wind** |
| **healthful exercise** |
| **sparkling sunlight** |
| **heavy, wet clothes** |
| **brilliant blue sky** |

Unpleasant

Cheerful

### Student Model

One of the worst places I've been in is the attic. Whenever I'm told to go get something from the attic, I try to squirm my way out of it. When I can't get out of it, my skin begins to crawl, I get nervous and start to sweat while ascending the stairs, and my breathing and pulse go wild when I reach the trapdoor to the attic.

Bryce Stoker, Frontier School, Moses Lake, Washington

*Which phrases tell the reader how Bryce reacts to the attic visit?*

# Activities

Here are some activities to help you apply what you have learned.

## 1. Guided Assignment

You have been asked to write a description of an amusement park for an ad campaign to attract teens as customers. Take a walk through the park, paying attention to the mood you think the park encourages. Take notes on the details that set the mood, and write a draft of a description. Then revise your description, adding other details and words that strengthen the mood you want to show. Ask a classmate to read your description and identify the mood you created.

PURPOSE    To explore how details create moods
AUDIENCE   Teen-agers
LENGTH     1 page

## 2. Open Assignment

You are the pilot of an experimental plane that has landed in an unfamiliar place. Walk around, taking notes as you explore. Write a description of the place to include in your flight log. Include the details that impressed you, and identify the mood they created. Imagine you have landed at one of the following locations, or choose another location:

- a desert
- the edge of a strange city
- an enormous lake
- a jungle

### COMPUTER OPTION

If you use a personal computer to write your descriptions for this assignment, find out if your word-processing program includes an electronic thesaurus. As you revise your descriptive writing, use the thesaurus to replace vague, dull words with clear, vivid words. Choose words and phrases that appeal to the five senses.

## 3. Cooperative Learning

In a group of four or six, talk about the many moods created by a place you all know very well. You may choose a nearby beach, the school gym, a park, or a public building such as a library or a courthouse. One member of the group should list the suggested moods. Then list descriptive details that group members think created those moods. To describe a beach, you might name relaxing as one mood, and list the details high waves, hot sand, salty tang, burning sun, and wheeling seagulls.

Finally, choose partners, and decide on a mood for a poem you will write about the place. Brainstorm, and list the mood and details you agree on. Work together to get a first line. Then discuss your ideas, and write new lines until your poem is finished. Share your poems with the whole group.

*Choosing Details to Create a Mood* **117**

**Organizing Details in a Description**

# *Up, Over, and Away*

Imagine you are a radio reporter covering a hot-air-balloon festival. Of course, your listeners cannot see the brightly colored balloons. Take a moment to write a script for your show, and describe the scene. Tell your listeners the position of each balloon.

Readers cannot see the subject of your descriptive writing, either. They rely on you to tell them the position of important details in a scene. Read the selection. Notice the order Scott O'Dell uses to identify the position of important characters in his description.

### Literature Model

On this mound, among the grasses and the plants, stood Rontu. He stood facing me, with his back to the sea cliff. In front of him in a half-circle were the wild dogs. At first I thought that the pack had driven him there against the cliff and were getting ready to attack him. But I soon saw that two dogs stood out from the rest of the pack, between it and Rontu. . .

Scott O'Dell, *Island of the Blue Dolphins*

*Why might the position of the dogs in relation to Rontu be important in this scene?*

# Deciding on Order

You can present details in various ways to give your reader a mental picture of a scene. Think about the location of each object and where it is in relation to other objects. How you describe them depends on your purpose. Describing a sky-scraper from bottom to top emphasizes the building's height. A description of the Grand Canyon might show details in the order a descending hiker sees them.

The pictures below show how details might be ordered to describe the photograph on page 118. Which order do you think would be most effective? Think of other ways you could describe the scene.

## Prewriting Tip

During the prewriting phase for a description, think about the order you will use to present details.

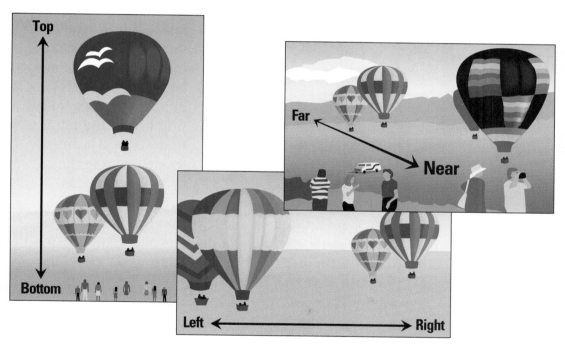

## • JOURNAL ACTIVITY •
### *Think It Through*

In your journal describe a room at home. How has the furniture been arranged? Why is it arranged the way it is? List three things you would change to make the room more convenient or to make it more attractive.

# Getting from Here to There

Transition words and phrases help show how each detail in a description relates to the others. You can use transitions to

In front of
Behind
To the right of
Next to

make your descriptions clearer. Look at the photograph and the phrases on this page. Think about how you can use these transitions to answer questions such as, Where is the diving platform in relation to the trees? and Where is the falling boy in relation to the other boys? Then read the literature model below to see how Mildred Taylor uses transition words and phrases to describe a scene.

## Literature Model

*The school building is presented first. Then the writer describes objects in relation to it.*

*Where did the writer place key transition words to show location?*

They were headed for the Jefferson Davis County School, a long white wooden building looming in the distance. **Behind** the building was a wide sports field around which were scattered rows of tiered gray-looking benches. **In front of** it were two yellow buses, our own tormentor and one that brought students from the other direction, and loitering students awaiting the knell of the morning bell. **In the very center** of the expansive front lawn, waving red, white, and blue with the emblem of the Confederacy emblazoned in its upper left-hand corner, was the Mississippi flag. **Directly below** it was the American flag.

Mildred D. Taylor, *Roll of Thunder, Hear My Cry*

# Activities

Here are some activities to help you apply what you have learned.

## 1. Guided Assignment

Imagine that someone has stolen this painting from the museum where you work. You have been asked to write a description of the painting for the police department. Decide on the order in which you will list details in the painting so the detectives can recognize it. Include transition words and phrases that show the position of the details you are describing.

| | |
|---|---|
| **PURPOSE** | To write a missing-painting bulletin |
| **AUDIENCE** | Police detectives |
| **LENGTH** | 1 page |

## 2. Open Assignment

Write a one-page description from an unusual viewpoint. Experiment with different kinds of order to make the scene more interesting. Select one of the following topics, or make up your own:

- Describe a loaded picnic table from an ant's point of view.
- Describe an imaginary attic or basement that you are seeing for the first time.

- Describe a place, such as a play lot or a sports arena. Order details from the center to the outside or from the edges to the center.
- Describe a spider web from the viewpoint of the spider who has just finished it. Make clear where the spider is in the web.

## 3. Mathematics

Draw a design using geometric shapes, such as lines, triangles, squares, rectangles, and circles. Write a description of your design. Use transition words that show where shapes are on the page and in relation to one another.

Nereyda García-Ferraz, *The Other Half,* 1989

## Who Is That, Anyway?

Like a jigsaw puzzle, a character is made up of pieces. Each piece is a detail: hair color, body shape, or the way a character smiles. The details come from a writer's imagination and from observation of real people. When they are put together, these pieces become a complete picture.

In most puzzles the pieces fit together in only one way. However, you can mix and match details in endless ways when you set out to create a character.

# How Does the Character Look?

Begin your description of a character by picturing that person in your mind. Decide which details will help readers see the character. Choose the words and the order that will help you describe these features.

The following passage tells the story of a Chinese-American woman who looks at a picture of her mother, taken long ago. She describes her mother as she appears in that picture.

## Literature Model

In this picture you can see why my mother looks displaced. She is clutching a large clam-shaped bag, as though someone might steal this from her as well if she is less watchful. She has on an ankle-length Chinese dress with modest vents at the side. And on top she is wearing a Westernized suit jacket, awkwardly stylish on my mother's small body, with its padded shoulders, wide lapels, and oversize cloth buttons. This was my mother's wedding dress, a gift from my father. In this outfit she looks as if she were neither coming from nor going to someplace. Her chin is bent down and you can see the precise part in her hair, a neat white line drawn from above her left brow then over the black horizon of her head.

Amy Tan, *The Joy Luck Club*

The speaker says that her mother looks "displaced." What is she wearing that supports this adjective?

### • JOURNAL ACTIVITY •
## Try It Out

Visualize several of the most memorable people you've known. List five or six details someone else would notice first about them.

# How Does the Character Act?

Describing a character's appearance doesn't give your readers a complete picture of the character. It would be like asking them to judge someone entirely on the way he or she looks rather than getting to know who the person really is. One way you learn about people is to observe the way they behave with other people.

A writer can reveal a character's personality by showing how the character interacts with others. In the draft below, a writer begins to fill out the character visualized on page 123. Instead of simply telling readers what Andy looks like, the writer shows how Andy behaves at a skateboarding park. What does Andy's treatment of other people say about him?

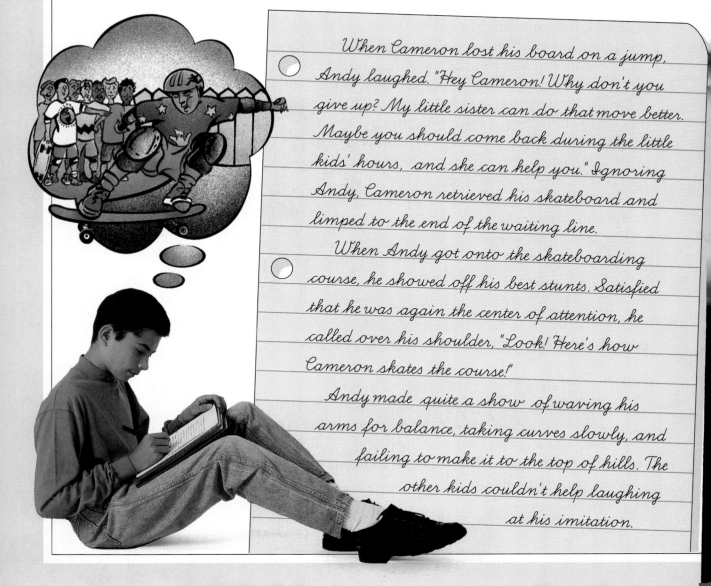

When Cameron lost his board on a jump, Andy laughed. "Hey Cameron! Why don't you give up? My little sister can do that move better. Maybe you should come back during the little kids' hours, and she can help you." Ignoring Andy, Cameron retrieved his skateboard and limped to the end of the waiting line.

When Andy got onto the skateboarding course, he showed off his best stunts. Satisfied that he was again the center of attention, he called over his shoulder, "Look! Here's how Cameron skates the course!"

Andy made quite a show of waving his arms for balance, taking curves slowly, and failing to make it to the top of hills. The other kids couldn't help laughing at his imitation.

# Activities

Here are some activities to help you apply what you have learned.

## 1. Guided Assignment

Write a description of the shoe-maker in this painting. Use the details you see to describe his personality and appearance. The following questions may help you:

- Which of the man's physical features stand out in the painting?
- What is the man doing? How do you think he feels about his work?
- What kind of person would be a good cobbler? What makes you think this?

PURPOSE    To elaborate on details in a painting

AUDIENCE   Your teacher and classmates

LENGTH     1 or 2 pages

Lilla Cabot Perry, *The Cobbler (Portrait of Luther N. Smith)*, 1928

## 2. Open Assignment

Write about an imaginary meeting with a person you have not met before. Describe the person's appearance and behavior. Write about one of the following subjects, or choose your own:

- a stubborn child for whom you are baby-sitting for the first time
- a new player on a rival team
- your favorite writer, whom you meet in a book store

## 3. Drama

In a small group brainstorm and list suggestions for characters who could appear in a play. Each group member should choose one character from the list. Working independently, write one-page descriptions of your characters. Describe their appearance and personalities. Then share your descriptions. Talk about what might happen if all of your characters came together in one place.

**Writing About Literature**
# Relating a Poem to Your Experience

## *In the Picture*

Poets are artists who use words to draw mental pictures. They share their thoughts and experiences with you, the reader. If you can put yourself into the picture the poet creates, a poem will be meaningful to you. Bring your experiences with you as you read the poem below. Try to see, hear, feel, taste, and smell the things that Gary Soto describes.

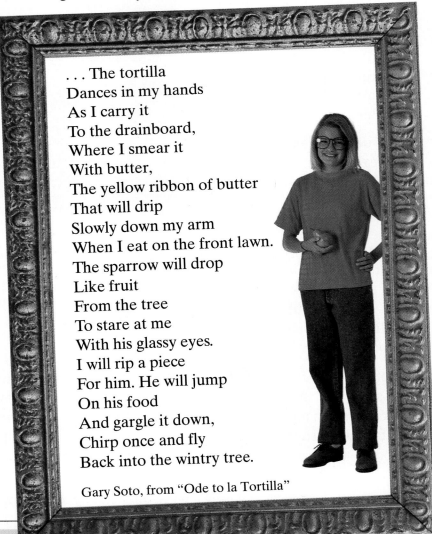

. . . The tortilla
Dances in my hands
As I carry it
To the drainboard,
Where I smear it
With butter,
The yellow ribbon of butter
That will drip
Slowly down my arm
When I eat on the front lawn.
The sparrow will drop
Like fruit
From the tree
To stare at me
With his glassy eyes.
I will rip a piece
For him. He will jump
On his food
And gargle it down,
Chirp once and fly
Back into the wintry tree.

Gary Soto, from "Ode to la Tortilla"

## Let a Poem Speak to You

Poets often use sensory language to share an impression. Look at the sensory details Gary Soto uses in "Ode to la Tortilla." He lets you feel what he feels as he prepares and eats his tortilla. You can experience "The yellow ribbon of butter/ That will drip/Slowly down my arm . . ."

To understand the meaning of a poem, you must relate it to what you already know about or have experienced. Recall a time when you tasted a wonderful food. How did it make you feel? Your own experience may help you understand how the speaker in the poem feels as he prepares and eats the tortilla.

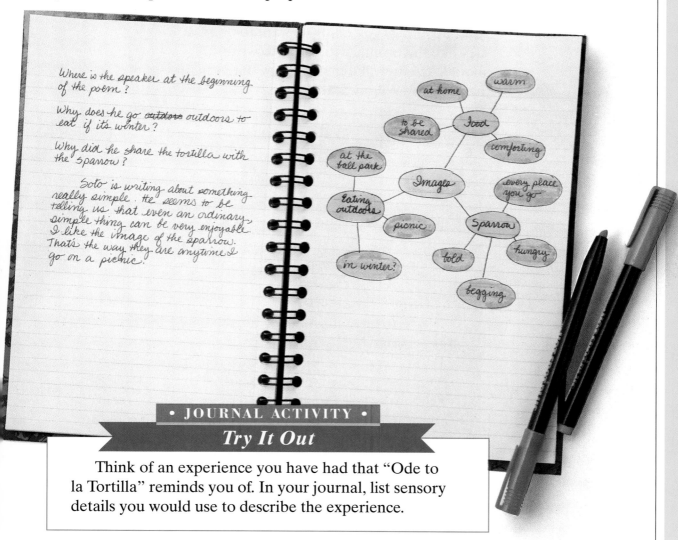

Where is the speaker at the beginning of the poem?

Why does he go ~~outdoors~~ outdoors to eat if it's winter?

Why did he share the tortilla with the sparrow?

Soto is writing about something really simple. He seems to be telling us that even an ordinary, simple thing can be very enjoyable. I like the image of the sparrow. That's the way they are anytime I go on a picnic.

- at home
- warm
- to be shared
- food
- comforting
- at the ball park
- Images
- every place you go
- Eating outdoors
- picnic
- Sparrow
- hungry
- in winter?
- bold
- begging

## • JOURNAL ACTIVITY •

### Try It Out

Think of an experience you have had that "Ode to la Tortilla" reminds you of. In your journal, list sensory details you would use to describe the experience.

## Talk to the Poet

You can carry on an imaginary conversation with the writer of a poem you have read. Tell the writer how the poem matches your own experiences. Write your ideas in your journal or in a letter. Then create a poem of your own. In your poem use a subject like the one the poet used, or borrow an image from the poem you read. For example, Gary Soto's subject is food, a very ordinary thing. Think about ordinary things in your life, things you enjoy or want to do. Are they like the ordinary things Soto writes about? Are they like the ordinary things in the poem by Willow Star Wright?

**Revising Tip**

When you revise, look carefully to see that you have used sensory language that makes your descriptions clear and easy to relate to.

*Notice that Willow names ordinary things in each line of her poem.*

*In which lines of the poem did the writer surprise you by combining unlike things?*

### Student Model

#### Daydreams

I am a ballerina who strives to be a doctor in the delivery room of a widely known hospital.

I like boys, and the fish in my aquarium are gold and swim around plastic, purple and green seaweed.

I hear people cheering, wasps buzzing and summer is just around the corner.

I want to go swimming or horseback riding on a large Arabian horse from the oasis.

I don't like fall or this poem I wrote moments ago that will eventually be put into a final draft.

I dream of the day when all nations declare world peace or when the guy I like finds out I am alive.

But for now I will just have to settle for being a ballerina.

Willow Star Wright, Oak Creek School, Cornville, Arizona

# Activities

Here are some activities to help you apply what you have learned.

## 1. Guided Assignment

Reread "Ode to la Tortilla" and "Daydreams." Then write a poem about an experience of your own.

- Choose an ordinary experience, possibly one from a Journal Activity.
- List sensory words or phrases that describe the experience. If you are thinking about dressing for a comfortable Saturday morning, you might list a favorite old sweatshirt; thick, warm socks; jeans so soft you can hardly feel them; and shoes that look older than you.
- Write your poem. Use details from your list.

PURPOSE   To discover how descriptive details work in a poem

AUDIENCE   Your teacher and classmates

LENGTH   A poem of 8–12 lines

## 2. Open Assignment

Find a descriptive poem that uses strong sensory language. Write what you think about the poem. Use one of the following questions, or come up with your own topic:

- Which images do you like best? Which are surprising? Familiar?
- How does this poem relate to things that happen in your life?

## 3. Cooperative Learning

In a small group read aloud a poem selected by a member of your group or by your teacher. Talk about what the poem means, and list the sensory images the poet uses. The questions in the Open Assignment on this page will help you with the discussion.

Next, group members can use various kinds of writing to relate the poem to their own experience.

One person could write a short story about the subject of the poem. Someone else could make a chart that lists images and shows drawings or photographs that use an image from the poem. A third person could write a short report about the poet. Someone else could write a journal entry telling what the poem means to him or her.

Share your responses to the poem. Discuss what you have learned.

### COMPUTER OPTION

When you are writing about a poem, use the split screen option to display two files at one time. Type your prewriting notes into one file. Open another file for your drafting work. Keep the first file on display as you write your draft. This way you can refer to both files without taking time to open and close files.

Virginia
Hamilton
*from*

# THE GATHERING

*In* The Gathering, *Virginia Hamilton presents four young mind-travelers, Justice and her brothers. They live in a universe where computers program themselves and everyone reads everyone else's thoughts. Hamilton makes this strange world real through detailed descriptions and the everyday conversations all brothers and sisters have. In the following selection, join them on Sona. Led by someone (something?) called Celester, they see Colossus for the first time.*

They traveled the triway system down to the Oneway level and beyond the hydrafields to the rim of the enormous geodesic[1] dome that covered Sona. Celester pointed out the dome's tubular structure that had all of its parts under tension but never stress. Then he led them inside a silitrex sphere which sat above an opening in the ground, like a stopper in a bottle. Once the sphere closed around them, it began descending with a pneumatic swishing sound of air under pressure. Soft light from Celester's eyes illuminated the sphere, for the vivid sundown of Sona was left above as they plunged.

The gaseous light streaming from his eyes spread about

[1] **geodesic** (je´ə des´ik) a structure having a strong surface made of bars that form a pattern of shapes having four or more sides

them. Fascinated, Thomas thrust his hand into the stream. Light piled up on his palm like soft ice-cream on a cone. Thomas gasped, jumping back, jerking his hand out of the stream. The piled light scattered and regrouped in the stream coming from Celester's eyes.

"Wow! Magic!" said Dorian.

Celester hummed a comic toning, entertaining them with the light.

"Whatever it was, it got hot," Thomas said. He eyed Celester suspiciously.

"A property of light is heat," toned Celester. "He who puts hand in fire will singe his fingertips."

"I get the message," Thomas muttered.

"Celester, you have powerful gifts," Justice said.

The sphere seemed to float momentarily; then it stopped with a soft jolt. A door slid open. Celester moved smoothly out ahead of them.

"Colossus is like no other machine," he toned as they followed him. "There are tooling mills above and below this level built by Colossus. And there are functioning machines nearby that helped to build Colossus itself."

They were in a place of vague light, vastly mysterious because of the dimness. They could make out steep, over-hanging slopes and a wide, deep trench stretching away from them. In the entire emptiness of the trench there was but one object. It had to be Colossus.

Leonardo da Vinci, sketch of an ornithopter, c. 1495–1510

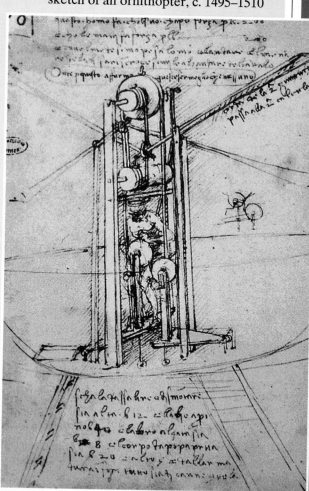

What was there they saw, yet did not see.

The Colossus that Celester saw never varied. It was shaded mauve,[2] deepening in pulsations to black. It greeted him, he thought, with the light emitting from its smooth surface. Celester lifted off the ground, moving to the trench. Higher and higher he went until he was halfway to the summit of Colossus. There he stood on space in conjunction with Colossus, as Colossus tuned Celester until Celester felt no desynchronization[3] of any of his half-million separate components. His brain was not yet middle-aged. His mind was peaceful.

Justice saw an enormous coiling, a Colossus whose awesome spring-release of time-force could whirl them home again. It changed form before her eyes. It was solid; it was ethereal. It was there, a brilliant silver coil, and it was not there.

Each of them saw Colossus differently. There before Thomas was what he loved, which was a science fiction. A silver space-ship was ready for lift-off. Upright in the trench, it was twenty stories high. Steam rose from it. He asked: Can I go, too?

Peter Blume, *Light of the World*, 1932

He understood that the ship knew his wish to be master of himself, to speak for himself without stuttering. Only the ship knew the violent feelings he had because of his stutter and because he wanted to be free of Justice. But here and now was not for him. His here and now would come. No, he could not go a-flying with the ship.

2 **mauve** (mōv) a mild shade of purple
3 **desynchronization** (de sin krə nə zā′shən) adjustment of parts so that their movement does not occur at the same time or rate of speed

Duster could not have comprehended a Colossus. But he had no need to name what he saw. It looked like his land of dust. He walked in it and the ground was moist under his feet. The area of the water pool was hardly recognizable. He knew it was water, glinting, refreshing to his senses, even though he was still a quarter-mile from it. But now, surrounding the pool on its banks were *things* growing in the dust. Nothing like them had ever grown. The pretty red, yellow. In an instant he knew the colors, knew to call them flowers, with greenery. Such bright growing extended three feet around the pool. He scented the plantings as he moved; the scent made him laugh. The odor was the best he'd smelled in all of the endless dust. He ran. He was there, putting his face down in the flowers.

A thought came, rising in his mind. Duster crawled to the water and thrust his hands under it, pulling his hands back toward himself on the bank. Drops of water did wet the shore. Duster stared at them. Suddenly he had his shove tool in his hand. It was a digger tool, sharp, broad and flat. He dipped the digger in the pool, then pulled it toward him in a straight line. He dug through the bank, half a hand under the dust. Water began flowing into the little ditch he made. Water filled the ditch and overflowed. That which was Colossus around Duster was aware of his learning. Now Duster knew how to keep moisture near the plantings. Tiny ferns grew quickly beside his first small irrigation ditch.

Then Duster was back in the underdome of Colossus. "Be wanting go to dust," he toned. "Where be my smooth-keep? Be wishing to be gone. Be doing to begin."

"It'll be okay, Duster," Levi said, patting his shoulder. He, too, had had a vision of Colossus. It had calmed him. He no longer feared being in the presence of such a wonder.

"Be touching leader, wrong," toned Duster to him. There was something of the old strength in his voice, which had made him leader of packens.

"It isn't like any machine I've even seen," Justice said about Colossus.

"That's the understatement of the year!" Thomas said in a hushed voice.

Dorian smiled to himself. He thought Colossus must be the biggest computer ever built. It had to be a hundred, two hundred feet high, if not higher. The lights flashing at the top of it and the tape reels going a mile a minute made him think of comets and stars. No sooner had he thought that Colossus could probably tape even their thoughts, than he heard the thought being transcribed[4] in a jumble of languages.

Smaller machines were connected to Colossus by what Dorian knew suddenly were coded physical quantities. They surrounded Colossus like flies, at a uniform height of about fifteen feet. They displayed differential equations and gave solutions to obscure problems through visuals, in electrical waves on fluorescent screens. Somehow the waves were transmitted to Colossus for it to read.

They do the small work of hydrafields, thought Dorian, of environments and life cycles. Colossus gives them direction, power.

They were all seeing Colossus differently but simultaneously. For Justice, it remained a brilliant silver coil. The space contained in the coiling caught her attention, causing her to go so near the trench she could have easily toppled in. Colossus was spectacular. It grew aware of her as distinct from the others. It saw her.

**4 transcribed** (tran skrībd') made a written copy

## For Discussion

1. How would you react to a machine like Colossus that could read your mind and grant your every wish? In what ways might this machine be harmful? In what ways might it do good?

2. Hamilton's make-believe world is like ours in some ways. How did you react when Duster discovered flowers? How did you feel when you learned Thomas wanted to stop stuttering?

## Readers Respond

The writer made Dorian seem real by showing the anxiety he had, knowing the robot could read their minds.

I enjoyed the way Dorian described Colossus. I would have written the story differently, showing Dorian in there by himself.

I would recommend this selection because every one of my friends enjoys science fiction.

**Admon Iramiya**

Colossus is something different to everyone. I like the way all of the characters use their imagination and picture Colossus. Duster is my favorite character because his vision of Colossus is the best—the way he smells his flowers and makes a ditch for irrigation.

The scene I remember most clearly is when Thomas touches the stream coming from Celester's eyes and sees it pile up "like soft ice-cream on a cone."

**Arti Patel**

### Did You Notice?

1. Did you notice that the writer brings her readers into this science fiction tale by describing what each character sees when in the presence of Colossus? Describe Colossus as you see it.

2. Consider how important a detail may be in science fiction and fantasy. For example, the writer states that Celester and Duster "tone," not "speak." How does this word help the reader to understand them? List phrases from the story that bring other characters to life.

# Writing Process in Action

## Your Ticket to Travel

A vivid description can transport you to places you've never dreamed of. In *The Gathering* Virginia Hamilton takes you to Sona, a place made lifelike through the magic of words.

Notice how effectively Hamilton organizes her description. What do *you* see when you look at Colossus? How can you apply the descriptive techniques Hamilton uses to your own writing?

The following assignment invites you to create a place as special as Sona, while developing your descriptive writing skills.

### • Assignment •

| | |
|---|---|
| Context | You've just visited a special place—real or imagined—that you want others to know about. You want to write an article for *Your Next Vacation*, a travel magazine for teens, while the details are still fresh in your memory. |
| Purpose | To write an article describing a special place |
| Audience | Teen-agers |
| Length | 2 or more pages |

In the next three pages you'll find advice on writing a description of a place. Read the lesson once to get an overview. Then refer to the appropriate section as you work through the writing process.

# 1. Prewriting

Not even the sky is a limit when you prewrite. Many experiences, knowledge, and emotions may come into play. But sometimes, with so much to draw from, it's hard to get started. The graphic on the right illustrates how freewriting helped one writer find a topic.

Once you've chosen a topic, continue prewriting to generate descriptive details. You might, for instance, take notes on a photograph or drawing of your special place. You might also make a list that compares and contrasts your topic with other places familiar to the reader. And, of course, you'll want to use all five senses to supply sensory impressions.

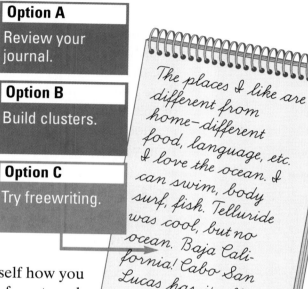

**Option A**
Review your journal.

**Option B**
Build clusters.

**Option C**
Try freewriting.

*The places I like are different from home—different food, language, etc. I love the ocean. I can swim, body surf, fish. Telluride was cool, but no ocean. Baja California! Cabo San Lucas has it all.*

# 2. Drafting

Before you begin drafting, ask yourself how you can best organize your prewriting notes for a travel article. Should you describe a typical day in your special place? Should you hit the attractions from the most well known to the least? Choose an appropriate method to help you get started. You can always change it later.

As you draft, make your descriptions vibrate with details. Appeal to your readers' senses. Share your excitement. Notice how effectively Virginia Hamilton describes Duster's pleasure in discovering *his* Colossus:

*B*   *ut now, surrounding the pool on its banks were things growing in the dust. Nothing like them had ever grown. The pretty red, yellow. In an instant he knew the colors, knew to call them flowers, with greenery. Such bright growing extended three feet around the pool. He scented the plantings as he moved; the scent made him laugh.*

Remember, your article should convince your audience that the place you're describing is special. In describing it, try capturing the scene's mood, as Hamilton does. Review pages 114–117 for tips on creating mood.

## 3. Revising

When you've finished your draft, put it aside for a day or two. Then pretend that you're the editor of *Your Next Vacation.* Your job is to find and analyze the article's strengths and weaknesses. Are the details clear? Does the language fit the audience? Are there helpful transitions between ideas? Do you feel the mood of the place? Does the opening make you eager to read on?

Look at the suggested revisions in the draft below. What revisions would you make?

**Question A**

Is the organization logical?

**Question B**

Are the details specific?

**Question C**

Is it clear why this place is special?

Even though it's small, there's lots to do in
Cabo San Lucas. After siesta you can Meet new friends at the Cabo
Wabo Cantina, owned by the rock group Van
Halen. In the cool of the morning, you can go
down to the dock to watch the fishing boats set
out in hope of catching something. ^which marlin or sailfish. Take a stroll to The center of
town features numerous craft shops. Here you can buy, or just admire,
unusual the black coral jewelry. And don't
pass up the weird but delicious food: spicy fish
tacos with freshly grated cabbage or chicken in
mole, a thick dark sauce flavored with
cinnamon and chocolate.

138

## 4. Editing

During editing, you'll locate and eliminate any errors in grammar, spelling, punctuation, and usage. Even one misspelled word can distract your audience from the value of the ideas and impressions you're offering. A well-edited and proofread paper communicates your professional attitude as a writer.

Use the checklist at the right to edit your work. There's a lot of satisfaction in discovering an error you've overlooked before. You might even find yourself laughing at some of the mistakes!

> Checklist
>
> 1. Have I avoided run-on sentences?
> 2. Are sentences complete?
> 3. Do my subjects and verbs agree?
> 4. Have I checked my spelling?
> 5. Have I used standard grammar and punctuation?

## 5. Presenting

The goal of writing is to communicate with an audience. From the very first, you had a particular audience in mind—teen-agers interested in travel. No doubt, many of your classmates fit this description. Share your work with one or more of them. If you get a positive reaction, talk with your teacher about submitting your article for publication. If others have written articles for *Your Next Vacation,* perhaps you can publish a class edition.

### Reflecting

As you know, adjectives and adverbs can help you turn a murky scene into a scene with sharp outlines and vibrant colors. In writing your description of a place, did you use any adjectives or adverbs that you don't ordinarily use? Will any of these words become "regulars" in your writing vocabulary?

# Portfolio & Reflection

## Summary

**Key concepts in descriptive writing include the following:**

- A strong description makes a vivid impression and creates a mood.
- Describing a person, place, or thing means using the senses and the imagination.
- Describing a scene involves ordered details and transition words that lead your reader to a mental picture of the scene.
- A description of a character includes both appearance and behavior.
- Your response to a poem may include sensory language from the poem.

## Your Writer's Portfolio

Look over the writing you did for this unit. Choose two pieces for your portfolio. Look for writing that does one or more of the following:

- uses details to create a mood
- gives life to a character through description
- uses position to order details
- gives your response to a poem that uses sensory language and details
- uses sensory language in a poem

## Reflection and Commentary

Think about what you have learned in this unit. Answer the following questions as you look over the two pieces of writing you chose. Write a page of "Comments on Descriptive Writing" for your portfolio.

1. Which details create a strong mood? To which senses do they appeal?
2. How does your use of transition words help your readers visualize the location of a person, place, or thing?
3. How does your descriptive writing combine sensory detail and imagination to create an impression?
4. Why, do you think, would readers find your description of a character vivid and exciting?
5. How do the sensory details you chose bring life to your poem?
6. Which senses involve your readers in the experience you described?

## Feedback

**If you had a chance to respond to the following student comment, what would you say or ask?**

*I write anywhere with anything on anything. I love writing in the morning because it gives me inspiration.*

Allison Troutman, Oak Creek School,
Cornville, Arizona

# Writing to Tell a Story

# Imagine That!

Marc Chagall, *My Village*, 1923–1924

# Bethancourt Writes

## User Friendly ▼

*"Writing stories is fun. You get to have adventures, except you're in control. And you get to use those swell remarks you don't think of until two days later and then say, 'Gee, I wish I'd said that.'"*

T. Ernesto Bethancourt

**W**hen novelist T. Ernesto Bethancourt's first portable computer fizzled out, he went shopping for a new one. "I started going to all the computer shows," Bethancourt said, "and I was amazed at all the things that were being done with computers. Before long I got heavily into the idea of artificial intelligence, and I thought what a great companion a computer could be. I said, 'Gee, what if the thing really had a personality and could be user friendly?'"

Like other imaginative ideas that flash on in Bethancourt's mind, this one turned into a fantasy short story. A fantasy involves characters, events, or settings that couldn't exist in everyday life. This fantasy is about a junior high school student and his best friend, a supercomputer built by his father. The computer frighteningly develops a mind of its own.

142

## Writing a Short Story

**1.** Planning the Story     **2.** Writing "User Friendly"     **3.** Revising the Story

### FOCUS

Creating a likable character facing a problem is one important part of writing a short story.

## 1 Planning the Story

Once Bethancourt knew he had a good idea, he began mulling it over. For six weeks he thought about characters and scenes.

All the while, Bethancourt followed his own map for short-story writing. "You create a hero or heroine and place the figure in a problem situation," he said. "Then you have your hero use his or her inner resources—courage, intelligence, wit—to resolve the conflict. After the conflict is resolved, the main character is in some way changed."

Following this plan, Bethancourt created a hero named Kevin. He modeled Kevin after a young friend of his—a quiet, smart boy with a sly sense of humor.

Bethancourt then broke his rough story line into individual scenes. He summarized each scene on an index card.

▼ *In the short story "User Friendly" Bethancourt creates the element of surprise by having the computer talk.*

GoodMorning,Kevin

In the opening scene, Kevin's computer, Louis, starts talking to him. This is the first hint of a problem. The story moves along as Kevin gets the brushoff from Ginny Linke, the girl he likes. And Kevin's troubles grow as

▼ *Writing down scene ideas on index cards helps Bethancourt organize the short story.*

Scene 1

In Kevin's room.

Introduce Kevin and Louis.

Louis "talks"!

Louis the computer continues to meddle in life. The problem of Louis is resolved in the final, surprising scene.

Once Bethancourt finished summarizing the scenes, he laid the index cards out on his desk. He looked for scenes that showed best the growing problem of Louis. Those scenes would get the most space in his story.

**INTERFACE** *Think about an idea for a story about traveling back in time. Who is your main character? What conflict is he or she involved in?*

## 2 "Writing User Friendly"

Scene 3

Kevin's confrontation with Chuck.

Kevin outsmarts the bully.

Last scene

At Kevin's house.

Dad pulls the plug on Louis.

With the events of the story now clearly in mind, Bethancourt began to write. He opened his story with Kevin, who wakes up, flips on his computer, eats breakfast, then notices a startling message on the screen: "When are you going to get me my voice module, Kevin?" Louis is talking to him!

Bethancourt accomplished several tasks in his opening scene. First of all, he introduced two main characters, Kevin and the computer, using dialogue to bring them

More important, I thought, what would *I* do next? It's one thing to play a trick or two, to get even, but Louis was going crazy! And I never wanted to harm Ginny, or even her stupid moose of a brother. She'd just hurt my feelings with that nerd remark.

"You have to disconnect Louis," I told myself. "There's no other way."

But why did I feel like such a rat about doing it? I guess because Louis was my friend . . . the only one I had.

◄ *Near the end of the story, Kevin faces a difficult decision about Louis.*

to life. Then he based events in everyday life to make the story believable. "The important thing in fantasy is that you've got to have a foot on the ground before you take off," Bethancourt said.

As Bethancourt moved into the middle of the story, he used action and dialogue to tell the story and build suspense. "This is largely a think story," he said. To balance that effect with adventure, Bethancourt said, "action was important. I had to show that Kevin wasn't a total dweeb. I did this by having him outsmart a jock who's trying to intimidate him."

Bethancourt also used words and actions to show Kevin's growing fear of Louis.

Bethancourt described the problem as follows: "The computer wants to grant Kevin everything. But it's scaring Kevin because Louis has no conscience."

How does Kevin resolve the problem? He realizes that he has to pull the plug on Louis, and he's ready to do it. But Bethancourt makes Kevin's father disarm the computer. "I couldn't have Kevin unplug this thing that cared for him so much," Bethancourt said.

**INTERFACE** *Bethancourt advises writers to "have a foot on the ground before you take off" into fantasy. If you were writing an adventure about building the first city on the moon, how would you make your story seem real?*

## 3 Revising the Story

▼ *After writing a draft, many writers—including Bethancourt—leave the draft alone for a period of time. After a week or so has passed, they then read the draft and revise.*

Like almost every writer, Bethancourt has a method for revising. After two days of writing, he goes back to page one. "I start from the top, and I rewrite it," he said. He lets this draft sit for at least a week before making final changes.

Some key parts of "User Friendly" came into being because of Bethancourt's careful revising. One example is the final scene between Kevin and the character Chuck. "In the first draft I had Kevin running away from Chuck," Bethancourt said. "I wanted more physical action. But when I looked at it, it wasn't as good as when Kevin simply outsmarted Chuck. So I cut the running away scene."

For Bethancourt, "the best writing is rewriting. The idea is to get something down on paper. It doesn't matter how long you write— you can always cut stuff out."

## 1. Fantasy Writing

**Brainstorm ideas for a story about something in your house—an appliance, a pet, a picture—that begins to behave strangely.**

- Jot down the name of an item at home that intrigues you.

- List the special qualities of that item. For example, your television might turn itself on.

- Expand one quality into an idea for a fantasy. For example, your radio might broadcast messages from another planet.

## 2. About Literature

**Write half a page explaining why a short story of your choice is so powerful.**

- Find three important scenes in your favorite story.

- Write a summary of each scene and what makes it effective. Consider elements like dialogue, action scenes, and qualities in the main character that make you care about him or her.

## 3. Cooperative Learning

**Write summaries of fantasy stories, and create an anthology for your classmates.**

- Meet with a small group of students to discuss ideas for the kinds of fantasy stories you want to summarize for your anthology.

- Each person should find and write summaries of two stories.

- Meet to share your story summaries. Decide which ones to include in your anthology. Discuss ideas for an introduction.

- Choose jobs for putting the anthology together. Ask two students to draft an introduction. Ask others to make copies of the summaries and to prepare art work for the cover.

- As a group, review the introduction and cover art. Revise the introduction, organize the contents, and write a title for your anthology.

- Assemble your anthology. Then present it to the class.

# Hanging by a Thread

Harold Lloyd in *Safety Last*, 1923

What happened here? How did this man get himself into this predicament? What will happen next? Who knows? The writer knows, and so will you when you see the movie.

When you write a story, or narrative, of your own, you answer the question What happened? Some stories are about events that really happened. Others are based on imagination. In either case, a story has a beginning, a middle, and an end.

## Who Did What?

Suppose that you've seen the movie in which this scene takes place, and a friend asks you what the movie is about. You would probably begin by telling what happened from the beginning of the movie to the end. This series of events is called the plot. If you've ever read a book that you just couldn't put down, the plot probably kept you reading to find out what would happen next.

As you talk about the events, you will find yourself talking about the characters. Characters are the people or animals that take part in the events. Notice how novelist Madeleine L'Engle introduces characters and plot in the following selection.

There are dragons in the twins' vegetable garden." Meg Murry took her head out of the refrigerator where she had been foraging for an after-school snack, and looked at her six-year-old brother. "What?"

"There are dragons in the twins' vegetable garden. Or there were. They've moved to the north pasture now."

. . . She took her sandwich materials and a bottle of milk and set them out on the kitchen table. Charles Wallace waited patiently. She looked at him, scowling with an anxiety she did not like to admit to herself, at the fresh rips in the knees of his blue jeans, the streaks of dirt grained deep in his shirt, a darkening bruise on the cheekbone under his left eye. "Okay, did the big boys jump you in the schoolyard this time, or when you got off the bus?"

"Meg, you aren't listening to me."

"I happen to care that you've been in school for two months now and not a single week has gone by that you haven't been roughed up. If you've been talking about dragons in the garden or wherever they are, I suppose that explains it."

"I haven't. Don't underestimate me. I didn't see them till I got home."

Madeleine L'Engle, *A Wind in the Door*

---

*What event begins the plot of this story?*

**Presenting Tip**

When reading aloud from a narrative with more than one character, try using a different voice for each character.

*What do you know about Meg and Charles Wallace by the end of the passage?*

---

• JOURNAL ACTIVITY •

*Try It Out*

Think of a story you have read or heard recently. In your journal list some of the major events of the plot. Then write down the names of the main characters, and list some of their personality traits.

# Where and When?

A story has characters and a plot. It also has a setting. The setting puts the characters in a certain place at a certain time. Stories can be set in the present, the past, or the future. How characters look and act and what happens in the story often depend upon the time when the events take place.

Where a story takes place may also affect what happens. A writer may set a story in a real place or in an imaginary one. A sailboat crossing a stormy lake can be a setting for a story. Other stories may take place in a summer camp, in a large city, or on another planet. Changing the setting will affect the kind of story you tell, as the illustrations below help you see.

## Contrasting Three Settings

A story about a cowboy who rides a horse on the range could be a traditional Western adventure story.

A story about a cowboy who rides a horse in the city might be a modern-day comedy.

A story about a cowboy who rides a horse on the moon would probably be a science fiction story.

Setting not only affects story events but also affects the way characters act. For example, the cowboy will probably act differently in each of the three settings illustrated here.

# Activities

Here are some activities to help you apply what you have learned.

### 1. Guided Assignment

Your class is writing a book of stories to be read to younger children at a day-care center. You want to write an imaginative, entertaining story that will keep the children interested. Think about some of your favorite stories when you were younger. If necessary, reread a few of these to help you remember them.

Decide on the characters, plot, and setting for your story. Then write a one- to two-page story. Be sure your writing is easy enough for a four- or five-year-old to understand.

PURPOSE    To create a children's story that is entertaining

AUDIENCE    Children at a day-care center

LENGTH    1–2 pages

#### COMPUTER OPTION

You may want to prepare more than one storybook so that the children at the day-care center can take them home. To make the book look appealing to the children, experiment with different type sizes and typefaces on your computer. Look at a few children's books to get some ideas about type. Also make sure that there is plenty of space between lines.

### 2. Open Assignment

Your aunt is a producer for a local television program. She is looking for offbeat, imaginative stories written by middle school students to produce for an after-school movie hour. Think of characters, a setting, and a plot that could be turned into a television movie. Use one of the ideas listed below or come up with an idea of your own for a story. Then write a one- to two-page story.

- a comedy about a family living in a new, strange place
- a mystery with a pair of identical-twin detectives
- an adventure story that takes place on an island

### 3. Cooperative Learning

Work with a small group to create a story. Brainstorm ideas for characters, plots, and settings. One person should write down a list of the group's ideas. As a group, choose ideas from the list for a story.

Have two group members write a brief story of one to two pages. Others can help out during the drafting and revising stages by providing suggestions. One or two group members might like to illustrate the story. As a group, decide how to present the story to the class.

# Another Fine Mess

This cow's problem can spark ideas that would make a great story. Jot down some ideas about how the cow got the barrel on her head. Then list a few ideas about how she can get rid of the barrel and what will happen to her next.

The plots of most good stories center on a problem faced by a character. Focusing on a problem that needs solving is one productive way to come up with story ideas.

## What's the Problem?

Look at the pictures at the top of the next page. Think about the problem involved in each situation. Take a few minutes to list or brainstorm some situations of your own. You can either use the pictures as a starting point or think of entirely new situations.

**Car Breaking Down**

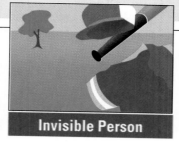
**Invisible Person**

**Monster in Town**

# What's the Solution?

Once you have a story idea you like, you can start developing it into a full-length story. Asking yourself questions like those listed in the chart below will help you plan a series of events. Some events will help solve the problem in your story. Other events may make the solution more difficult.

As you answer these questions, let your imagination run wild. It is your story, and anything can happen! The journal entry to the right shows how one student answered questions about her story idea—a monster terrorizing Middleville.

| Questions About Story Ideas |
| --- |
| 1. What is the problem? |
| 2. What characters does it involve? |
| 3. What happened before? |
| 4. What will happen next? |
| 5. What is the solution to the problem? |

*Problem*—monster terrorizes Middleville

*Characters*—monster, Patrice (14-year-old girl), Matt (her 10-year-old brother)

*Before*—monster was lonely and came to town

*Next*—everyone scared of monster, except Patrice and Matt

*Solution*—Patrice and Matt put monster on a basketball team

### • JOURNAL ACTIVITY •
## Try It Out

Think of a problem that you can build a story around. List one or two events leading up to the problem. Then list the solution and one or two events that happen afterward.

# Who's Involved?

## Grammar
## Editing Tip

As you edit, check your story for appropriate use of personal pronouns. You can review the rules on pages 384–385.

Once you have some ideas, try them out to see if they will work for a story. Many writers try out story ideas by focusing on a particular character. What kind of a problem is that character likely to have? How would he or she try to solve the problem?

The paragraphs below involve Mellissa, who tells the story in the first person, and Eddie, who lives in an abandoned bus. Here Mellissa learns the results of her efforts to befriend Eddie. The excerpt begins with Mellissa's father telling her some news.

### Literature Model

*When does Mellissa sense that Eddie faces a problem?*

After the reporter left Eddie's place today, Hendrikson showed up with a bunch of people. They barged right into the bus." He stopped, embarrassed. "Like I did tonight, I guess. Anyway, they told Eddie that the city was going to help him by moving him into the newest senior citizen housing complex."

I didn't like the sound of it. "They can't do that! Eddie will never go for it. He hates apartments. He told me. He likes to be free."

"I know. And I don't blame him. . . . But anyway, the thing that really upset him is they told him he can't take Shadow with him."

*At what point does Mellissa recognize the seriousness of the problem?*

"Why not?"

"No dogs allowed."

Incredible! "Shadow isn't just a dog. He's like a relative to Eddie. They need each other."

"They don't care. He's a dog and they don't allow any animals."

Gloria Gonzalez, *The Glad Man*

Imagine that you are the author, Gloria Gonzalez, answering the questions in the chart on page 153. How many possible solutions to Mellissa and Eddie's problem can you think of?

# Activities

Here are some activities to help you apply what you have learned.

## 1. Guided Assignment

You are a prisoner in the tower shown in this painting. A servant has agreed to smuggle a message out to your family. Make the message a story telling how you got into this situation. Provide a solution by suggesting how your family might help you escape.

PURPOSE    To write a story about a predicament you are in

AUDIENCE    Your family

LENGTH    2 pages

Detail of folio 104 of "Princes of the World Proceeding to the Court of the Emperor in Constantinople" from *La Fleur des Histoires* Part II, Artist unknown, c. 1455–1460

## 2. Open Assignment

Your job on an advertising campaign is to show how a product helped solve a problem. Write a one- to two-page story telling how someone handled a problem by using one of the products below or another one of your choosing.

- skateboard
- book bag
- portable stereo

## 3. Social Studies

Suppose that the year is 1500, and you are a Native American from one of the Plains groups. Because of a long, harsh winter, food is scarce. You are concerned about how the food shortage affects your family. Refer to the questions on page 153 as you think of a way to solve this problem. Then write a one- or two-page story. Explain the problem. What caused it? What can be done to solve it?

## Just Write

Your story will eventually bring together plot, setting, and characters. As you draft, you may want to focus on one of these elements. Review your prewriting notes, and choose the element that seems most striking. Then start writing about this element, and notice how the other elements find their way into the story. Other helpful drafting tips are listed in the illustration below.

### Drafting Tips

Start writing, and keep writing.

Let your story tell itself.

Try to see and hear your story as you are writing it.

Worry about punctuation, grammar, and spelling later.

Take a break if you get stuck.

These paragraphs are part of a story called "Project: Brainwave." As you read, notice how Rick Harrison lets the story tell itself.

### Student Model

How does this list of choices move the plot along?

This computer stores the memories and experiences of the entire human race. *Beep!* You may choose from five categories. *Beep!* They are: 1. Mystery, *beep!* 2. Adventure, *beep!* 3. Paradise, *beep!* 4. Romance, *beep!* and 5. Sports, *beep!*"

. . . I figured I deserved a vacation. So I chose Paradise. But as I reached for the headset, my wrist accidentally hit the Mystery button as well. Before I knew it, for the second time that day, everything went black.

Rick Harrison, Mt. Pleasant Middle School, Livingston, New Jersey; first appeared in *Merlyn's Pen: The National Magazine of Student Writing*

Here are some activities to help you apply what you have learned.

## 1. Guided Assignment

Your county or state will hold a fair this summer. One of the biggest events of the fair is the tall-tale contest. Contestants have two minutes to tell the funniest and most outlandish story they can think of.

Brainstorm or list ideas for your tall tale. Then use a chart like the one on page 165 to fill in details about characters, plot, and setting. Finally, draft your tall tale. If time allows, break into small groups to tell your stories aloud.

PURPOSE   To entertain and amaze an audience with a tall tale

AUDIENCE   People attending the fair

LENGTH   1–2 pages, tellable in 2 minutes

### COMPUTER OPTION

If you have software that creates tables and charts, use it to create a chart for your tall tale. The software will allow you to customize the size of your rows and columns. You can then print out a blank chart and fill it in by hand. You might also try filling in the chart on the screen. When you are ready to draft your story, you may find it easier to work from a neat, well-designed chart.

## 2. Open Assignment

Select at least one character, one setting, and one plot event from the list below. Or use your writing from the journal activity on page 165. Plan and draft a story of one or two pages using the elements you selected.

- Henry, a twelve-year-old
- Marcia, a thirty-year-old mother of twins

- the American Revolution
- the year 2100

- A girl discovers she can talk with animals.
- A person wakes up looking like a different person.

## 3. Cooperative Learning

Working in a small group, have each group member start with an empty chart like the one on page 165. Label each row Characters, Setting, or Plot. Fill in the Character row of the chart. Then pass the chart to the person on your right. That person will fill in the next row on your chart. You, in turn, will receive another chart from the person on your left. Keep passing the charts around until group members have completed every row. Then draft a story using your own chart, which now includes the ideas of your classmates. Share your completed stories with one another.

# Evaluating a Story Opening

## *Getting off the Ground*

> ### *Literature Model*
>
> **W**ill you please stop walking up and down like that?" said Warren Moore from the couch. "It won't do any of us any good. Think of our blessings; we're airtight, aren't we?"
>
> Mark Brandon whirled and ground his teeth at him. "I'm glad you feel happy about that," he spat out viciously. "Of course, you don't know that our air supply will last only three days." He resumed his interrupted stride with a defiant air.
>
> Isaac Asimov, "Marooned off Vesta"

*What makes this a good story beginning?*

Notice how Isaac Asimov plunges into a tense scene to open this story, the first he ever published. He tells very little about the situation—directly. Yet, because Asimov's writing lets you hear and see the characters, you learn a great deal. You know that the men are stranded in an airtight vehicle with enough air for only three days. Furthermore, they disagree on what to do.

Asimov was only a teen-ager when he wrote this story. Yet the opening kept the editor of a science fiction magazine reading long enough to decide to publish the story.

## *Grabbing Attention*

Starting to read a story doesn't always mean finishing it. Think about what makes you keep reading a story. Is it an exciting plot? Intriguing characters? An unusual writing style? Consider these questions as you read the following paragraphs written by a student.

## Student Model

*I* only remember two things from when I was seven: The time I got a bingo chip stuck up my nose and had to go to the hospital to have it removed, and the fights I had with my sister, Jane. We used to argue endlessly.

When Mom and Dad weren't around, I'd always give her the "now I'M the boss" speech, she'd do something like pour shampoo in my sock drawer, and we'd both end up tearing each other's hair out. Then when Mom and Dad got back, I'd run to them and say, "YOU take care of her—I'm running away!" Jane would then waltz in and say, sweet as pie, "What's going on?"

Renee Albe, Maplewood, New Jersey
First appeared in *Cricket* magazine

*Do you think this is an effective story beginning? Why?*

*Renee uses dialogue to develop her characters and advance the story.*

Some writers work and rework the beginning of a story until they get it just the way they want it. They feel that once they have a beginning, the rest of the story will fall into place. Other writers like to draft the entire story first. Then they read it through for the catchiest line or the first dramatic moment and move that to the beginning.

**Prewriting Tip**

To come up with ideas for a story beginning, think about the most interesting part of your story.

### • JOURNAL ACTIVITY •
### *Think It Through*

Look at the opening paragraphs of four or five stories you enjoyed reading recently. What elements in each opening did you find interesting? Record your answers in your journal.

## Making an Impact

Sometimes revising a story opening means looking at what you've already written to find the best beginning. You might look for the most engaging sentences and start your story at that point, as in the paper on the left below.

You can also keep the beginning you have but just make a few changes, as in the paper on the right. Cutting unimportant words or adding descriptive details can give more impact to your story beginning.

Either approach works well. You may try both methods several times before you write a beginning that satisfies you.

*What did the writer achieve by beginning where she did?*

*Which of the revised openings do you find more effective? Why?*

It was a lovely spring morning
when Kathy and I set out on the
bike trip we'd planned for so long.
I'd been so excited over breakfast
I'd hardly been able to eat.
   It had never occurred to either
of us that anything would go
wrong. So *Start Here* when my rear tire went
flat, I stood by the side of the road
and watched helplessly as Kathy
and her yellow bike receded into
the distance.

It was a lovely spring *The* morning
when Kathy and I set out on the *overnight*
bike trip we'd planned for so long,
I'd been so excited over breakfast. *was too* *to eat*
I'd hardly been able to eat.
   It had never occurred to either
of us that anything would go *I was already starving*
wrong. So when my rear tire went *only two hours into the trip*
flat, I stood by the side of the road
and watched helplessly as Kathy *and my lunch disappeared*
and her yellow bike receded into *over a hill*
the distance.

# *Activities*

Here are some activities to help you apply what you have learned.

## 1. Guided Assignment

Your teacher has asked you to write a story. Look in your journal at some of your story ideas for previous lessons in this unit. Select one that you would like to develop. Brainstorm ways that the story can begin. When you have at least three ideas for openings, choose one. Then draft and revise a possible beginning for the story you've selected.

PURPOSE   To grab readers' attention with an exciting story opening
AUDIENCE   Your teacher
LENGTH   1–2 paragraphs

## 2. Open Assignment

Look back in your journal at your writing for the activity on page 169. Choose one of the story beginnings you've listed. Think about ways the beginning of the story could be revised. Try rewriting the opening, using some of your ideas. How does your opening compare with the original?

## 3. Art

The painting on this page shows a familiar scene—children playing outside

Allan Rohan Crite, *Last Game at Dusk,* 1939

in the evening. Spend ten minutes brainstorming ideas about characters, plot, and setting based on the painting. Select one of your story ideas, and plan and draft a story opening. Then revise the beginning of your story for impact. You might want to refer to page 170 for different ways to reuse your story beginning.

*Evaluating a Story Opening* **171**

## Using a Different Approach

Writing a story of your own is just one way to respond. Use your imagination to explore other possibilities. You can write a poem about how the story made you feel. You can write an advice column, advising a character what to do to get out of a tricky situation. Suppose that you have a chance to interview a character. You may begin by writing down the questions you'd ask, and you might go so far as to imagine the character's answers.

Perhaps you are intrigued by a certain topic that the story suggests. One writer was fascinated by the phoenix in "A Leg Full of Rubies" and wanted to find out more about it. The journal entry below shows his response.

The story inspired this writer to do some additional reading to find out more about the phoenix.

I just finished reading a story about a phoenix. This was the first time I've heard about a phoenix. My teacher said it's a mythical bird and that it's in other stories, too. I checked out a book from the library that tells about different myths. It says that the phoenix lives for five hundred years! At the end of that time it builds a nest and goes up in flames. Out of the ashes comes a new phoenix.

In the story I read the phoenix is evil. But I don't think it would always be an evil bird. I'd like to write a story about a phoenix, but the bird wouldn't be evil. Because it lives for so long, it would probably be very wise. The phoenix could be an adviser to different rulers for hundreds of years.

# Activities

Here are some activities to help you apply what you have learned.

## 1. Guided Assignment

You have been given the chance to play Theseus or Dr. Kilvaney in a dramatic production of "A Leg Full of Rubies." Your drama coach has asked you to write about your character so that you can better understand and portray him.

Write a brief story, making up what happened to your character before the scene on page 172.

**PURPOSE**   To understand a character by writing a story
**AUDIENCE**   Yourself
**LENGTH**   1–2 pages

## 2. Open Assignment

Select a short story you would like to respond to. You can choose a new story or one you have already read. After reading or reviewing the story, brainstorm to come up with ideas for responding to it. Review the suggestions in this lesson, or think of your own ideas. After choosing a method you like, write a one- or two-page response.

## 3. Social Studies

This vase shows one Chinese interpretation of the phoenix. How is this

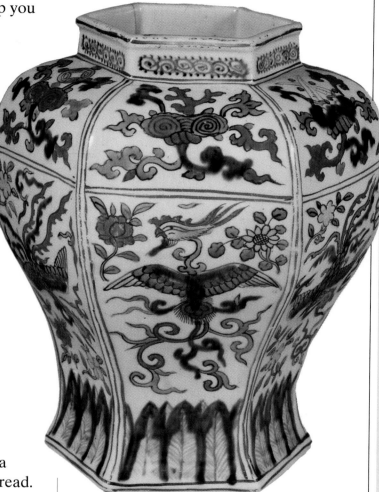

Ming dynasty, China, Five-color vase, Lung-ch'ing period, A.D. 1567–1572

image different from the idea you had of the phoenix when you read the excerpt on page 172? Use your school or public library to find out about the phoenix myth in Asian or Native American culture or in another culture.

*Writing About Literature: Responding to a Short Story*   **175**

*Marjorie Agosín*

# A Huge Black Umbrella

---

*"A Huge Black Umbrella" is the story of Delfina,[1] a special woman who lived an extraordinary life. Just as Delfina's ragged umbrella somehow protected her from rain, her strength of character guided her through misfortune. This fictional narrative is taken from* Where Angels Glide at Dawn, *a collection of short stories by Latin American writers.*

---

When she arrived at our house she was covered by a huge black umbrella. A white gardenia hung from her left ear. My sister Cynthia and I were bewitched by the sight of her. We were a little afraid, too. She seemed like an enormous fish or a shipwrecked lady far from home. Certainly, her umbrella was useless in the rain since it was ripped in many places, which let the rainwater fall on her—water from one of the few downpours of that surprisingly dry summer. It was the summer in which my sister and I understood why magical things happen, such as the arrival of Delfina Nahuenhual.[2]

---

1 **Delphina** (Del fēn′ ə)
2 **Nahuenhual** (Nə′ wen əl)

My mother welcomed her, and Delfina, with a certain bold-ness, explained that she always traveled accompanied by that enormous umbrella, which protected her from the sun, elves, and little girls like us. My mother's delicate lips smiled. From that moment my mother and Delfina developed a much friend-lier relationship than is usual between "the lady of the house" and "her servant."

Delfina Nahuenhual—we had to call her by her full name—was one of the few survivors of the Chilean earthquake in the south of Chile. She had lost her children, house, her wedding gown, chickens and two of her favorite lemon trees. All she could rescue was that huge black umbrella covered with dust and forgotten things.

In the evenings she usually lit a small stove for cooking; the fire gave off a very lovely, sweet light. Then she wrapped her-self up in an enormous shawl of blue wool that wasn't scratchy and she put a few slices of potato on her temples to protect her-self from sickness and cold drafts.

As we sat by the stove, Delfina Nahuenhual told stories about tormented souls and frogs that became princes. Her gen-erous lap rocked us back and forth. We were peaceful children who felt the healing power of her love. After she thought we were asleep, Delfina Nahuenhual would write long letters that she would later number and wrap up in newspaper. She kept the letters in an old pot that was filled with garlic, cumin,[3] and slivers of lemon rind.

My sister and I always wanted to read those letters and learn the name and address of the person who would receive them. So whenever Delfina Nahuenhual was busy in the kitchen, we tried peeking into the pot to discover what she was hiding.

But we never managed to read the letters. Delfina Nahuenhual would smile at us and shoo us along with the end of her broom.

3 **cumin** (kum' in) the fruits from a small plant in the parsley family, used for flavoring, pickles, soups, etc.

For many years, Delfina continued to tell us stories next to the stove. Not long after my brother Mario, the spoiled one of the family, was born, Delfina Nahuenhual told us she was tired and that she wanted to return to the south of Chile. She said she now had some savings and a chicken, which was enough to live on. I thought that she wanted to die and go to heaven because she had decided to return to the mosses and clays of her land.

I remember that I cried a lot when we said good-bye. My brother Mario clung to her full skirt, not wanting to be separated from the wise woman who for us, was never a servant. When she bent over to give me a kiss, she said that I must give her letters to the person to whom she had addressed them but that I could keep the pot.

For many years I kept her little pot like a precious secret, a kind of magical lamp in which my childhood was captured. When I wanted to remember her, I rubbed the pot, I smelled it, and all my fears, including my fear of darkness, vanished. After she had left I began to understand that my childhood had gone with her. Now more than ever I miss the dish of lentils[4] that she prepared for good luck and prosperity on New Year's Eve. I miss the smell of her skin and her magical stories.

Many years later, my sister Cynthia had her first daughter. Mario went traveling abroad and I decided to spend my honeymoon on Easter Island, that remote island in the middle of the Pacific Ocean, six hours by plane from Chile. It is a place full of mysterious, gigantic statues called Moais.[5] Ever since I was a child, I had been fascinated by those eerie statues, their enormous figures seeming to spring from the earth, just as Delfina Nahuenhual and her huge black umbrella did when she first came to my house. I carried her letters, which I had long ago taken from the small earthen pot and placed in a large moss-green chest along with the few cloves of garlic that still remained. As a grown-up I never had the urge to read the letters. I only knew that they should be delivered to someone.

4 **lentils** (lent′ lz) plants in the family to which peas and beans belong
5 **Moais** (Mō′ īz)

One morning when the sun shone even in the darkest corner of my hotel room, I went to the address written on Delfina's letters. It was a leper[6] colony, one of the few that still exist. A very somber employee opened the door and quickly took the packet of five hundred letters. I asked if the addressee was still alive and he said of course, but that I couldn't meet the person. When I gave him the letters, it seemed as though I had lost one of my most valuable possessions, perhaps even the last memories of my dear Delfina Nahuenhual's life.

So I never did meet the person to whom Delfina Nahuenhual wrote her letters nor learned why she spent her sleepless nights writing them. I only learned that he was a leper on Easter Island, that he was still alive and, perhaps, still reads the letters, the dreams of love Delfina Nahuenhual had each night. When I returned home, I knew at last that Delfina Nahuenhual was content, because when I looked up, as she had taught me to do, I saw a huge black umbrella hovering in the cloudy sky.

Pierre-Auguste Renoir, *The Umbrellas*, 1880–1885

6 **leper** (lep'ər) a person having a severe skin disease that attacks and deforms skin, flesh, and nerves

Frida Kahlo, *Self-Portrait with Monkey*, 1940

## For Discussion

1. Imagine you are the narrator of this story and you see Delfina again. What would you talk about? Why?

2. The small earthen pot always reminded the narrator of Delfina. Is there some object that reminds you of another person? What is it about the item that makes you think of the person?

# Readers Respond

At the beginning, the character of Delfina captured my attention. She seemed like such an odd person, and I wanted to find out what she was really like. By the end, however, I still hadn't found out much about her. I think the author should have developed the character of Delfina better.

**Maria Concepción**

When Delfina first arrives, she is covered by the huge black umbrella. She seems to put a spell over the narrator, a spell that hangs like a black cloud. At the end the narrator realizes that Delfina has always been there and that Delfina's spirit acts like an umbrella, covering and protecting.

I like this story because it's very much like real life. Some people might feel alone in the world. They might not realize that there are people to help them or protect them. But at some point in their lives, they realize that there's a cover—another person or a memory of a person—to help them out.

**Trina Chu**

## Do You Agree?

1. Do you agree with Maria that Delfina's character should have been better developed? Why or why not?

2. Think of a person you know, or imagine someone, who would make a fascinating character for a story. In your journal write your ideas about the character's appearance, interests, and personality.

# *Writing Process in Action*

## Very Special People

Some people are unforgettable. Knowing them can change the way you see the world and yourself.

In "The Huge Black Umbrella," on pages 176–180, Delfina Nahuenhual was a special person to the narrator. The narrator doesn't understand Delfina, but she tells her story so that we can see Delfina and be just as mystified and fascinated.

This assignment gives you a chance to think and write about a special person in your life.

### • Assignment •

| | |
|---|---|
| Context | You have been asked to write a story based on a special person you have known well. Write about one event that makes this person special to you. Your story will be converted into a short scene for a student playwrights' lab. |
| Purpose | To show in a story how you feel about a special person |
| Audience | Student playwrights |
| Length | 2 or more pages |

The following pages offer advice on how to approach this assignment. After you've read them once, don't hesitate to return to them for review.

182

# 1. Prewriting

Whom will you write about? You could choose a close friend, a relative, a teacher, or a camp counselor. Look through photo albums, letters, journals, or collections of objects to help you decide whom you want to write about. Brainstorming may help you explore what you want to say about the person. Look at pages 148–151 for tips about brainstorming. Your goal is to find specific details about the person and your experiences with her or him to use in your story.

**Option A**

Look at important objects or mementos.

**Option B**

Review your journal.

**Option C**

Browse through a photo album.

My swimming trophies bear my name, but they should bear this name, too: Glenn Williams. I was afraid of the water until the summer he taught me to swim. His soft voice and steady gaze calmed me.

# 2. Drafting

After noting details about your subject, you need to look through your prewriting to get an idea of how to start your story. A strong opening paragraph will make the person you're writing about sound interesting from the very beginning. Don't try to tell readers everything about your subject in the first paragraph. Choose a few details that set your character apart.

Notice the details in the following paragraph that would let you recognize Delfina Nahuenhual right away if you happened to meet her:

W*hen she arrived at our house she was covered by a huge black umbrella. A white gardenia hung from her left ear. My sister Cynthia and I were bewitched by the sight of her. We were a little afraid, too. She seemed like an enormous fish or a shipwrecked lady far from home.*

Delfina's huge black umbrella and hanging gardenia make her hard to miss. In addition, the narrator tells us how she and her sister responded to Delfina. They were fascinated yet a little afraid.

As you draft your story, keep your focus on the person you're writing about. If you get stuck, look again at your prewriting notes for fresh ideas. The most important thing to remember at the drafting stage is to get your ideas on paper. You can make changes later.

## 3. Revising

As you read your draft, check whether every detail, sentence, and paragraph helps build your story. Review the assignment when you're ready to revise. Have you stayed on track?

Before you begin to revise your work, you may want to ask a teacher or friend to read your draft. Also, reading your draft out loud can help you decide what changes to make. Think about questions like the ones below as you see that all parts of your story work together smoothly.

**Question A**

Does every sentence contribute to the story?

**Question B**

Does the action of my story move along clearly?

**Question C**

Do the details let readers picture my subject?

*I didn't even want to go to camp that summer. I hated the counselor who registered me, but as soon as I found out that Mr.* the tall man with big ears who greeted us *Williams was going to be my swimming teacher, I knew the summer would be all right.*

yet sure

*He talked in a soft, voice that forced you to lean toward him. He wore a whistle like every other swimming teacher I'd ever had, but I never heard him use it.*

## 4. Editing

Many writers will let their work sit for a day before they begin to edit. During the editing stage, you can fix any errors that might muddy the ideas and feelings you want to express. For instance, if your story contains dialogue, you'll want to make sure your readers can follow who is speaking. Look again at page 162 to review suggestions for writing dialogue. Also see pages 536–537 to check your usage of quotation marks.

This checklist will help you catch errors you might otherwise overlook. You'll want your story to reflect your hard work, so read and reread your work with care. If some part of it still doesn't sound right, fix it.

*Checklist*

1. *Have I chosen vivid details that bring my subject to life?*
2. *Are all my sentences complete?*
3. *Is the time order of events clear?*
4. *If I've used dialogue, is it apparent who speaks when?*

## 5. Presenting

Before you send your story to the playwrights' lab, ask someone else who knows your subject to read it. Your reader may have some last-minute suggestions to contribute. Consider putting your story in a folder or clear plastic sleeve. If you have a photograph of the person you've written about, include it with your story.

### Reflecting

Writing about a person you've known is one way to use events from your life to create a story. Did the writing help you think about the role of other people in your life? How have you been changed by other special people in your life?

# Portfolio & Reflection

## Summary

**Key concepts in writing a story include the following:**

- Characters, plot, and setting are the three basic elements of a story.
- The plot of a story is the series of events that focuses on the problem faced by a character.
- Brainstorming and listing are useful prewriting techniques for story writing.
- Arranging story events in time order helps the reader follow the action.
- Dialogue can help a reader understand the moods, interests, and personalities of different characters in a story.
- An effective story beginning includes descriptive details, action, or dialogue that grabs the reader's attention.

## Your Writer's Portfolio

Look over the writing you did for this unit. Choose two pieces for your portfolio. Look for writing that does one or more of the following:

- grows out of your prewriting ideas
- includes believable characters, an intriguing setting, and a clear plot
- contains an imaginative solution to a problem faced by the main character
- relates a series of events in time order
- includes lively, realistic dialogue that reveals what characters are like
- has a beginning that makes the reader want to read the whole story

## Reflection and Commentary

Think about what you learned in this unit. Answer the following questions as you look over the two pieces of writing you chose. Write a page of "Comments on Writing a Story" for your portfolio.

1. What prewriting techniques helped you most in finding your story ideas?
2. Did you answer the question What happened? in an imaginative way?
3. Does the dialogue you wrote sound like real speech?
4. In your opinion, what is special about the stories you picked? Why would others enjoy reading them?

## Feedback

**If you had a chance to respond to the following student comment, what would you say or ask?**

*I really like writing stories because anything can happen.*

Sarah Maguire, Maplewood Middle School,
Menasha, Wisconsin

# Writing to Inform and Explain

# Inquiring Minds

Mark Tansey, *Secret of the Sphinx*, 1984

Contrast w/wolf-eel

- can crawl through crevices

## Two Lefts and a Right

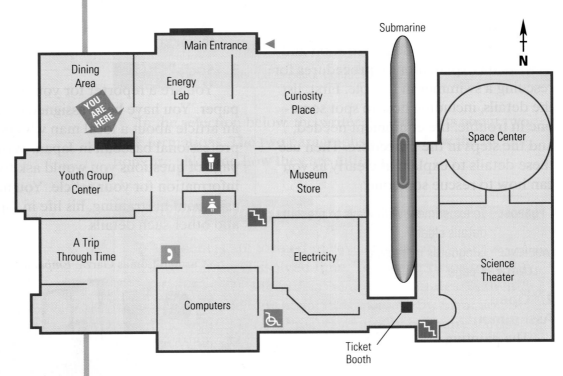

- At the pay phones, turn left.
- Leave by the door on the opposite side.
- Pass the ticket booth, and turn left immediately.
- Go into the Energy Lab, and turn right immediately.
- Pass the Science Theater. Turn right into the Space Center.
- Enter the Electricity exhibit.

You may not think the order in which you present information is very important—until you need to use that information! Look at the directions to the Space Center. The information is out of order, making the directions useless. On a sheet of paper, write the steps of these directions in an order that seems helpful.

# Getting Organized

How you organize information in expository writing depends on what you want to say. You may want to arrange events in the order in which they happened. You may want to list facts in order of importance. You may want to tell about places and things according to their position. You may even want to list items according to how much you like or dislike them.

Examine the diagram below, and think about how you could organize the information if you were going to write about the planets. You could choose to group them by temperature, according to their distance from the sun, or in several other ways.

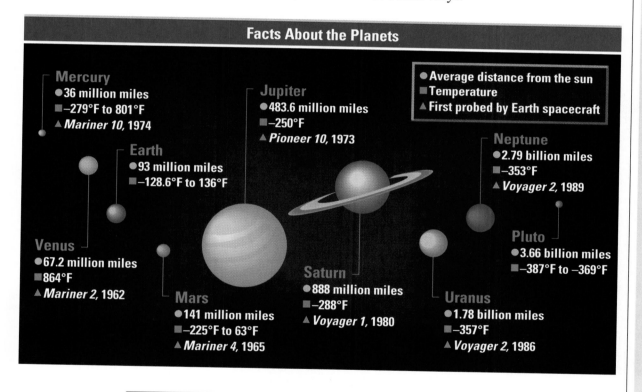

**Facts About the Planets**

- Average distance from the sun
- Temperature
- First probed by Earth spacecraft

**Mercury**
- 36 million miles
- −279°F to 801°F
- *Mariner 10,* 1974

**Earth**
- 93 million miles
- −128.6°F to 136°F

**Venus**
- 67.2 million miles
- 864°F
- *Mariner 2,* 1962

**Mars**
- 141 million miles
- −225°F to 63°F
- *Mariner 4,* 1965

**Jupiter**
- 483.6 million miles
- −250°F
- *Pioneer 10,* 1973

**Saturn**
- 888 million miles
- −288°F
- *Voyager 1,* 1980

**Uranus**
- 1.78 billion miles
- −357°F
- *Voyager 2,* 1986

**Neptune**
- 2.79 billion miles
- −353°F
- *Voyager 2,* 1989

**Pluto**
- 3.66 billion miles
- −387°F to −369°F

- JOURNAL ACTIVITY •

## Try It Out

In your journal, note five or six important events that happened in the past year. Then list the events in order of their importance.

# Details, Details!

**DRAFTING TIP**

When you draft the introductory paragraph of an explanation, you may want to use a striking example to raise your readers' interest.

Details in expository writing are important. Details can include facts, examples, reasons, and statistics (various kinds of numerical information). The chart below highlights different kinds of details.

| Kinds of Details | |
| --- | --- |
| Facts | Mercury is nearer the sun than any other planet in our solar system. |
| Statistics | Mercury rotates once in about 59 Earth days. Its orbit around the sun takes about 88 Earth days. These numbers mean that a day on Mercury lasts about two-thirds of its year. |
| Examples | The temperature on Mercury could melt lead. |
| Reasons | Because it is so close to the sun, Mercury is extremely hot. |

The writer of the following passage uses details to explain temperatures on Mercury. As you read, look for facts, statistics, examples, and reasons.

## Literature Model

In what way do the details help you understand why Mercury is so hot?

Mercury is dry, hot, and almost airless. The sun's rays are about seven times as strong on Mercury as they are on the earth. The sun also appears about 2½ times as large in Mercury's sky as in the earth's. Mercury does not have enough gases in its atmosphere to reduce the amount of heat and light it receives from the sun.

"Mercury," *The World Book Encyclopedia*

# Activities

Here are some activities to help you apply what you have learned.

## 1. Guided Assignment

At the right is a drawing for a remote-controlled exploratory space vehicle. It is designed to travel to a planet, gather information, and send the information back to Earth. Imagine that you are the scientist who built this vehicle for exploring the surface of Mars. You are to prepare a brief paper for other scientists, explaining what this vehicle can do. First, explain what powers your vehicle and how it moves. Next, tell how the vehicle will conduct tests. Finally, explain how it will communicate information to Earth.

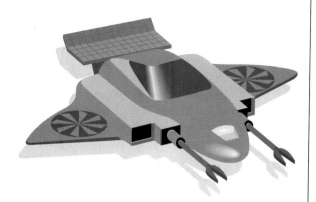

| | |
|---|---|
| **PURPOSE** | To show your ability to explain a process clearly |
| **AUDIENCE** | Other scientists |
| **LENGTH** | 1–2 pages |

## 2. Open Assignment

Write one or two pages explaining how you go about any of the following activities or an activity of your own choosing. Arrange the steps in time order, in order of importance, or in the order of your likes and dislikes.

- your morning routine before school
- chores you do around home on the weekend
- the walk from where you live to where one of your friends lives

## 3. Cooperative Learning

In a small group discuss an imaginary island on which you are shipwrecked. You need to know what the island is like, so you decide to explore it. Agree on the way you will divide up the island for exploration. Then, working individually, explore your part of the island. List your discoveries in order of importance to the shipwrecked group. Come together again, and share your notes on what each of you found. Make a map of the island, and mark your discoveries on the map. List the things you found that will be important to you all.

### COMPUTER OPTION

Tables and charts can help you organize information and make it clear for your reader. If your word-processing program allows you to create graphics, try using this option. Make a chart that identifies the parts of the island and what you found in each part.

# Writing About Similarities and Differences

## *Anything in Common?*

Can you tell one fish from another? If you were planning an aquarium, one decision you'd need to make is whether to have freshwater or saltwater fish. Your choice would affect everything from the price of your collection to the design of your aquarium.

*Notice the writer's use of "on the other hand." Does this phrase signal similarities or differences?*

*After reading this comparison and contrast, which type of fish do you think would be more interesting?*

### Model

Aquarium fish are cold-blooded, so they cannot adjust to abrupt changes in water temperature. As a result, you must keep the water temperature steady in any aquarium. The water's composition may be different, though, depending on the kind of fish you have. Marine (saltwater) fish need exactly the right amount of salt and other compounds dissolved in their water. Freshwater fish, on the other hand, cannot tolerate much salt. In general, marine fish are more delicate and more expensive. Many people think they are worth the extra trouble, however, because of their glorious colors and exotic shapes.

# Looking Closely

On the surface, two things often may seem alike. When you examine them closely, however, you find differences. For example, two four-door, American-made cars may be alike in many ways, but every model and style is different from the others.

When you look at ways in which two things are alike, you are comparing them. When you examine their differences, you are contrasting them. Making a clear, complete comparison-contrast list or diagram can help you identify likenesses and differences.

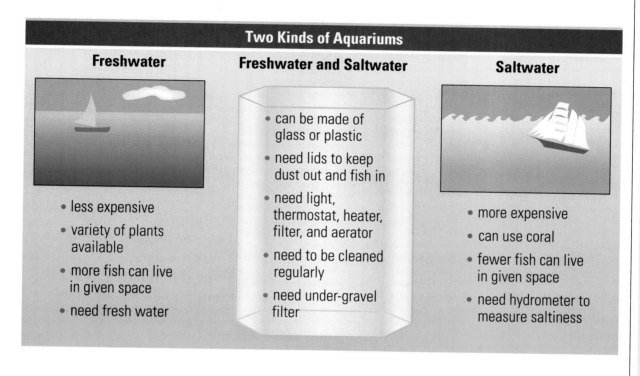

**Two Kinds of Aquariums**

**Freshwater**

- less expensive
- variety of plants available
- more fish can live in given space
- need fresh water

**Freshwater and Saltwater**

- can be made of glass or plastic
- need lids to keep dust out and fish in
- need light, thermostat, heater, filter, and aerator
- need to be cleaned regularly
- need under-gravel filter

**Saltwater**

- more expensive
- can use coral
- fewer fish can live in given space
- need hydrometer to measure saltiness

## • JOURNAL ACTIVITY •
### Think It Through

Think about talking with a friend or relative face to face and talking with that same person on the telephone. In your journal, list how the experiences are alike and how they are different. Write a few sentences telling which method of communication you prefer and why.

# Drawing Comparisons

When you know how two things are alike and different, you can begin to organize your ideas for a written explanation. The chart below shows one way to organize details. It compares and contrasts two insects feature by feature. The passage following the chart also uses a feature-by-feature comparison.

## Grammar
### Editing Tip

A comparison-contrast statement may include the adjectives *more, most, less,* and *least* to show degrees of difference. See pages 408–409.

| Comparing Two Insects | | |
|---|---|---|
| **Feature** | **Centipede** | **Millipede** |
| **Legs** | 1 pair per segment | 2 pairs per segment |
| **Food** | snails, slugs, worms | plants |
| **Danger** | poisonous | harmless |
| **Movement** | quick | moderate |

### Literature Model

*Notice the writer's use of the word "whereas." Does the word signal likenesses or differences?*

Compare the centipede and millipede below. The centipede has one pair of jointed legs per segment, whereas the millipede has two pairs of legs per segment. Centipedes hunt for their food and have a pair of poison claws used to inject venom into their prey. Centipedes feed on snails, slugs, and worms. Their bites are very painful to humans. Millipedes don't move as quickly as centipedes and feed on plants.

Lucy Daniel, Edward Paul Ortleb, Alton Biggs,
*Merrill Life Science*

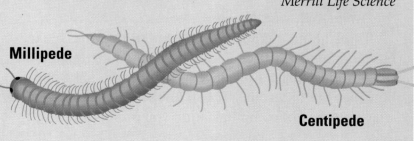

Millipede

Centipede

# Activities

Here are some activities to help you apply what you have learned.

## 1. Guided Assignment

Imagine you have a twin brother or sister who is like you in some ways but not in others. Your family will soon be going on a vacation. Make a diagram or chart showing activities both you and your twin like and activities you don't agree on. Write a letter to your twin explaining the diagram and suggesting vacation plans that you both can agree on and can propose to your parents.

Lilla Cabot Perry, *The Visit*, 1899

PURPOSE   To plan a successful vacation
AUDIENCE   Your family
LENGTH   1–2 pages

## 2. Open Assignment

The painting on this page shows a Japanese woman receiving a visitor. Your way of welcoming someone to your home may be different from hers, but the two welcomes will be alike in some ways. Compare and contrast this scene with a welcome you have received or given. List your observations. Then write one or two pages explaining how the two welcomes are alike and different. These features may guide your comparison and contrast:

- clothing
- words
- food

## 3. Music and Drama

Imagine that you belong to a group that has been asked to select music for your end-of-the-year school program. Name two songs you would suggest. Compare and contrast them feature by feature. For each song, you might explain the message, identify the likely audience, describe the tempo, and try to capture the mood.

*Writing About Similarities and Differences*   **205**

# Explaining How Something Works

## Talk About Complicated!

You've probably never seen an apparatus as complicated as this one. For all its multiple moving pieces and dizzying action, the end result is pretty simple. Can you figure out what it is? Follow the steps in order from A to Q. By putting items in the proper order, you can make complicated ideas clear.

## Step by Step

Sometimes cartoonists have fun drawing sequences like the one above. Who would think the process of hitting a golf ball could be so complicated? This machine is imaginary, but it illustrates the importance of explaining steps in the proper order when you want to show how something works.

Consider a real process, such as operating canal locks. Notice the way the following passage explains how the locks work.

irst, a lock is filled with water by opening the filling valve. From the higher water level, the boat enters the first set of gates. The upper gates open easily because the water pressure is the same on both sides. After the upper gates are closed, water is pumped out of the lock through the drain valve. The water level begins to lower. Because of the angle of the gates, the higher water pressure at each level keeps them shut. When the water level in the lock is the same as it is on the lower part of the river, the lower gates open and the boat continues its journey.

*Which words does the writer use to signal the order in which the locks work?*

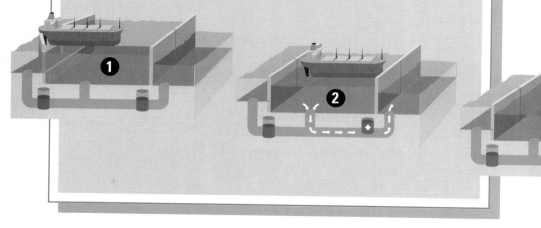

Could ships travel through locks if the gates opened out of order? Hardly! Nor will your writing about a process work if you put the steps in the wrong order.

### • JOURNAL ACTIVITY •
### *Think It Through*

An old saying states, "The difference between a dream and a plan is that one is written down." In your journal write down one of your dreams—for a career, a trip, or something else. Then list in time order the steps you would take to realize that dream.

# Guiding Your Reader

### Prewriting Tip

When you are planning to write about a process, brainstorm with other people to make sure you have identified all steps in the process.

Once you've placed the steps of a process in the correct order, you should select the transition words and phrases that will help readers follow your explanation. When you explain a process, transitions show how the steps are related to each other. Common transition words include *first, next, after, later, while, second, initially,* and *finally.*

You also can make your writing clear to readers by breaking up long passages into smaller paragraphs. This approach helps readers find your main ideas and keep them in order. Notice how the writer of the following paragraph revised it, making new paragraph breaks, rearranging steps, and adding transition words.

*How do the transition words added here help the reader?*

> The hydroelectric dam is the latest method of harnessing the power of rivers. It is designed to ~~uses~~ generate electricity ~~with running water~~. *First,* Water from the dam's reservoir passes through large pipes called penstocks. ~~The powerhouse is where electricity is generated.~~ *then* The water flows to a powerhouse built on the other side of the dam.
>
> *Next,* The force of the water spins a large water wheel called a turbine. *Finally,* The turbine's action produces electricity, which goes out on power lines to homes, schools, *factories,* and businesses.

# Activities

Here are some activities to help you apply what you have learned.

## 1. Guided Assignment

Since you were small, you probably have handled toys and other objects that have wheels. By this time you have come to understand how wheels work.

Imagine that you have been asked to write an article for the "How Things Work" column of a popular children's magazine. Your topic is "How the Wheels of a Bicycle Work." Your readers may know almost nothing about bicycles. Tell what makes the wheels revolve and what causes the machine to move forward. Be sure you explain each step of the process in the order it happens. If you wish, you may use sketches or diagrams to illustrate what you have written.

PURPOSE    To explain how a bicycle works
AUDIENCE    Young readers
LENGTH    1–2 pages

### COMPUTER OPTION

Some software contains desk-top publishing capabilities that let you lay out your page to look like a magazine's or newspaper's. Try designing a magazine column for your article. Be sure to include a headline, a byline, and room for your diagrams or sketches. Be creative!

## 2. Open Assignment

Select a question from the list below, or write one of your own. Then answer the question, putting the steps in the order you would follow. Explain each step thoroughly, and use transition words to help guide your reader.

- How would you entertain your favorite sports or television star if he or she were to spend the day in your hometown?
- If you could spend a day exactly as you want, what would you do?
- What do you wish you could explain to somebody if you had the opportunity?

## 3. Cooperative Learning

In a small group, plan a five-day camping trip. Discuss places to camp, and decide where you will go. Then list the tasks you will have to perform before your group begins the trip. For example, you might need to plan for shelter, cooking equipment, transportation, a route to the campsite, and first-aid equipment.

Brainstorm other planning tasks. Assign one or more tasks to each group member. Working individually, write a one-page explanation of how you would accomplish your task. Include the steps you would take, and put the steps in the order you would follow. When the group regathers, discuss the tasks, and share your explanations. Be sure that all needs have been taken care of.

# *Blame It on the Weather*

Weather affects the way you dress, what you do for fun, even the way you feel. Of course, natural events cause changes in the weather. For example, volcanic eruptions can spew enough ash into the air to partially block the sunlight. In turn, this reduction in sunlight can cause colder temperatures in much of the world. The freezing weather that may result can ruin crops, as explained in the excerpt below. Ours is a world of causes and effects.

### *Literature Model*

*What cause-and-effect relationship does the first sentence suggest?*

*Note the writer's use of statistics to show the effect of the cold weather.*

*T*he coldest December temperatures in a century could wreak havoc with consumers' budgets this winter. Freezing weather has decimated [ruined] up to a third of Florida's citrus and 90 percent of the state's winter vegetable crop, estimates Doyle Conner, Florida's agriculture commissioner. Experts say that will translate into sharply higher prices for orange juice, grapefruits, and tomatoes.

*Newsweek*, January 8, 1990

# Just Because

The passage on the previous page shows how a natural event—a cause—resulted in a problem—an effect. A cause is an identifiable condition or event. An effect is something that happens as a direct result of that condition or event. A cause precedes an effect. But of course every event that precedes another isn't necessarily a cause.

Sometimes it seems that one event causes another, when it really doesn't. Be careful not to mislead your readers. Before you write, make sure that something is the direct result of something else. Study the following chart, and note why some statements are not examples of cause and effect.

### Grammar
### Editing Tip

When you edit, try combining a cause and its effect in a complex sentence. For help see pages 448–451.

## Understanding Cause and Effect

| Cause | | Effect |
|---|---|---|
| **Cause** Lightning tends to strike the tallest object in the area. |  | **Effect** Single trees in open fields are often hit by lightning. |

This is true cause and effect. The cause is a condition that comes before and brings about the effect.

| **Cause** Scientists hope someday to probe the planet Pluto. |  | **Effect** Scientists have collected information about the planets. |

A probe of Pluto did not precede the collection of information.

| **Cause** In the spring melting snow filllled the reservoir. |  | **Effect** This summer the city has a water shortage. |

Melting snow preceded the water shortage but did not cause it.

## • JOURNAL ACTIVITY •
### Try It Out

Watch the television news, and look for cause-and-effect relationships the reporters identify. List three or four. In your journal write about why one of them is a true example of a cause-and-effect relationship.

## One Thing Leads to Another

Sometimes a cause and its effect form part of a chain of events. One cause may lead to an effect, and that effect may in turn change circumstances and lead to another effect. The diagram shows how this chain works. The passage below the diagram also shows a cause-and-effect chain.

Below-freezing weather occurs.

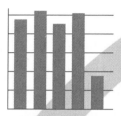

Fewer oranges are available than in previous years.

Consumers want as many oranges as before, but few are available, so prices ris

Frost damages the oranges, and much of the crop is lost.

A rise in the price of oranges makes orange juice more expensive.

### Model

*Is the "indoor air" mentioned in the first sentence a cause, an effect, or both?*

I ndoor air in winter has several effects on the human body. As the outdoor temperature drops, heat must be added indoors for comfort. However, added heat causes the indoor air to hold less moisture. This drier air often causes health problems such as asthma or nosebleeds. People moving about in rooms where the air is too dry may also be irritated by static electricity, which is common when air moisture is low.

# Activities

Here are some activities to help you apply what you have learned.

## 1. Guided Assignment

As a new mayor, you want to present a plan for tackling a major issue, such as ecology, transportation, or education. You must be sure that the city council understands what is causing a particular problem and how that problem is causing other problems. For example:

Waldo Pierce, *Fire at East Orrington*, 1940

- Lack of city planning has caused a shortage of parks.
- Having few parks is the cause of children playing in the streets.
- Children's playing in the streets has led to accidents.

Write a speech explaining your plan to attack these causes and to produce good effects.

PURPOSE   To use cause-and-effect analysis
          to present a plan
AUDIENCE  The city council
LENGTH    1–2 pages

## 2. Open Assignment

Study the painting above, or choose another painting of an event that shows people responding to an emergency. Write a one- or two-page answer to one of these questions:

- What may have caused the event?
- What may be some effects of the event?

## 3. Social Studies

Conduct some research on a fire that happened a long time ago. You may choose one you have heard about from people in your area. Or read about the fire in Chicago on October 8, 1871, or the one in Peshtigo, Wisconsin, on the same date. Use at least one book and one periodical to discover a possible cause and several effects of the fire on the area and the people who lived there.

**Reports: Narrowing a Topic**

## *Limiting the Field*

You probably recognize most of the sports represented by these pictures, and you may want to find out about other sports. But you can't play them all at once. Choosing a report topic is like choosing a sport; you can't do (or say) everything.

### *What to Write About?*

A research report is a kind of expository writing. Because a report should cover a topic thoroughly, you'll need information from many sources. This search for information is research. After you've gathered the information, you must organize it so that your readers will find it clear and useful.

Business people conduct research and then write reports that show how their companies are doing. Scientists write reports to explain new discoveries to the world. Journalists investigate events and report on them. When you're planning a research report, keep three things in mind:

1. Select a topic that you care about.
2. Narrow the topic so that you can cover it thoroughly.
3. Plan on using several sources of information.

The diagram below shows how you can focus your topic. Outdoor sports can be interesting, but the focus is too broad. There are just too many outdoor sports to cover thoroughly. You can narrow your topic, however, and focus on a single sport— bicycling. But even this narrowed topic includes too much information for one report. You can cover one part of bicycling—bicycle safety. Experience in writing reports will help you gain a clearer sense of how much information you can cover.

> **Drafting Tip**
>
> When drafting, remember that visual aids such as photos, maps, and charts can help your reader grasp your points.

## • JOURNAL ACTIVITY •
### *Think It Through*

Think of what you covered today in one class on one topic. Next, narrow the topic, and jot the revised topic down. Write about it in your journal, and explain why you narrowed it.

## Who's Out There?

A report on bicycle safety could have a wide audience. Who's the audience for the report you're planning? It may be your class or the readers of your local paper or an adult community group. Turn back to page 56, and review ways to determine the purpose and audience of your writing.

The next time you are driving your car, think for a moment about others who are sharing the road. More and more people are riding bicycles these days, and too many of them are in accidents with moving cars. In a recent year 460,000 people were injured in such accidents, and as many as 1,100 cyclists have been killed each year. Make the roads safe for all who use them.

Bike riding can be fun, but it also carries some responsibility. The next time you jump on your bike and get ready to take off, remember to (1) ride with the traffic and keep to the right; (2) never ride double on a bicycle; (3) wear a helmet, and; (4) wear light colored clothes, put reflective strips on your clothes and your bike, and use a bike light when light is poor.

These examples show how you can tailor a report to two different audiences. The paragraph on the left is intended for drivers. Its purpose is to make drivers aware of the frequency of serious car-bicycle accidents. The paragraph on the right is directed toward cyclists. The writer reminds bicycle riders of some basic safety rules. The purpose is to get readers to think about and follow precautions.

# *Activities*

Here are some activities to help you apply what you have learned.

## 1. Guided Assignment

The painting shows several types of farming in California. Notice that the artist focuses on orange growing. She chose one part of a topic and provided more details about it. This is what writers often do.

Select one of the broad topics from the list below, or choose one of your own. Write an explanation of how you would narrow the topic to emphasize one part. List some details you would include about your topic

- plants growing where you live
- places of interest in your town
- clubs in your school
- American inventors

| | |
|---|---|
| PURPOSE | To explore techniques for focusing on a topic |
| AUDIENCE | Classmates |
| LENGTH | 1 page |

## 2. Open Assignment

Write a report about books you think make good reading for first-grade children. Use the library as a resource. Narrow your topic to a particular type of book, such as easy-reading books or picture books. Write one page about the type of book you chose.

## 3. Science

This painting was made in the 1930s. The only modern machine it shows is a tractor. Since then, what machines have been invented to help workers in the orange groves? Do some reading, and write a short report on what you find.

Maxine Albro, *California Agriculture*, 1934

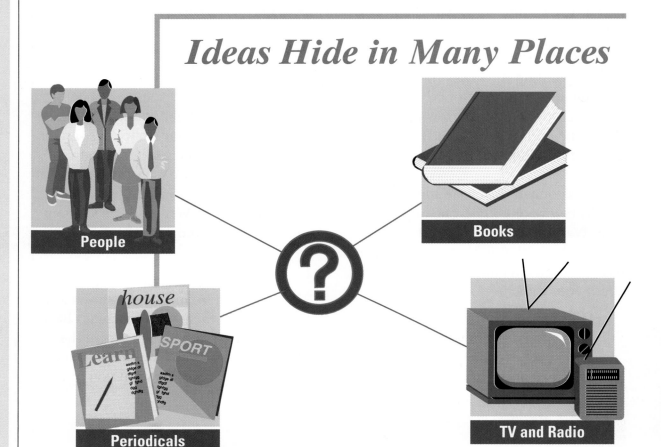

*Ideas Hide in Many Places*

You've selected a topic and are ready to begin your research. Now a big question mark appears in your mind. The question mark stands for your next consideration: Where will I find the information I need?

## Getting the Information

To make the most of the information available for your report, consult several sources. This research will increase your knowledge of the topic you've selected and help you write a good report. You may find information that interests you but doesn't fit in your report. Note it in your journal. Even though you can't use the information this time, you'll have it for future use.

When you're researching a topic, the library can be your best resource. There you'll find a variety of informative materials:

- books on all subjects
- reference books, such as almanacs, atlases, dictionaries, and encyclopedias
- magazines on special subjects
- newspapers
- videotapes, audiotapes, and compact discs

### Revising Tip

When revising, check transitions between paragraphs. Good transitions show how one paragraph relates to the next.

Your library also has indexes that list books, tapes, and magazine articles according to subject.

A good place to start your investigation of printed sources is an encyclopedia. An encyclopedia article can give you a broad view of your topic. It also can point you in the direction of sources you hadn't thought of. The encyclopedia is only a place to begin, however. To explore your topic fully, you'll need to look further.

People are also an important source for a research report. Interviews with knowledgeable people can provide you with information you could never find anywhere else. Most people are pleased when you ask them to share their knowledge.

When possible, your research should include primary sources. A primary source may be a person close to the event or original material you're studying. For example, a friend who lives on a farm is a primary source for a report on farm life. Another type of primary source would be a journal, letter, or document written during the period you're studying. Books and magazines are generally considered secondary sources. Another writer gathered information and shaped it in a certain way.

### • JOURNAL ACTIVITY •
#### Try It Out

How many sources of information do you consult in a single day without realizing it? Think of the types of sources mentioned above. List in your journal the sources you might run across in a typical day.

# A Clear Trail

Now that you've started reading to get an overview for your research report, you'll need to take notes. Note cards will help you put accurate details in your report. They also will provide a record of the information source. At the top of a card, write the topic you're researching. Be sure to include the source's title, its publication date, and the author's name. Then take notes on the card as you read—not later! For each piece of information you write down, write the page number on which you found it. Begin another card each time you begin reading a new source or start a new topic.

Look at the notes for a report on bicycling.

*Each card contains notes on a different topic.*

*This primary source is an informal but helpful interview.*

*Quotation marks indicate exact words.*

### Note cards

**Accidents**
Most accidents occur
— on bright, sunny days, because more cyclists are out;
— on Saturday;
— late in the afternoon.
*Better Bicycling for Boys* Sullivan, 1984, pp. 47-

**Safety Rules**
The most important rules are
— keep to the side of the road.
— Make right turns from the right lane and left turns from the left lane.
— Use hand signals to indicate turns.
"Ride in a straight line; don't weave in and out."
*Better Bicycling for Boys and Girls*, George Sullivan, 1984, pp. 46-47

**Local Problems**
Interview with friend, who bikes to work
1. Watch out for corners with four-way stop signs. Some drivers don't wait for bikes.
2. Bike path through the park has huge potholes. Be careful.
3. There's a dog next door to the grocery store. He got loose last week and grabbed my ankle!

---

## Tips for Taking Notes

- Keep your notes in one place—a journal, notebook, or file.

- With every note include the information source (title, author, publication date, and page numbers). Write this down immediately.

- List main ideas and details to support them. Record dates and names exactly.

- Write in your own words. If you copy words from a source, use quotation marks in your report to show that you're quoting directly.

# Activities

Here are some activities to help you apply what you've learned.

## 1. Guided Assignment

Imagine that you're working with a veterinarian who is writing a booklet on pet care. You are to research the care received by pets in your area. One source of information will be your own observations.

Recall pets you've seen in your neighborhood. Make one or two pages of notes about how the animals are treated and where they are housed and exercised. Also note what you observe about their physical condition.

PURPOSE   To practice observation and note-taking skills

AUDIENCE  Yourself

LENGTH    1–2 pages of journal notes

### COMPUTER OPTION

You can create a note file for this project. Create a table, using one column for each kind of observation you intend to make. Then type in the information from each day's study. When you want to refer to the notes, print them out. Or use your window option to put them on the screen while you write on another file.

## 2. Open Assignment

Imagine that you have been assigned to write a research report. It can be about fire prevention, recycling efforts, or another topic of your choice. Once you have chosen a topic, narrow it. Write your topic at the top of a page. Look at the sources you listed in the Journal Activity and at those listed below. Consider each source and explain in writing why it would or would not help you write on your topic.

- this year's almanac
- your local newspaper
- an interview with a police officer

## 3. Cooperative Learning

In a small group discuss and select three or four topics for brief research. For example, you might want to know a team's won-lost record, the most popular TV shows among teens, or the two most important crops grown in the farming region nearest your home.

Brainstorm possible sources of information for each topic as one group member lists your suggestions. Then each group member should select one of the suggested topics.

Working independently, each group member should research his or her topic. Use note cards to keep track of details and sources.

Come together again, and share information about each topic. List the sources you used. Note how frequently each source was used, and discuss which sources were most helpful.

*Reports: Turning to Helpful Sources*   **221**

# *In Their Own Words*

Think of all the things you've learned by talking with people. People, especially experts, can be a great source of information for research reports. An interview with an expert can give you details, dates, and stories to strengthen your report. An interview also may uncover ideas for further research.

An Illinois writer heard about a program to promote safety among bicycle riders in Schaumburg, Illinois. He became curious about this program. Who ran it? What did it do? An interview with an expert answered many of his questions.

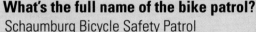

### Interview with Schaumburg Police Intern Becky Stiefvater

**What's the full name of the bike patrol?**
Schaumburg Bicycle Safety Patrol

**How does it operate?**
We have six people, and we divide up into three teams of two. We ride around, and we look for kids who go through stop signs or are riding on the wrong side of the road or riding two people on a bike made for one—anything that's against the village ordinance.

**What happens to them?**
We're capable of issuing a warning ticket or a notice to appear in "bike court." We set up an actual court setup for them, and they get assignments like community service.

**When you're off-duty, do you ride a bike?**
Sometimes I do, but usually, since I'm riding eight hours a day, I opt for my car.

# Take More Than a Pencil

Whom should you interview for the report you're planning? Your parents and teachers might have suggestions. Your librarian might know a local group, such as a historical society or a business association, that can help you.

Once you've identified an expert, you have some planning to do before you conduct your interview. First, you must contact the person to see if and when an interview is possible. Set up an appointment. Be courteous. Your interviewee is doing you a favor by setting aside the time to talk.

Do some preliminary research, and prepare your interview questions ahead of time. Ask yourself what you expect to learn through the interview. Do you want to discover new developments? Do you want personal observations or stories? Many of the most effective interview questions are open-ended; that is, they ask for more than a yes or no answer. Note how the interviewer used open-ended questions when talking with Mrs. Rodriguez.

## Revising Tip

When revising, consider your audience. What do they already know about your topic? What parts of the interview should you include in your report to interest them?

Interview: Mrs. Bianca Rodriguez
Founder of the Ready Riders Bike Safety Club
East side of town; weekly club meetings at the fieldhouse

1. Why did you organize this club?

2. What do you mean by <u>bike safety</u>?

3. How can kids contact you to join the club?

4. What are the benefits of joining this club?

How do the questions show that the interviewer prepared for this conversation?

## • JOURNAL ACTIVITY •
### Try It Out

How would you interview yourself? In your journal write five open-ended questions an interviewer might ask you. Then answer them as honestly as you can.

## *Listen and Question*

When you conduct your interview, you can use a notebook or a tape recorder or both. If you use a notebook, you may have time only to write down the most important points. A tape recorder can copy everything said. Using both may strengthen your report. On tape you'll have a record of the speaker's exact words; on paper you'll have a record of your strongest impressions.

When you meet your expert, thank him or her for taking the time to talk. If you can, conduct the interview in a quiet place. The more privacy you have, the more easily you can talk. Before ending the interview, make sure you have the information you need.

Other hints for a good interview are listed below. Look at the last hint on the list. Immediately after your interview, while the information is fresh in your memory, look at your notes again. Mark the notes that need more research. Add notes about other things you remember. Make sure all numbers and names are correct. Also write down your personal impressions. Did you enjoy the interview? Do you like or trust your interviewee? Though these impressions won't be part of a report, they might help you interpret your information.

### Tips for Conducting an Interview

- Prepare your questions ahead of time.

- Arrive on time, dressed properly.

- Listen carefully to the answers.

- If you don't understand an answer, politely ask for an explanation.

- Ask follow-up questions.

- Immediately after the interview, write out your notes fully, and organize them.

# Activities

Here are some activities to help you apply what you have learned.

## 1. Guided Assignment

A graduate of your school is now the governor. She has agreed to speak at graduation. As a member of the graduation committee, you have been assigned to introduce her. Write to the governor's office. Ask for information you can share with the audience as you make the introduction. Include eight to ten questions for the governor to answer. Keep in mind how valuable her time is, and don't ask for information you could find in print. Write questions that may be answered briefly but that will allow the governor to give you as many details as time permits.

PURPOSE   To structure interview questions
AUDIENCE   The governor
LENGTH   8–10 questions

## 2. Open Assignment

Choose a famous person you would like to interview. The person may be alive or dead and may be from any field—film, music, sports, science, or another field of your choice. Write eight to ten questions that explore the person's opinions on a topic in his or her field.

## 3. Cooperative Learning

In groups of four, conduct an exercise in interviewing. Have the people in your group pair off. One pair will be observers. The other pair will be interviewer and interviewee. You might choose one of these interviewing situations:

- a coach and a student reporter on requirements for student athletes
- a teacher and a student who is considering being a teacher

The interviewer should take notes. The observers also should take notes, focusing on the strengths and weaknesses of the interview.

Working individually, those who took notes should check their notes and write a few sentences in which they evaluate the interview. The interviewee also should write an evaluation of the interview.

Gather as a group again, and share notes. Then discuss strengths and weaknesses of interviewing.

### COMPUTER OPTION

Use your computer to write and organize questions for your interview. First, list questions as they come to mind. When you cannot think of more questions, organize your material. Block or highlight each question, and move it to the place in your list where it will be most effective. Continue until all of the questions you wrote are in a logical order. Then write additional questions under any item you may want to follow up or clarify.

*Reports: Conducting an Interview*   **225**

# *Getting It Together*

Having gathered details and ideas, you've completed your research. You have the raw materials for a report. Now you must decide whether the information you've collected fits what you want to say. Then you must plan how to organize it most effectively.

When you started your research, you knew what you wanted to write about. By now you know the big idea you want your reader to understand. Your next task is to decide how to organize the information in your report so that you get that big idea across.

## *What Are You Trying to Prove?*

All research reports have a thesis statement. The thesis statement is a sentence that tells briefly and clearly the central idea of the whole report. It tells what you want to show, prove, or explain, and it gives your report a focus.

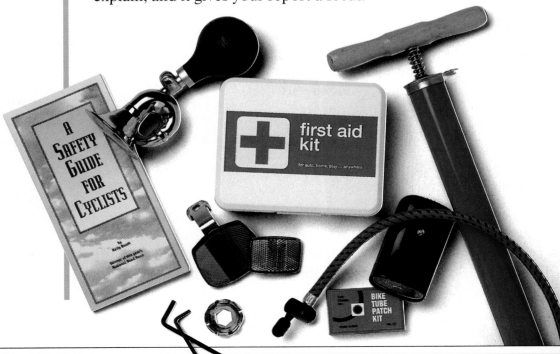

When you begin to organize your report, think about what you want to say. Write a thesis statement. Work with the sentence until you're satisfied that it says just what you want your readers to know. Then list the ideas that support your thesis statement, and organize them to form a working outline. Finally, organize the details from your reading and interview notes, and add these to your outline.

Now you're ready to begin drafting your report. Write from your notes in the order shown in your outline. The information from your research and interviews will help you support your thesis statement and write a strong report.

Thesis Statement: Bike safety includes careful riding, regular maintenance, and proper equipment.

   I. Introduction
   II. Traffic regulations
      A. Ride on the right side of the road.
      B. Don't weave in and out.
      C. Ride single file.
      D. Obey traffic signs, and use hand signals.
   III. Maintenance of your bike
   IV. Wearing a helmet

*When you write an outline, use roman numerals to indicate main ideas and letters to indicate supporting details.*

**• JOURNAL ACTIVITY •**
*Think It Through*

Think about the information you gathered through research but cannot use. From this information write three sentences you could use to develop a thesis statement for a different report.

# The Parts of a Report

Every report has three parts: the introduction, the body, and the conclusion. Each part has a specific purpose. An example of each part and its purpose appears below. (The picture shows only a section of the report on safety.) When you work on your report, look at your notes, and decide which part they belong in.

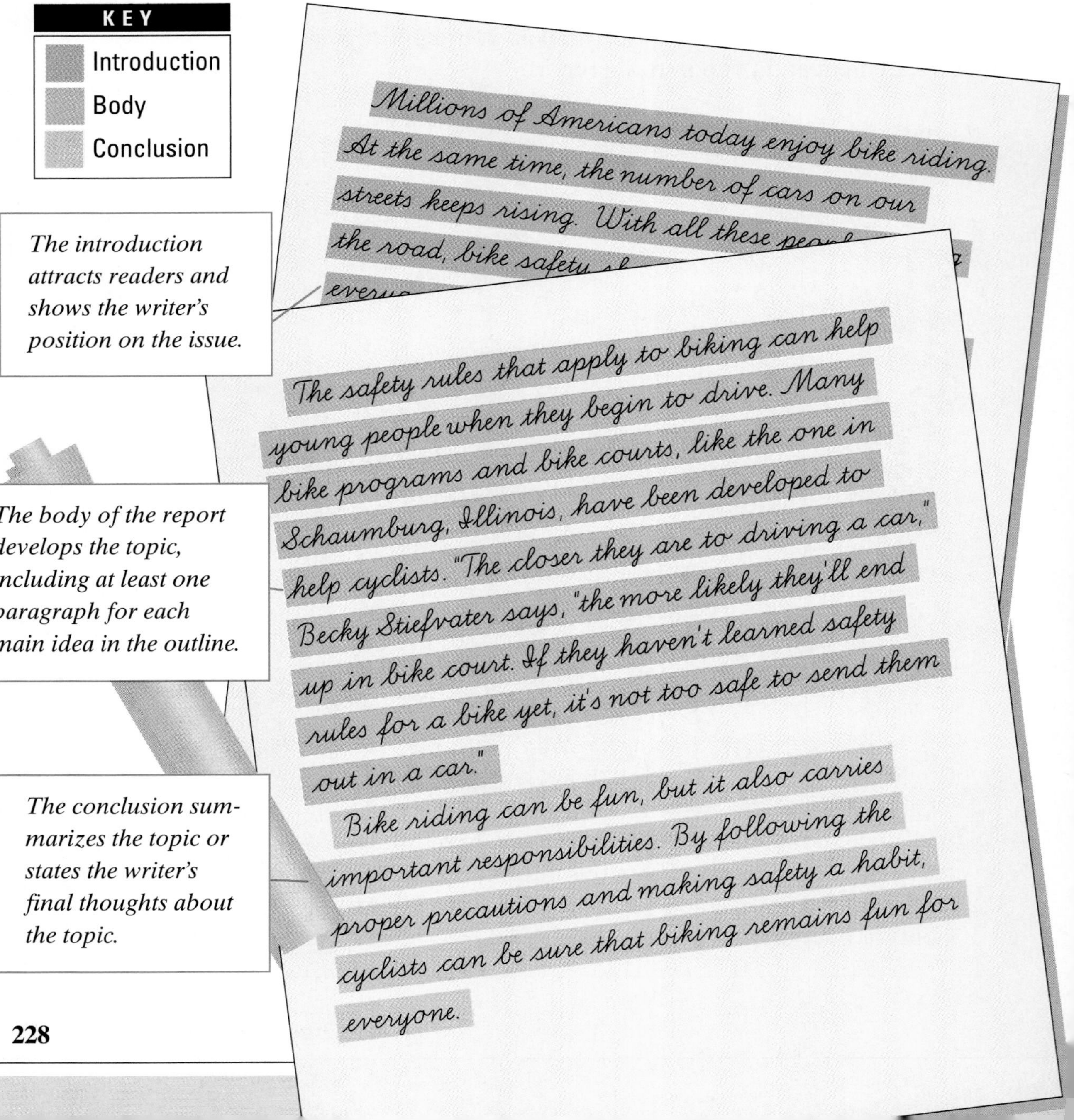

**KEY**

- Introduction
- Body
- Conclusion

*The introduction attracts readers and shows the writer's position on the issue.*

*The body of the report develops the topic, including at least one paragraph for each main idea in the outline.*

*The conclusion summarizes the topic or states the writer's final thoughts about the topic.*

Millions of Americans today enjoy bike riding. At the same time, the number of cars on our streets keeps rising. With all these people on the road, bike safety sh... everyo...

The safety rules that apply to biking can help young people when they begin to drive. Many bike programs and bike courts, like the one in Schaumburg, Illinois, have been developed to help cyclists. "The closer they are to driving a car," Becky Stiefvater says, "the more likely they'll end up in bike court. If they haven't learned safety rules for a bike yet, it's not too safe to send them out in a car."

Bike riding can be fun, but it also carries important responsibilities. By following the proper precautions and making safety a habit, cyclists can be sure that biking remains fun for everyone.

# *Activities*

Here are some activities to help you apply what you have learned.

## 1. Guided Assignment

A science magazine for middle-school students is planning an issue on ecology, dams, and waterways. The editor has asked you to write an article for the issue. The outline below represents information the editor wants, and the notes contain information you can include if you find it useful. Write an introductory paragraph that catches the reader's attention and explains what you intend to say in your report. Then write one page based on Part I of the outline.

**Outline**
I. Early dams
   A. Purpose
   B. Materials
II. Hydroelectric dams
   A. Parts
   B. Purpose
III. Present concerns about damage to ecology

**Notes**
Dams stop the flow of running water, create lakes, store water for later use.

Ancient people built dams, using wood, earth, and rock. They discovered ways to release the water a little at a time.

Later, people built dams for power, releasing water that turned wheels.

Rainy seasons may be followed by dry spells. Farmers need water throughout the growing season. Releasing water from dams allows farmers to irrigate fields.

PURPOSE  To write a short article based on notes and an outline
AUDIENCE  Middle-grade students
LENGTH  1 page

## 2. Cooperative Learning

In a small group brainstorm a list of sports that you think are good activities for people your age. Then narrow the topic, and agree on a few sports to cover in a report. Next, have each group member research one sport. Working independently, research the advantages of your sport for young people. Meet again, and share your notes. Agree on a thesis statement, and organize your group report by making an outline. Then work independently again to complete each item on the outline. One member may write an introduction, one a conclusion. Each of the other members should write about one of the sports listed.

Come together once more, and share your writing. Discuss details to add to or remove from each part of the report. Make sure every part supports the thesis statement you wrote at the beginning. Then gather together the parts of the report, and present the finished product to the whole class.

# Making Something Good Even Better

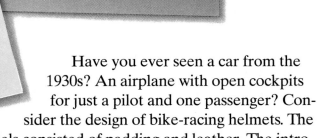

Have you ever seen a car from the 1930s? An airplane with open cockpits for just a pilot and one passenger? Consider the design of bike-racing helmets. The old models consisted of padding and leather. The introduction of plastics allowed manufacturers to produce stronger and lighter helmets. Testing led to improvements that made helmets not only fit riders well but also keep them cool. It seems that the early version of just about anything can stand improvement.

Your research report probably can stand improvement, too. By revising the report, you can test and strengthen the presentation of your ideas.

# Getting It Right

When revising your report, check each part to be sure it fulfills its purpose and makes your report effective. The introduction, the body, and the conclusion should engage and inform your readers. For a discussion of other revision strategies, turn back to page 69.

Because reports are based on facts and other details, there's another step to revising—checking these details.

☑ Are all dates, names, and numbers correct?
☑ Are quotations accurate?
☑ Are notes clear? (If not, go back to the source.)

### Grammar
### Editing Tip

In editing, check the form of all irregular verbs. For more information see pages 374–377.

Proper clothing *and equipment* can also make a difference in bicycle safety. *According to one study,* Only 21 *12* percent of accidents involve a car and a bike. The rest occur when cyclists fall from their bikes. *or are thrown* Because of this, *, when riding,* cyclists wear *themselves* experts recommend that bike helmets to protect against brain injuries.

*Note: name an expert*

*How do the writer's revisions improve this part of the report on cycling safety?*

## • JOURNAL ACTIVITY •
### Think It Through

Think about your work as you revise your report. Look again at the revision guidelines on page 69. In your journal, note the guidelines you have found most helpful, and tell why they worked for you.

## Telling the World

When you started your report assignment, all you had was a topic you were curious about. Now, after all your hard work, you have more knowledge and an informative report. You're ready to share what you've learned.

You can share your work in a variety of ways. Bind your report in book form, present it on a computer disk, put it into a notebook binder, post it on a bulletin board, or print it as part of a class newsletter or magazine. Who will read your work? What will interest them? Think of things to include—covers, graphics, clippings, photographs—that will make your report attractive. Then share it with others!

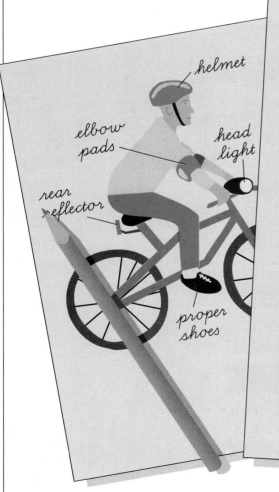

helmet

elbow pads

head light

rear reflector

proper shoes

Another safeguard that people often ignore is proper bike maintenance. Cyclists should inspect their bikes regularly to make sure the tires, brakes, handlebars, seats, and spokes are in proper shape. Some repairs can be done easily by the cyclist, but regular inspections at a bike repair shop are also recommended.

Proper clothing and equipment can also make a difference in bicycle safety. According to one study, only 12 percent of accidents involve a car and a bike. The rest occur when cyclists fall or are thrown from their bikes. Because of this, experts such as those from the National Safe Kids Campaign recommend that, when riding, cyclists wear bike helmets. The helmets protect against brain injuries.

# *Activities*

Here are some activities to help you apply what you have learned.

## 1. Guided Assignment

In an old folder, you found the draft shown below. Read the material. Decide how you could revise it. Then rewrite it, and add a brief introduction. Include a thesis statement and at least one example.

### Bike Dangers

Many injuries and deaths occur each year. We could have avoided them if people were aware of bike safety. The National Safety Council says 80 percent of cyclists killed or injured were breaking traffic laws. About 20 percent were riding bikes with mechanical defects. Bike safety is really easy, and so this shouldn't happen.

**PURPOSE**  To freshen your perspective on a topic
**AUDIENCE**  Your classmates
**LENGTH**  1 page

## 2. Open Assignment

The antique figure shown here advertised a bicycle shop almost a century ago. Find a picture of a modern bicycle. Think about how bikes have changed. Then draft, revise, and edit a report on the changes.

## 3. Art

Merchants often advertised with figures like the one pictured here instead of with words because many of their

Amidée T. Thibault, *Trade Sign: Bicycle, Livery, Carriage and Paint Shop*, 1895–1905

customers could not read. Merchants still represent product names by using symbols, called logos. Select a logo that interests you. Research, draft, revise, and edit a short report on the logo. Find information in an encyclopedia or a magazine, or request information from the company that owns the logo. Write about the logo's origin and meaning, and tell why you think it is effective.

*Reports: Revising and Presenting*  **233**

As you begin to draft, always keep your focus in mind. Put your ideas on paper, referring to your notes as necessary. You'll have time to change things later, if you wish.

## 3. Revising

Are you remembering the audience for your informative account? How will these people feel about your draft? Check the assignment on page 244 to make sure you are staying on track.

Does your draft give an objective view of the people in your town? These questions as well as the questions below can help as you consider changes to your draft. Also, you can return to pages 226–233 for ideas about different ways of organizing and presenting information.

**Question A**

Have I clearly explained unfamiliar terms?

**Question B**

Do all the details fit my main idea?

**Question C**

Have I organized my information effectively?

The people of Fairfield enjoy diversity among their neighbors. The Mexican festival, Cinco de Mayo, is a yearly highlight for neighbors of many different ethnic origins. At the August art fair at Library Plaza, you'll find the works of (Add Cinco de Mayo details) local painters who may be senior citizens, or hospital patients, college students. In "Life Steps," the annual walkathon for diabetes research, Scandinavian-Americans, African Americans, and Laotian-Americans Hmong to name just a few—join forces as friends.

## 4. Editing

Small mistakes can cause confusion, especially in expository writing. So take the time to make an accuracy check of your draft. You can do the editing yourself. Also, you might ask a friend to be a peer reviewer.

One way to edit is to read the draft closely, looking out for anything that just doesn't seem right. You may find it easier, however, to use a checklist such as the one shown here. If so, consider the questions, one by one, as you read your draft. Use proofreading marks to make changes. With this method you may have to read your draft several times, but your audience will appreciate your efforts.

*Checklist*

1. *Are quotations and other facts correct?*
2. *Have I used exact nouns and verbs?*
3. *Is there a variety of sentence types?*
4. *Have I used standard spelling, capitalization, and punctuation?*

## 5. Presenting

You might find it helpful to first present your account to two long-time residents of your town. Have them read your work separately and comment about its thoroughness. Do they agree with what you've said about your subject?

Once you're happy with your account, you may want to prepare a set of photographs to accompany it. Perhaps you might combine your work with that of other students, and have compiled copies of *The People of (your town or city)* bound for your school or town library.

### Reflecting

Think about what you've discovered during this assignment. You've probably gained some knowledge of the different types of people in your town. What other details would you like to learn?

*Writing Process in Action* **247**

# Portfolio & Reflection

## Summary

**Key concepts in expository writing include the following:**

- Strong expository writing is clear and concise and follows a sensible order.
- Cause-and-effect writing explains how one event causes another.
- Identifying likenesses and differences helps make informative writing clear.
- Prewriting for a report includes narrowing the topic, doing research, conducting interviews, and taking notes.
- Facts, statistics, reasons, and examples strengthen expository writing.
- Careful editing of a report will help with an effective presentation.

## Your Writer's Portfolio

Look over the writing you did for this unit. Choose two pieces for your portfolio. Look for writing that does one or more of the following:

- uses sensible order in an explanation
- uses a chart or diagram to show likenesses and differences
- is based on notes from your research or from an interview
- supports a main idea by using facts, statistics, or examples
- is based on reading about people

## Reflection and Commentary

Think about what you have learned in this unit. Answer the following questions as you look over the two pieces of writing you chose. Write a page of "Comments on Expository Writing" for your portfolio.

1. How does the writing explain how something works or why something happened?
2. How does the order help your audience understand your main idea?
3. What have you found through your research that you would like to learn more about?
4. How did you use facts, statistics, and examples to support your ideas?

## Feedback

**If you had a chance to respond to the following student comment, what would you say or ask?**

*Brainstorming is how I usually come up with topics for writing. I usually take a topic that sounds interesting and then work it into an idea I can write about.*

Brad Kimmel, Springman Junior High School, Glenview, Illinois

# A Better Place

John Sloan, *Sally, Sarah and Sadie, Peter and Paul*, 1915

# Carson Delivers a Wake-Up Call

*"When I returned to this country from a year in Australia, I saw so many young people who were focusing on the wrong things and weren't going anywhere. In a land of such opportunity, to see people squandering these opportunities, really gets you. . . . I had to see if there was a way to wake people up."*

Dr. Benjamin S. Carson

A t The Johns Hopkins Hospital in Baltimore, Maryland, Dr. Benjamin Carson is about to deliver another wake-up call. Nearly 800 middle-school students pack Turner Auditorium, the biggest hall at the hospital. To many people the man who's about to walk through the doors is a hero—a poor student who turned his life around and became a world-famous children's brain surgeon.

For the last four years Carson has taken time from his medical work to talk to kids about success. More than ten thousand students have visited Carson at Johns Hopkins Hospital. Thousands

**Preparing a Speech**

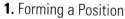

**1.** Forming a Position

**2.** Preparing His Case

**3.** Presenting His Story

### FOCUS

Successful persuaders state a clear position and back it up with facts and solid opinions.

▼ *Reading books instead of watching television is a major point in Dr. Carson's message.*

more have heard Carson speak as he travels around the country, carrying his message. Today Dr. Carson enters the hall wearing a white jacket over surgical scrubs. With a ready smile he begins the story of his rise to the position of famous surgeon, urging others to follow.

## 1 Forming a Position

Like all persuasive speakers, Carson has taken a stand on an important issue: He believes that by turning off the television and by reading, reading, reading, any student can become a winner.

Carson bases his position on the facts and experiences of his life. When Carson was ten years old, he was in trouble. He didn't care about school. But Carson's mother came up with a plan to change all that. She told her children they could watch only two or three television shows a week. In their free time they had to read two library books

Yet if you use it frequently, it becomes firm and enlarged and very powerful." Reading, he says, demands that you use your mind to make sense of words, sentences, and ideas. It makes you into a literate person who can express ideas.

Why is this important? "You have a great deal more confidence when you know you can express something," Carson says. "You probably know two people who have seen the same thing, but one knows how to express himself and the other doesn't. That becomes a pattern through life. Clearly the person who is able to state a position will be seen as the brighter individual. When it comes time for opportunities to be granted, the person who can express himself will almost always be chosen."

and give her book reports on each one.

Carson went along, grumpily at first. But he quickly saw results. In a year and a half he zoomed to the top of his class. He knew he was on his way.

From these and later experiences Carson developed his position on reading. "The key thing about reading is what it does for the mind," he says. "I liken the mind to a muscle, which becomes flabby and weak if it's not used.

**INTERFACE** *Dr. Carson has developed a philosophy of life he calls "Think Big." He believes that reading is key to success. What experiences in your life support his point of view?*

# 2 Preparing His Case

To persuade people of another point of view, speakers like Carson often organize evidence into strong arguments. Example, such as Carson's personal story, is one form of persuasive evidence. Carson begins his story by describing his mother's reading plan and his journey into the world of the mind. He started reading about animals and plants. Soon he became fascinated by rocks.

"One day we were in science class," Carson says, "and the science teacher held up a dark glassy rock. He said, 'Does anybody know what this is?' I didn't put my hand up because I figured one of the smart kids would answer the question. I looked around, and nobody had their hand up, and I said, 'Humph.' I knew what it was because I'd been reading about this stuff, so I put my hand up. And I said 'That's obsidian.'"

Carson then tells how he talked about obsidian. But, most important, he describes his classmates' reaction. "For the first time I could see in my classmates' eyes a look of admiration," he says. "This was a totally new experience

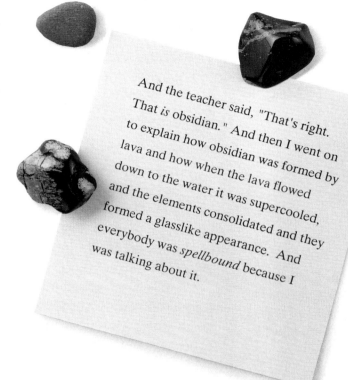

And the teacher said, "That's right. That *is* obsidian." And then I went on to explain how obsidian was formed by lava and how when the lava flowed down to the water it was supercooled, and the elements consolidated and they formed a glasslike appearance. And everybody was *spellbound* because I was talking about it.

for me; and I said 'I like this; I can deal with this.' From that point on I couldn't get enough to read."

Carson says he chooses to tell a story because "people can remember stories and the points they make. I want to make it very clear that I had the very same experiences these students have had. Then they can say this guy clearly knows what he's talking about. He's clearly been where I am or have been and is where I'd like to be in the future.

▲ *Realizing the power of knowledge was a turning point in young Ben Carson's life. This strongly persuasive moment is shown in a transcript of Dr. Carson's speech.*

*Case Study: Speech* **253**

"I also need for them to understand that knowledge is power, not only in the eyes of teachers, but in the eyes of their friends. It's not a thing to be ashamed of."

**INTERFACE** *Dr. Carson believes that pressure from classmates can work for people as well as against them. Do you agree? Find examples to support your position.*

## 3 Presenting His Story

In making his presentation, Carson speaks softly and honestly, never preaching or raising his voice. Yet his ideas and his tone help change students' minds.

"This way of speaking is effective because students believe the story is true," he says. "That's the bottom line. This is real. This is not made up in Hollywood. The fact that students can identify with me makes them believe success is possible for them, too."

Carson's story is powerful medicine. "I get tons of letters all the time, and almost everywhere I go people come up to me and say they've heard me or seen me," Carson says.

Schools in California, Texas, and other states have also started Ben Carson Reading Clubs—and the clubs work. An eighth-grade club member said to Carson one day, "Because I didn't read, I thought I was kind of dumb. Now I know better."

▼ *Mountains of letters from young students all around the world are the evidence of Dr. Carson's ability to persuade.*

Dr. Ben Carson
Johns Hopkins Hospital
600 North Wolfe Street
Baltimore, Md. 21287-7509

Dr. Benjamin Carson
Johns Hopkins Hospi
600 North Wolfe Str
Baltimore, Md. 21287.

Dr. Ben Carson
Johns Hopkins Hospital
600 North Wolfe Stree
Baltimore, Md. 2128

# ON ASSIGNMENT

## 1. Persuasive Writing

**Develop a position for a debate on a twelve-month school year.**

- Jot down all the reasons you can think of to persuade people that schools should be open twelve months. Then write down reasons to stay on a nine-month school year.

- If necessary, do library research to gather evidence to strengthen your position. Consider, for example, articles on America's ability to compete with other nations.

- Review your notes. Will you argue for or against the idea?

## 2. About Literature

**Describe the most persuasive person you've heard or read about, and explain his or her techniques for changing minds.**

- Brainstorm a list of people that have affected your thinking. Consider public figures, such as John F. Kennedy, Barbara Jordan, or Sandra Day O'Connor.

- Choose one person from the list you developed. Jot down notes explaining what specific words and actions this person used to affect you.

- Use your notes to write an explanation of how the person you chose persuaded you to adopt a new point of view.

## 3. Cooperative Learning

**Plan a campaign to persuade students at your school to form a Ben Carson Reading Club.**

- Meet as a group to define jobs for this campaign. You'll need writers, editors, artists, and speakers.

- Plan your club and set its goals. Discuss your membership campaign. You'll need to make posters and give a persuasive speech.

- Assign jobs to each member of your group. Writers can prepare a draft of the persuasive speech and slogans for posters. Artists can design the posters.

- Meet as a group to review the speech draft and suggest improvements.

- Present your posters and speech to the class for feedback.

**Using Persuasive Writing**

## *Join Our Cause*

Many topics probably make you feel strong emotions—anger, frustration, excitement. Maybe you feel strongly about animal rights. Perhaps you think that school dress codes are out of date. When you have a strong belief, you can use words to try to persuade others to share it. Read the following passage, part of an advertisement by a group that wants to save dolphins.

### *Literature Model*

The ancient Greeks respected the dolphins for their kindness and intelligence. In fact, it was a crime punishable by death to harm or kill a dolphin. Today, though, over 100,000 dolphins are being needlessly killed every year, caught by tuna fishermen and driftnets.

Together we saved over 50,000 dolphins last year. But hundreds of thousands are still endangered. You can make the difference. Please join us.

Write us for further information and for a list of dolphin-safe tuna brands.

The Dolphin Project, Earth Island Institute

*What exactly does the writer want you to do?*

# Do You Agree?

A persuasive writer tries to get you to agree with what she or he writes. Persuasive writing can also call you to action. The Dolphin Project, for example, wants readers to agree that tuna fishers harm dolphins. The members of the organization want people to help them by joining their group and eating dolphin-safe tuna. Read the two statements below. Think about the writer's purpose in making each statement.

> *What does the writer want you to do?*

> *Join the Ten-Mile Walkathon, and walk to preserve our city's parks.*

> *A vegetarian diet is the most healthful and most humane way to eat.*

> *What two words do you think carry the writer's message most clearly?*

Persuasive writers choose words that will have a certain effect on their readers. When you read persuasive writing, think about the special words and phrases the writer uses to persuade you to agree or to act.

# Anywhere You Look

## Presenting Tip

In the presenting stage consider the different forms in which you can present your persuasive statement, such as an ad, an editorial, or a speech.

Magazines, newspapers, books, posters, letters, television programs—almost anything you read, see, or hear can include persuasion. All these forms of persuasion try to get the reader, viewer, or listener to agree or to take action. Consider what an ad for a new cereal tries to persuade you to do. Think about what action an editorial on sun exposure encourages you to take.

The illustration below shows everyday examples of persuasion. Think about what kinds of persuasion each labeled item might include. For example, some items contain written forms of persuasion. Other items, like the radio, contain forms of persuasion you hear rather than read. As you look at the illustration, picture a room in your house, your school, or another place where you spend time. What sources of persuasive writing can you find there?

**Where to Find Persuasion**

Poster · Television · Newspaper · Book · Advertisement · Radio · Magazine

# Activities

Here are some activities to help you apply what you have learned.

## 1. Guided Assignment

Suppose that you belong to an organization that helps the homeless in your area. The group is planning a fund-raising event, such as a car wash, a bake sale, or a charity auction. You've been asked to write a persuasive statement for a poster advertising the event. Write a statement that will persuade people in your neighborhood to attend your fund raiser. Choose words that will convince readers that this is an event not to be missed.

PURPOSE    To persuade readers to attend a fund-raising event

AUDIENCE   Adult and teen-age community members

LENGTH     3–5 lines

## 2. Open Assignment

Many products sell widely because they are linked to a well-known and successful persuasive statement. For example, you are probably familiar with catchy slogans used by soft-drink companies, sneaker manufacturers, and automobile makers. Choose two of the following products, or two others of your choice. Write persuasive slogans that you think will help sell those products.

- in-line skates
- dog food
- a solar-powered calculator
- a line of exercise clothing
- a music magazine
- oatmeal cookies
- waterproof boots
- lipstick

### COMPUTER OPTION

If you have access to a computer graphics program, you might use it to create a professional-looking ad for your persuasive statement. Use the graphics program to design art. Type in your slogan, and choose a typeface that will catch your reader's eye.

## 3. Cooperative Learning

Persuasive writing plays an important role in an election campaign. Meet with a small group of classmates to plan an imaginary campaign for president of your class. Decide who in your group will be the candidate. As a group, brainstorm ideas for a persuasive statement to use in the campaign. The statement should try to convince your audience—classmates outside your group—that your candidate is the best person for the job. One group member should list the group's ideas. Continue brainstorming until the group comes up with four or five statements. Then discuss how persuasive each statement is. Finally, choose which persuasive statement you will use for the campaign.

*Using Persuasive Writing*    **259**

# 6.2 | Forming an Opinion

## *If You Want to Know What I Think . . .*

Take a few minutes to think of some everyday situations that you have strong opinions about. Write down a few of them and your opinions on them. Opinions about everyday situations often inspire entertaining pieces of persuasive writing. Notice the position Andy Rooney takes in his humorous piece on cats.

---

**Literature Model**

### CATS ARE FOR THE BIRDS

I have never met a cat I liked.
As an animal lover, I'm constantly disappointed with myself when there's a cat around.

Don't think I haven't tried to love cats, because I have. I always try to win their affection or, at the very least, try to establish some sort of relationship. Nothing. A cat will walk on my lap, jump on a table next to me where my host has put a dish of corn chips, or rub against my pants, but there is never any warmth in the cat's gesture.

"He likes you," the host will say.

Well, if those cats I've met like me, they have a plenty strange way of showing it. If I got the kind of affection from the people I like that I get from cats whose owners think they like me, I'd leave home.

Andy Rooney, *Not That You Asked . . .*

*What does the writer think of cats?*

*Do you agree or disagree with the writer's opinion? Why?*

# What's Your Topic?

Rooney takes many of his topics from everyday life. Experiences from your daily life can inspire strong opinions, too. Look over the list of situations you brainstormed. Which of them do you feel strongly enough about to use as a topic for persuasive writing?

Besides brainstorming, you can use freewriting to help you find a topic. Start by writing names of people, places, or things. Then jot down notes about each. For example, you might write "tents" and then write "cold, not waterproof, hard to set up, difficult to fold." When you finish making notes, you'll probably have at least one topic about which you have a strong opinion.

Journal entries also can help you find a topic. In the journal entry shown here, the writer has circled possible topics. The questions in the chart below can help you decide whether to write about a topic.

*The only things I wanted for my birthday were my (own phone) and a job at the mall. I know I'm (too) (young for a job,) and Mom doesn't want to get me a phone. Still, the day wasn't a total loss. I heard about a program that trains (teen-age baby sitters,) and now I'm old enough to sign up.*

## Questions for Choosing a Topic

| 1 | Is this a topic that makes me feel strongly? |
|---|---|
| 2 | Is this a topic that could have more than one side, a topic on which people might disagree? |
| 3 | Do I have enough to say to persuade others to accept my position? |

## • JOURNAL ACTIVITY •
### Try It Out

Look through your journal for possible persuasive-writing topics. When you have found two or three topics, use the questions above to decide which topic will work best for you.

## *Where Do You Stand?*

Once you have a topic, think about your position on it. You should know as much about your topic as possible. Sometimes, when you learn more about a topic, your position on it changes. Other times you may discover that a topic doesn't offer much reason for disagreement. That is, your opinion on it is similar to everyone else's. Exploring a topic helps you discover whether it's suitable for a writing project.

You can use a chart like the one below to explore your persuasive-writing topic. List the pros—reasons that people might agree with your opinion. Then list the cons—reasons that they might disagree with you. A pro-and-con chart can help you organize your thoughts and make your opinion clearer. It can also help you think about why or how others might argue against your opinion.

**Revising Tip**

In the revising stage make sure you have organized your persuasive writing in a sensible way.

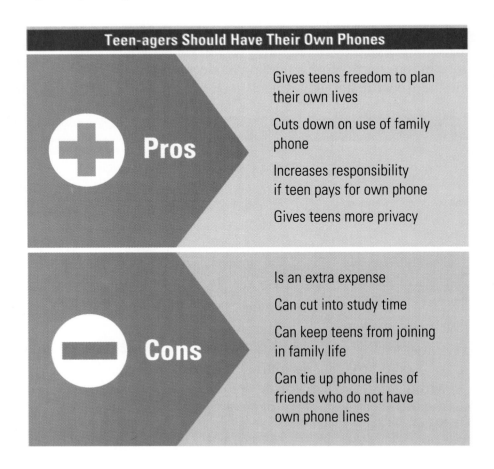

**Teen-agers Should Have Their Own Phones**

**Pros**
- Gives teens freedom to plan their own lives
- Cuts down on use of family phone
- Increases responsibility if teen pays for own phone
- Gives teens more privacy

**Cons**
- Is an extra expense
- Can cut into study time
- Can keep teens from joining in family life
- Can tie up phone lines of friends who do not have own phone lines

Here are some activities to help you apply what you have learned.

## 1. Guided Assignment

Suppose that people want to build a road through the area shown in this painting. The road will connect two cities, making travel and business transactions between the cities easier. But it will also alter the area's natural beauty. What opinion do you have about this proposed construction? Take a few minutes to jot down your ideas. Then make a pro-and-con chart like the one on page 262. List three pros to support your opinion and three cons to oppose it.

| | |
|---|---|
| **PURPOSE** | To clarify and explore an opinion about a topic |
| **AUDIENCE** | Yourself |
| **LENGTH** | 3 pro statements and 3 con statements |

## 2. Open Assignment

Many famous people claim that fame is not as wonderful as it seems. Choose one of the pathways to fame listed in the next column, or choose another career path. Then brainstorm pros and cons of life in that career. First, list all your beliefs about why this career would be worth pursuing. Then list all your doubts about it.

- musician
- actor
- athlete

## 3. Social Studies

Think of a time in the United States' past when you might like to have lived. Make a chart detailing the pros and cons of living at that time. Then determine whether you would still like to live during that time. Write your opinion in a few paragraphs.

Pierre–Auguste Renoir, *Path in the High Grass,* 1874

# Where's Your Backup?

Suppose that you and your classmates want to use your school's public-address system to broadcast music. The music would be heard only in nonclassroom areas and only before school and during class breaks. You feel that students should have charge of the music service, perhaps under a teacher's supervision. You have quite a job of persuading ahead of you.

You must convince teachers and administrators that a student-run music service is a good idea, one that they should seriously consider. You must also convince them that it won't interfere with learning time. Your best bet is to write a persuasive proposal, using evidence to back up your position.

# Lend Support

If you want to persuade others to agree with your position, you can show them evidence that supports it. Your position and supporting evidence make up your argument.

You want your argument to be as strong as possible. First, test your argument by listing the pros and cons to discover possible arguments against it. Then look over your list for any weak links—places where your evidence is unconvincing. Decide how to strengthen those links.

The chart below shows several types of evidence you can use to support an argument. Your argument can include more than one example of each type.

| Types of Evidence | | |
|---|---|---|
| **Type** | **Definition** | **Example** |
| **Fact** | something known to be true | The school already has the equipment needed for a music broadcast. |
| **Statistic** | fact expressed in numbers | A school poll shows that 84 percent of students are in favor of a music broadcast. |
| **Example** | particular instance or event | Two other schools in our area have similar broadcasts. |
| **Opinion** | personal judgment based on feelings or beliefs | Students should play a mix of popular, jazz, and classical music. |
| **Reason** | sensible explanation | The music service will expose students to music they might not otherwise hear. |

## • JOURNAL ACTIVITY •
### Think It Through

Look in a recent newspaper for an editorial. Identify the argument or position it presents. In your journal list the types of evidence the writer uses to support his or her position. Which piece of evidence do you find most convincing?

# Consider Your Audience

When you're preparing an argument, your choice of evidence should suit your audience. For instance, you might use one type of evidence to persuade a friend to go on a camping trip. You might use different evidence to persuade your parents to let you go on the same trip.

After you determine your audience, consider the following questions. They'll help you decide which evidence will most strongly convince your audience.

- How much does my audience know about my topic?
- How much does my audience care about my topic?
- What evidence will appeal most to my readers?
- What evidence will my readers find most convincing?

Your purpose for writing will also affect your choice of evidence. Consider what results you want to achieve through your writing. Then decide what evidence works best to either make your audience agree with you or get them to take action. Notice how David Rauen considered audience and purpose in this piece of persuasive writing.

## Grammar
### Editing Tip

In the editing stage make sure you have correctly copied the numbers used in any statistical evidence.

*What's the purpose of David's writing?*

*What evidence does he use to persuade his audience?*

## Student Model

I think wearing uniforms is a bad idea because it brings down the morale of the students. First of all, we feel uncomfortable in the uniforms. The pants are itchy. By the end of the day, our feet hurt from the school shoes. Secondly, wearing uniforms makes us feel like robots. After a few weeks we get tired of seeing the same colors and outfits every day. I believe the students at our school are responsible enough to choose what they wear. I think the principal should let students have a say about the school's uniform policy.

David Rauen, Hope Lutheran School,
Chicago, Illinois

# Activities

Here are some activities to help you apply what you have learned.

## 1. Guided Assignment

Suppose you want to start your own business, such as designing jewelry or tutoring younger students. To get your business going, though, you need to persuade a relative or friend to loan you money. Gather at least three types of evidence to support your argument. Then write a few paragraphs to persuade your audience.

Nancy Holt, *Sun Tunnels,* 1973–1976

| | |
|---|---|
| PURPOSE | To obtain a loan for your business |
| AUDIENCE | Your choice |
| LENGTH | 2–3 paragraphs |

## 2. Open Assignment

Suppose that, as a casting agent, you need to persuade an actor to appear in a movie. Choose an actor and one of the movie types listed below. Ask yourself the questions on page 266 as you gather evidence to support your argument. Write a one-page persuasive letter to the actor.

- a murder mystery
- a romance
- a comedy

## 3. Art

The concrete tunnel shown here is one of four placed in the Utah desert by the artist. Each tunnel measures eighteen feet in length and more than nine feet in diameter, big enough for a person to walk through. In the upper half of each tunnel, the artist cut holes in the pattern of certain constellations. These holes cause light in the tunnel to change constantly.

Imagine that you have visited this work of art. Write a letter trying to persuade a friend to visit or not visit this site. Base your argument on the information given here.

# A Call for Change

Suppose that you're meeting friends at a movie theater or a restaurant. When you get there, however, you can't get in. Violinist Itzhak Perlman, who's handicapped, finds himself in this situation often.

### Literature Model

*What change does the writer want? What evidence does he use to support his position?*

I've been in public buildings throughout the world, and it's clear that the people who design them have no idea what it feels like to use crutches or sit in a wheelchair. One of the great architectural catastrophes of all time, from the point of view of any concertgoer, much less one who is disabled, is the Sydney Opera House in Sydney, Australia. A design contest was held and the winner was an architect who had conceived a truly fantastic-looking place with about a hundred steps leading to the entrance. There is no elevator—not for the general public, not for the poor musicians who have to lug instruments up all those stairs, and certainly not for the disabled. Why couldn't the prize have been given to the best design that was also barrier-free? Why, when it's possible to make *everyone* comfortable, is so little attention paid to accessibility?

Itzhak Perlman, "To Help the Handicapped, Talk to Them," *Glamour*, March 1987

# Stating Your Position

When you write persuasively, you almost always include a main idea—your opinion. You can express your main idea in a topic sentence, which generally appears either at the beginning or the end of your opening paragraph. In the piece on the facing page, Perlman begins with a clearly focused topic sentence and gives strong evidence to support his opinion.

> The Whitebridge movie complex should have an entrance ramp. It has twelve theaters, four concession stands, and video games. You can see any movie, eat any snack, or play any game you want—if you can walk up a flight of stairs.

Where is the topic sentence in this paragraph?

> The other day my friend Tiffany and I went to Lily's Snacks. Tiffany uses a wheelchair to get around. I was shocked to realize that she couldn't come in with me. There are three steps to the door but no ramp. Why isn't Lily's accessible to everyone?

What is the main idea of this paragraph?

## • JOURNAL ACTIVITY •
## Try It Out

Think of somewhere you like to go that would be impossible to visit if you use a wheelchair. In your journal write how such a situation would make you feel. Then jot down possible solutions to the problem.

# Three-Part Persuasion

The structure of a persuasive-writing piece can resemble the three-part structure of a report. The introduction states the topic and your opinion on it. The body provides evidence to support your opinion. The conclusion summarizes your argument and suggests action.

To make your persuasive writing strong, place your most convincing evidence where it best supports your point. Sometimes the argument works best when you present the strongest evidence first. Other times you may make your point more persuasively by putting the strongest evidence last. Notice how Justin Pinegar introduces his topic and gets his opinion across.

## Grammar

### Editing Tip

When you edit, make sure all your sentences express complete thoughts. Review the rules for sentences and fragments on pages 324–325.

## Tips for Structuring a Persuasive Piece

| | |
|---|---|
| 1 | Decide how to arrange your evidence. |
| 2 | Write a strong opening that states your position. |
| 3 | Present all your supporting evidence. |
| 4 | Sum up your argument, and give your conclusions. |

## Student Model

*How does Justin draw his audience into his argument?*

*I*magine that it is the year 2080. You are walking through a forest, when you see a five-legged frog jump out of a pool of orange and green water. Suddenly you realize that this is the first animal life you've seen on your walk. You are seeing one of the effects of toxic waste, caused by a world that relied too much on technology. Although many machines serve good purposes, we are relying too much on technology to solve our problems. We need to moderate technology now, before it is too late.

Justin Pinegar, Frontier Junior High School,
Moses Lake, Washington

Here are some activities to help you apply what you have learned.

## 1. Guided Assignment

Suppose that city budget cuts will force your public library to close on weekends. Draft a letter to your mayor to protest the closing. State your position in a topic sentence, and gather evidence for your argument. Make sure your letter has a strong opening and a conclusion that calls for action.

| | |
|---|---|
| PURPOSE | To persuade the mayor to keep the library open |
| AUDIENCE | Mayor of your city |
| LENGTH | 1 page |

## 2. Open Assignment

A local businessperson has donated a large amount of money to your school. Think about what could be done with the money. Choose one of the ideas below, or come up with your own. Draft an editorial for the school newspaper to convince readers of your opinion.

- new sports equipment
- videocassette recorders and educational videos
- a student lounge

## 3. Music

This painting from 1889 shows the first time that women played in an orchestra in Japan. Imagine that you are one of these musicians in the time just before women were allowed to play. Write a letter trying to persuade the conductor to let women muscians perform in the orchestra.

Chikanobu, *Concert of European Orchestra,* central panel of triptych, c. 1889

# Polishing an Argument

## *Now I Get It!*

The draft of your persuasive writing probably contains many solid ideas. But just as with any other writing you do, you should review your draft to be sure it makes sense. You want your argument not only to grab your readers' attention but also to hold it. If your argument lacks sensible connections between ideas and convincing evidence, your audience will feel confused and will probably lose interest in your topic. Review and revise your writing so that your readers will grasp your ideas.

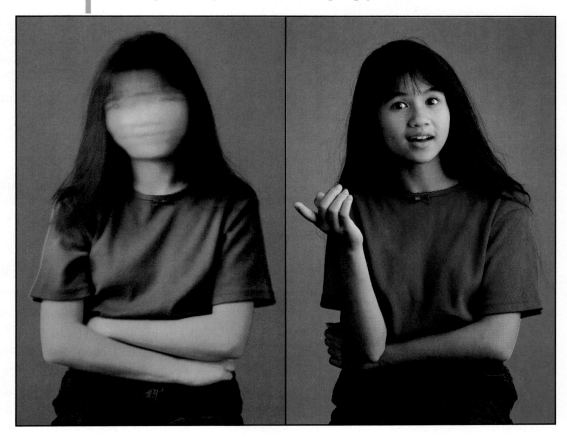

# The Big Picture

When you begin to revise your writing, you want to look first at the big picture, the whole argument. Ask yourself, Have I stated and supported my argument clearly? One way to answer this question is to have a peer reviewer evaluate your writing. The draft below shows how one writer revised her work after a peer reviewer evaluated it. Whether you or a peer reviewer looks at your work, the following questions will help you evaluate persuasive writing:

- Is the position stated clearly?
- Does the introduction grab attention?
- Is the evidence persuasive, and is it in the best order?
- Is enough evidence included?

Sally Lu should win the Student Community Service Award. Her efforts have helped bring the people in our community closer together. She started the Chinese-to-English Program to help Chinese children new to our area learn English. ~~She is a winning baseball and tennis player.~~ She also arranged a Get-Acquainted Night to bring the Chinese community into contact with other area groups. Vote for Sally Lu.

*Why did the peer reviewer suggest removing this sentence?*

*What does this sentence add to the paragraph?*

## • JOURNAL ACTIVITY •
### Try It Out

Think of a teacher who deserves to win a Teacher of the Year award. In your journal draft a brief persuasive piece explaining why that person should win. Then review your writing to make sure you have provided evidence to support your position.

## Winning Words

**Prewriting Tip**

In the prewriting stage brainstorm a list of strong words that apply to your topic. You can then refer to your list when you draft or when you revise for word choice.

When you write to persuade, word choice can make a big difference. Think about which bike ad makes you more likely to buy: "It's a great bike—and cheap, too!" or "It's the bike used by professional cyclists—at a price that won't break the bank!" Aim for strong words and phrases that grab your readers' attention. Look at the word changes made to this draft.

*How do these changes affect the writing?*

> the best
> David Lopez is a good candidate for school
>                high              both students and
> president. He gets good grades and teachers
> trust                              takes part in
> like him. Students too. He belongs to several
>
> school clubs: Theater Club, Chess Club, and
>                                    also
> Woodworking Club. He plays on the
>                        Above all
> basketball team. He wants to make our
>
> school a better place.

## Where to Say It

**Forms of Persuasive Writing**

school newspaper editorials

school campaign posters

letters to the editor of a magazine

book reviews

You can present written arguments in many forms. Some possibilities appear on the left. The form you choose will depend upon what you want to say and what you want your readers to think or do. When you choose the form for your persuasive writing, consider your audience and your purpose.

# Activities

Here are some activities to help you apply what you have learned.

## 1. Guided Assignment

Your town council is considering two names for a new park: Sunset Park and Katherine Smith Memorial Park. The council has asked the community to help choose the park's name. Write an editorial for the local newspaper stating your opinion on which name the council should choose. Defend your position with evidence. When you have completed your editorial, revise it, paying special attention to word choice.

PURPOSE   To choose a name for a park
AUDIENCE   Local newspaper readers and town council members
LENGTH   ½–1 page

### COMPUTER OPTION

As you revise your editorial for effective word choice, you may wish to use the thesaurus function on your computer. The thesaurus suggests synonyms, words of similar meaning. Identify any words in your draft that you want to replace. Then look in the thesaurus for synonyms that may be more precise.

## 2. Open Assignment

Think of what concerns you most about the environment. It could be the thinning of the ozone layer, the pollution of the ocean, or another problem of your choice. Consider the evidence you will need to persuade your classmates to take action. To present your argument, pick one of the forms of persuasive writing listed below, or choose another form. Then draft and revise a piece of persuasive writing that calls for action.

- a poster
- a letter to the editor of your school newspaper
- a leaflet

## 3. Cooperative Learning

Imagine that you and a group of classmates are a team of scientists. You have just discovered a cure for a rare form of cancer. Unfortunately, the medicine is made from the leaves of a tree found only in the Brazilian rain forest. To make your medicine, you have to destroy part of the unique forest. Your team must decide what action to take and must present the decision in writing to a meeting of scientists. With your classmates, gather information to support your position. Then work as a group to draft and revise your argument.

## *Look at That!*

When your favorite band comes to town for a concert, you can find out about it in several ways. You might hear a radio announcement or read a newspaper ad. You'll probably see posters splashed all over town. By the time the concert takes place, everyone in town knows about it. That's the result of good publicity.

Publicity includes posters, radio ads, flyers, and other printed or spoken forms of persuasion. If you want to get the word out about an event or cause, publicize it.

# Getting Noticed

The first goal of publicity writing is to capture your readers' attention. After all, no one will know about your event if the publicity isn't noticeable. A striking visual image on a poster can make someone stop and stare. A short, snappy slogan on a flyer can invite someone to read. Think about any posters, flyers, leaflets, or other forms of publicity you've seen recently. What images or language made you notice them? What statements did they make?

**Publicity should:**  ❶ Get people's attention.  ❷ Include all important information.  ❸ Get results.

When you plan to write publicity, you must think about your purpose. Decide what message you want to get across. Then think about your audience—whom you want to read your writing. Once you have your purpose and audience in mind, consider what kind of language will most appeal to your audience. You need to present all the necessary information in as few words as possible. Remember, too, that images often grab attention and convey ideas more immediately than words. Think about how your words and images can work together. You want your audience to understand your idea in one reading and to react to it positively.

## • JOURNAL ACTIVITY •
### *Try It Out*

Look through recent newspapers and magazines. Clip any photographs or drawings that seem especially eye-catching. Tape or paste one or more of these images into your journal. Jot down ideas for possible persuasive statements to go with them. One of the images could inspire a poster or other kind of publicity.

# Posting Your Message

Posters make highly visual and effective attention grabbers. A poster can be the perfect way to persuade people to attend a school play or to recycle cans and bottles. This illustration shows four different uses for posters. What other uses for posters can you think of?

## Grammar
### Editing Tip

Check capitalization carefully when you edit. Because posters use few words, any mistakes stand out. To review capitalization guidelines, see pages 514–519.

**Uses for Posters**

KAREN JONES

CLASS PRESIDENT

**Get votes.**

LOST

KAYO

123-4567

**Find a lost pet.**

CIRCUS

**Advertise an event.**

Support Our Band

**Explain a cause.**

Remembering your purpose for the poster helps you decide what information to include. For example, if you're advertising for a lost pet, you'll need to write a description of the animal and perhaps provide a picture. You'll want to note whether it answers to its name and whether it bites. You'll need to write your name and telephone number and the amount of any reward you might offer. Your information should appear in a format that is easy to read and understand. That way, should a person find your pet, he or she will be able to return the animal to you.

# Activities

Here are some activities to help you apply what you have learned.

## 1. Guided Assignment

Think of how you might use this painting to advertise a circus coming to your town. Decide which form of publicity you will use—a poster, a leaflet, a flyer, or another form. Write a slogan that will work with the art to attract people's attention. Include information about the circus, such as its name and where and when it will perform.

PURPOSE    To draw a crowd by writing publicity

AUDIENCE    Adults and children

LENGTH    1 slogan, 3–5 lines of information

## 2. Open Assignment

Travel posters try to lure people to visit certain places. Design a poster for one of the places listed below or for another place of your choice. Make a drawing or find a photo of the place your poster will advertise. Write a slogan that will make people think, "I want to go there!" Include all necessary information about the trip.

- Tokyo
- Mexico City
- your town

## 3. Health and Safety

Make a leaflet to advertise a food that is not only tasty, but also healthful. Choose a visual image to draw readers' attention. You might cut one out of a magazine or draw one yourself. Think of a slogan that will make your readers' mouths water. Be sure you include information, such as statistics, to support your claim that the food is a healthful choice.

Kathy Jakobsen, *Circus Parade,* 1979

## Where There's Smoke . . .

Have you ever been in a public place where you found yourself coughing and your eyes watering because of cigarette smoke? If so, you probably felt angry or annoyed. You may have thought there was nothing you could do about the problem, but there was!

*Model*

Dear Sir or Madam:

   My friends and I ate at El Jardín last Friday evening, and it upset us to find that your restaurant does not have a No Smoking section. The people at the tables on either side of us were smoking. Because the air around our table was full of smoke, we found it impossible to enjoy our dinner. We had to breathe the smoke, which is dangerous as well as unpleasant.

   I suggest that you set aside one section of your restaurant as a Smoking area. That way, customers who do not smoke will find it possible to enjoy your good food in a clean, smoke-free environment.

                              Sincerely,

                              *Julia Mendoza*

                              Julia Mendoza

*What is the writer's complaint?*

*What solution does the writer suggest?*

# *Putting Together Your Letter*

A letter of complaint has the same purpose as other kinds of persuasive writing. You present an argument, trying to persuade your reader to act. In a letter of complaint, you should state the problem, explain how it happened, and propose a reasonable solution.

You can use these steps to write a letter of complaint about many different situations. For example, you can complain about a product that broke too soon or about food that was spoiled when you bought it. When you write a letter of complaint, use the business-letter form, like that of the letter shown here.

*Heading: your address and the date*

*Inside address: the name and address of the person to whom you are writing*

71 Union Street
Tempe, AZ 85281
October 17, 199–

Sergeant Samuel Kincaid
Precinct 4
1106 Fortieth Street
Tempe, AZ 85281

*Body: explains the problem and suggests a solution*

Dear Sergeant Kincaid:

I want to call your attention to the dangerous intersection at Oak Street and First Avenue. Yesterday my younger sister was almost hit by a car speeding through the intersection. Because there are stop signs only on Oak Street, many drivers drive too fast through the intersection.

Would you please look into this problem? Perhaps stop signs can be placed on the First Avenue corners.

*Greeting: begins with "Dear" and includes the name of the person to whom you are writing, followed by a colon*

*Closing: final words of the letter, such as "Sincerely," followed by a comma*

Sincerely,

Peter Raymond

Peter Raymond

*Signature: your signed name followed by your typed name*

• JOURNAL ACTIVITY •
### *Think It Through*

Consider how you might feel if you received a letter like the one above. In your journal write about this feeling and about what you might do in response.

## Grammar
### Editing Tip

As you edit your letter, see that verb tenses agree with any special subjects, such as business names. To review subject-verb agreement for special subjects, see pages 480–481.

# Making a Good Impression

Think about how you might react if you got a letter that was threatening, rude, or insulting. You probably wouldn't want to help the writer, even if the writer's anger was justified. When you write a letter of complaint, use language that will persuade your readers to take action, not make them angry. Notice the difference in language in the sentences below. How would you react to each of them?

| Using Appropriate Language ||
| Inappropriate | Appropriate |
| --- | --- |
| I waited all day in the rain for concert tickets only to find that you stupid people advertised more tickets than you really had. I'll never use your ticket service again! | Your ad led me to believe that there would be plenty of tickets for next week's concert. I suggest that in the future you correctly advertise the number of tickets available. |

As you write, remember your purpose. Explain your problem and propose a solution. Your explanation of the problem should be clear and easy to follow, and your wording should be reasonable. The overall impression of your letter should be calm, businesslike, and organized, as is the letter shown below.

### Student Model

*What is the writer's complaint?*

*What solution does she offer for the problem?*

For years I have been a content subscriber to *Outdoor Adventures*, but recently I have not been pleased. Neither the July nor the August issue has been delivered to my home.

I am writing to request that you deliver these issues when you deliver the September edition of the magazine. Thank you for your time.

Laurie Hedlund, Springman Junior High School,
Glenview, Illinois

# Activities

Here are some activities to help you apply what you have learned.

## 1. Guided Assignment

Suppose that you bought a tape player by mail order. When it arrived, you found it played everything at high speed. Write a letter of complaint to the manufacturer of the tape player.

In your letter state the problem, explain how it happened, and offer a solution. Remember to use reasonable, businesslike language so that your complaint will be well received. Be sure to use the business-letter form, shown on page 281.

PURPOSE To identify a problem by writing a letter of complaint

AUDIENCE The manufacturer of the tape player

LENGTH 1 page

## 2. Open Assignment

You can probably think of several actions by the federal government that upset or angered you. Write a letter to the president, complaining about government action on one of the topics below or another topic of your choice. Be sure to suggest a reasonable solution to the problem.

- the environment
- poverty
- unemployment
- education

## COMPUTER OPTION

When you write a letter to a government official, you might want to send it to other officials. Doing so might strengthen the letter's impact. You can use the merge function on your computer to insert different inside addresses and greetings for your letter. That way, you can send your letter to several government representatives, such as your senator or state representative, without having to retype it.

## 3. Cooperative Learning

With a group of classmates, discuss advertisements that you find unpleasant or offensive. After discussing several ads, focus on one. Then divide your group into two smaller groups. Write a letter of complaint to the company sponsoring one such ad. One group can write the part of the letter describing the problem with the ad. The other group can suggest a solution to the problem—a way to change the ad so that it will no longer offend readers or viewers.

Meet again as a single group to combine the smaller groups' writing into one letter. Be sure to follow the business-letter form. As a group decide whether you will send your letter to the company.

*Writing a Letter of Complaint* **283**

# Writing a Movie Review

## A Must See

"The best movie of the summer." "I give it four stars!" "A real nail biter. Don't miss this movie!" Sometimes a movie review can make you feel that you have to see the film. Other times a review might convince you that you'd rather stare at a blank wall for two hours than sit through the movie.

Read the following movie review by a student. As you read, think about how Kimberly Knapp tries to convince you of her opinion.

### Student Model

I enjoyed the movie *Honey, I Shrunk the Kids*. The special effects were very entertaining, especially the scene where the miniature kids rode on insects. I also thought the characters were realistic. In the beginning of the movie, the kids fought with each other. They behaved like real brothers and sisters. The movie had a lesson because at the end the kids had learned to get along with each other.

Kimberly Knapp, Hope Lutheran School,
Chicago, Illinois

*Does the reviewer convince you that the movie is worth seeing? Why or why not?*

# Weigh the Elements

Movie reviews are written mostly for people who haven't seen the movie. An effective review gives readers enough information to help them decide whether to see the film. It provides brief background information about the actors and other people involved in making the movie. A review usually discusses specific elements—characters, plot, acting, and visual effects. The illustration on the right explains these elements. The review also states an opinion about the movie.

You usually know whether you like a film. But you may not have considered why you reached that conclusion. Think about how the film's elements affected your opinion. Ask yourself how each element worked in the movie. Take notes as you watch the movie or just after you view it. Your notes about each element can result in judgments such as the following:

- The characters of the boy and girl were realistic, but the father's actions and words made him seem cartoonish.
- The plot was complicated, but good characters and smooth writing made it easy to follow.

**Characters**
The people or animals that appear in the movie

**Plot**
What happens in the movie

**Acting**
The way actors portray the characters

**Visual Effects**
Techniques used to create illusions and mood

## • JOURNAL ACTIVITY •
### Think It Through

Think of a movie you have seen recently that has special effects. Then consider how these effects influenced your opinion of the movie. Write your thoughts in your journal.

# In Other Words

A movie reviewer doesn't have to come right out and say, "I loved this film" or "This movie was terrible." The reviewer's language often expresses his or her opinion without stating it directly. For example, read the following passage from a review of director George Lucas's movie *Star Wars*. Notice how the reviewer chooses words that reveal her opinion of the film rather than state it directly.

## Literature Model

*What does the reviewer think of the film?*

L ucas' talents lie more in the realm of film technique than film writing. The plot is a simplistic "shoot-em-up" war story of good *versus* evil, with stock characters such as the innocent hero, the beautiful damsel in distress, and the rogue with the heart of gold. The characters are shallow and always overshadowed by the technical aspects of the film and their dialogue is cartoonish and awkward. Although the sparse story line, weak characters, and lack of strong dialogue are obvious flaws, the visual effects are well done and so overwhelming that the impact of the film as a whole is not marred.

*What words does the reviewer use to convince you of her opinion?*

Ruth L. Hirayama,
Star Wars, *Magill's Survey of Cinema*

# Activities

Here are some activities to help you apply what you have learned.

## 1. Guided Assignment

Think of a movie you have seen recently. Write a review of it for your school newspaper. State your opinion clearly, and back it up with convincing evidence. Point out which elements of the movie led you to think as you do. Perhaps you enjoyed the movie because of its fast-paced and suspenseful plot. Or maybe you disliked the movie because the characters seemed unrealistic or because the special effects were amateurish.

Be sure to include background information about the movie. When appropriate, use words that allow you to reveal your opinion rather than state it directly.

PURPOSE   To write a movie review
AUDIENCE  Readers of school newspaper
LENGTH    ½–1 page

## 2. Open Assignment

Most movies can be grouped into types according to certain characteristics. Pick one of the types listed here, or choose another type. Write a one-page review of this type as a whole. Discuss the elements that movies of this type share. Explain how the movies' similarities help define the type to which they belong. Give your opinion of the type.

- westerns
- comedies
- horror movies
- science fiction movies

## 3. Cooperative Learning

In a group of four students, choose a movie that you have all seen to review. Brainstorm together to come up with ideas about characters, plot, acting, and visual effects. Each person should choose a different element and take notes on the group's ideas about that element. Then each person should write about the element he or she chose. Meet again to discuss your writing. Then combine the group's writing about the separate elements into a review of the movie as a whole. If you like, share your review with other class members.

### COMPUTER OPTION

If your computer has a newspaper layout feature, your group can join other groups of students to publish your movie reviews. You can name your publication, design the heading, and determine the placement of each review. If you wish to rank each movie, create a box on the page, and in the box show how the movies are ranked. Use asterisks to indicate the ranking—four asterisks for excellent, three for good, and so on.

Bel Kaufman

# The Liberry

*Is it true that Americans don't read anymore? Even if you don't enjoy reading, chances are you spend at least some time in the public library. However, for better or worse, decreased funding from city budgets has changed the way libraries serve local communities. In this essay, best-selling novelist Bel Kaufman presents her view on books and the libraries of New York City.*

A small boy in one of William Saroyan's stories finds himself in the public library for the first time. He looks around in awe: "All them books," he says, "and something written in each one!"

I remember myself as a 12-year-old, newly arrived from Russia, groping toward the mastery of the English language in my neighborhood library. Guided by no reading lists, informed by no book reviews, I had no use for the card catalogue, since I worked each shelf alphabetically, burrowing my way from one end of the stacks to the other, relentless as a mole. I read by trial and error, through trash and treasure; like a true addict, I was interested not so much in quality as in getting the stuff.

Sometimes I would stumble upon a book that was special; a book unrequired, unrecommended, unspoiled by teacher-imposed chores—"Name 3 . . . Answer the following . . ."—a book to be read for sheer pleasure.

Where else was it allowed, even encouraged, to thumb through a book, to linger on a page without being shooed away from handling the merchandise? This was merchandise to be handled. I was not fooled by the stiff, impassive maroon and dark-green library bindings; I nosed out the good ones. If the pages were worn and dog-eared, if the card tucked into its paper pocket inside the cover was stamped with lots of dates, I knew I had a winner.

Those dates linked me to the anonymous fellowship of other readers whose hands had turned the pages I was turning, who sometimes left penciled clues in the margins: a philosophic "How True!"—a succinct[1] "Stinks."

Here, within walls built book by solid book, we sat in silent kinship, the only sounds shuffling of feet, scraping of chairs, an occasional loud whisper, and the librarian's stern "Shhh!"

The librarian was always there, unobtrusive[2] and omniscient, ready for any question: Where to find a book about Eskimos? A history of submarines? A best-selling novel?—unruffled even by a request I once overheard in the children's section: "Have you got a book for an eight-year-old with tonsils?"

I am remembering this because today the public libraries are becoming less and less available to the people who need them most. Already shut part of the time, their hours reduced by 50 percent in the last five years, their budgets further curtailed as of July 1, and still threatened with continued cuts in staff and services, the public libraries have suffered more in the city's financial squeeze than any other major public-service agencies.

The first priority of our nation, according to former New York State Commissioner of Education, James E. Allen, is the right to read. Educators are inundating our schools with massive surveys, innovative techniques and expensive gimmicks

---

1 **succinct** (sək singkt′) clearly and briefly stated
2 **unobtrusive** (un əb tro͞o′ siv) not calling attention to oneself

to combat illiteracy and improve the reading skills of our children—at the same time that our public libraries are gradually closing their doors.

What are our priorities? Name 3.

It seems to me that especially now, when there are so many people in our city whose language is not English, whose homes are barren of books, who are daily seduced by clamorous offers of instant diversion, especially now we must hold on to something that will endure when the movie is over, the television set broken, the class dismissed for the last time.

For many, the public library is the only quiet place in an unquiet world; a refuge from the violence and ugliness outside; the only space available for privacy of work or thought. For many it is the only exposure to books waiting on open shelves to be taken home, free of charge.

As a former student put it: "In a liberry it's hard to avoid reading."

When I taught English in high school, I used to ask my students to bring a library card to class, on the chance that if they had one they might use it. One boy brought in his aunt's. "Aw, I ain't gonna use it," he cheerfully assured me, "I just brought it to *show* you!"

Still—some did make use of their cards, if only because they were *there*. Some enter the library today because it is *there*. Inside are all them books, and something written in each one. How sad for our city if the sign on the door should say CLOSED.

---

### For Discussion

1. In what ways are libraries important to you? How would you react if libraries were closed permanently? Why?

2. If you were a taxpayer, would you be willing to pay higher taxes so that your local library could serve your community better? Give reasons for your answer.

## Readers Respond

I agree that libraries should get the money they need to buy new books and to remain open. I think people should read this piece so they're reminded that libraries are important and need to be supported. It might also give them a greater interest in picking up a book and reading.

**Jeffrey Johnson**

I liked the beginning of the piece because it made me realize that not everyone has an opportunity to go into a library, much less read a book. I'm an avid reader, and I think I would be lost without books.

The writer got my attention by pointing out that so many libraries are closing down. I agree with James E. Allen that education is our first national priority. I didn't realize that libraries are on such tight budgets.

Although I like this piece and agree with it, I think the writer should have told readers how to help the libraries. Perhaps she wrote the way she did to make people more aware of the problem.

**Alina Braica**

### Do You Agree?

1. Do you agree that the writer made a convincing argument about the difficulties facing libraries? What evidence do you find most persuasive? Least persuasive?

2. Do you think public libraries are facing a serious problem? Write your opinion in your journal. Think of at least two arguments to oppose your opinion, and write them down. Then write responses to the arguments.

# *Writing Process in Action*

## Patriots All

Bel Kaufman's essay "The Liberry" suggests that public libraries *are* the United States. In this single institution Kaufman finds the threads of important national values, from the immigrant experience to self-improvement to freedom of thought. It's a hard argument to beat.

This assignment invites you to write persuasively about how to save something uniquely and irreplaceably American. It's up to you to decide What *is* America?

### • Assignment •

| | |
|---|---|
| Context | Your class is planning to publish This Is America, a magazine devoted to saving institutions, traditions, and culture unique and irreplaceable to the fabric that is America. |
| Purpose | To save something uniquely American with powerful persuasive writing |
| Audience | The readers of This Is America, your classmates and teacher |
| Length | 3–4 pages |

For advice on approaching this assignment, read the next few pages. You need not remember it all. Return to these pages during the writing process when you need help.

# 1. Prewriting

It's hard to miss the passion in Bel Kaufman's writing. In fact it seems at first that her argument is based only on strong emotions and childhood memories. But then the emotion-driven first part of the essay leads neatly into an argument based on more traditional evidence: reasons, facts, and statistics.

As you prewrite, think about taking a cue from Kaufman. Try to find a topic that means something to you —a topic you can support with a variety of reasons. The chart on page 261 can help you test topic ideas.

Finally, use the options at the right to help you settle on a topic. (The arrow points to a real-life example.)

**Option A**

Freewrite for ideas.

**Option B**

Brainstorm with a peer reviewer.

**Option C**

Explore your journal.

*My dream of running for the Hawks next year. Not if the high school can't pay for sports. Photos of Hawk teams since the forties: the same jerseys. What's more American than high school sports?*

# 2. Drafting

Before you begin turning your prewriting notes into a draft, think back briefly to the literature selection by Bel Kaufman. Consider how you want your audience to see you in your writing. Are you a victim, a success story (like Kaufman), a supporter of a cause, an expert, a common citizen, a problem solver? It's important to choose a stance that matches the point you want to make. Don't pretend to be an expert if you're not. But if you are an expert, let your audience know it loud and clear.

Now it's time to lay out your position and gather evidence. You can start by reviewing the chart on page 262. Once you're clear about your opinion on your topic, review pages 264–267 for suggestions on how to gather evidence for your position. The chart on page 265 should be especially helpful. Finally, review page 270 for suggestions on how to organize your persuasive piece.

Before you begin drafting, take a few minutes to review pages 64–67. Remember, your goal is to get your argument down on paper. You can go back and fix any problems later.

## 3. Revising

Revising your persuasive piece requires as much objectivity as you can muster. You need to put yourself in your audience's shoes and see if your argument really holds up. First, though, you should go back to page 292 and make sure that you've followed the basic assignment.

Now that you're ready to start revising, review pages 68–71, especially the checklist for evaluating a draft, on page 69. You may also want to have a peer reviewer look at your work. Make sure you have a good sense of the strengths and weaknesses of your draft before you start to make revisions.

Once you begin revising, you'll probably need to answer all the questions below. Where you start is up to you.

**Question A**

Is my position stated clearly?

**Question B**

Is my evidence in the best and most persuasive order?

**Question C**

Does the introduction grab attention?

The pictures appear in the _polished glass_ showcases in front of the auditorium. They show the Ticu City —in the same staged pose, in the same crimson Hawks track team, over more than sixty _and black jerseys—_ seasons. Now there might not be any more _to record_ seasons. _can name the faces photographed in every season_ I have known everyone on the team since my sister ran, the year I entered grade school. That's when I decided to become a running Hawk. My dream was to come true next year, but then the school budget talks began.

## 4. Editing

You may have heard the expression "reinventing the wheel" to describe duplicated efforts. The expression couldn't be more apt for describing how some writers approach the editing stage of the writing process. Do yourself a favor. Use pages 80–83, especially the editing checklist on page 81, as a step-by-step guide to editing your writing. This will save you both time and effort.

Finally, think about the language of your persuasive piece. Have you used the most persuasive language and chosen the most effective words? Will your words grab readers' attention and hold it? Look at page 274 for suggestions on this aspect of your edit.

*Checklist*

1. Have I chosen a strong topic?
2. Have I used a stance that fits the point I want to make?
3. Have I used precise language?
4. Have I used standard spelling and capitalization?

## 5. Presenting

What would an edition of *This Is America* look like if your class were to put out an edition? You might exchange papers with your classmates to see the range of topics and forms your classmates used to express their view of what America is.

Finally, evaluate your work. Is there a means of presenting it that you haven't considered? Maybe you wrote a letter that you could publish in a local newspaper. Perhaps you wrote an essay that could find a home in a teen magazine. Whatever you do, be sure to consider including this piece in your portfolio.

### Reflecting

One decision this assignment left up to you was the focus your writing would take. How much consideration did you give to the topic in this assignment? If you were to do this assignment again, would you change the focus of your piece?

# Portfolio & Reflection

## Summary

**Key concepts in persuasive writing include the following:**

- Persuasive writing should get the reader to agree or to take action.
- Creating a pro-and-con chart is one useful way to explore a topic.
- An opinion and the evidence that supports it make up an argument.
- Opinions in persuasive writing are often stated in topic sentences.
- Publicity uses persuasive words and images to appeal to an audience.
- A letter of complaint states and explains a problem and suggests a solution.
- Characters, plot, acting, and visual effects are some elements to consider when writing a movie review.

## Your Writer's Portfolio

Look over the writing you did for this unit. Choose two pieces for your portfolio. Look for writing that does one or more of the following:

- uses different types of evidence to support an opinion
- states an opinion in a clear topic sentence
- shows the effects of revisions for precise word choice
- uses effective words and images to publicize an event or idea
- uses reasonable language and business-letter format to air a complaint
- provides examples from a movie to support an opinion about a movie

## Reflection and Commentary

Think about what you learned in this unit. Answer the following questions as you look over the two pieces of writing you chose. Write a page of "Comments on Persuasive Writing" for your portfolio.

1. What prewriting technique helped you most to find or to explore persuasive-writing topics?
2. What types of evidence did you use to support your opinion?
3. Did you present your strongest evidence first? Last? What worked best about the order you chose?
4. What was special about the persuasive pieces you chose?

##  Feedback

**If you had a chance to respond to the following student comment, what would you say or ask?**

*I like school writing assignments because you get to see the different directions other people take with the same topic.*

Nicole Berg, Oak Creek Junior High School, Cornville, Arizona

# Grammar, Usage, and Mechanics

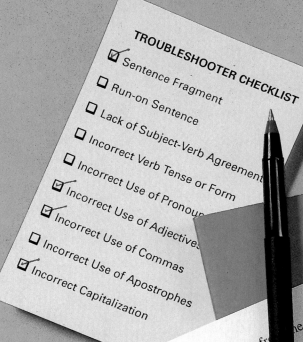

**TROUBLESHOOTER CHECKLIST**

☑ Sentence Fragment

☐ Run-on Sentence

☐ Lack of Subject-Verb Agreement

☐ Incorrect Verb Tense or Form

☑ Incorrect Use of Pronouns

☑ Incorrect Use of Adjectives

☐ Incorrect Use of Commas

☑ Incorrect Use of Apostrophes

☐ Incorrect Capitalization

The empty lot across from the Shop-Good Market that

Broad street is an eyesore and health hazard. We propose that

the community develop the lot to make a space for a large

community a play lot use the lot should be developed

explains why we think it should be done. People in the

Describes how that the empty lot is unsafe.

neighborhood that the empty lot is unsafe.

# Part 2 Grammar, Usage, and Mechanics

# Troubleshooter

This Troubleshooter is designed to help you correct the common errors that your teacher is likely to mark. Use the Table of Contents below to locate quickly a lesson on a specific error. Your teacher may mark errors with the handwritten codes in the left-hand column.

## 7.1    Sentence Fragment

*Fragment that lacks a subject*

*frag*    Lucy bought a new tennis racket. Wanted to play today.

*frag*    Oscar wrote a long essay. Read it in class.

*frag*    My dog buried the bone. Dug it up later.

**SOLUTION**

**Lucy bought a tennis racket. She wanted to play today.**

**Oscar wrote a long essay. He read it in class.**

**My dog buried the bone. He dug it up later.**

Add a subject to the fragment to make a complete sentence.

*Fragment that lacks a predicate*

*frag*    The beach is closed. The pool now, too.

*frag*    Spring is near. Flowers soon.

*frag*    Marla wore a coat. That red woolen coat.

## PROBLEM 3

### Fragment that lacks both a subject and a predicate

*frag*    Sophia ran very fast. (During the relay race.)

*frag*    My mother called me on the phone. (At two o'clock.)

*frag*    Ceara rode the sled. (Down the hill.)

## SOLUTION

**Sophia ran very fast during the relay race.**

**My mother called me on the phone at two o'clock.**

**Ceara rode the sled down the hill.**

Combine the fragment with another sentence.

*If you need more help in avoiding sentence fragments, turn to pages 324–325.*

## 7.2　Run-on Sentence

**Two main clauses separated only by a comma**

*run-on* Janet's book was published, it has twelve chapters.

*run-on* Jorge trained hard for the race, he expects to win.

### SOLUTION A

**Janet's book was published. It has twelve chapters.**

Replace the comma with a period or other end mark.
Begin the second sentence with a capital letter.

### SOLUTION B

**Jorge trained hard for the race; he expects to win.**

Place a semicolon between the main clauses.

**Two main clauses with no punctuation between them**

*run-on* Ravi went on vacation he will be home soon.

*run-on* Stanley left the party early he drove home.

## SOLUTION A

**Ravi went on vacation. He will be home soon.**

Separate the main clauses with a period or other end mark. Begin the second sentence with a capital letter.

## SOLUTION B

**Stanley left the party early; he drove home.**

Place a semicolon between the main clauses.

## PROBLEM 3

*Two main clauses with no comma before the coordinating conjunction*

*run-on*  Vanna is going to Canada and her sister is going, too.

*run-on*  Barry can leave today but he must return tomorrow.

## SOLUTION

**Vanna is going to Canada, and her sister is going, too.**

**Barry can leave today, but he must return tomorrow.**

Add a comma before the coordinating conjunction.

**Need More Help?** *If you need more help in avoiding run-on sentences, turn to pages 332–333.*

## 7.3   Lack of Subject-Verb Agreement

PROBLEM 1

*A subject that is separated from the verb by an intervening prepositional phrase*

*agr*   One of the books (were) sold.

*agr*   The actors in the play (is) good.

### SOLUTION

**One of the books was sold.**

**The actors in the play are good.**

Ignore a prepositional phrase that comes between a subject and a verb. Make sure that the verb agrees with the subject of the sentence. The subject is never the object of the preposition.

PROBLEM 2

*A sentence that begins with* here *or* there

*agr*   There (is) the books you want.

*agr*   Here (come) the school bus.

*agr*   There (is) trees in your backyard.

**There are the books you want.**

**Here comes the school bus.**

**There are trees in your backyard.**

The subject is never *here* or *there*. In sentences that begin with *here* or *there,* look for the subject *after* the verb. The verb must agree with the subject.

## PROBLEM 3

*An indefinite pronoun as the subject*

*agr*    Several of the paintings (is) oils.

*agr*    Each of the books (are) autographed.

*agr*    All of my effort (were) worthwhile.

Some indefinite pronouns are singular, some are plural, and some can be either singular or plural, depending upon the noun they refer to.

### SOLUTION

**Several of the paintings are oils.**

**Each of the books is autographed.**

**All of my effort was worthwhile.**

Determine whether the indefinite pronoun is singular or plural, and make the verb agree.

*A compound subject that is joined by* and

*agr*    The car and the bus (was) hit by lightning.

*agr*    Bacon and eggs (were) served for breakfast.

### SOLUTION A

**The car and the bus were hit by lightning.**

If the parts of the compound subject do not belong to one unit or if they refer to different people or things, use a plural verb.

### SOLUTION B

**Bacon and eggs was served for breakfast.**

If the parts of the compound subject belong to one unit or if both parts refer to the same person or thing, use a singular verb.

## PROBLEM 5

*A compound subject that is joined by* or *or* nor

*agr*    Either a dog or a cat (make) a good pet.

*agr*    Neither raisins nor an apple (make) a complete meal.

*agr*    Either Jim or his friends (is) bringing the cake.

**Either a dog or a cat makes a good pet.**

**Neither raisins nor an apple makes a complete meal.**

**Either Jim or his friends are bringing the cake.**

Make the verb agree with the subject that is closer to it.

*If you need more help with subject-verb agreement, turn to pages 476–485.*

## 7.4    Incorrect Verb Tense or Form

### PROBLEM 1

*An incorrect or missing verb ending*

*tense*    Have you ever (walk) all the way to school?

*tense*    Last Saturday we (pack) for our camping trip.

*tense*    Yesterday we (hope) for rain.

### SOLUTION

**Have you ever walked all the way to school?**

**Last Saturday we packed for our camping trip.**

**Yesterday we hoped for rain.**

Add -*ed* to a regular verb to form the past tense and the past participle.

### PROBLEM 2

*An improperly formed irregular verb*

*tense*    The water in the pond (freezed) overnight.

*tense*    Elena has (bringed) the girls to the dance.

*tense*    I (teared) my coat on the nail.

The past and past participle forms of irregular verbs vary. Memorize these forms, or look them up.

**SOLUTION**

**The water in the pond froze overnight.**

**Elena has brought the girls to the dance.**

**I tore my coat on the nail.**

Use the correct past or past participle form of an irregular verb.

## PROBLEM 3

*Confusion between the past form and the past participle*

*tense*   Diana had already (went) home when we arrived.

**SOLUTION**

**Diana had already gone home when we arrived.**

Use the past participle form of an irregular verb, not the past form, when you use the auxiliary verb *have.*

*If you need more help with correct verb forms, turn to pages 358–377.*

## 7.5    Incorrect Use of Pronouns

### PROBLEM 1

*A pronoun that refers to more than one antecedent*

*pro*    David always beats Hector to school, but (he) still gets there on time.

*pro*    When Tess leaves with Emma, (she) is home by noon.

### SOLUTION

**David always beats Hector to school, but Hector still gets there on time.**

**When Tess leaves with Emma, Tess is home by noon.**

Rewrite the sentence, substituting a noun for the pronoun.

### PROBLEM 2

*Object pronouns as subjects*

*pro*    Velma and (me) went to the mountains today.

*pro*    (Her) and Glen rode to the farm on a bus.

*pro*    Terry and (them) read that book last year.

**Velma and I went to the mountains today.**

**She and Glen rode to the farm on a bus.**

**Terry and they read that book last year.**

Use a subject pronoun in the subject part of a sentence.

## PROBLEM 3

*Subject pronouns as objects*

pro   Jane will be at home with Akiko and ⓘ.

pro   Please help (she) and ⓘ with the house painting.

pro   Bart would like ⓘ and George to go to the movie.

## SOLUTION

**Jane will be at home with Akiko and me.**

**Please help her and me with the house painting.**

**Bart would like me and George to go to the movie.**

Use an object pronoun as the object of a verb or preposition.

**Need More Help?**

*If you need more help with the correct use of pronouns, turn to pages 384–397.*

## 7.6    Incorrect Use of Adjectives

### PROBLEM 1

*Incorrect use of* good, better, best

> *adj*    The weather can't get (more good) than this.
>
> *adj*    This is the (most good) book in the library.
>
> *adj*    This is a (more) better exercise for you than that one.

#### SOLUTION

**The weather can't get better than this.**

**This is the best book in the library.**

**This is a better exercise for you than that one.**

The comparative and superlative forms of *good* are *better* and *best*. Do not use *more* or *most* before irregular forms of comparative and superlative adjectives.

### PROBLEM 2

*Incorrect use of* bad, worse, worst

> *adj*    This is the (baddest) movie I've ever seen.
>
> *adj*    These shoes are (more bad) than those shoes.
>
> *adj*    Yesterday I ate the (most) worst food I've ever tasted.

## PROBLEM 3

*Incorrect use of comparative and superlative adjectives*

*adj*    Maple Drive is (more) wider than Elm Street.

*adj*    Daphne lives in the (most) smallest house in town.

## SOLUTION

**Maple Drive is wider than Elm Street.**

**Daphne lives in the smallest house in town.**

Do not use both *-er* and *more* or *-est* and *most* at the same time.

**Need More Help?**    *If you need more help with the incorrect use of adjectives, turn to pages 408–411.*

## PROBLEM 1

*Missing commas in a series of three or more items*

*com* We visited the museum◡the zoo◡and the aquarium.

*com* Sam drove down the block◡around the corner◡ and into the parking lot.

### SOLUTION

**We visited the museum, the zoo, and the aquarium.**

**Sam drove down the block, around the corner, and into the parking lot.**

Use commas to separate three or more items in a series.

## PROBLEM 2

*Missing commas with direct quotations*

*com* "Biology class◡" said Ms. Blas◡"meets tomorrow."

*com* "Let's rake the leaves◡" said Ben◡"before we leave."

**"Biology class," said Ms. Blas, "meets tomorrow."**

**"Let's rake the leaves," said Ben, "before we leave."**

The first part of an interrupted quotation ends with a comma, followed by quotation marks. The interrupting words are also followed by a comma.

## PROBLEM 3

*Missing commas with nonessential appositives*

*com*    Our house,a split-level,was painted last year.

*com*    My bicycle,a black ten-speed,was shipped to Alaska

### SOLUTION

**Our house, a split-level, was painted last year.**

**My bicycle, a black ten-speed, was shipped to Alaska.**

Determine whether the appositive is truly not essential to the meaning of the sentence. If it is not essential, set off the appositive with commas.

**Need More Help?**

*If you need more help with commas, turn to pages 528–533.*

## 7.8    Incorrect Use of Apostrophes

### Singular possessive nouns

*apos*    (Chriss) son borrowed the neighbor's rake.

*apos*    The (womans) report is on the desk.

*apos*    (Ettas) book is in (Ians) house.

**SOLUTION**

**Chris's son borrowed the neighbor's rake.**

**The woman's report is on the desk.**

**Etta's book is in Ian's house.**

Use an apostrophe and an -*s* to form the possessive of a singular noun, even one that ends in *s*.

**PROBLEM 2**

### Plural possessive nouns ending in -s

*apos*    The (drivers) maps are in their cars.

*apos*    The two (pilots) orders are to land in Springfield.

*apos*    The (cats) owner fed them milk.

## PROBLEM 3

*Plural possessive nouns not ending in -s*

*apos*  The (mens) department is at the rear of the store.

*apos*  Ida Stark is known as the (peoples) candidate.

## PROBLEM 4

*Possessive personal pronouns*

*apos*  The hat is (your's), but the jacket is (her's).

**The hat is yours, but the jacket is hers.**

Do not use an apostrophe with any of the possessive personal pronouns.

## PROBLEM 5

*Confusion between* its *and* it's

*apos* (Its) going to be a beautiful morning.

*apos* Turn the rowboat over on (it's) side.

### SOLUTION

**It's going to be a beautiful morning.**

**Turn the rowboat over on its side.**

Do not use an apostrophe to form the possessive of *it*. Use an apostrophe to form the contraction of *it is.*

*If you need more help with apostrophes and possessives, turn to pages 538–539.*

# 7.9    Incorrect Capitalization

**Words referring to ethnic groups, nationalities, and languages**

*cap*    Mr. Dunn has studied several (asian) cultures.

*cap*    The (arabic) language is a difficult language to learn.

*cap*    Pierre is a (canadian) who speaks (russian).

### SOLUTION

**Mr. Dunn has studied several Asian cultures.**

**The Arabic language is a difficult language to learn.**

**Pierre is a Canadian who speaks Russian.**

Capitalize proper nouns and adjectives that refer to ethnic groups, nationalities, and languages.

**Words that show family relationships**

*cap*    Denise told (uncle) Evan to go to the theater.

*cap*    Yesterday (mom) fixed the car.

**PROBLEM 3**

*The first word of a direct quotation*

*cap* "We didn't leave the house until evening," said Rosa.

*cap* Peter said, "please wash the dishes before you leave."

**SOLUTION**

**"We didn't leave the house until evening," said Rosa.**

**Peter said, "Please wash the dishes before you leave."**

Capitalize the first word in a direct quotation. A direct quotation gives the speaker's exact words.

**Need More Help?**

*If you need more help in capitalizing, turn to pages 512–519.*

# UNIT 8
# Subjects, Predicates, and Sentences

Kay O'Rourke, *The Porcupine Preferred Patented Roses*, 1991

## 8.1 Kinds of Sentences

A **sentence** is a group of words that expresses a complete thought.

Different kinds of sentences have different purposes. A sentence can make a statement, ask a question, give a command, or express strong feeling. All sentences begin with a capital letter and end with a punctuation mark, which is determined by the purpose of that sentence.

A **declarative sentence** makes a statement. It ends with a period.

> Ecologists study relationships in nature.

An **interrogative sentence** asks a question. It ends with a question mark.

> Do animals and plants depend on each other?

An **exclamatory sentence** expresses strong feeling. It ends with an exclamation point.

> What important work ecologists do!

An **imperative sentence** gives a command or makes a request. It ends with a period.

> Look at these animals.

Ecologists often do research in the field.

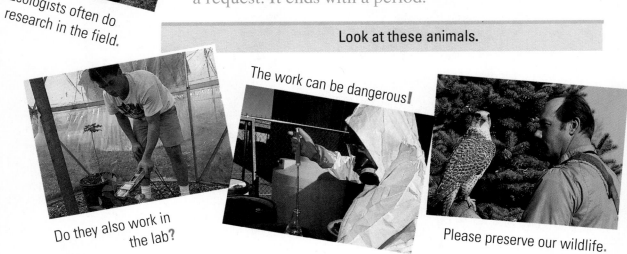

Do they also work in the lab?

The work can be dangerous!

Please preserve our wildlife.

## Exercise 1

**Identifying Kinds of Sentences**   Write each sentence.
Then write whether it is *declarative, interrogative,
exclamatory,* or *imperative.*

1. Ecologists study the world's population.
2. They also study the world's food supply.
3. Do ecologists study air pollution, too?
4. They tell us about the effects of air pollution.
5. Have ecologists also studied water pollution?
6. Examine the source of the water supply.
7. What an exciting field this is!

## Exercise 2

**Punctuating Different Kinds of Sentences**   Write
each sentence. Add capital letters and punctuation marks
where necessary.

1. ecologists and other experts study the effects of air
   pollution and water pollution on wildlife
2. look to the oceans for food in the future
3. what fascinating work marine biologists do
4. what other kinds of information do ecologists use
5. they use knowledge from physics and mathematics
6. ecologists often speak to private organizations about
   the importance of a clean environment
7. students of ecology learn about the cycles of nature
8. think about becoming an ecologist

### Writing Link

Have you seen any examples of pollution in the area
where you live? Describe the pollution and its impact on
the area. Try to use each kind of sentence.

## 8.2 Sentences and Sentence Fragments

Every sentence has two parts: a subject and a predicate.

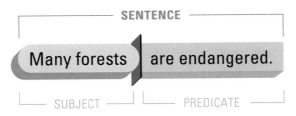

SENTENCE

Many forests | are endangered.

SUBJECT | PREDICATE

The **subject part** of a sentence names whom or what the sentence is about.

The **predicate part** of the sentence tells what the subject does or has. It can also describe what the subject is or is like.

A sentence must have both a subject and a predicate to express a complete thought. A group of words that does not have both a subject and predicate is an incomplete sentence, or sentence fragment.

A **sentence fragment** is a group of words that lacks a subject, a predicate, or both. A fragment does not express a complete thought.

You often use sentence fragments when you speak. You should use complete sentences, however, in anything you write for school or business.

| Correcting Sentence Fragments | | |
| --- | --- | --- |
| Fragment | Problem | Sentence |
| Lush forests. | The fragment lacks a predicate. *What do the lush forests do?* | Lush forests provide scenic land for recreation. |
| Inhabits the woodlands. | The fragment lacks a subject. *Who or what inhabits the woodlands?* | Wildlife inhabits the woodlands. |
| For animals. | The fragment lacks both a subject and a predicate. | Forests provide shelter for animals. |

## Exercise 3

**Identifying Sentences and Fragments**    Explain why each group of words is a *sentence* or a *sentence fragment*.

1. Tall trees provide shade.
2. Groves of birches.
3. Under the shelter of trees.
4. Many plants grow in a forest.
5. Healthy forest land.
6. Forests provide benefits.
7. Among the trees.
8. Hardwood makes sturdy furniture.

## Exercise 4

**Identifying Subjects and Predicates**    Write each numbered item. Underline each subject part once and each predicate part twice. If the item is not a complete sentence, write *sentence fragment*.

1. Acres of forest land support many kinds of wildlife.
2. Giant redwood trees grow in the Pacific Northwest.
3. Pines are common in the South.
4. Forests of red and white pine.
5. Oak trees dominate the East.
6. Forests of evergreens cover parts of Asia.
7. Of birches and pines.
8. Forests can provide food and shelter.
9. The tall trees of an ancient forest.

### Writing Link

Recall the last time you went to a wooded area. Write a paragraph describing what you saw. Identify the subjects and predicates.

## 8.3　Subjects and Predicates

A sentence consists of a subject and a predicate, which together express a complete thought. Both a subject and a predicate may consist of more than one word.

| Complete Subject | Complete Predicate |
|---|---|
| The capable foresters | study forests closely. |
| Foresters | are guardians of the environment. |

The **complete subject** includes all of the words in the subject of a sentence.

The **complete predicate** includes all of the words in the predicate of a sentence.

Not all of the words in the subject or the predicate are of equal importance.

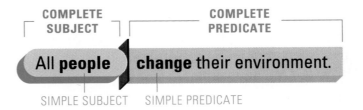

The **simple subject** is the main word or group of words in the complete subject.

The simple subject is usually a noun or a pronoun. A **noun** is a word that names a person, a place, a thing, or an idea. A **pronoun** is a word that takes the place of one or more nouns.

The **simple predicate** is the main word or group of words in the complete predicate.

The simple predicate is always a verb. A **verb** is a word that expresses an action or a state of being.

Sometimes the simple subject is also the complete subject. Similarly, the simple predicate may also be the complete predicate.

## Exercise 5

**Identifying Complete Subjects and Complete Predicates** Write each sentence. Underline each complete subject once and each complete predicate twice.

1. Capable loggers cut only certain trees.
2. Some simple procedures preserve the conditions of the forest.
3. Several foresters study the trees in this region.
4. Their careful observations are useful to ecologists.
5. Their plans for lumber production seem reasonable.

## Exercise 6

**Identifying Simple Subjects and Simple Predicates** Write each sentence. Underline each simple subject once and each simple predicate twice.

1. Scientists control changes in the environment.
2. Ecologists counteract the effects of forest fires, erosion, and floods.
3. Everyone near a forest benefits from these efforts.
4. Careful people preserve natural resources.
5. Biologists observe the growth of plants.
6. Farmers improve the soil on their land.
7. The soil provides crops with valuable nutrients.
8. Some crops take few nutrients from the soil.
9. Lush, green fields are a farmer's delight.
10. A temperate climate always helps.

### *Writing Link*

Think about how people use forests. Write a paragraph in which you describe several uses. Go back and look at the various subjects and predicates you used.

## 8.4     Identifying the Subject

Most statements begin with the subject.

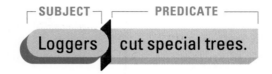

Not all sentences begin with the subject, however. Many questions begin with a word that is part of the predicate. The subject comes next, followed by the rest of the predicate.

To locate the subject of a question, it helps to rearrange the words to form a statement.

| Predicate | Subject | Predicate |
|---|---|---|
| Do | most people | understand the delicate balance of nature? |
| | Most people | do understand the delicate balance of nature. |

The predicate also precedes the subject in statements beginning with *There is, There are,* or *Here is.*

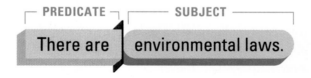

In commands, the subject is usually not stated. The predicate is the entire sentence. The word *you* is understood to be the subject.

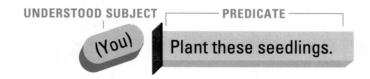

**Finding the Subject**   Write each sentence. Underline the complete subject, rewording the sentence if necessary. Write the word *(You)* before each command.

1. The production of clean timber takes several years.
2. Lumber companies buy large amounts of timber.
3. Some simple procedures protect the conditions of the forest.
4. Growers of trees divide the forest into several sections.
5. Loggers work one section each year.
6. The workers cut individual trees.
7. Do the loggers leave some trees?
8. Think of the heavy chain saws.
9. Do plants sprout easily in the region?
10. Here is a book about ecology.
11. In the library are other interesting books on the subject.
12. Many kinds of bacteria help the environment.
13. Do human beings change their environment?
14. Green plants need a certain amount of light.
15. Do ecologists study animal populations?
16. Scientists reduce the number of undesirable insects.
17. Look at the new plants in this region.
18. Some ecologists look for new methods of farming.
19. There are many helpful agricultural advances.
20. Learn about them when you have time.

### Writing Link

Describe the actions your family and neighbors have taken or could take to protect the environment. Find the subjects in your sentences.

## 8.5 Compound Subjects and Predicates

A sentence may have more than one simple subject or simple predicate.

A **compound subject** has two or more simple subjects that have the same predicate. The subjects are joined by *and*, *or*, or *but*.

COMPOUND SUBJECT

**Rangers** and **loggers** study forest conditions.

When the two simple subjects are joined by *and* or by *both . . . and*, the compound subject is plural and takes the plural form of the verb. In the sentence above, the verb *study* agrees with the plural compound subject.

When simple subjects are joined by *or,* the compound subject may be singular or plural. The verb must agree with the nearer simple subject.

> A ranger or **one** of his assistants **is** always on watch in the observation tower.
>
> A ranger or his **assistants are** always on watch in the observation tower.

A **compound predicate** has two or more simple predicates, or verbs, that have the same subject. The simple predicates are connected by *and*, *or*, or *but*.

COMPOUND PREDICATE

Rangers **explore** and **protect** the forest.

*Explore* and *protect* are the simple predicates, or verbs, in the compound predicate. The plural noun *rangers* is the subject of both verbs. Notice that both verbs agree with the plural noun in the subject.

**Identifying Compound Subjects and Predicates**
Write each sentence. Write whether the sentence has a
*compound subject* or a *compound predicate*.

1. Trees and grass hold soil in place.
2. Scientists observe and study the effects of erosion.
3. Plants and minerals enrich the soil.
4. Erosion destroys and wastes valuable land.
5. Winds and rain sometimes harm the earth.

**Making Subjects and Verbs Agree**   Write each
sentence. Use the correct form of the verb in parentheses.

1. Rachel Carson and other biologists (warns, warn)
   people about the dangers of air pollution.
2. Plants and trees (releases, release) oxygen.
3. Some chemicals (fights, fight) and (controls,
   control) pests.
4. Humans and animals often (eats, eat) the same foods.
5. The chemicals (travels, travel) and (mixes, mix) in the
   food chain.
6. Either smog or acid rain (injures, injure) the earth.
7. Air pollution and water pollution (affects, affect)
   the soil.
8. Either the scientist or the laboratory workers
   (studies, study) the effects of pollution.

### Writing Link

Describe the impact of winds on people, buildings,
and nature. Use at least one compound subject and one
compound predicate.

## 8.6 Simple and Compound Sentences

A **simple sentence** has one subject and one predicate.

SIMPLE SENTENCE

Rachel Carson wrote *Silent Spring*.

A simple sentence may have a compound subject, a compound predicate, or both, as in the following example.

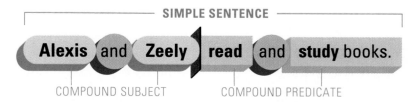

SIMPLE SENTENCE

Alexis and Zeely read and study books.

COMPOUND SUBJECT        COMPOUND PREDICATE

A **compound sentence** is a sentence that contains two or more simple sentences joined by a comma and a coordinating conjunction or by a semicolon.

A compound sentence has two complete subjects and two complete predicates.

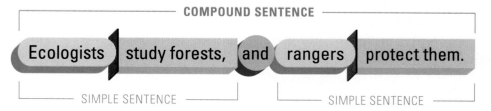

COMPOUND SENTENCE

Ecologists study forests, and rangers protect them.

SIMPLE SENTENCE        SIMPLE SENTENCE

A run-on sentence is two or more sentences incorrectly written as one sentence. To correct a run-on, write separate sentences, or combine the sentences as shown below.

| Correcting Run-On Sentences | |
|---|---|
| **Run-On** | **Correct** |
| Ecologists study nature they protect it. Ecologists study nature, they protect it. | Ecologists study nature. **T**hey protect it. Ecologists study nature, **and** they protect it. Ecologists study nature**;** they protect it. |

**Identifying Simple and Compound Sentences**
Write whether each sentence is *simple*, *compound*, or
*run-on*. If it is a run-on sentence, rewrite it correctly.

1. Ecologists study forests, their research provides
   important information for the rangers.
2. Ecologists study and work in modern, well-equipped
   laboratories.
3. The laboratories develop new instruments of science
   the instruments must work well in the field.
4. Some problems arise in forest environments;
   ecologists develop solutions to these problems.
5. Neither the animals' homes nor their food sources
   escape the effects of the unwise use of resources.
6. Small plants grow under tall trees and provide food
   for the smaller animals of the forest.
7. Sometimes animals can return to the forest after a
   disaster; this heartens ecologists.
8. Soil and leaves may be losing elements.
9. The burning of gas, oil, and coal pollutes the air and
   perhaps causes acid rain.
10. Lakes in Canada and forests in the United States are
    harmed by acid rain.
11. Scientists develop antipollution devices farmers use
    natural fertilizers.
12. The Environmental Protection Agency establishes
    and enforces clean-air standards.

### Writing Link

Imagine you are on a camping trip. Describe what you
would do to make sure you didn't cause any destruction
to the forest. Use compound sentences.

# $\mathcal{G}$rammar Workshop

## Subjects, Predicates, and Sentences

In *Water Sky* by Jean Craighead George, Lincoln Noah, a young half-Inuit boy from Massachusetts, visits the whaling village where his father once lived. There Lincoln observes how a community can live in harmony with its environment. In this passage the boy learns about the relationship that exists between whales and humans from an Inuit whaling captain, Vincent Ologak. The passage has been annotated to show some of the sentence structures covered in this unit.

### Literature Model

#### *from* WATER SKY
*by Jean Craighead George*

Compound predicate → Vincent  folded  his arms and  stood  beside him.

Compound sentence → "Lincoln Noah," he said, "I have something very important to say to you."  His eyes were soft, and his strength seemed to have returned.

"A whale is coming to you."

Complete subject → " A whale  is coming to me, Vincent Ologak? I do not understand."

Complete predicate → "The animals  give themselves to the Eskimos . They let us kill them. They then become us: our blood, our voices, our spirits. They join us in our bodies. That is

Declarative sentence → what they wish.  We are all one "

Lincoln tried to understand. Vincent continued.

"When your father left my igloo many years ago, he asked me what he could do to thank me. And so I said to him: Name your first son Lincoln, for the great protector of men. And give him a second name, Noah, for the great protector of animals." ➡

> "He never told me that," Lincoln said. "I sure wish he had. I always hated my name. Kids made fun of it." He paused. "I guess I never asked about it."
>
> "Lincoln Noah is a fine name all right. I knew someday there would be a whale who would come to one named Lincoln Noah. I have waited and waited for you to grow up and the whale to grow old."

— Simple predicate (told)

— Simple sentence (He paused.)

## Grammar Workshop Exercise 1

**Writing Sentences from Fragments**   On your paper correct each fragment by writing a complete sentence.

SAMPLE   Vincent said something important to Lincoln. Talked about the bond between men and animals.

ANSWER   He talked about the bond between men and animals.

1. Ologak believed that a whale would come to Lincoln Noah. Did not understand.
2. The whaling captain knew Lincoln's father. Had lived in Ologak's igloo.
3. Lincoln's father was grateful to Ologak. Wanted to thank the whaling captain.
4. Ologak named the boy. Lincoln and Noah.
5. Lincoln Noah had always hated his name. The other kids.

## Grammar Workshop Exercise 2

**Identifying Subjects and Predicates**   Rewrite each question as a statement. Then underline each simple subject once and each simple predicate twice.

SAMPLE   Do laws protect certain kinds of whales?

ANSWER   <u>Laws</u> <u>do protect</u> certain kinds of whales. ➡

1. Are whales mammals?
2. Have people hunted whales since prehistoric times?
3. Can a whale produce and locate sounds underwater?
4. Do some whales grow to be one hundred feet long?
5. Are dolphins and porpoises classified as whales?

## Grammar Workshop Exercise 3

**Writing Compound Sentences**    On your paper combine each pair of simple sentences to form a compound sentence by using *and, but,* or *or.*

1. Lincoln's father had lived in the village. He wanted his son to spend time there, too.
2. The whale hunters had to locate and spear a whale. People in their village would starve.
3. Lincoln hunted for the whale. He killed it.
4. Lincoln loved the Inuit community. He felt he should return to his life in Massachusetts.

## Grammar Workshop Exercise 4

**Proofreading**    The following passage is about Siwidi, a mythological hero of the Kwakiutl Indians. The whale mask opposite was used in ceremonial dances to reenact that hero's adventures. Rewrite the passage, correcting the errors in spelling, capitalization, punctuation, grammar, and usage. There are ten errors in all.

### The Legend of Siwidi
[1]Siwidi acquired many wonderful gifts during his adventures in an undersea kingdom [2]These gifts enabled siwidi to change his appearance. [3]When the hero rose from the sea he apeared to his people as a whale with an eagle on its back and a double tail. [4]The people chased  this great creature in their canoes. [5]But couldn't catch ➡

it. [6] As a result of his undersea adventures, siwidi became known as "Born-to-Be-Head-of-the-World."

[7] The Kwakiutl people developed a dance to celabrate Siwidi's appearance as a whale. [8] Throughout the dance the performer imitate the movements of a whale and wears a large whale mask. [9] Vincent Ologak of *Water Sky* showed his respect for whales by recognizing the bond between animal's and people's. [10] Likewise, the dance reflects the respect the Kwakiutl people have for Siwidi and for all whales.

**Artist unknown, Kwakiutl, Whale mask, nineteenth century**

# Subjects, Predicates, and Sentences

## Kinds of Sentences

[pages 322–323]

Write each sentence. Use punctuation marks where needed. Then write whether the sentence is *declarative, interrogative, imperative,* or *exclamatory.*

1. Scientists improve the quality of trees
2. Do they want more trees with rapid growth rates
3. How tall the giant redwoods grow
4. Please do not litter the forests
5. I would like to be a forest ranger

## Sentences and Fragments; Subjects and Predicates; Identifying the Subject

[pages 324–329]

Write each complete sentence. Underline the complete subject once and the complete predicate twice. Write (*you*) before a command. If the group of words is not a complete sentence, write *fragment.*

6. Do laws protect rare animals?
7. The ecology club.
8. Some people preserve natural resources.
9. Inform the public about our wildlife.
10. There is a great natural resource.

## Compound Subjects and Predicates; Simple and Compound Sentences

[pages 330–333]

Write each sentence. If the sentence has a compound subject, draw one line under each simple subject. If the sentence has a compound predicate, draw two lines under each simple predicate. If it is a compound sentence, circle each simple sentence.

11. Some animals feed on bark and branches; they damage trees.
12. Livestock needs grass and shrubs, and woodlands provide this food.
13. Large herds of animals arrive and endanger the food supply.
14. Foresters regulate the use of the lands, or animals roam elsewhere.
15. Regulations protect the lands, but these laws and ordinances require enforcement.

## Writing for Review

Imagine that you're a forest ranger. Write an entry in your journal, describing a typical day's activities. Use each of the four kinds of sentences as well as a compound sentence.

# Nouns

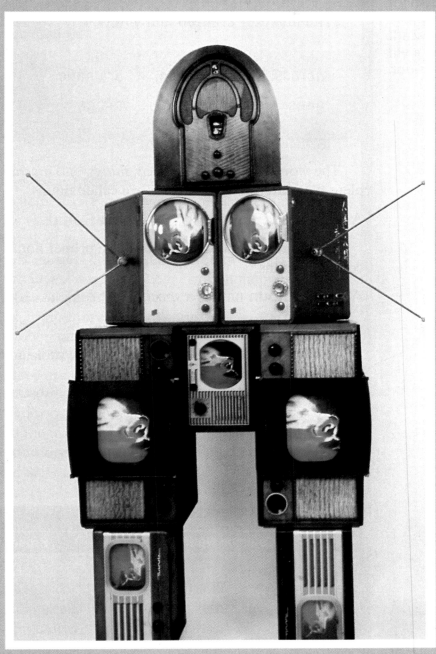

Nam June Paik, *Family of Robot: Grandmother*, 1986

**Using Appositives**   Rewrite each sentence below, inserting the appositive or appositive phrase in parentheses. Remember to add commas where needed.

SAMPLE   *Apollo 8* orbited the moon ten times. (a highly sophisticated spacecraft)

ANSWER   *Apollo 8,* a highly sophisticated spacecraft, orbited the moon ten times.

1. Frank Borman, James Lovell, and William Anders took pictures of the moon. (the crew of *Apollo 8*)
2. They were the first human beings to see the moon's far side. (a cold, forbidding place)
3. Borman was a veteran of several other space missions. (the commander of the crew)
4. During a Christmas Eve broadcast, half a billion people listened to the conversation between the crew and mission control. (an incredible dialogue)
5. For the first time in history, people orbited another celestial body. (the moon)

**Proofreading**   The following passage is about the space shuttle *Challenger,* the subject of the work on the next page. Rewrite the passage, correcting the errors in spelling, capitalization, punctuation, grammar, and usage. There are ten errors in all.

### Challenger's *Last Flight*

¹In Challenger's *Last Flight* artist Robert McCall pays tribute to the final mission of the space shuttle *challenger.* ²Just seconds after liftoff on January 28, 1986 an explosion tore the space shuttle apart, killing it's seven crew members.

³However, the space program had experienced tragedy befour. ⁴During a test of the *Apollo 1* ➡

command module, 3 astronauts died in a fire on the launching pad. [5]Nonetheless, scientist's continued to improve the spacecraft. [6]Within two years after the fire, *Apollo 8* orbited the moon. [7]About seven months later, *Apollo 11* carried the first men to the moon [8]*Challenger's Last Flight* celebrate the human spirit.

**Robert McCall, Challenger's *Last Flight,* 1987**

# Unit 9 Review

## Nouns

### Kinds of Nouns

[pages 340–343]

Write each noun in the following sentences. Write whether it is a *common noun* or *proper noun*. Then write whether any common nouns are *compound nouns*.

1. Napoleon Bonaparte needed food for his armies.
2. The commander in chief offered a prize for the best process for preserving food.
3. Nicholas-François Appert experimented in his kitchen for ten years.
4. This man had a brainstorm regarding the preservation of foodstuff.
5. People once had success using salt and smoke to preserve meat.

### Distinguishing Plurals, Possessives, and Contractions

[pages 344–347]

Write each of the following sentences. Use the correct word in parentheses to complete the sentence. Then write whether the noun is *plural, singular, possessive, plural possessive,* or a *contraction.*

6. The (telescopes, telescope's) a Dutch invention.
7. We do not know the (inventors', inventor's) name.
8. Galileo Gallilei pointed his telescope at the (planets, planet's).
9. Galileo taught (courses, course's) in astronomy.
10. All (astronomers', astronomers) debt to him is immeasurable.

### Collective Nouns; Appositives

[pages 348–351]

Underline the appositive or appositive phrase in the following sentences. Add commas where needed. Circle each collective noun, and write whether it is *singular* or *plural.*

11. Jacques Cousteau a French scientist explores the sea.
12. He created *The Silent World* a film.
13. The French public has honored him on several occasions.
14. Cousteau an inventor as well as an explorer created the aqualung.
15. His support team have diverse skills.

### Writing for Review

Imagine that you are a deep-sea diver. Describe one of your dives.

Artist unknown, Mughal, *Mihrdukht Shoots Her Bow at the Ring*, c. 1562–1577

## 10.1 Action Verbs

**ACTION
VERB**

Many sports are games of fast action. The action in sports can be named by verbs. If a word expresses action and tells what a subject does, it is an action verb.

An **action verb** is a word that names an action. It may contain more than one word.

Notice the action verbs in the following paragraph.

> Sports experts **write** about the football player Jim Thorpe even today. Thorpe **blocked** like a tank. He **tackled** like a tornado. In every game Thorpe **attacked** his opponents with all his might. He **caught** the ball skillfully and **charged** ahead fearlessly. Experts still **remember** and **honor** Thorpe's greatness.

Action verbs can express physical actions, like writing and running, or mental activities, such as thinking and remembering.

| Action Verbs | |
|---|---|
| **Physical** | write, block, tackle, attack, catch, charge |
| **Mental** | remember, honor |

Tonio **remembered** Thorpe's famous play . . .

*Have, has,* and *had* are often used before other verbs. They can also be used as action verbs when they name what the subject owns or holds.

> These players **have** red uniforms.
> The pitcher **has** a sore arm.
> The stadium **had** an electronic scoreboard.
> Our cheerleader **had** a megaphone.

. . .as he **snared** the ball.

**Identifying Action Verbs**   Write each of the following sentences. Underline each action verb, and write whether it expresses a *physical* or a *mental* action.

1. Althea Gibson learned tennis on the streets of Harlem.
2. She won her first championship in her hometown of New York City.
3. In 1949 Gibson entered college.
4. Later in New York City she enjoyed a ticker tape parade in her honor.
5. In 1874 Mary E. Outerbridge observed tennis being played in Bermuda.
6. She brought a net, some tennis balls, and some racquets back to the United States.
7. Maud Wilson won the first women's championship at Wimbledon in 1884.
8. Ellen Hansen earned  the first singles crown at the U.S. Open in 1887.
9. Suzanne Lenglen of France developed an athletic style of play.
10. In 1926 Lenglen starred in the first U.S. professional tennis tour.
11. Helen Wills Moody set a record of eight Wimbledon singles titles.
12. Many players prefer clay courts.
13. We compared the players' styles.

### Writing Link

Imagine that you are competing in a championship game. Write an entry in your journal describing your experience.

## 10.2 Transitive and Intransitive Verbs

Every sentence has a subject and a predicate. In some sentences the predicate consists of only an action verb.

> The punter **kicks**.

Usually sentences provide more information. The predicate often names who or what received the action of the verb.

The punter **kicks** the **football**

DIRECT OBJECT

In the sentence above, *football* receives the action of the verb *kicks*. It answers the question *what?* after the action verb. It is called a direct object.

A **direct object** receives the action of a verb. It answers the question *whom?* or *what?* after an action verb.

A verb can also have a compound direct object. That is, it can have more than one direct object.

> The team carried **gloves** and **bats** into the stadium.

Sometimes the action verb does not have a direct object.

> The team played well.

In the sentence above, *well* does not answer the question *whom?* or *what?* after the verb *played*. Therefore, it is not a direct object. Action verbs that have direct objects are called transitive verbs. Action verbs that do not have direct objects are called intransitive verbs.

A **transitive verb** has a direct object.

An **intransitive verb** does not have a direct object.

## Exercise 2

### Distinguishing Transitive and Intransitive Verbs

Write each sentence. Underline each action verb once. If the verb has a direct object, write *transitive*. If it does not, write *intransitive*. Underline each direct object twice.

1. Jim Thorpe ran fast as a boy in Oklahoma.
2. Thorpe came from a Native American family.
3. In 1909 Jim Thorpe entered Carlisle College.
4. Thorpe played football there under Coach Pop Warner.
5. He starred as the starting halfback on the team.
6. In 1912 Thorpe scored 129 points.
7. Thorpe entered the 1912 Olympics.
8. He participated in the decathlon and the pentathlon.
9. He competed against many other athletes.
10. He jumped higher and farther than the others.
11. Thorpe ran with great strength and concentration.
12. Other track athletes copied Jim Thorpe's style.
13. Thorpe defeated his rivals in the ten events of the decathlon.
14. He even set world records.
15. He served as the first president of the football association.
16. Thorpe retired from football in 1929, at the age of forty-one.
17. Many regard Thorpe as the best all-around athlete ever.

### *Writing Link*

What type of sports facilities does your town have? Write a description of a facility that you might like to use. Use both transitive and intransitive verbs.

## 10.3  Verbs with Indirect Objects

Nouns or pronouns that answer the question *whom?* or *what?* after an action verb are called direct objects.

> Michael Jordan led his **team** to the championship.
> Michael Jordan tossed the **ball**.

Sometimes two kind of objects follow an action verb. The object that directly receives the action of the verb is the direct object. The object that tells *to whom* or *for whom* the action is done is called the indirect object.

An **indirect object** answers the question *to whom?* or *for whom?* an action is done.

Michael Jordan **shows** his **teammates** new shots.

INDIRECT OBJECT

The direct object in the sentence above is *shots*. The indirect object is *teammates*. *Teammates* answers the question *to whom?* after the action verb *shows*.

An indirect object appears only in a sentence that has a direct object. Two easy clues will help you recognize indirect objects. First, the indirect object always comes before a direct object. Second, you can add *to* or *for* before the indirect object and change its position. The sentence will still make sense.

> The helper gives the **players** towels.
> The helper gives the towels **to the players**.

You can figure out that in the first sentence *players* is the indirect object. First, it comes before the direct object. Second, its position can be changed to follow the word *to*.

**Distinguishing Direct and Indirect Objects**    Write each sentence. Underline each direct object once. If the sentence contains an indirect object, underline it twice.

1. The university sent the tournament some of its best players.
2. One player earned his team a three-point edge.
3. The rookie played a good game.
4. In the first game of the season, the teams showed their fans some skillful plays.
5. Many fans paid the players tribute with colorful banners.
6. The coach gave the players new instructions.
7. The players executed some fancy shots.
8. Students from many different schools cheered their favorite players.
9. Mr. Romero refereed the game.
10. Clayton's shooting skill gave his team's offense a potent weapon.
11. Several players gave him a pat on the back.
12. A top reporter wrote an article about the game for the *Times Gazette.*
13. She asked Clayton some questions about his game.
14. Clayton explained his strategy to her.
15. The coach gave his players all the credit.
16. The team, in turn, praised its coach.

### Writing Link

Imagine that you are on the basketball team for the first time. Write a paragraph describing your feelings during your first game. Use direct objects and indirect objects in your sentences.

## 10.4　Linking Verbs and Predicate Words

Action verbs tell what the subject of a sentence does. Other verbs tell what the subject is or is like. These verbs are called linking verbs.

A **linking verb** connects the subject of a sentence with a noun or an adjective in the predicate.

John McGraw **was** the manager.

LINKING VERB

LINKING VERB

In the sentence above, the word *was* is a linking verb. It connects, or links, the subject, *John McGraw,* to a word in the predicate, *manager.*

A **predicate noun** is a noun that follows a linking verb. It tells what the subject is.

A **predicate adjective** is an adjective that follows a linking verb. It describes the subject by telling what it is like.

---

Sam is a **pitcher.** [predicate noun]
The pitcher is **skillful.** [predicate adjective]

---

| Common Linking Verbs | | | |
| --- | --- | --- | --- |
| be | appear | turn | smell |
| become | look | taste | sound |
| seem | grow | feel | |

Many of these verbs can also be used as action verbs.

---

Chandra **turned** thirteen. [linking verb]
The car **turned** the corner. [action verb]

---

**Identifying Action and Linking Verbs and Predicate Nouns and Adjectives**   Write each sentence. Under-line each verb, and write whether it is an *action verb* or a *linking verb*. If it is a linking verb, write whether it is followed by a *predicate noun* or a *predicate adjective.*

**GRAMMAR HINT**

To see whether a verb is a linking verb, replace it with the correct form of *be: Ahmad* appears *happy. Ahmad* is *happy.*

1. Our pitcher appears nervous today.
2. The catcher ran very quickly.
3. She caught the ball.
4. The pitcher was a good hitter.
5. The player at third base threw the baseball.
6. Fans of the team grew ecstatic.
7. The ball flew into the bleachers.
8. Fans of the home team seem confident today.
9. The home team was the winner yesterday.
10. They tasted victory for the first time this season.
11. Today's winners become members of the state's Hall of Fame.
12. The players on both teams seem eager at the start of the game.
13. The mayor walks onto the field.
14. She is an honorary member of the team.
15. The player sounds thrilled.
16. He announces his plans.
17. These athletes are also students.
18. They divide their time between the playing field and the library.

### *Writing Link*

Imagine that you are a sportscaster. What do you do to prepare to announce a game? Write a description of your job. Use action and linking verbs.

## 10.5 Present, Past, and Future Tenses

A verb changes its form to show tense and to agree with its subject. The **tense** of a verb tells when an action takes place.

The **present tense** of a verb names an action that happens regularly. It can also express a general truth.

In the present tense the base form of a verb is used with all subjects except singular nouns and the words *he, she,* and *it.* When the subject is a singular noun or *he, she,* or *it, -s* is usually added to the verb.

| Present Tense Forms of the Verb *Race* | |
|---|---|
| **Singular** | **Plural** |
| I **race.** | We **race.** |
| You **race.** | You **race.** |
| He, she, *or* it **races.** | They **race.** |

The **past tense** of a verb names an action that already happened.

The past tense of many verbs is formed by adding *-ed* to the base form of the verb.

The runner **trained** yesterday.

The **future tense** of a verb names an action that will take place in the future.

In the future tense the word *will* is used with the verb. Sometimes *shall* is used when the pronoun *I* or *we* is the subject.

| Future Tense Forms of the Verb *Go* | |
|---|---|
| **Singular** | **Plural** |
| I **will (shall) go.** | We **will (shall) go.** |
| You **will go.** | You **will go.** |
| He, she, *or* it **will go.** | They **will go.** |

**Distinguishing Present, Past, and Future**   Write each sentence. Use the correct tense of the verb in parentheses. Then write whether it is in the *present, past,* or *future tense.*

1. Wilma Rudolph (enter) many races in the 1950s.
2. During her youth Rudolph (suffer) many difficulties.
3. Today Wilma Rudolph (encourage) other young runners.
4. In future years people (remember) her success on the track.
5. At an early age Wilma Rudolph (learn) the importance of good health.
6. The young Wilma (want) an active life.
7. As a girl she (enjoy) several different sports.
8. She (triumph) over many illnesses.
9. For years she (train) long and hard.
10. In 1960 Rudolph (receive) an Olympic medal in track.
11. This great runner no longer (describe) sports on television.
12. Even today, however, she (inspire) many young athletes.
13. In the years ahead, young runners (follow) Rudolph's example.
14. Sportswriters of the future (include) Rudolph's name in the history of sports.

### Writing Link

Write about someone in sports whom you admire. Describe why he or she is important to you. Use the present, past, and future tenses.

## 10.6    Main Verbs and Helping Verbs

Verbs have four principal parts that are used to form all tenses. The chart below shows how the principal parts of most verbs are formed.

| Principal Parts of the Verb *Jump* | | | |
|---|---|---|---|
| **Base Form** | **Present Participle** | **Past Form** | **Past Participle** |
| jump | jumping | jumped | jumped |

The principal parts of a verb are often combined with helping verbs to form verb phrases.

A **helping verb** is a verb that helps the main verb to tell about an action or make a statement.

A **verb phrase** consists of one or more helping verbs followed by a main verb.

> The students **are jumping** rope now.

In the sentence above, the word *are* is the helping verb, and the present participle *jumping* is the main verb. Together they form a verb phrase.

The most common helping verbs are *be, have,* and *do.* Forms of the helping verb *be* include *am, is,* and *are* in the present and *was* and *were* in the past. They combine with the present participle of the main verb.

Forms of the helping verb *have* include *have* and *has* in the present and *had* in the past. They combine with the past participle form of a verb.

| *Have* and the Past Participle | | | |
|---|---|---|---|
| **Present** | | **Past** | |
| **Singular** | **Plural** | **Plural** | **Singular** |
| I **have** jumped. | We **have** jumped. | I **had** jumped. | We **had** jumped. |
| You **have** jumped. | You **have** jumped. | You **had** jumped. | You **had** jumped. |
| She **has** jumped. | They **have** jumped. | She **had** jumped. | They **had** jumped. |

**Using Helping Verbs and Present and Past Participles**   Write each sentence. Use the correct helping verb shown in parentheses. Underline the verb phrase in the sentence, and draw a second line under the participle. Then write whether it is a *present participle* or a *past participle*.

1. Champions (were, had) making archery a more popular sport.
2. The equipment (are, has) changed very little.
3. Many people (are, have) playing in tournaments each year.
4. Tournaments (have, are) increased people's interest in archery.
5. The archers in the competition (are, have) practicing every day.
6. Archers (were, had) marking their targets.
7. We (are, have) learning about archery this year.
8. Archers (are, have) working hard in today's competition.
9. That archer (is, has) earning the most points today.
10. She (is, has) scored several bull's-eyes.
11. Sarafina's arrow (is, has) landed away from the target.
12. Some archers (are, have) bringing new arrows.
13. Her concentration (is, has) improved greatly.
14. Last year archery (had, was) taking up most of her free time.

**GRAMMAR HINT**

The main verb is always the last verb in a verb phrase. The first verb shows present, past, or future tense.

### Writing Link

Write a paragraph about the qualities an athlete should possess to excel at your favorite game or sport. Use verb phrases.

## 10.7 Progressive Forms

You know that the present tense of a verb names an action that occurs repeatedly. To describe an action that is taking place right now, you use the present progressive form of the verb.

The **present progressive form** of a verb names an action or condition that is continuing in the present.

> I **am enjoying** this baseball game at Candlestick Park.
> The home team **is winning** at the moment.

The present progressive form of a verb consists of the present participle of the main verb and the helping verb *am, are,* or *is.*

| Present Progressive Form | |
|---|---|
| **Singular** | **Plural** |
| I **am looking.** | We **are looking.** |
| You **are looking.** | You **are looking.** |
| He, she, *or* it **is looking.** | They **are looking.** |

The past progressive names an action that was continuing at some point in the past.

The **past progressive form** of a verb names an action or condition that continued for some time in the past.

> They **were winning** the game.

The past progressive form of a verb consists of the present participle and the helping verb *was* or *were.*

| Past Progressive Form | |
|---|---|
| **Singular** | **Plural** |
| I **was trying.** | We **were trying.** |
| You **were trying.** | You **were trying.** |
| He, she, *or* it **was trying.** | They **were trying.** |

## Exercise 7

**Using Present and Past Progressive Forms**
Write each sentence. Use the present progressive or past progressive form of the verb given in parentheses.

1. I (watch) a great soccer game on television now.
2. The players (try) very hard.
3. Yesterday fans (cheer) this same team.
4. We saw a film clip in which the team (look) for the bus.
5. The coach (laugh) at the players.
6. They (climb) into the wrong bus.

## Exercise 8

**Using the Progressive Forms** Write each sentence. If the verb is in the present tense, change it to the present progressive form. If the verb is in the past tense, change it to the past progressive form.

1. The soccer coach plans a team for the next season.
2. She asked players from other teams to the tryouts.
3. Many new players tried out also.
4. Some players train for the next season.
5. My friend watched the players at the tryouts.
6. Some players stand by the goal post.
7. The players kick the ball back and forth.
8. Several players exercised.
9. A goalie inspected the field.
10. Some enthusiastic players practice daily.

### Writing Link

In a paragraph describe a sports event. Use some progressive forms.

## 10.8  Perfect Tenses

The **present perfect tense** of a verb names an action that happened at an indefinite time in the past. It also tells about an action that happened in the past and is still happening now.

> My family **has attended** many sports events.
> We **have watched** baseball games for years.

The present perfect tense consists of the helping verb *have* or *has* and the past participle of the main verb.

| Present Perfect Tense | |
|---|---|
| **Singular** | **Plural** |
| I **have watched.** | We **have watched.** |
| You **have watched.** | You **have watched.** |
| He, she, *or* it **has watched.** | They **have watched.** |

The **past perfect tense** of a verb names an action that happened before another action or event in the past.

The past perfect tense is often used in sentences that contain a past tense verb in another part of the sentence.

> By the time we found our seats, the game **had** already **started.**
> I **had** never **seen** a baseball game before.

The past perfect tense of a verb consists of the helping verb *had* and the past participle of the main verb.

| Past Perfect Tense | |
|---|---|
| **Singular** | **Plural** |
| I **had studied.** | We **had studied.** |
| You **had studied.** | You **had studied.** |
| He, she, *or* it **had studied.** | They **had studied.** |

## Exercise 9

**Using the Present Perfect Tense**   Write each sentence. Use the present perfect tense of the verb in parentheses to complete the sentence.

1. Some players (start) their warm-up routines.
2. They (arrive) in time to hear the coach's instructions.
3. The coach (watch) the games.
4. She (call) an early practice this evening.
5. Most players (agree) to the new rules.
6. They (arrive) at school early for more practice.
7. The students (hope) for a victory.
8. The star (develop) a sore ankle, however.

## Exercise 10

**Using the Past Perfect Tense**   Write each sentence. Use the past perfect tense of the verb in parentheses.

1. The skater (earn) a medal by the age of six.
2. She (want) a place on her school's skating team.
3. The speed skater (try) twice before.
4. She (practice) daily.
5. The team (welcome) her into the group.
6. They (wish) her the best of luck.
7. The spectators (notice) the new skater.
8. Her skating (improve) dramatically.
9. They were pleased that she (win) a place on the team.

### Writing Link

Describe a recent gym class that was especially challenging or memorable. Use the present and past perfect tenses.

## 10.9    Irregular Verbs

The irregular verbs below are grouped according to the way their past form and past participle are formed.

| Irregular Verbs | | | |
| --- | --- | --- | --- |
| Pattern | Base Form | Past Form | Past Participle |
| One vowel changes to form the past and the past participle. | begin | began | begun |
| | drink | drank | drunk |
| | ring | rang | rung |
| | shrink | shrank *or* shrunk | shrunk |
| | sing | sang | sung |
| | spring | sprang *or* sprung | sprung |
| | swim | swam | swum |
| The past form and past participle are the same. | bring | brought | brought |
| | buy | bought | bought |
| | catch | caught | caught |
| | creep | crept | crept |
| | feel | felt | felt |
| | get | got | got *or* gotten |
| | keep | kept | kept |
| | lay | laid | laid |
| | lead | led | led |
| | leave | left | left |
| | lend | lent | lent |
| | lose | lost | lost |
| | make | made | made |
| | pay | paid | paid |
| | say | said | said |
| | seek | sought | sought |
| | sell | sold | sold |
| | sit | sat | sat |
| | sleep | slept | slept |
| | swing | swung | swung |
| | teach | taught | taught |
| | think | thought | thought |
| | win | won | won |

throw
threw
thrown

fling
flung
flung

win
won
won

**Using the Past and Past Participle of Irregular Verbs**
Write each sentence, using the past tense or the past participle of the verb in parentheses to complete the sentence.

1. The public first (sing) Sonja Henie's praises in the 1920s.
2. Experts have (say) that she made figure skating popular.
3. Sports historians have (think) highly of her.
4. She (get) gold medals at the 1928, 1932, and 1936 Olympic games.
5. Other skaters, too, have (make) a name for themselves in figure skating.
6. They have (bring) high standards to the sport.
7. Ballet has (lend) many movements to figure skating.
8. Last night the skater (spring) onto the rink.
9. The silver skate blades (ring) on the ice.
10. The skater has (lead) her partner onto the ice.
11. The skater's partner has (catch) the woman expertly.
12. We (feel) the excitement of the moment.
13. Errors have (creep) into some skaters' routines.
14. The judges (begin) their voting after each performance.
15. The coach had (teach) the skaters as well as possible.
16. That skating team (win) last year's gold medal.
17. One judge has (seek) the opinion of another judge.
18. We (think) that each skater did his or her best.

### *Writing Link*

Write about your favorite event or sport at the Olympic games. Use several irregular verbs in the past tense and in one of the perfect tenses.

## 10.10  More Irregular Verbs

| Irregular Verbs | | | |
|---|---|---|---|
| **Pattern** | **Base Form** | **Past Form** | **Past Participle** |
| The base form and the past participle are the same. | become<br>come<br>run | became<br>came<br>ran | become<br>come<br>run |
| The past form ends in -*ew* and the past participle ends in -*wn.* | blow<br>draw<br>fly<br>grow<br>know<br>throw | blew<br>drew<br>flew<br>grew<br>knew<br>threw | blown<br>drawn<br>flown<br>grown<br>known<br>thrown |
| The past participle ends in -*en.* | bite<br>break<br>choose<br>drive<br>eat<br>fall<br>give<br>ride<br>rise<br>see<br>speak<br>steal<br>take<br>write | bit<br>broke<br>chose<br>drove<br>ate<br>fell<br>gave<br>rode<br>rose<br>saw<br>spoke<br>stole<br>took<br>wrote | bitten *or* bit<br>broken<br>chosen<br>driven<br>eaten<br>fallen<br>given<br>ridden<br>risen<br>seen<br>spoken<br>stolen<br>taken<br>written |
| The past form and the past participle do not follow any pattern. | am, are, is<br>do<br>go<br>tear<br>wear | was, were<br>did<br>went<br>tore<br>wore | been<br>done<br>gone<br>torn<br>worn |
| The base form, past form, and past participle are all the same. | cut<br>let | cut<br>let | cut<br>let |

**Using the Past and Past Participle of Irregular Verbs**
Write each sentence. Use the past tense or the past participle of the verb in parentheses to complete the sentence.

1. I have (see) several games of handball in the city recently.
2. When I realized the excitement of the game, I (know) handball was for me.
3. The champion (break) the old record.
4. She has (throw) the ball to a fan in the crowd.
5. The winner (give) a victory speech.
6. She (rise) from her chair to say a few words to the audience.
7. Several of us have (choose) to join a handball club.
8. Gail has (speak) with the director.
9. He has (write) out her membership card.
10. He also (give) Gail a few visitors' passes.
11. The handball (fly) across the room.
12. Juan (drive) the shot against the front wall.
13. One of the players has (tear) her sweatshirt.
14. A player has (fall) during an exciting play.
15. The director (draw) the foul lines across the handball court.
16. Two players have (choose) a date for their next game.
17. Gail (become) interested in handball last year and now plays regularly.

### Writing Link

In a paragraph describe a story or movie that involves a sport. Use several irregular verbs in the past tense and in one of the perfect tenses.

# *Grammar* Workshop

## Verbs

Douglas, the hero of this novel, craves a new pair of sporty tennis shoes. In this passage, which has been annotated to show various concepts covered in the unit, he tries to persuade a shoe-store owner to sell him a pair.

### Literature Model

#### *from* DANDELION WINE

*by Ray Bradbury*

"Please!" Douglas held out his hand. "Mr. Sanderson, now could you kind of rock back and forth a little, sponge around, bounce kind of, while I <u>tell</u> you the rest? It's this: I give you my money, you give <u>me</u> the shoes, I owe you a dollar. But, Mr. Sanderson, *but*—soon as I get those shoes on, you know what *happens*?"

"What?"

"Bang! I deliver your <u>packages</u>, pick up packages, bring you coffee, burn your trash, run to the post office, telegraph office, library! You'<u>ll see</u> twelve of me in and out, in and out, every minute. Feel those shoes, Mr. Sanderson, *feel* how fast they'd take me? All those springs inside? Feel all the running inside? Feel how they kind of grab hold and can't let you alone and don't like you just *standing* there? Feel how quick I'd be doing the things you'd rather not bother with? You stay in the nice cool store while I'<u>m jumping</u> all around town! But it's not me really, it's the <u>shoes</u>. They're going like mad down alleys, cutting corners, and back! There they go!"

Action verb — *tell*
Indirect object — *me*
Direct object — *packages*
Future tense — *'ll see*
Present progressive form — *'m jumping*
Predicate noun — *shoes*

**Identifying Action and Linking Verbs**   Write each sentence. Circle each verb, and write whether it is an *action verb* or a *linking verb*. Then write whether the underlined word after the verb is a *direct object*, an *indirect object*, a *predicate noun*, or a *predicate adjective*.

SAMPLE   Douglas does not have enough <u>money</u> for the sneakers.

ANSWER   Douglas (does) not (have) enough <u>money</u> for the sneakers. (action verb, direct object)

1. The shoes were too <u>expensive</u> for Douglas.
2. How will he pay <u>Mr. Sanderson</u> the additional dollar for the shoes?
3. Douglas asked a <u>favor</u> of Mr. Sanderson.
4. Mr. Sanderson must wear a <u>pair</u> of sneakers from the store; that was the <u>favor</u> Douglas asked.
5. Did Mr. Sanderson feel <u>good</u> in the sneakers?

**Identifying Verb Tenses and Forms**   Write each sentence. Identify the tense or form of the underlined verb.

SAMPLE   Douglas and his father and brother <u>are picking</u> dandelions for wine.

ANSWER   Douglas and his father and brother <u>are picking</u> dandelions for wine. (present progressive form)

1. Bradbury <u>is writing</u> about a special summer in the twelfth year of Douglas's life.
2. Douglas <u>has</u> just <u>made</u> a new discovery.
3. He <u>had</u> always <u>known</u>, of course, that he <u>was</u> alive.
4. Douglas <u>was hoping</u> that he would be aware of feeling exhausted.
5. After this Douglas <u>will</u> never <u>be</u> the same again.

**Using Helping Verbs**   Write each sentence, using the correct form of the helping verb in parentheses.

SAMPLE      Many kinds of shoes (are, were) worn for sports today.

ANSWER      Many kinds of shoes are worn for sports today.

1. Basic sports shoes (was, were) once called sneakers.
2. Today many people (do, did) not wear the same pair of sneakers for different sports or exercises.
3. The name *tennis shoes* (is, has) no longer meant to refer to walking shoes or track shoes.
4. Shoe manufacturers (did, have) created a slightly different shoe style for each sport.
5. What kind of shoes (do, has) you wear?

**Proofreading**   The following passage is about the artist Gregg Spears, whose painting appears on the next page. Rewrite the passage, correcting the errors in spelling, capitalization, punctuation, grammar, and usage. There are ten errors in all.

### Gregg Spears

[1] Like bradbury's book *Dandelion Wine,* Gregg Spears's *My Back Porch* deal with lifes everyday happenings. [2] Such comon occurrences are the themes around which Spears creates his paintings.

[3] Spears was born in Chicago, and It is there that most of his art have been exhibited. [4] Gregg Spears has participate in exhibits at the DuSable Museum of African-American History and [5] The chicago Cultural Center.

[6] The place where Spears has his studio are an abandoned building that was rebuilt.

**Gregg Spears,** *My Back Porch,* **1992**

## Verbs

### Transitive and Intransitive Verbs; Direct and Indirect Objects; Linking Verbs

[pages 360–365]

Underline each verb once. If it is an action verb, tell whether it is *transitive* or *intransitive*. If it is transitive, underline the direct object twice. Circle any indirect objects. If the verb is a linking verb with a predicate word, circle the predicate word, and tell whether it is a *predicate noun* or a *predicate adjective*.

1. Asian monks developed karate.
2. It is a combination of art and sport.
3. Karate evolved rapidly.
4. Masters taught students different forms of self-defense.
5. Karate became popular worldwide.

### Tenses and Forms; Main and Helping Verbs

[pages 366–373]

Underline each verb or verb phrase, and circle any helping verbs. Then indicate the tense or form of the verb: *present, past,* or *future tense; present progressive* or *past progressive form; present perfect* or *past perfect tense.*

6. The canoe has provided transportation.
7. People are using canoes for recreation, too.
8. Canoes had carried explorers.
9. That canoe trip was exciting.
10. Rapids have challenged experts.
11. We canoe every weekend.
12. Last week we paddled for hours.
13. We shall go again next week.
14. The race has ended already.
15. Someone is paddling still.

### Irregular Verbs

[pages 374–377]

Write each sentence. Use the past tense or the past participle of the verb in parentheses.

16. The team has (take) on several new players.
17. The team has (draw) young skaters together for years.
18. Some of the skaters (grow) into professionals.
19. Some amateurs had (go) to special camps for training.
20. The hockey player has (swing) her stick at the puck.

### Writing for Review

Imagine that you have just interviewed your favorite sports figure. Write a short report describing the interview.

# Pronouns

Diego Velázquez, *The Fable of Arachne*, 1644–1648

**Writing Sentences with Interrogative Pronouns**
The following sentences are about figures in Egyptian mythology. Rewrite each question, using the correct interrogative pronoun in parentheses.

1. Nut represented the heavens. (What, Which) did Nut represent?
2. Geb was the earth god. (Who, Whom) was Geb?
3. Nut and Geb married, but Re, the sun god, opposed their marriage. (Which, What) did Re oppose?
4. Re ordered Shu, the god of the air, to separate Nut from Geb. (Who, Whom) did Re order to separate Nut from Geb?
5. Shu's action raised the heavens from the earth. (Whose, What) action raised the heavens?

**Proofreading**   The following passage is about chariot racing. This event inspired *Charioteers,* the Greek vase shown on the next page. Rewrite the passage, correcting the errors in spelling, capitalization, punctuation, grammar, and usage. There are ten errors in all.

### *Charioteers*

[1]A four-horse chariot race became part of the anceint Olympics in 680 B.C. [2]The race proved to be so popular that they became the opening spectacle at the Games. [3]As many as forty chariot drivers competed in the race [4]Each chariot driver were hired by the owner of the chariot and horses. [5]Sometimes a owner entered up to seven chariots in the same race.

[6]The competitors has to run laps down a straight track for a total distance of nearly nine miles. [7]When the four horses puling a chariot turned around to double back down the track, the chariot would swing wildly. ➡

[8]As phaethon discovered when he tried to drive the chariot of the sun god, the horses were very hard to control. [9]Spills and collisions occured frequently. [10]As a result very few of the chariot drivers managed to finish the race.

**Artist unknown, Greece, *Charioteers*, fifth century** B.C.

# Pronouns

## Pronouns and Antecedents

[pages 384–387]

Use the correct pronoun in each blank. Underline the antecedent of each pronoun.

1. Athens was a naval power. _____ controlled the sea.
2. Spartan soldiers were well disciplined. Sparta trained _____ well.
3. Athens and Sparta competed. _____ fought for years.
4. Alexander the Great wanted to control Greece. _____ conquered it.
5. His army got to India. _____ fell, too.

## Using Pronouns Correctly

[pages 388–389]

Choose the correct pronoun. Identify it as a *subject* or *object pronoun*.

6. Tell Mari and (I, me) about Troy.
7. (She, Her) and Ana read the *Iliad*.
8. The hero is (he, him).
9. (He, Him) and Hector fought.
10. The victors were (they, them).

## Possessive Pronouns

[pages 390–391]

Replace the underlined word or words in each sentence with the correct possessive pronoun or pronouns.

11. The city of Troy was <u>the Trojans'</u>.
12. The Greeks sent <u>the Greeks'</u> ships to Troy.
13. Odysseus helped defeat Troy with <u>Odysseus's</u> Trojan horse.
14. Everyone is writing <u>everyone's</u> report on the Trojan war.
15. Many presented <u>many students'</u> interpretation of the *Iliad*.

## Reflexive, Intensive, and Interrogative Pronouns

[pages 394–397]

Choose the correct pronoun. Indicate whether it is *reflexive, intensive,* or *interrogative.*

16. I bought (me, myself) a collection of myths.
17. The myths (they, themselves) are old.
18. (Who, Whom) is the sun god in Greek mythology?
19. (Who, Whom) does Atalanta marry?
20. The ancient Greeks (theirselves., themselves) had a tradition of oral storytelling.

## Writing for Review

Imagine you're touring Greece. Write a post card describing your first day there. Use as many kinds of pronouns as you can.

Joseph Stella, *The Brooklyn Bridge: Variation on an Old Theme*, 1939

## Grammar Workshop Exercise 3

### Using Comparative and Superlative Modifiers
The following sentences discuss Egyptian mummies and Tutankhamen's tomb. Write each sentence, correctly inserting the comparative or superlative form of the adverb or adjective in parentheses.

1. The contents of the Annex were in even (bad) disarray than the Antechamber.
2. The (early) mummies of all occurred naturally when people buried their dead in dry, sandy areas.
3. When they dried out quickly, the bodies lasted (long) than they would have lasted otherwise.
4. Drying out the body before burial meant that it would be (good) preserved than usual.
5. Wood, clay, and stone figures of servants were placed inside the tomb; but these figures were (small) than the dead person they were to serve.
6. The pyramids could not keep out tomb robbers; in fact, the pyramids attracted attention and made the graves even (little) secure than they were before.

## Grammar Workshop Exercise 4

**Proofreading**    The following passage is about Charles Simonds, whose sculpture *Untitled* appears on the next page. Rewrite the passage, correcting the errors in spelling, capitalization, punctuation, grammar, and usage. There are ten errors in all.

### *Charles Simonds*
[1]Charles Simonds created this here sculpture from clay. [2]He use only water, glue, and the simplest tools to form the clay into both landscape and architecture. [3]The color of the clay helps define and seperate different parts of this sculptures. [4]In many of his most simple works, the Color distinctions are very basic: red clay for landscape ➡

and gray clay for stone. [5]Simonds miniature dwellings demonstrate a interest in how people live and how their beliefs affect the structures they create. [6]Clay is the material Simonds has been comfortablest with since childhood. [7]While saveing money and increasing the variety of soil types and colors, Simonds enjoys the pleasure of recycling clays and sands from around the world.

[8]Simonds's sculptures convey a sense of history but they are his own archaeological interpretations. [9]They are not miniature reconstructions of actual buildings or sites.

**Charles Simonds, *Untitled,* 1982**

# Unit 12 Review

## Adjectives and Adverbs

### Adjectives

[pages 404–413]

Write each sentence. Use the correct adjective form given in parentheses. Underline the noun that each of those adjectives modifies.

1. At one time the Empire State Building was the (most tallest, tallest) building in the world.
2. The Statue of Liberty was a gift from the (french, French) people.
3. The shape of (the, an) Eiffel Tower is more unusual than the shape of the Leaning Tower of Pisa.
4. Which of the two stadiums is (more larger, larger)?
5. (That, Those) stadium has the (goodest, best) facilities in the world.

### Adverbs

[pages 414–421]

Write each sentence. Underline each adverb once and each intensifier twice. Then write whether the adverb describes an *action verb*, an *adverb*, or an *adjective*.

6. Architects work extremely carefully on their plans for buildings.
7. Groups of architects quite often collaborate on building plans.
8. They work toward the most successful plan they can produce.
9. A successful building meets the needs of its tenants most completely and most satisfactorily.
10. Especially ambitious architects work eagerly to create new and improved buildings.

### Avoiding Double Negatives

[pages 422–423]

Write each sentence. Use the word or words that correctly complete the sentence.

11. Hardly (any, no) country has more cathedrals than France has.
12. The world hadn't (never, ever) seen such majestic architecture.
13. Scarcely (no one, anyone) misses a visit to a church in Paris.
14. Tourists (can, can't) never forget the size of these magnificent cathedrals.
15. A tourist does not usually forget to carry (no, a) camera.

### Writing for Review

Imagine a city of the future. Describe what you think the architecture will look like. Be sure to include adjectives and adverbs in your writing. Check your description carefully, and be sure to correct any double negatives.

Artemisia Gentileschi, *Self-Portrait as the Allegory of Painting,* 1630

## 13.1 Prepositions and Prepositional Phrases

A **preposition** is a word that relates a noun or a pronoun to some other word in a sentence.

> The paint **on** the canvas will dry very slowly.

The word *on* in the sentence above is a preposition. It shows the relationship of the nouns *paint* and *canvas*.

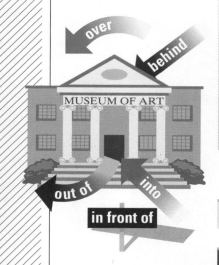

### Commonly Used Prepositions

| | | | | |
|---|---|---|---|---|
| about | before | during | off | to |
| above | behind | for | on | toward |
| across | below | from | onto | under |
| after | beneath | in | out | until |
| against | beside | inside | outside | up |
| along | between | into | over | upon |
| among | beyond | like | since | with |
| around | by | near | through | within |
| at | down | of | throughout | without |

A preposition can consist of more than one word.

> You can use acrylic paint **instead of** oils.

### Compound Prepositions

| | | | |
|---|---|---|---|
| according to | aside from | in front of | instead of |
| across from | because of | in place of | on account of |
| along with | far from | in spite of | on top of |

A **prepositional phrase** is a group of words that begins with a preposition and ends with a noun or pronoun, which is called the **object of the preposition.**

> Michelangelo was born **in a small town**.

**Identifying Prepositional Phrases and Objects of Prepositions**  Write each sentence, and underline each prepositional phrase. Draw a second line under the preposition, and circle the object of the preposition.

1. Some artists study Michelangelo's work for inspiration.
2. His work had a great influence on many other artists.
3. Artists see perfection in his paintings.
4. They also see it in his sculpture.
5. Architects study building designs by Michelangelo.
6. Most think him the embodiment of genius.
7. He painted the ceiling of the Sistine Chapel.
8. The chapel work was completed in three years.
9. His fellow artists honored him after this project.
10. Michelangelo was a man with many artistic talents.
11. He carved sculpture from marble.
12. His *David* is one of his best-known statues.
13. According to art historians, the *Pietà* in Rome is Michelangelo's only signed sculpture.
14. Among his other statues are *Victory* and *Cupid Kneeling*.
15. Michelangelo sometimes painted on wet plaster.
16. The artist designed a dome for Saint Peter's Church.
17. Michelangelo once worked with Leonardo da Vinci.
18. Michelangelo was also the author of many poems.
19. He is often considered the creator of the Renaissance.

**GRAMMAR HINT**

A preposition is always the first word in a prepositional phrase. The preposition is always followed by a noun or a pronoun object.

### Writing Link

Identify an artist whose work you like, and briefly describe the kind of art the artist creates and your reasons for liking it. Use prepositional phrases.

## 13.2   Pronouns as Objects of Prepositions

When a pronoun is the object of a preposition, remember to use an object pronoun and not a subject pronoun.

> Nick handed the easel to Martha. Nick handed the
>     easel to **her**.

In the example above, the object pronoun *her* replaces *Martha* as the object of the preposition *to*.

Sometimes a preposition will have a compound object consisting of a noun and pronoun. Remember to use an object pronoun in a compound object.

> I borrowed the palette from Nick and Martha. I borrowed the
>     palette from Nick and **her**.
> Lloyd painted with Ayisha and **me**.

Object pronouns are used in the sentences above. In the second sentence *Nick and her* is the compound object of the preposition *from*. In the third sentence *Ayisha and me* is the compound object of the preposition *with*.

If you are unsure about whether to use a subject pronoun or an object pronoun, try saying the sentence aloud with only the pronoun following the preposition.

> I borrowed the palette from **her**.
> Lloyd painted with **me**.

The subject pronoun *who* is never the object of a preposition; only the object pronoun *whom* can be an object.

> The artist of **whom** I spoke has a show at the Whitney Museum.
> To **whom** did you lend the turpentine?

**Using Pronouns After Prepositions**    Write each sentence, using the correct pronoun in parentheses. Be sure each pronoun you choose makes sense in the sentence.

1. A paper on Rembrandt has been assigned to Bernard and (she, her).
2. Rembrandt is an artist about (who, whom) many historians have written.
3. According to H. W. Janson and (them, they), Rembrandt's early work is highly realistic.
4. Bernard and Laticia showed some slides to Nina and (I, me).
5. Then we set a series of pictures in front of Bernard and (she, her).
6. We asked if they could tell the difference between the artist Caravaggio and (he, him).
7. Aside from Bernard, Laticia, and (us, we), no one recognized Rembrandt's work.
8. In the 1600s everyone in Amsterdam wanted his or her portrait painted by (him, he).
9. Rembrandt painted many portraits of his wife, his son, and (they, them).
10. It was a pointed out by Janson and (them, they) that Rembrandt's lighting is dramatic.
11. Rembrandt's self-portraits were described by Nina and (she, her).

### Writing Link

In a paragraph describe the kind of work you would create if you were an artist. Use pronouns as objects of prepositions in your writing.

## 13.3   Prepositional Phrases as Adjectives and Adverbs

An **adjective phrase** is a prepositional phrase that modifies, or describes, a noun or a pronoun.

The fabrics **from the Orient** were quite beautiful.

These ancient hangings are tapestries **from other lands.**

In the first sentence above, the prepositional phrase *from the Orient* describes the subject of the sentence, *fabrics*. In the second sentence the prepositional phrase *from other lands* describes the noun in the predicate, *tapestries*.

An **adverb phrase** is a prepositional phrase that modifies, or describes, a verb, an adjective, or another adverb.

| Adverb Phrases Modifying a Verb, an Adjective, and an Adverb | |
|---|---|
| **Describes a verb** | The women are weaving **on looms.** |
| **Describes an adjective** | That fabric looks great **on you.** |
| **Describes an adverb** | She weaves fabric well **for her age.** |

An adverb phrase tells *when, where,* or *how* an action takes place. The prepositional phrases in the chart below all modify the verb *work*.

| How Adverb Phrases Modify Verbs | |
|---|---|
| **When?** | Weavers work **during the day.** |
| **Where?** | They work **in shops.** |
| **How?** | They work **with care.** |

Adverb phrases can usually be moved to the beginning of the sentence.

**Identifying Adjective and Adverb Phrases**   Write each sentence. Underline each prepositional phrase, and write whether it is an *adjective phrase* or an *adverb phrase*.

1. Weavers around the world practice an ancient craft.
2. Early weavers worked with long strands of grass.
3. Old paintings from Egypt show that weaving had developed by 5000 B.C.
4. Tapestries with complex patterns hang in museums.
5. These tapestries often illustrate stories about great people.
6. The famous *Bayeux Tapestry* illustrates William the Conqueror's invasion of England.
7. Medieval weavers worked for kings and queens.
8. Hopi men traditionally wove clothing for the women.
9. Pueblo, Navaho, and Hopi women wore woven sashes during ceremonial dances.
10. Many people today have taken an interest in the craft.
11. They often may be found around the country diligently at work.
12. Contemporary weavers use a variety of materials in their work.
13. Young weavers usually begin with simple patterns.
14. Patterns from many nations teach the necessary skills.
15. Weavers may become famous for their designs.
16. A tapestry made at home may become valuable after a while.

### *Writing Link*

Describe one of your hobbies. Use as many adjective and adverb phrases as you can.

## 13.4 Conjunctions

A **coordinating conjunction** is a single word used to connect parts of a sentence, such as words or phrases. *And, but, or, for,* and *nor* are used as coordinating conjunctions.

| Using Coordinating Conjunctions | |
|---|---|
| **Compound Subject** | Ann **or** Flo studied art. |
| **Compound Predicate** | Georgia O'Keeffe studied art **and** taught it. |
| **Compound Object of a Preposition** | Art appeals to you **and** me. |
| **Compound Sentence** | Grandma Moses never went to art school, **but** her work is quite professional. |

*Yet* and *so* are not coordinating conjunctions, except when they are used with *and*.

To make a relationship between words or groups of words especially strong, use a correlative conjunction.

**Correlative conjunctions** are pairs of words used to connect words or phrases in a sentence. Correlative conjunctions include *both . . . and, either . . . or, neither . . . nor,* and *not only . . . but also.*

**Both** New York **and** Paris are major art centers.

When a compound subject is joined by *and,* it is a plural subject. The verb must agree with the plural subject.

When a compound subject is joined by *or* or *nor,* the verb must agree with the nearest part of the subject.

Jaime **and** Sue are artists.
**Neither** the twins **nor** Carla **is** a good painter.

**Identifying Conjunctions**   Underline each conjunction. Write whether it joins a *compound subject*, a *compound predicate*, a *compound object of a preposition*, or a *compound sentence.*

1. Mari mixed the paint, for she wanted various colors.
2. Nora rented a studio and painted there on weekends.
3. Both a painter and a sculptor need good lighting.
4. The painter took many lessons, but students now learn from her.
5. Yvonne will attend the high school of art and design.

## Exercise 5

**Making Compound Subjects and Verbs Agree**
Write each sentence, using the correct verb form. Underline each coordinating or correlative conjunction.

1. Both the sketch and the painting (is, are) beautiful.
2. The painters or the sculptor (enter, enters) the exhibition.
3. Neither the students nor their teacher (attends, attend) the show.
4. The judge and the artist (have, has) different opinions.
5. Either a famous painter or some critics (is, are) judging the show.
6. Neither this canvas nor the frame (look, looks) sturdy.
7. Watercolors or oils (provides, provide) rich tones.

### GRAMMAR HINT

Coordinating conjunctions are "glue" words that link two or more elements of the same kind.

### Writing Link

Describe a special exhibition or event held at your school. Note all of the conjunctions you use.

Awesome!

Great!

Gee!

Wow!

Sometimes people express very strong feelings in a short exclamation that may not be a complete sentence. These exclamations are called interjections.

An **interjection** is a word or group of words that expresses strong feeling. It has no grammatical connection to any other words in the sentence.

Any part of speech can be used as an interjection. These are some of the more common interjections.

| Common Interjections | | | |
|---|---|---|---|
| aha | good grief | oh | well |
| alas | ha | oh, no | what |
| awesome | hey | oops | whoops |
| come on | hooray | ouch | wow |
| gee | look | phew | yes |

An interjection that expresses a very strong feeling may stand alone, either before or after a sentence. Such interjections are followed by an exclamation mark.

**Oh, no!** The art museum is closed today.

When an interjection expresses a milder feeling, it appears as part of the sentence. It is separated from the rest of the sentence with a comma.

**Oh, well,** I'll just have to go tomorrow.

Interjections should be used sparingly. Overusing them will spoil their effectiveness.

**Identifying Interjections**  Write the sentences below. Underline each interjection.

1. Oh, I am going to be late for my painting class.
2. My! I have never seen anyone who could sketch that fast.
3. It certainly is hard work to stretch this canvas tight. Phew!
4. We may be able to get an interview with a famous artist. Hooray!
5. Golly, I hope she will autograph one of her prints for me.
6. Wow! The colors in that painting hurt my eyes.
7. Hey! Where are you going?
8. Yes! That one's definitely my favorite.
9. Come on, I want to show you a painting by Salvador Dali.
10. Have you ever seen such images? Look!
11. That clock looks as though it melted. Awesome!
12. No way! I prefer this painting by Chagall.
13. Oops, those people seem to be floating.
14. Well, don't you think these artists make Picasso look staid?
15. Gee, I don't know.
16. Really! He seems so old-fashioned by comparison.
17. I would like to see a few more paintings; however, it is time to leave, alas.

## Writing Link

Think of an action-filled movie you have seen recently, and describe the action that takes place. Write a list of interjections you could use.

## 13.6    Finding All the Parts of Speech

Artist unknown, China, *Woman Painting*, 18th c.

Each word in a sentence performs a particular job. Each word can be put into a particular category called a **part of speech.** The part of speech of a word depends on the job that the word performs in the sentence. The same word may be classified as one part of speech in one sentence and as a different part of speech in another.

You have learned about all eight parts of speech. They include *nouns, pronouns, verbs, adjectives, adverbs, prepositions, conjunctions,* and *interjections.* The following sentence contains at least one example of each part of speech.

> Gee, she is artistic and paints well with watercolors.

| Parts of Speech | | |
|---|---|---|
| **Word** | **Part of Speech** | **Function** |
| **Gee** | Interjection | Expresses strong feeling |
| **she** | Pronoun | Takes the place of a noun |
| **is** | Linking verb | Links *she* with *artistic* |
| **artistic** | Adjective | Describes the subject *she* |
| **and** | Conjunction | Joins two parts of compound predicate |
| **paints** | Action verb | Names an action |
| **well** | Adverb | Describes the verb *paints* |
| **with** | Preposition | Relates the words *paints* and *watercolors* |
| **watercolors** | Noun | Object of the preposition *with* |

**Identifying Parts of Speech**    Write each underlined word and its part of speech.

1. I often sculpt with colored clays.
2. Sometimes the clay dries too quickly.
3. Wow! That statue is enormous.
4. Does Aretha sculpt with clay or stone?
5. He does not sculpt realistic heads.

**Using Parts of Speech**    Complete each sentence below by supplying a word whose part of speech is indicated in parentheses. Be sure your finished sentences make sense.

1. Hector, Marisol, and (proper noun) visited a museum of art (preposition) New York City.
2. (Pronoun) saw a great many (common noun).
3. Hector liked the Impressionist paintings (adverb).
4. (Pronoun) thought Claude Monet's paintings were (adjective).
5. Marisol (action verb) two Americans: Mary Cassatt (conjunction) Winslow Homer.
6. (Adverb) they (action verb) the Post-Impressionists.
7. Hector loved (correlative conjunction) van Gogh (correlative conjunction) Rousseau.
8. "(Interjection)!" said Marisol. "I think we've (action verb) too much art."

### Writing Link

Describe a visit to an art museum. Use all of the parts of speech in your description.

# *Grammar* Workshop

## Prepositions, Conjunctions, and Interjections

This Chinese-American folk tale tells the story of a painted horse that comes to life. The passage has been annotated to show some of the parts of speech covered in this unit.

**Literature Model**

### *from* THE MAGICAL HORSE

*by Laurence Yep*

Preposition

    As the boy sat with his body aching from the hard work and eating his cold rice, he gazed up at the painting. His father had caught the horse as if it were sus-

Prepositional phrase (adverb phrase)

pended upon one hoof . And as he watched, the horse's sides seemed to heave in the moonlight—as if it were breathing in the incense. On a whim, Sunny set out feed for his painted horse just as he did for the other animals.

    He slept among the beasts for warmth, so he was not surprised when he felt an animal's warm breath blow

Pronoun as subject of the preposition *on*

on him . When a nose nudged him, he sat up irritated, intending to shove the creature away, but his hand paused in the air.

Prepositional phrase (adjective phrase)

    By the light of the moon , he saw a silvery horse standing over him. He looked over at the wall where the painting had been

Coordinating conjunction

and saw that the canvas was empty. The next thing he knew, he was on the back of the horse, his hands clinging to the flying mane, the horse's hooves booming rhythmically along a road that gleamed like a silver ribbon winding up into the sky.

## Grammar Workshop Exercise 1

**Using Prepositions** The following sentences are based on the passage from "The Magical Horse." Rewrite each sentence, inserting the correct prepositional phrase in parentheses.

1. The horse (on the canvas, with the canvas) seemed to be breathing.
2. Sunny set out food (for he, for him).
3. The boy lay down and slept (among the animals, between the animals).
4. When he woke up, the empty canvas stood (in the wall, against the wall).
5. The horse and the boy galloped (down the road, through the road).

## Grammar Workshop Exercise 2

**Using Conjunctions** Rewrite each sentence, inserting the most appropriate conjunction (word or word pair) in the blank or blanks provided.

SAMPLE     The father wanted to create a perfect horse, _____ _____ he painted without resting.

ANSWER     The father wanted to create a perfect horse, and so he painted without resting.

1. When the painting was finished, _____ Sunny _____ his father admired the magnificent horse.
2. _____ Sunny _____ his father knew that the horse would come to life.
3. The father was old _____ tired from hard work.
4. The painter died, _____ his spirit entered into the horse in the painting.
5. Sunny _____ _____ buried his father, _____ _____ earned the money for the funeral.

*Prepositions, Conjunctions, and Interjections*   **443**

## Grammar Workshop Exercise 3

**Using Interjections**   The following sentences are based on passages in "The Magical Horse" that do not appear in this textbook. Rewrite each sentence, inserting an appropriate interjection in the blank. More than one answer may be possible.

SAMPLE     "_____!" cried Sunny when he rode the horse for the first time.

ANSWER     "Hooray!" cried Sunny when he rode the horse for the first time.

1. Sunny woke up the next morning and found that the feed for the painted horse was gone. "_____!" exclaimed the boy. "It wasn't a dream."
2. Every night Sunny called out "_____! Let's go for a ride."
3. One evening the boy said, "_____, I'd like to see the king's palace."
4. "_____!" shouted the prince to his servant as the horse sped past the palace.
5. _____, the prince decided then and there to take the horse away from Sunny.

## Grammar Workshop Exercise 4

**Proofreading**   The following passage is about artist Helen Oji, whose work appears on the next page. Rewrite the passage, correcting the errors in spelling, capitalization, punctuation, grammar, and usage. There are ten errors in all.

### Helen Oji

[1]Helen Oji paint subjects found in nature. [2]The artist has painted a series of volcanoes, a group of fish swimming in swiftly moving water and a brightly colored bird in flight. [3]Oji expresses her subject matter in a explosive style charactarized by movement and ➡

intense energy.

⁴In paintings such as *H.P.*, the artist uses drammatic colors—fiery reds and flashes of white, to help achieve this energy. ⁵In addition, the works bold, thick brush strokes help rise the picture from the canvas. ⁶Like the magical horse in Laurence Yep's folk tail, the horse in the painting looks as if it is about to leap off the canvas

**Helen Oji, *H.P.*, 1986**

# Prepositions, Conjunctions, and Interjections

## Prepositions and Prepositional Phrases

[pages 430–431]

Underline each prepositional phrase, and write whether it is an adverb phrase or an adjective phrase. Circle the preposition, and draw a second line under the object of the preposition.

1. Georgia O'Keeffe was born in Wisconsin.
2. She showed talent at an early age.
3. O'Keeffe often painted pictures of local scenery.
4. She has served as a role model for my friends and me.
5. O'Keeffe worked well into her old age.

## Conjunctions

[pages 436–437]

Write each sentence. Then underline each conjunction. Write whether it joins a *compound subject, compound predicate, compound object of a preposition,* or *compound sentence.*

6. Most artists gravitate to a specific medium, but others are versatile.
7. Some artists have talents for both painting and sculpture.
8. Charcoal or pastels are the preferred materials of other artists.
9. Many painters and sculptors either create plans or draw sketches for large works.
10. Daniel would like to work as an artist and teach in a local university.

## Interjections; Parts of Speech

[pages 438–441]

Identify the part of speech of each underlined word.

11. <u>Fiddlesticks</u>, this <u>clay</u> is drying too quickly.
12. Oh, <u>you</u> have so much artistic talent.
13. <u>Goodness</u>! It <u>takes</u> such a long time to make a statue.
14. These <u>two</u> colors <u>simply</u> do not go well together.
15. What an exciting day this <u>is</u> for me.

## Writing for Review

Imagine that you are interviewing a well-known artist. Make a list of questions you would ask. Note the different parts of speech you have used.

# Clauses and Complex Sentences

Fernand Léger, Sketch for *The Railway Crossing*, 1919

## 14.1    Sentences and Clauses

A **sentence** is a group of words that expresses a complete thought.

A **simple sentence** has one complete subject and one complete predicate.

The **complete subject** names whom or what the sentence is about. The **complete predicate** tells what the subject does or has. Sometimes it tells what the subject is or is like.

| Complete Subject | Complete Predicate |
|---|---|
| Some people | travel. |
| Neither cars nor jets | are completely safe. |
| Trains and buses | carry passengers and transport luggage. |
| Freight trains | transport products to various cities. |

A **compound sentence** is a sentence that contains two or more simple sentences. Each simple sentence is called a main clause.

A **main clause** has a subject and a predicate and can stand alone as a sentence.

In the compound sentences below, each main clause is in black; the connecting elements are highlighted in red.

Millions of people live in cities, **but** many others reside in the suburbs.
Most people travel to work, **and** many of them use public transportation.
Commuters take trains, buses, and cars; some even fly.
Helicopters are often used to monitor traffic conditions, **but** computers can more accurately predict traveling time.

A comma precedes the conjunction in a compound sentence. A semicolon joins the two main clauses if they are not joined by a conjunction.

## Exercise 1

### Identifying Simple and Compound Sentences

Identify each sentence as *simple* or *compound*.

1. The growth of railroads changed the lives of many Americans.
2. Workers moved out of crowded cities, and commuters used trains.
3. Family members moved across the country, but trains reunited them.
4. Soon America became a nation of travelers.
5. Some travel to work; others travel for pleasure.
6. Today airplanes provide greater ease of travel.

## Exercise 2

### Punctuating Simple and Compound Sentences

Write each sentence, and underline each main clause. Add a comma or a semicolon as needed.

1. About four million miles of roadways exist in the United States and problems with them do arise.
2. Accidents cause delays poor road conditions often result in traffic jams.
3. Radio listeners hear traffic reports and can avoid trouble spots.
4. Drivers take detours around these trouble spots.
5. Detours are often long and they can be hazardous.
6. Delays are unpleasant but safety comes first.
7. Travel is a way of life for many people.

### *Writing Link*

In a letter to a friend, write about a trip you would like to take. Use both simple and compound sentences.

## 14.2    Complex Sentences

A **main clause** has a subject and a predicate and can stand alone as a sentence.

Sometimes sentences have more than one clause, and only one of the clauses is a main clause. The other clause is a subordinate clause.

A **subordinate clause** is a group of words that has a subject and a predicate but does not express a complete thought and cannot stand alone as a sentence. It is always combined with a main clause.

A sentence with a main clause and a subordinate clause is a complex sentence. In each complex sentence below, the main clause is in light type, and the subordinate clause is in dark type.

> **When the sun set,** the caravans stopped for the night.
> The dromedary has one hump, **which stores fat.**
> Most people know **that camels are stubborn.**

A **complex sentence** is a sentence that has one main clause and one or more subordinate clauses.

Subordinate clauses can function in three ways: as adjectives, as adverbs, or as nouns. In the examples above, the first sentence has an adverb clause, the second has an adjective clause, and the third has a noun clause. Such clauses can be used in the same ways that adjectives, adverbs, and nouns are used.

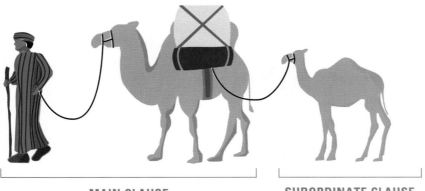

The mother camel carried the load, **while the baby camel walked behind**

MAIN CLAUSE          SUBORDINATE CLAUSE

**Identifying Complex Sentences** Write each sentence, and underline the main clause. Then identify each sentence as *complex* or *not complex.*

1. Camels are useful because they cross the desert easily.
2. Camels provide necessary transportation in the desert.
3. The Bactrian camel is the camel that has two humps.
4. Camels have double eyelashes, which protect their eyes from blowing sand.
5. Camels are stubborn animals, but they are also hard workers.
6. The camels usually used for riding are dromedaries, which have only one hump.
7. The Bactrian camel has two humps and is solidly built.
8. Camels survive desert life because they can live with little water.
9. People have found that camels can survive sandstorms.
10. Until the sun sets, camels maintain a 105-degree temperature.
11. We have learned that the camel's temperature drops to 93 degrees at night.
12. For short periods both dromedaries and Bactrian camels can exist on fat from their humps.

### *Writing Link*

Imagine that you are traveling by camel in the desert. In a paragraph that includes some complex sentences, describe your trip.

## 14.3　Adjective Clauses

Sometimes a subordinate clause acts an adjective.

Ed's bicycle, **which he bought on sale,** is a ten-speed.

The price **that he paid** was incredibly low.

Each subordinate clause in dark type in these sentences is an adjective clause. An adjective clause adds information about a noun or pronoun in the main clause.

An **adjective clause** is a subordinate clause that modifies, or describes, a noun or pronoun in the main clause of a complex sentence.

An adjective clause is usually introduced by a relative pronoun. Relative pronouns signal that a clause is a subordinate clause and cannot stand alone.

| Relative Pronouns | | | |
|---|---|---|---|
| that | who | whose | what |
| which | whom | whoever | |

An adjective clause can also begin with *where* or *when*.

Allene likes trails **where she can see flowers.**

A relative pronoun that begins an adjective clause can be the subject of the clause.

Allene bought the ten-speed **that is the most popular.**
She is a person **who truly loves bicycling.**

In the first sentence above, *that* is the subject of the adjective clause. In the second sentence *who* is the subject of the adjective clause.

**Identifying Adjective Clauses**   Write each sentence. Underline each adjective clause once and each relative pronoun twice. Circle the noun that each adjective clause modifies.

1. Most bicyclists who ride in cities follow safety rules.
2. Reckless bicyclists ignore the rules that others obey.
3. Moira has a new helmet, which she wears for protection.
4. People who ride bicycles often use them for pleasure or sport.
5. Bicycle racing, which is very popular today, began in the last century.
6. There are many people whose main interest is bicycling.
7. Some amateurs who practice a great deal become professionals.
8. Cautious cyclists proceed carefully through crosswalks that are crowded.
9. Many messenger services that depend upon speed use cyclists.
10. Some people who live in large cities commute by bicycle.
11. Certain bicycles that people ride can be folded and taken indoors.
12. People who ride bicycles regularly get excellent exercise.

**GRAMMAR HINT**

An adjective clause always follows the noun it modifies. It should not be moved far from that noun.

## Writing Link

Imagine that you're riding your bike through a city. List the laws that you must obey, and explain why. Use several adjective clauses in your writing.

## 14.4   Adverb Clauses

Sometimes a subordinate clause is an adverb clause. It may add information about the verb in the main clause. An adverb clause tells *how, when, where, why,* or *under what conditions* the action occurs.

> **Before Julia bought a bicycle,** she compared models.
>
> She likes ten-speeds **because they are versatile.**

Julia crossed the finish line . . .

before the other bicyclists arrived.

In the first sentence above, the adverb clause *Before Julia bought a bicycle* modifies the verb *compared.* The adverb clause tells when Julia compared bicycles. In the second sentence the adverb clause *because they are versatile* modifies the verb *likes.* The adverb clause tells *why* she likes ten-speeds.

An **adverb clause** is a subordinate clause that often modifies, or describes, the verb in the main clause of a complex sentence.

An adverb clause is introduced by a subordinating conjunction. Subordinating conjunctions signal that a clause is a subordinate clause and cannot stand alone. Some common subordinating conjunctions are listed below.

| Subordinating Conjunctions | | | |
| --- | --- | --- | --- |
| after | before | though | whenever |
| although | if | unless | where |
| as | since | until | whereas |
| because | than | when | wherever |

You usually do not use a comma before an adverb clause that comes at the end of a sentence. When an adverb clause introduces a sentence, however, you do use a comma after the adverb clause.

**Identifying Adverb Clauses**  Write each sentence.
Underline each adverb clause once and each
subordinating conjunction twice. Circle the verb
that each adverb clause modifies.

1. When gasoline prices rose, many people used
   bicycles.
2. Bicyclists behave dangerously when they speed.
3. At crosswalks cautious cyclists reduce speed before
   they proceed.
4. At stoplights cyclists should proceed after the light
   has turned green.
5. Before automobiles were available, some people
   rode bicycles.
6. Travelers covered miles easily when they used this
   simple vehicle.
7. Professional bicyclists ride wherever they find a good
   area.
8. After they finish work, many people commute by
   bicycle to their homes.
9. Many messengers use bicycles when they make local
   deliveries.
10. These messengers often face heavy traffic while they
    are working.
11. Because they often carry heavy bags, messengers
    must ride cautiously.
12. Today you will see cycling messengers whenever you
    visit a large city.

**GRAMMAR HINT**

Most adverb
clauses modify the
verb in the main
clause. They can
usually be placed
before or after the
main clause.

### Writing Link

Using some adverb clauses, write a paragraph describing the bicycle you would like to own.

# Grammar Workshop

## Clauses and Complex Sentences

The following passage is taken from *The Pearl,* a novel by John Steinbeck. This celebrated American author won the Pulitzer Prize in 1940 for *The Grapes of Wrath.* In 1962 Steinbeck won the Nobel Prize for literature. Set on the coast of the Gulf of Mexico, the tale is constructed around a young fisherman named Kino who discovers an extraordinary pearl. In this passage Kino and his wife, Juana, are preparing to paddle Kino's canoe out to the oyster beds. The passage has been annotated to show some of the kinds of clauses and sentences covered in this unit.

### Literature Model

#### *from* THE PEARL

#### *by John Steinbeck*

Kino and Juana came slowly down to the beach and to Kino's canoe, which was the one thing of value he owned in the world. It was very old. Kino's grandfather had brought it from Nayarit, and he had given it to Kino's father, and so it had come to Kino . It was at once property and source of food, for a man with a boat can guarantee a woman that she will eat something. It is the bulwark against starvation. And every year Kino refinished his canoe with the hard shell-like plaster by the secret method that had also come to him from his father . Now he came to the canoe and touched the bow tenderly as he always did. He laid his diving rock and his basket and the two ropes in the sand by the canoe. And he folded his blanket and laid it in the bow.

Compound sentence — Kino's grandfather had brought it from Nayarit, and he had given it to Kino's father, and so it had come to Kino

Noun clause — that she will eat something

Complex sentence — And every year Kino refinished his canoe with the hard shell-like plaster by the secret method that had also come to him from his father

Adverb clause — as he always did

Simple sentence — And he folded his blanket and laid it in the bow

**Identifying Sentences and Clauses**   Write each sentence, and identify it as *compound* or *complex*. If it is complex, underline the subordinate clause.

SAMPLE   Steinbeck's story *The Pearl* is about a man and woman who are very poor.

ANSWER   Steinbeck's story *The Pearl* is about a man and woman <u>who are very poor</u>. (complex)

1. The canoe is the most valuable thing that Kino owns.
2. The canoe was very old, and it had belonged to Kino's father and grandfather.
3. Kino touched the canoe tenderly whenever he came down to the beach.
4. The boat was a special kind of property that could ensure a person a source of food.
5. Kino refinished his boat every year; he wanted to keep it in good condition.

**Identifying Clauses**   Write each sentence. Underline each subordinate clause once and the word that the clause modifies twice. Then write whether the clause acts as an *adjective* or *adverb*.

SAMPLE   A good canoe is very important to a simple man who fishes for a living.

ANSWER   A good canoe is very important to a simple <u>man</u> <u>who fishes for a living</u>. (adjective)

1. Early canoes were made from tree trunks, which dwellers in the Caribbean islands hollowed out.
2. The North American peoples also used canoes, which they made from birchbark and wooden frames.
3. Birchbark canoes provided excellent transportation because they were light and relatively fast. ➡

4. When they explored parts of North America, Marquette and Joliet traveled in birchbark canoes.
5. Today's canoes, which are used for recreation, are made from aluminum, canvas, fiberglass, and wood.

## Grammar Workshop Exercise 3

**Writing Complex Sentences**   Write each sentence below, using the correct relative pronoun or subordinating conjunction in parentheses.

1. John Steinbeck, (who, which) wrote *The Pearl*, has written many novels.
2. Steinbeck was born and raised in southern California, (whatever, where) many of his stories take place.
3. Steinbeck worked at a series of temporary jobs (while, as if) he attended Stanford University.
4. The characters in Steinbeck's novels were based on people (whom, which) he knew and respected.

## Grammar Workshop Exercise 4

**Proofreading**   The following passage is about the artist Paul Sierra, whose painting *A Place in Time* appears on the next page. Rewrite the passage, correcting the errors in spelling, capitalization, punctuation, grammar, and usage. There are ten errors in all.

### *Paul Sierra*

[1]Born in Cuba in 1944, Paul Sierra was expected to enter a profession. [2]Although he receives little encouragement he spent hours drawing in notebooks and reading books on painting. [3]When he was sixteen, Sierra moved to the United States, were he lived first in miami and then in Chicago. [4]The only formal art training that Sierra recieved was three years at the Art Institute Of ➡

Chicago, where he enrolled in 1963. ⁵today Sierra worked as creative director of a small advertising agency. ⁶He feels that his job allow him the freedom to paint for himself rather than for the expectation of others. ⁷He says, I only hope to live long enough to make a good painting."

**Paul Sierra, *A Place in Time,* 1989**

# Clauses and Complex Sentences

## Sentences and Clauses

[pages 448–449]

Write each sentence. Write whether it is *simple* or *compound*. If it is a compound sentence, underline each main clause.

1. Ancient hunters dragged their loads on crude sleds.
2. Oxen pulled the heavy sleds.
3. Some loads were manageable; heavy loads proved more difficult.
4. Eventually the concept of the wheel emerged, and wheels were used for transportation.
5. Did people originally attach only two wheels to sleds and carts?

## Complex Sentences

[pages 450–451]

Write each sentence. Underline each main clause once and each subordinate clause twice.

6. Wherever canals link oceans, ships sail from country to country.
7. Tugboats pull some vessels through canals because the vessels are especially large.
8. Large ships sail quickly when a canal has a lock system.
9. The canal lock behind the ship closes after the ship is in the channel.
10. When the water flows out into the ocean, the ship leaves the canal.

## Adjective, Adverb, and Noun Clauses

[pages 452–457]

Write each sentence. Underline each subordinate clause, and write whether it is an *adjective clause,* an *adverb clause,* or a *noun clause.*

11. The automobile, which is popular today, developed through a series of inventions.
12. When the first steam-driven wagon was invented in the eighteenth century, the history of the automobile began.
13. This vehicle had an engine that rested on a single wheel.
14. Whoever designed the vehicle created it for hauling weapons.
15. The first automobile traveled at three miles per hour as it cruised through the streets of Paris.

## Writing for Review

Imagine that you are taking a cross-country bus ride. Write a post card to a friend, describing a typical day on the trip. Use at least one of each kind of subordinate clause: adjective, adverb, and noun.

Frank Romero, *Still Life with Red Car*, 1986

The **soaring**
biplane

flew over
the clouds.

## 15.1    Participles and Participial Phrases

A present participle is formed by adding *-ing* to a verb. A past participle is usually formed by adding *-ed* to a verb.

A participle can function as the main verb in a verb phrase or as an adjective to modify nouns or pronouns.

> The biplane was **soaring.**
> The flight had **astounded** skeptics.
> The **soaring** biplane flew 120 feet.

In the first sentence above, the present participle *soaring* is the main verb, and *was* is the helping verb. In the second sentence the past participle *astounded* is the main verb, and *had* is the helping verb. In the third sentence the present participle *soaring* is used as an adjective to describe the noun *biplane*.

Sometimes a participle that is used as an adjective is part of a phrase called a participial phrase.

> **Sailing across the dunes,** the *Flyer* made history.

A **participial phrase** is a group of words that includes a participle and other words that complete its meaning.

A participial phrase that begins a sentence is always set off with a comma. Participial phrases in other places may or may not need commas. If the phrase is necessary to identify the modified word, it should not be set off with commas. If the phrase simply gives additional information about the modified word, it should be set off with commas.

> The biplane **displayed here** is a model of the *Flyer.*
> The model, **shaped with care,** attracts many visitors.

A participial phrase can appear before or after the word it describes. Place the phrase as close as possible to the modified word; otherwise, the meaning of the sentence may be unclear.

## Exercise 1

**Identifying Participles**   Write each sentence. Underline each participle, and write whether it is *part of a verb phrase* or is used as an *adjective.*

1. People have considered the flying Wright brothers the first pilots.
2. Otto Lilienthal did pioneering work.
3. In the 1890s he had experimented with gliders.
4. The Wrights had learned of his work.
5. Soon they were experimenting in North Carolina.
6. In 1903 they built an advanced model.

## Exercise 2

**Identifying Participial Phrases**   Underline each participial phrase. Then draw two lines under the word that the phrase describes. Add commas as needed.

1. Witnessed by only a few the first successful flight gained little recognition for the Wright brothers.
2. The brothers, however, were inventors committed to their work.
3. Later flights lasting up to five minutes each attracted attention.
4. Working hard the Wrights built a wooden biplane.
5. By 1908 the Wright brothers had signed a government contract financing their invention.
6. Flown by bold pilots airplanes thrill the public.

### Writing Link

Imagine that you are a newspaper reporter covering the Wright brothers' first flight. Write your story. Use some participial phrases.

## 15.2 Gerunds and Gerund Phrases

The previous lesson explains that the present participle may be used as an adjective. A verb form ending in *-ing* may also serve as a noun, in which case it is called a *gerund*.

A **gerund** is a verb form that ends in *-ing* and is used as a noun.

Sometimes a gerund functions as the subject of the sentence.

**Moving** involves a lot of work.

At other times a gerund functions as the direct object of a verb. Remember, a direct object of a verb receives the action of the verb. It answers the question *whom?* or *what?* after an action verb.

People enjoy **traveling.**

Do not confuse gerunds with other verb forms that end in *-ing.* You can tell them apart by distinguishing their functions in a sentence. A verb form ending in *-ing* may be the main verb in a verb phrase. It may be used as an adjective to describe a noun or pronoun. It also may function as a noun. Then it is called a gerund.

Megan has been **packing.** [main verb in a verb phrase]
She will take an **exciting** trip. [participle used as adjective]
**Traveling** will be fast. [gerund]

In some sentences a gerund is part of a gerund phrase.

A **gerund phrase** is a group of words that includes a gerund and other words that complete its meaning.

Many jobs require **long-distance traveling.**
**Choosing the best mode of travel** takes some consideration.

## Exercise 3

**Identifying Verbals**   Write each sentence. Then write whether the underlined word is the *main verb in a verb phrase*, a *participle used as an adjective*, or a *gerund*.

1. Commerce requires <u>moving</u> goods between places.
2. People had been <u>transporting</u> objects long before the invention of the wheel.
3. <u>Trading</u> presented problems.
4. Ancient merchants depended on animal transportation for their <u>growing</u> businesses.
5. People began <u>using</u> litters for heavy packages.

## Exercise 4

**Identifying Gerunds**   Underline each gerund or gerund phrase. Write whether it is used as a *subject* or a *direct object*.

1. Hauling packages on these litters simplified work.
2. Workers started using logs as rollers for litters.
3. Eventually people began floating crude rafts of logs.
4. Transporting various goods on these vehicles created new problems.
5. Steering these rafts was difficult.
6. Raft builders liked experimenting with the design.
7. Adding a wall of logs along each edge of the raft formed a boat.
8. Shipping goods became easier with the rafts.

### *Writing Link*

Imagine a new method of transportation, and explain it in a letter to a friend. Identify any gerunds that you use in your letter.

# Grammar Workshop

## Verbals

*Amelia Earhart: Flight Around the World* by Peggy Mann is a biography of one of the world's most famous aviators. One of Earhart's greatest achievements occurred in 1932, when she became the first woman to successfully complete a solo flight across the Atlantic Ocean. The following excerpt from the book describes the early part of that historic flight. The passage has been annotated to show some of the types of verbals covered in this unit.

### Literature Model

#### from AMELIA EARHART:
#### FLIGHT AROUND THE WORLD
##### by Peggy Mann

At first the flight seemed a dream coming true. The view was vast and lovely. As she looked about, she felt she was gulping beauty. The clouds were marvelous shapes in white, some trailing shimmering veils. In the distance the highest peaks of the fog mountains were tinted pink with the **setting** sun. *[Present participle]*

Gradually she flew into darkness, star-flecked, with moonlight **shimmering through the endless skies**. *[Participial phrase]*

Then, suddenly, the dream turned into nightmare. Something happened that had never occurred in all her twelve years of **flying**. The dials of the altimeter started **to spin crazily**. She could no longer tell how high she was above the sea. And she was flying through thick darkness—flying into a storm. *[Gerund / Infinitive phrase]*

**Using Participles**   Rewrite each sentence, inserting the participle or participial phrase in parentheses.

SAMPLE   Amelia Earhart watched the earth fade from view. (gazing down from the cockpit)

ANSWER   Gazing down from the cockpit, Amelia Earhart watched the earth fade from view.

1. She was awestruck by the beauty. (breathtaking)
2. The stars danced in the night sky. (twinkling)
3. Clouds glowed warmly in the sunset. (pink-tinted)
4. Earhart encountered some rough weather. (traveling across the Atlantic)
5. The pilot peered into the darkness. (flying through the storm)

**Using Gerunds**   Write a sentence that answers each question. Use the word or words in parentheses in your answer.

SAMPLE   What is Amelia Earhart best known for? (pioneering aviation for women)

ANSWER   Amelia Earhart is best known for pioneering aviation for women.

1. What filled Earhart with wonder when she was a young girl? (seeing an airplane in the sky)
2. What was Earhart's passion? (flying)
3. By what means did Earhart first achieve fame? (flying across the Atlantic as a passenger in 1928)
4. What action gained Earhart renewed respect in 1935? (becoming the first person to successfully fly from Hawaii to California)

**Using Infinitives** Write a sentence that answers each question, using the word or words in parentheses.

1. What did Amelia Earhart set out to do in 1937? (to fly around the world)
2. Why did Fred Noonan accompany Earhart on the flight? (to serve as her navigator)
3. What did the pair manage to do before they ran into trouble? (to complete two thirds of their journey)
4. What have searchers been unable to do ever since? (to find a trace of Earhart)

**Proofreading** The following passage is about Yvonne Jacquette, whose painting appears on the next page. Rewrite the passage, correcting the errors in spelling, capitalization, punctuation, grammar, and usage. There are ten errors in all.

### Yvonne Jacquette

[1]Born in 1934 in Pittsburgh, Pennsylvania Yvonne Jacquette began her artistic career by painting landscapes. [2]In time, however, she became facsinated with painting these scenes as seen from a distance. [3]Eventualy the artist began painting country and city landscapes from the vantage point of a single-engine plane? [4]While flying high above the earth, Jacquette selects a particuliar view and makes sketches of them. [5]She uses these drawings two help her create her paintings. [6]In *Clouds over Farmland, Forked Tree Masses* Jacquette has painted the view overlooking a stretch of rural landscape. [7]With it's images of cloud shapes, the painting could illustrate what Amelia Earhart sees on her solo flight across the Atlantic ocean.

**Yvonne Jacquette, *Clouds over Farmland, Forked Tree Masses,* 1988**

# Unit 15 Review

## Verbals

### Participles and Participial Phrases

[pages 464–465]

Write each sentence. Then underline each participle or participial phrase, and write whether it is used as an *adjective* or as *part of a verb phrase*.

1. Exciting stories of pioneer days are still popular.
2. People were traveling across the continent in Conestoga wagons.
3. The Conestoga wagon, or covered wagon, was a home on wheels.
4. Living in the wagons for long periods, pioneers became exhausted.
5. The Conestoga wagon, plodding across the plains, covered ground slowly.

### Gerunds and Gerund Phrases

[pages 466–467]

Write each sentence. Then underline each gerund phrase, and write whether it is used as the *subject* or the *direct object* in the sentence.

6. Pulling busloads of people was difficult for the horses.
7. New York City began installing a system for streetcars.

8. Operating streetcars as a means of transportation did not occur in Britain until 1860.
9. People in San Francisco tried moving the cars by a cable beneath the street.
10. Riding streetcars is a good way to get around San Francisco.

### Infinitives and Infinitive Phrases

[pages 468–469]

Write each sentence. Then underline each infinitive or infinitive phrase, and write whether it is used as the *subject* or the *direct object* in the sentence.

11. To arrive at their destinations quickly is important to passengers.
12. Jet aircraft promised to provide a fast ride for them.
13. Business people like to fly from city to city in one day.
14. The noise and pollution of early jets started to offend the public.
15. To improve planes became a goal of manufacturers.

### Writing for Review

Write a paragraph describing a trip on your favorite mode of transporation. Try to use participial phrases, gerund phrases, and infinitive phrases.

René Magritte, *Victory*, 1939

## 16.1  Making Subjects and Verbs Agree

A subject and its verb are the basic parts of a sentence. A singular noun subject calls for a singular form of the verb. A plural noun subject calls for a plural form of the verb. The subject and its verb are said to agree in number. Read the sentences below. You can see that the subjects and verbs agree in number.

Notice that in the present tense the singular form of the verb usually ends in *-s* or *-es*.

A **rose blooms.**

SINGULAR
SUBJECT

SINGULAR
VERB

| Subject and Verb Agreement | |
|---|---|
| **Singular** | **Plural** |
| A **poet explores** beauty. | **Poets explore** beauty. |
| The **theme touches** readers. | The **themes touch** readers. |
| **Robert Frost writes** about farms. | **Frost and Robinson write** about farms. |

Verbs and subject pronouns must also agree. Look at the chart below, and notice how the verb changes. In the present tense the *-s* ending is used with the subject pronouns *it, he,* and *she.*

The **roses bloom.**

PLURAL
SUBJECT

PLURAL
VERB

| Subject Pronoun and Verb Agreement | |
|---|---|
| **Singular** | **Plural** |
| I **read.** | We **read.** |
| You **read.** | You **read.** |
| He, she, it **reads.** | They **read.** |

The irregular verbs *be, do,* and *have* can be main verbs or helping verbs. They must agree with the subject, regardless of whether they are main verbs or helping verbs.

I **am** a poet. They **are** talking to a poet. He **is** a poet.
She **does** well. She **does** write poetry. They **do** write.
He **has** books. He **has** read poetry. They **have** written.

**Identifying the Correct Verb Form**  Write each sentence. Complete it by choosing the correct form of the verb in parentheses.

**GRAMMAR HINT**

In verb phrases it is the helping verb that must agree with the subject.

1. This book (contain, contains) poems by Frost.
2. Frost (has, have) a great reputation as a lyric poet.
3. Readers (find, finds) his use of symbols interesting.
4. He (was, were) a teacher in his youth.
5. Most libraries (has, have) collections of Frost's work.
6. Certainly our local library (do, does).
7. Students (talk, talks) about Frost's poem "Fire and Ice."
8. This poem (is, are) rather bleak.
9. Several works (share, shares) common themes.
10. Robert Frost's poems (do, does) much for the American spirit.
11. They (have, has) meaning for us today.
12. Some people (think, thinks) his poems are cold.
13. Most people (do, does) admire his work, however.
14. Frost's poetry (do, does) require close study.
15. Even his short poems (have, has) hidden meanings.
16. Certain poems (is, are) apparently simple.
17. His poetry (focus, focuses) on ordinary people.
18. Most students (have, has) read some of his work.
19. His book *In the Clearing* (have, has) some of his most beautiful poems.
20. Frost's poetry (continue, continues) to be popular.

### Writing Link

Describe some writers you admire. Why do you like their work? Write a paragraph explaining your choice. Be sure that each verb agrees with its subject.

## 16.2    Problems with Locating the Subject

Making a subject and its verb agree is easy when the verb directly follows the subject. Sometimes, however, a prepositional phrase comes between the subject and the verb.

> The **city**, in all its moods, **inspires** poets.
> The **cities** of the Midwest **inspire** poets.

In the first sentence above, *in all its moods* is a prepositional phrase. The singular verb *inspires* agrees with the subject of the sentence, *city,* and not with the plural noun *moods,* which is the object of the preposition. In the second sentence, *of the Midwest* is a prepositional phrase. The plural verb *inspire* agrees with the plural subject *cities,* and not with the noun *Midwest,* which is the object of the preposition.

Some sentences begin with *here* or *there. Here* or *there* is never the subject of a sentence. Look for the subject after the verb.

> There **is** a great **poem** about Chicago.

To more easily identify the subject, rearrange the sentence so that the subject and verb are in their usual order.

> A great **poem** there **is** about Chicago.

In some interrogative sentences a helping verb may come before the subject. The subject appears between the helping verb and the main verb.

> **Do** these **poems interest** you?

You can check the subject-verb agreement by making the sentence declarative.

> These **poems do interest** you.

## Exercise 2

**Identifying the Correct Verb Form**   Write each sentence. Complete it by choosing the correct form of the verb in parentheses.

1. The writer of these poems (is, are) Carl Sandburg.
2. This son of Swedish immigrants  (is, are) famous.
3. Ideas for his work (arise, arises) from his travels.
4. His days in Puerto Rico (inspire, inspires) his earliest poems.
5. Does the young man (succeed, succeeds) in his career?
6. Critics around the world (praise, praises) his work.
7. Poems about modern industry (is, are) unusual.

## Exercise 3

**Making Subjects and Verbs Agree**   Write each sentence. Underline the subject once and its verb twice. If they agree, write *correct*. If they do not agree, correct the verb.

1. These lines of the poem describes the city.
2. Here is the phrase "Hog butcher of the world."
3. Does it introduce a certain viewpoint?
4. A list of adjectives are in another line.
5. Sandburg, with a few words, show us the city.
6. There are longer phrases after the introduction.
7. Among the long phrases a string of verbs appear.

GRAMMAR HINT

By deleting a prepositional phrase that comes between a subject and a verb, you can more easily check for subject-verb agreement.

### Writing Link

Where would you go if you wanted to be able to write without being disturbed? Write a paragraph describing that place. Be sure that your subjects and verbs agree.

## 16.3   Collective Nouns and Other Special Subjects

It is difficult to tell whether certain special subjects are singular or plural. For example, collective nouns follow special agreement rules. A collective noun names a group. The noun has a singular meaning when used to tell about a group that acts as a unit. The noun has a plural meaning when used to describe members of the group acting as individuals.

The class . . .

. . . **studies** modern poetry.

> The **audience sits** in silence. [one group, singular]
> The **audience sit** on chairs and pillows. [individuals, plural]

Certain nouns, such as *mumps* and *mathematics,* end in *-s* but take a singular verb. Other nouns that name one thing, such as *pliers* and *binoculars,* end in *-s* but take a plural verb.

> **News is** important to us all. [singular]
> **Scissors are** useful and often attractive. [plural]

The class . . .

. . . **study** for their exams.

When the subject refers to an amount as a single unit, it is singular. When the subject refers to a number of individual units, it is plural.

> **Fifty years seems** a long time. [single unit]
> **Fifty years pass** quickly. [individual units]
> **Five dollars is** the admission price. [single unit]
> **Five dollars are** on the table. [individual units]

A title of a book or work of art is always singular even if a noun within the title is plural.

> **"The Victors" is** a poem by Denise Levertov. [one poem]
> ***Collected Earlier Poems* was** published in 1979. [one book]

**Identifying the Correct Verb Form**   Write each sentence. Complete it by choosing the correct form of the verb in parentheses.

1. The crowd (gather, gathers) outside the room.
2. The crowd (look, looks) at their programs.
3. Ten minutes (seem, seems) a long time.
4. The audience (find, finds) their seats.
5. The class (attend, attends) the poetry reading.
6. Our class (is, are) in the first row.
7. The class (discuss, discusses) the Pulitzer Prize among themselves.
8. A committee (award, awards) the prize each year.
9. The committee (accept, accepts) nominations of American poets.
10. A thousand dollars (is, are) the amount of the prize.
11. The audience (include, includes) the poet laureate of the United States.
12. His book *Promises* (win, wins) a prize for Robert Penn Warren.
13. Two dollars (is, are) the price of admission.
14. The poetry club (read, reads) their favorite poems.
15. *Winter Trees* (is, are) a book by Sylvia Plath.
16. *Winter Trees* (contain, contains) some of Plath's best poems.
17. News of other events (is, are) posted at the reading.
18. "Women" (is, are) a poem by Alice Walker.

**GRAMMAR HINT**

You can decide whether to use a singular or a plural verb by substituting *it* or *they* for the collective noun.

### Writing Link

Suppose that you are a poet and have just won a prize for poetry. Write your acceptance speech. Be sure that your subjects and verbs agree.

# Usage Workshop

## Subject-Verb Agreement

In this passage from "Robert Frost: Visit to a Poet," Octavio Paz describes the wooded area near Robert Frost's cabin in Vermont. The passage has been annotated to show examples of subject-verb agreement.

### Literature Model

#### from ROBERT FROST: VISIT TO A POET

*by Octavio Paz*
*translated from the Spanish by Michael Schmidt*

After the word *there* a singular noun subject follows its singular verb

Agreement between a singular subject and verb that have a prepositional phrase between them

Agreement between a singular pronoun subject and a singular verb

In the air there was a scent of green, hot growth, thirsty. Not a tree, not a leaf stirred. A few clouds rested heavily, anchored in a blue, waveless gulf. A bird sang. I hesitated: "How much nicer it would be to stretch out under this elm! The sound of water is worth more than all the poets' words." I walked on for another ten minutes. . . . When I reached the top I could see the whole little valley; the blue mountains, the stream, the luminously green flatland, and, at the very bottom, the forest. The wind began to blow; everything swayed, almost cheerfully. All the leaves sang. I went toward the cabin. It was a little wooden shack, old, the paint flaked, grayed by the years. The windows were curtainless; I made a way through the underbrush and looked in. Inside, sitting in an easy chair, was an old man. Resting beside him was a woolly dog. When he saw me the man stood up and beckoned me to come around the other side. I did so and found him waiting for me at the door of his cabin.

**Making Verbs Agree with Their Subjects**   Rewrite each sentence, choosing the correct form of the verb in parentheses.

SAMPLE   The path winding toward Robert Frost's cabin (bakes, bake) under the hot sun.

ANSWER   The path winding toward Robert Frost's cabin bakes under the hot sun.

1. There (is, are) a few clouds hanging heavily overhead.
2. Octavio Paz, walking through the undergrowth, (stops, stop) to listen to a flock of birds.
3. The flock (continues, continue) to sing their songs after Paz walks on toward the cabin.
4. Beside Robert Frost (lies, lie) his dog.
5. Does Frost's cabin (seems, seem) remote?

**Making Verbs Agree with Indefinite Pronoun Subjects**   Rewrite each sentence, choosing the correct form of the verb in parentheses.

SAMPLE   Most of Robert Frost's poetry (deals, deal) with the landscape of New England.

ANSWER   Most of Robert Frost's poetry deals with the landscape of New England.

1. Many (praises, praise) the poet for his graceful style.
2. Everyone (recalls, recall) that he won the Pulitzer Prize for poetry four times.
3. Some of us (remembers, remember) that Frost read a poem at the inauguration of President Kennedy.
4. All of Frost's poems (is, are) written in simple, straightforward language.
5. Each (requires, require) careful reading.

**Making Verbs Agree with Compound Subjects**

The following sentences are about Octavio Paz's visit with Robert Frost. Rewrite each sentence, choosing the correct form of the verb in parentheses.

SAMPLE    Robert Frost and Octavio Paz (talks, talk) about the different landscapes of their countries.

ANSWER    Robert Frost and Octavio Paz talk about the different landscapes of their countries.

1. According to Frost, either fear or loneliness (drives, drive) people away from the countryside.
2. According to both men, failure or liberating adventures (awaits, await) every poet.
3. Neither Frost nor Paz (trusts, trust) people who cannot laugh at themselves.
4. Both Frost and Paz (enjoys, enjoy) rereading books.
5. Toward the end of the visit, Paz, Frost, and Frost's dog (walks, walk) back down the hill.

**Proofreading**    The following passage is about French artist Pierre Bonnard, whose work appears on the next page. Rewrite the passage, correcting the errors in spelling, capitalization, punctuation, grammar, and usage. There are ten errors in all.

### Pierre Bonnard

[1] Pierre Bonnard (1867–1947) began his career as 1 of the french artists who rejected the bright colors and broken brush strokes of a popular style of art. [2] By the early 1900s, however Bonnard had changed his mind. [3] Thus the Artist began painting scenes of everyday life ussing brighter colors and textured brush strokes. [4] *Dining Room in the Country* reflect Bonnard's ➡

change of style. [5] Full of light and color, the painting captures the effect of sunlight streeming into a room [6] With it's view of the trees and woods below, the picture could represent what Octavio Paz saw when he reached Robert Frosts cabin.

**Pierre Bonnard, *Dining Room in the Country,* 1913**

## Subject-Verb Agreement

### Making Subjects and Verbs Agree [pages 476–479]

Write each sentence. Underline the subject once and its verb twice. If they agree, write *correct*. If they do not agree, correct the verb.

1. Kenneth Koch teach poetry.
2. This poet works in the schools of New York City.
3. His books includes *When the Sun Tries to Go On*.
4. Koch are also a professor at Columbia University.
5. Koch's poems delights people of all ages.
6. Children write about their dreams and wishes.
7. The poems of Ogden Nash is delightful.
8. There are many funny ideas in his poems.
9. One of his books is *Hard Lines*.
10. A poem from *Hard Lines* discuss billboards.

### Collective Nouns; Indefinite Pronouns; Compound Subjects

[pages 480–485]

Write each sentence. Complete the sentence by choosing the correct form of the verb in parentheses.

11. My family (hold, holds) poetry readings for friends and neighbors on Sunday nights.
12. My family (read, reads) their favorite works aloud.
13. Sometimes two weeks (pass, passes) between our readings.
14. Everyone (know, knows) the poetry of E. E. Cummings.
15. Few (use, uses) capitalization and punctuation so oddly.
16. *Tulips and Chimneys* (is, are) one of the volumes of poetry that E.E. Cummings published.
17. Many of his poems (has, have) unusual spacing.
18. Songs and ballads (is, are) important forms of American poetry.
19. Dangerous outlaws and admirable heroes (appear, appears) in many ballads.
20. Love or adventure (form, forms) the focus of ballads, songs, and even long narrative poems.

### Writing for Review

Write a simple four-line poem on any subject that is familiar to you. Reread your poem to make sure that the subjects and verbs agree.

Andō Hiroshige, *Scenery of Kuwara,* c. 1850

## 17.1　Using Troublesome Words I

Like all languages English contains a number of confusing expressions. The following glossary will help you understand some of the more troublesome ones.

| Word | Meaning | Example |
|------|---------|---------|
| accept | "to receive" | Most stores readily **accept** credit cards as well as cash. |
| except | "other than" | I have no money **except** a dollar. |
| all ready | "completely prepared" | I am **all ready** to go shopping. |
| already | "before" or "by this time" | I **already** spent all of my allowance for this week. |
| all together | "in a group" | We will shop **all together**. |
| altogether | "completely" | The shirts I liked were **altogether** too costly. |
| a lot | "very much" It is two words. Because its meaning is vague, avoid using it. | **A lot** of us are thrifty. [vague]<br>Many of us are thrifty. [more precise] |
| beside | "next to" | The shoe store is **beside** the bank. |
| besides | "in addition to" | **Besides** shoes they sell socks. |
| between | Use *between* for two people or things. | Choose **between** two styles. |
| among | Use *among* when talking about groups of three or more. | Distribute the suits **among** the seven stores. |
| bring | "to carry from a distant place to a closer one" | We **bring** goods into this country. |
| take | "to carry from a nearby place to a more distant one" | They **take** goods from this country to other lands. |
| choose | "to select" | We **choose** items to import. |
| chose | "selected" | Buyers **chose** silk last year. |
| in | "inside" | Factories are often **in** cities. |
| into | indicates movement from outside to a point within | Imports come **into** a country. |

**Choosing the Correct Word**   Write each sentence. Choose the correct word or words in parentheses.

1. Most countries (accept, except) foreign goods.
2. Trade (between, among) China and the United States has grown.
3. Food distribution has (all ready, already) improved in China.
4. Jan (choose, chose) silk from Hong Kong.
5. (Bring, Take) enough money, or yuan, with you when you go to Canton.
6. The buyers flew (all together, altogether) to Shanghai.

**Using the Correct Word**   Write each sentence. Use the correct word or words from the lesson. A definition of the word appears in parentheses.

1. Nigeria _____ to lower the price of oil. (selected)
2. Oil is loaded on tankers _____ the docks. (next to)
3. That tanker is _____ to sail to foreign lands. (completely prepared)
4. Nigeria produces most of its major foods _____ fish. (other than)
5. _____ oil, Nigeria exports rubber. (in addition to)
6. He will _____ our order to the mill. (carry to a distant place)

### Writing Link

In a paragraph describe products you use that are made in Asia. Use some of the words from the lesson.

**Making Usage Choices**   The following sentences are based on passages in *The Clay Marble* that do not appear in this textbook. Rewrite each sentence, choosing the correct word in parentheses.

SAMPLE    When fighting broke out close to the refugee camp, Dara and Jantu became separated from (their, they're) families.

ANSWER    When fighting broke out close to the refugee camp, Dara and Jantu became separated from their families.

1. Jantu, (who's, whose) baby brother was hurt, had to go to the hospital with him.
2. Dara was afraid to (leave, let) her friend.
3. (Than, Then) she remembered the magic marble.
4. Bravely the girl (choose, chose) to look for her family on her own.
5. Dara's determination, rather (than, then) the marble, gave her the courage to find them.

**Proofreading**   The following passage is about the cultivation of tea in China, which is illustrated in the work on the next page. Rewrite the passage, correcting the errors in spelling, capitalization, punctuation, grammar, and usage. There are ten errors in all.

### Tea Cultivation in Ancient China

[1]By the 800s the cultivation of tea into China was subject to well established procedures and traditions.  The seeds first had to be planted in sandy soil to leave them drain properly. [3]when the seeds sprouted, the farmers lightly watered the plants, using the same water in which the seeds had been washed.  [4]The figures in *Tea Cultivation* are watering the young tea plants and fertilizing it. ➡

[5]According to Lu Yü, who's essay on tea helped popularize tea cultivation in the 700s, fertilizer made from the wastes of silkworms was prefered.

[6]Rice is another major crop grown in China and in many other asian countries. [7]To Dara and her family in *The Clay Marble*, rice meaned life. [8]The rice given to them at the refugee camp inabled them to return to their war-torn home in Cambodia and rebuild their lives.

**Artist unknown, China,** *Tea Cultivation,* **nineteenth century**

# Unit 17 Review

## Glossary of Special Usage Problems

### Using Troublesome Words I

[pages 492–493]

Complete each sentence by choosing the correct word or words.

1. Tourism is (all ready, already) a big industry in Mexico.
2. (Between, Among) Mexico's exports are oil, timber, and sugar.
3. In Veracruz freighters unload goods (beside, besides) the docks.
4. Oil and gas have (all together, altogether) enriched Mexico.
5. Many visitors (bring, take) Mexican pottery home with them.
6. Yesterday we (choose, chose) a rug.
7. Tour guides are (bringing, taking) us on a visit to a ranch.
8. Trade talks (between, among) Mexico and the United States began.
9. By December summer in Brazil has (all ready, already) begun.
10. Brazilian hotels (accept, except) many visitors during Mardi Gras.
11. Crowds pour (in, into) the streets.
12. People work (altogether, all together) during the harvest.
13. Farmers (bring, take) their produce to market.
14. (Beside, Besides) sugar Brazil produces coffee and beef.
15. Lumber mills (accept, except) logs.

### Using Troublesome Words II

[pages 494–495]

Write each sentence. Use the correct form of the glossary word that is defined in the parentheses.

16. Autoworkers _____ new computer techniques. (to receive knowledge)
17. The designer _____ the new model on the table. (to place)
18. The automakers claim that _____ car is the best. (belonging to them)
19. Engineers _____ about car design. (to give knowledge)
20. In some racing cars the driver can _____ almost flat. (to recline)
21. Workers _____ car frames out of the paint pit. (to cause to go up)
22. When the paint is dried, _____ the surface is polished. (at that time)
23. _____ steel was used to make your car. (belonging to them)
24. Automakers _____ robots rivet parts together. (to permit)
25. The robots mainly rivet the _____ parts together. (not firmly attached)

### Writing for Review

Find the difference between *emigrate* and *immigrate* and *weather* and *whether*. Use each word in a sentence.

Paul Gauguin, *The Meal*, 1891

Every sentence contains a subject and a predicate. To diagram a sentence, first draw a horizontal line. Then draw a vertical line that crosses the horizontal line.

To the left of the vertical line, write the simple subject. To the right of the vertical line, write the simple predicate. Use capital letters as they appear in the sentence, but do not use punctuation.

**Apples grow.**

| Apples | grow |

Be sure to write only the simple subject and the simple predicate in this part of the diagram. Remember that the simple predicate can include a helping verb.

Some **apples are falling** already.

| apples | are falling |

**Exercise 1**

**Diagraming Simple Subjects and Simple Predicates**
Diagram each simple subject and simple predicate.

1. Apples fell.
2. They have ripened.
3. Joan tastes one.
4. Workers pick the fruit.
5. Some people are resting.
6. The orchard is busy.

The simple subject and simple predicate of the four kinds of sentences are diagramed below. Notice that the location of the simple subject and simple predicate in a sentence diagram is always the same regardless of the word order in the sentence.

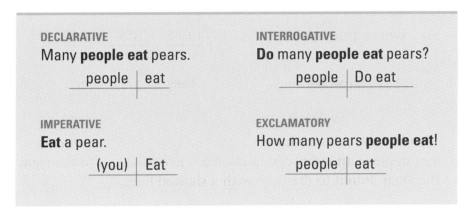

DECLARATIVE
Many **people eat** pears.

people | eat

INTERROGATIVE
**Do** many **people eat** pears?

people | Do eat

IMPERATIVE
**Eat** a pear.

(you) | Eat

EXCLAMATORY
How many pears **people eat**!

people | eat

Notice that in an interrogative sentence the subject often comes between the two parts of a verb phrase. In an imperative sentence the simple subject is the understood *you*.

### Exercise 2

**Diagraming Sentences**    Diagram the simple subject and the simple predicate of each sentence.

1. I brought a pear for lunch.
2. Do you like pears?
3. Taste this one.
4. This pear is delicious.
5. How delicious this pear is!
6. Pears are good in salads.
7. Do you eat pears often?
8. Try some pear juice.
9. Have you ever eaten pear pie?

*Diagraming the Four Kinds of Sentences*    **503**

Pineapples in many stores.

## 19.4  Capitalizing Other Proper Nouns and Adjectives

Many nouns besides the names of people and places are proper nouns. Adjectives that are formed from proper nouns are called proper adjectives. For example, the proper adjective *Egyptian* is formed from the proper noun *Egypt*.

RULE 1:  Capitalize the names of clubs, organizations, businesses, institutions, and political parties.

Data Corporation        Boy Scouts        Republican party

RULE 2:  Capitalize brand names but not the nouns following them.

Cruncho peanut butter        Spiffy cleaning fluid

RULE 3:  Capitalize the names of important historical events, periods of time, and documents.

Battle of Yorktown        Bronze Age        Bill of Rights

RULE 4:  Capitalize names of days of the week, months of the year, and holidays. Do not capitalize names of the seasons.

Thursday        April        Memorial Day        summer

RULE 5:  Capitalize the first word, the last word, and all important words in the title of a book, play, short story, poem, essay, article, film, television series, song, magazine, newspaper, and chapter of a book.

*A Wrinkle in Time*        "The Raven"        *Washington Post*

RULE 6:  Capitalize the names of ethnic groups, nationalities, and languages.

Asian        German        Spanish

RULE 7:  Capitalize proper adjectives that are formed from the names of ethnic groups and nationalities.

Asian languages        Italian food

## Exercise 6

**Capitalizing Proper Nouns and Adjectives**   Write the following items. Use capital letters where needed.

1. sierra club
2. thanksgiving day
3. colorado river
4. *los angeles times*
5. war of 1812
6. halloween
7. the middle ages
8. sneezo tissues
9. october
10. french horn
11. world war II
12. *national geographic*

## Exercise 7

**Using Capital Letters**   Write each sentence, using capital letters where needed for proper nouns and adjectives. Write *correct* if the sentence has no errors.

1. James Marshall found gold in California on january 24, 1848.
2. In the spring thousands of prospectors arrived at Sutter's Mill.
3. Hawaiian, japanese, chinese, european, and american fortune seekers joined the rush.
4. Have you read *the california gold rush*?
5. A similar rush to Colorado took place in 1858.
6. In 1859 a newspaper called the *rocky mountain news* reported on the search for gold in Colorado.
7. Long after the civil war gold was found in Alaska.

### Writing Link

In a paragraph relate the time and place of your birth. Mention other important dates in your life, and explain their importance.

# *Mechanics* Workshop

## Capitalization

In "The Pomegranate Trees," a short story by William Saroyan, the narrator's uncle Melik attempts to grow pomegranates in the middle of a desert. In the following excerpt from the story, the narrator reflects on his uncle's dream of creating a garden on the land. The passage has been annotated to show some of the rules of capitalization covered in this unit.

### *Literature Model*

### *from* THE POMEGRANATE TREES

#### *by William Saroyan*

Name of a person →

My uncle Melik was just about the worst farmer that ever lived. He was too imaginative and poetic for his own good. What he wanted was beauty. He wanted to plant it and see it grow. I myself planted over one hundred pomegranate trees for my uncle one year back there in the good old days of poetry and youth in the world. I

Brand name →

drove a John Deere tractor, too, and so did my uncle. It was all pure esthetics, not agriculture. My uncle just liked the idea of planting trees and watching them grow.

Only they wouldn't grow. It was on account of the soil. The soil was desert soil. It was dry. My uncle waved

Name of a language →

at the six hundred and eighty acres of desert he had

First word of a direct quotation that is a complete sentence →

bought and he said in the most poetic Armenian anybody ever heard, "Here in this awful desolation a garden shall flower, fountains of cold water shall bubble out of the earth, and all things of beauty shall come into being."

The pronoun *I* →

"Yes, sir," I said.

**Capitalizing Sentences**   Write each sentence, correcting any errors in capitalization.

| SAMPLE | Uncle Melik said, "here in this awful desolation a garden shall flower." |
|--------|--------------------------------------------------------------------------|
| ANSWER | Uncle Melik said, "Here in this awful desolation a garden shall flower." |

1. uncle Melik wanted to bring beauty to the desert.
2. "I think you understand," he said, "Why I bought this land."
3. "Yes," I said, "you want to plant a garden here."
4. The narrator thought That his uncle was a poet.
5. "most farmers don't try to grow pomegranate trees on dry desert land," explained the narrator.

**Capitalizing Names and Titles and Other Proper Nouns**   Write each sentence, correcting any errors in capitalization.

| SAMPLE | Uncle Melik purchased land at the foot of the sierra nevada. |
|--------|---------------------------------------------------------------|
| ANSWER | Uncle Melik purchased land at the foot of the Sierra Nevada. |

1. The narrator's uncle in "the Pomegranate Trees" hired workers to clear the land.
2. Uncle Melik also bought a John Deere Tractor.
3. The men followed uncle Melik's instructions.
4. The narrator asked his Uncle Melik why he wanted to plant pomegranate trees.
5. Pomegranates aren't well known in america.
6. The narrator said, "He knew i would understand the impulse that was driving him to ruin."

**Capitalizing Proper Nouns and Proper Adjectives**
Write each of the following sentences, correcting any
errors in capitalization.

SAMPLE    The narrator's armenian uncle planted
          hundreds of pomegranate trees.
ANSWER    The narrator's Armenian uncle planted
          hundreds of pomegranate trees.

1. Like the pioneers of the far west, Uncle Melik tried
   to realize his dreams.
2. He wanted to create a garden on the west coast.
3. The pomegranates didn't sell because the american
   people didn't know what they were.
4. Eventually Melik had to give the land back to mr.
   Griffith, the man who had sold it to him.
5. At the end of the story, the pomegranate trees died,
   and cactus returned to the Western desert land.

**Proofreading**   The following passage is about artist
Rudy Fernandez, whose work appears on the next page.
Rewrite the passage, correcting the errors in spelling,
capitalization, punctuation, grammar, and usage. There
are ten errors in all.

### *Rudy Fernandez*

[1]Rudy Fernandez was born in 1948 and grew up into
the southwest. [2]The mexican-American artist therefore
feels an intense affection for the area's landscape. [3]He
especially loves the high deserts of new mexico. [4]Many of
Fernandez' paintings capture the beauty of the dessert
landscape.
  [5]In *Hot and Cold: Cold,* for example Fernandez celebrates the desert by using abstract images of a flowering
cactus. [6]the simply drawn cactus glows warmly against ➡

against the blue background. [7]Like Uncle Melik in "The Pomegranate Trees," Fernandez believes that beauty can survive in the desert. [8]Fernandez shows that the plants and flowers that grows naturally in the desert have their own beauty.

**Rudy Fernandez,** *Hot and Cold: Cold,* **1987**

# Capitalization

## Capitalizing Sentences and Quotations

[pages 512–513]

Write each sentence. Use capital letters where needed.

1. one of our greatest presidents was Abraham Lincoln.
2. he became a lawyer in 1836.
3. Darby asked, "where did Lincoln practice law?"
4. "he practiced law throughout Illinois," Ms. Angola said.
5. "he also tried cases before the state court," said Josh.

## Capitalizing Names and Titles of People and Places

[pages 514–517]

Write each sentence. Use capital letters where needed.

1. The steamboat was invented by robert fulton.
2. It made river transportation faster, i think.
3. My teacher, mr. avery, said that the steamboat ushered in a new era.
4. Even napoleon bonaparte found this invention remarkable.
5. In 1807 fulton's steamboat journeyed down the hudson river.

6. In 1955 uncle john made the same voyage.
7. Fulton called his boat *clermont*.
8. In 1825 the erie canal opened a route from albany to buffalo.
9. Did the *clermont* steam from new york city to lake erie?
10. The erie canal is still part of the new york state canal system.

## Capitalizing Other Proper Nouns and Adjectives

[pages 518–519]

Write each sentence. Use capital letters where needed.

1. Clara Barton, an american nurse, was born on christmas day, 1821.
2. During the franco-prussian war Barton was a battlefield nurse.
3. After returning to the United States, she established the american red cross.
4. The red cross aided the soldiers during world war II.
5. The american red cross headquarters is in washington, d.c.

## Writing for Review

Imagine that you saw Fulton's first steamboat voyage in 1807. Write a report describing the event.

Claude Monet, *Saint-Lazare Train Station, the Normandy Train*, 1877

## 20.1 Using the Period and Other End Marks

Different end marks are used with the different types of sentences. The period is used for declarative and imperative sentences. The question mark is used for interrogative sentences, and the exclamation point is used for exclamatory sentences.

RULE 1: Use a period at the end of a declarative sentence. A declarative sentence makes a statement.

> I enjoy traveling by train.
> Almost every country in the world has at least one major railroad line.

RULE 2: Use a period at the end of an imperative sentence. An imperative sentence gives a command or makes a request.

> Read about Russia's long rail system. [command]
> Please explain the meaning of the word *railroad*. [request]

RULE 3: Use a question mark at the end of an interrogative sentence. An interrogative sentence asks a question.

> Do we still use steam trains in this country?
> Why are diesel engines used now?

RULE 4: Use an exclamation point at the end of an exclamatory sentence. An exclamatory sentence expresses strong feeling.

> What a high-speed train this is!
> How fast it moves!

RULE 5: Use an exclamation point at the end of an interjection. An interjection is a word or group of words that expresses strong emotion.

| | | |
|---|---|---|
| My! | Alas! | Oops! |
| Well! | Whew! | Ssh! |
| Gee! | Ouch! | Oh, no! |

## Exercise 1

**Using End Marks** Add the correct end mark to each sentence, and then write whether the sentence is *declarative, imperative, interrogative,* or *exclamatory.*

1. Railroads provide an important means of transportation
2. Are we going to learn about the history of railroads
3. When was the first steam locomotive invented
4. Read about railroads in your book
5. An English inventor named Richard Trevithick built the first steam locomotive
6. Please tell me about the race between a horse and the tiny steam locomotive called the *Tom Thumb*
7. What an exciting race that was
8. In 1830 Peter Cooper built the *Tom Thumb*
9. This small locomotive raced against a horse but lost
10. The *Tom Thumb* led until an engine belt slipped
11. What a disappointment for Peter Cooper
12. Railroads grew rapidly in the mid-nineteenth century
13. Did these early railroads have high accident rates
14. As a safety measure George Westinghouse developed an air brake for railroads
15. Explain the difference between an air brake and a hand brake
16. What a wonderful invention the air brake was
17. Isn't rail travel still a wonderful way to see the country

### Writing Link

Imagine that you're riding aross the country by rail in 1870. Write a paragraph describing your trip. Use the different end marks in your paragraph.

## 20.2　Using Commas I

Commas make sentences easier to understand because they signal a pause or separation between parts of a sentence.

**RULE 1:**　Use commas to separate three or more words, phrases, or clauses in a series.

Columbus commanded the *Niña,* the *Pinta,* and the *Santa Maria*.

**RULE 2:**　Use a comma to show a pause after an introductory word.

Yes, ancient ships had few cabins for passengers.

**RULE 3:**　Use a comma after two or more introductory prepositional phrases.

For years people crossed the ocean in ships. [one prepositional phrase—*For years*]

For thousands of years, shipbuilders constructed large ships. [two prepositional phrases—*For thousands* and *of years*]

**RULE 4:**　Use a comma after introductory participles and introductory participial phrases.

Daydreaming, I found myself on an ancient ship.
Traveling the Mediterranean, the Minoans became seafarers.

**RULE 5:**　Use commas to set off words that interrupt the flow of thought in a sentence.

Ships, you might imagine, were invented thousands of years ago.

**RULE 6:**　Use commas to set off an appositive if it is not essential to the meaning of the sentence.

The Egyptians, the inventors of sails, built barges from planks of wood. [The appositive, *the inventors of sails,* is not essential to the meaning of the sentence.]

**RULE 7:**　Use commas to set off names used in direct address.

Ms. Mar, did the Romans have a large merchant fleet?

**Using Commas**   Add any needed commas to the following sentences. Write *correct* if a sentence needs no changes.

1. Packet ships clipper ships and ocean liners are three kinds of ships.
2. By the early part of the nineteenth century trade between the United States and Europe had grown.
3. At that time American shipowners built packet ships for carrying cargo and passengers.
4. Packet ships you might imagine were not comfortable.
5. The first packet ship a ship that measured about one hundred feet did not travel very fast.
6. In the 1850s clipper ships the most beautiful of all sailing ships provided speed and comfort.
7. Driving at top speed the captain of a clipper could cut through the water at twenty knots Ramón.
8. The age of the huge swift and luxurious ocean liner began in the early 1900s.
9. Beginning in the late 1940s airplanes attracted passengers.
10. Most ocean liners Sally could not compete with airplanes.
11. Yes in the 1960s some European shipping companies tried to compete with jet planes.
12. Juanita do you enjoy sailing?
13. Yes I love to go sailing.

**GRAMMAR HINT**

Be sure not to forget the second comma when you use a pair of commas to set off an appositive or a group of words that interupts the flow of thought in a sentence.

### Writing Link

Which country would you like to visit? Describe a boat trip to the country of your choice. Be sure to use commas correctly.

## 20.3　Using Commas II

It is important to use commas correctly in sentences with clauses. A clause is a group of words that has a subject and a predicate and is used as part of a sentence. A main clause can stand alone as a sentence. A subordinate clause cannot stand alone as a sentence.

A compound sentence has two or more main clauses joined by the conjunction *and, or,* or *but.*

**RULE 8:**　Use a comma before *and, or,* or *but* when they join main clauses.

> Camels can travel great distances, and their strength enables them to carry heavy loads.
> Camels can live alone, but most travel in small herds.
> Camel's hair is used for making blankets, or it is woven into cloth for suits and coats.

When one or more subordinate clauses are joined with a main clause, the new sentence is called a complex sentence. An adverb clause is a subordinate clause that tells how, when, why, or where an action takes place.

**RULE 9:**　Use a comma after an adverb clause that introduces a sentence. Adverb clauses begin with subordinating conjunctions such as *after, although, as, because, before, considering (that), if, in order that, since, so that, though, unless, until, when, whenever, where, wherever, whether,* or *while.*

> Since camels are the main means of transportation in many dry areas, they are called ships of the desert.

Do not use a comma with an adverb clause that comes at the end of a sentence.

> Nomads take good care of their camels since these animals are vital to their way of life.

## Exercise 3

**Using Commas with Clauses**   Write each sentence. Add a comma or commas where needed. For a sentence that needs no commas, write *correct*.

1. Millions of people depend on camels since these animals supply so many needs.
2. In the desert camels pull plows or they turn water wheels.
3. Because they carry nomads to places without roads camels are highly valued in the desert.
4. These animals walk easily on soft sand and they go where trucks cannot pass.
5. When camels travel they go without water for days.
6. If camels pass through sandstorms their nostrils shut.
7. Wherever nomads go they travel by camel because this animal provides the best means of transportation.
8. Camels seem strange to us because they are not native to our country.
9. When a person mounts a camel the beast usually whines.
10. Until a camel begins moving it grunts and groans.
11. After a camel starts walking it carries its load quietly.
12. Since camels do not work willingly they never learn obedience.
13. If camels become upset they may bite.
14. Because camels are easily annoyed they often bite or they kick with their hind legs.

### Writing Link

Would you prefer to travel across the desert by camel or by car? Describe your journey in a paragraph that uses a compound sentence and a complex sentence.

## 20.4  Using Commas III

Several rules for using commas—including those for punctuating dates and addresses, titles, direct quotations, and salutations—are a matter of standard usage.

**RULE 10:** Use commas before and after the year when it is used with both the month and the day. Do not use a comma if only the month and the year are given.

> The bus trip began on July 5, 1992, and lasted four weeks.
> The journey ended in August 1992.

**RULE 11:** Use commas before and after the name of a state or a country when it is used with the name of a city. Do not use a comma after the state if it is used with a ZIP code.

> People came from as far away as Buffalo, New York, to travel with the tour.
> The address on the envelope was as follows: 136 East Main St., Huntington, NY 11743.

**RULE 12:** Use a comma or pair of commas to set off an abbreviated title or degree following a person's name.

> Carol Warren, M.D., studied the effects of motion sickness.

**RULE 13:** Use a comma before *too* when *too* means "also."

> Dr. Warren rode on the bus with us, too.

**RULE 14:** Use a comma or pair of commas to set off a direct quotation.

> Kerry said, "Buses are more efficient than cars."
> "Train travel," Sarah said, "is pleasant and safe."

**RULE 15:** Use a comma after the salutation of a friendly letter and after the closing of both a friendly and a business letter.

> Dear Dad,                Your pal,                Yours truly,

**RULE 16:** Use a comma to prevent misreading.

> Instead of two, five teachers made the trip.

**Using Commas**    Write each sentence. Add a comma or commas where needed.

1. A letter from Troy, New York arrived in May 1992.
2. Alan said "I'm planning a tour of Canada."
3. "I hope" said Nora "that we can go in July."
4. The bus will go from New York to Quebec City Canada and then back to the United States.
5. Pamela Chin M.A. will lead the tour.

**Using Commas**    Add any needed commas to each of the following numbered items.

[1] 98 Heritage Road
[2] Somers New York 10589
[3] August 8 1993

[4] Dear Keith

[5] I have just returned from a terrific bus trip. [6] We went from Troy New York to Quebec City Canada. [7] Mike went too. [8] On the bus I read a terrific book about Quebec by Carlos Espinoza Ph.D. [9] Instead of three four hours were allotted for our meals. [10] Andy says "Wish you were here."

[11] Your friend
*Ahmad*

## Writing Link

Write a letter describing a bus trip from Chicago to San Diego. Use commas correctly.

## 20.5  Using Semicolons and Colons

The semicolon and the colon are punctuation marks that separate parts of a sentence that might otherwise be confused.

RULE 1:   Use a semicolon to join parts of a compound sentence when a conjunction such as *and, but,* or *or* is not used.

> In the 1890s the electric car became the most popular car in America; people liked electric cars because they ran quietly and cleanly.

RULE 2:   Use a semicolon to join parts of a compound sentence when the main clauses are long and are subdivided by commas, even if the clauses are joined by a coordinating conjunction such as *and, but,* or *or.*

> Before the invention of the automobile, people rode horses, bicycles, or streetcars for short distances; and they took horse-drawn carriages, trains, or boats for longer trips.

RULE 3:   Use a colon to introduce a list of items that ends a sentence. Use a phrase such as *these, the following* or *as follows* before the list.

> A few years ago you could order a car only in **the following** colors: black, white, blue, and brown.

Do not use a colon immediately after a verb or a preposition. Either leave out the colon, or reword the sentence.

> Large automobile companies **sell** cars, trucks, and vans.
> Most of the world's cars are built **in** the United States, Japan, or Europe.

RULE 4:   Use a colon to separate the hour and the minute when you write the time of day.

> Ms. Cole starts her car at 7:15 each morning.

RULE 5:   Use a colon after the salutation of a business letter.

> Dear Sir or Madam:            Dear Ms. Delgado:

Tasha drove downtown at rush hour

she found a parking space in front of the library.

## Exercise 6

**Using Semicolons and Colons**   Add any needed semicolons or colons to the following sentences. Write *correct* if the sentence needs no changes.

1. Large automobile clubs aid travelers these travelers often write to the clubs for information.
2. I wrote to one of these organizations last month it promised to send me a packet of information.
3. Within a week the organization sent me the following items a road map, a guidebook, and a car manual.
4. I plan to leave next Saturday at 530 in the morning.
5. For possible emergencies I am taking these items a flashlight, a first-aid kit, and a spare tire.

## Exercise 7

**Using Semicolons and Colons**   Use semicolons or colons to punctuate the following numbered items.

[1] Dear Sir or Madam

[2] I am planning a trip I am, therefore, seeking information about Virginia, Tennessee, and North Carolina. [3] I would like to visit these cities Richmond, Raleigh, and Atlanta. [4] Please send the following a road map and a guidebook.

Sincerely,
*An-Mei Cho*

### Writing Link

Describe what you would do to plan a successful trip. Use a colon and semicolon in your sentences.

## 20.6    Using Quotation Marks and Italics

Quotation marks enclose a person's exact words as well as the titles of some works. Italic type—a special slanted type that is used in printing—identifies titles of other works. You can show italics on a typewriter or with handwriting by underlining.

RULE 1:    Use quotation marks before and after a direct quotation.

"For centuries people dreamed of flying," Iris said.

RULE 2:    Use quotation marks with a divided quotation.

"Leonardo da Vinci," said Ray, "drew plans of flying machines."

RULE 3:    Use a comma or commas to separate a phrase such as *he said* from the quotation itself. Place the comma outside opening quotation marks, but inside closing quotation marks.

Chan said, "Orville and Wilbur Wright invented the airplane."
"It was a great advance for civilization," Lou said.

RULE 4:    Place a period inside closing quotation marks.

Ed said, "An Air Force captain made the first supersonic flight."

RULE 5:    Place a question mark or an exclamation point inside the quotation marks when it is part of the quotation.

Amy asked, "When did jumbo jets begin carrying passengers?"

RULE 6:    Place a question mark or an exclamation point outside the quotation marks when it is part of the entire sentence.

Did I really hear Sam say, "Jumbo jets are just big airplanes"?

RULE 7:    Use quotation marks for the title of a short story, essay, poem, song, magazine or newspaper article, or book chapter.

"Araby" [short story]          "Trees" [poem]

RULE 8:    Use italics (underlining) to identify the title of a book, play, film, television series, magazine, or newspaper.

*The Pearl* [book]          *Seventeen* [magazine]

**Punctuating Titles**   Correctly add quotation marks or underlining for italics for each of the following.

1. Through the Tunnel (short story)
2. The Denver Post (newspaper)
3. Dream Variations (poem)
4. Much Ado About Nothing (play)
5. Kilimanjaro (essay)
6. Nova (television series)
7. Hook (film)

**Using Quotation Marks and Italics**   Add quotation marks, italics, and other punctuation marks where needed in the following sentences.

1. Dolores said Supersonic planes travel at great speeds
2. Only spacecraft added Randy travel faster than these airplanes
3. Supersonic transports cross the Atlantic in three hours explained Ms. Chu.
4. Dolores shouted What an exciting ride that must be
5. Randy asked Is that plane a supersonic transport
6. Ms. Chu answered Yes a supersonic transport appeared in the film Airport
7. Isn't that plane called the Concorde asked Akira.
8. Have you read Carl Sandburg's poem Fog

### *Writing Link*

Write an imaginary dialogue between an air-traffic controller and a pilot trying to land at a busy airport at rush hour.

## 20.7    Using Apostrophes

An apostrophe shows possession; the missing letters within a contraction; and the plurals of letters, numbers, or words when they refer to themselves.

RULE 1:    Use an apostrophe and an *s* (*'s*) to form the possessive of a singular noun.

James + **'s** = James**'s**          nation + **'s** = nation**'s**

RULE 2:    Use an apostrophe and an *s* (*'s*) to form the possessive of a plural noun that does not end in *s*.

men + **'s** = men**'s**          geese + **'s** = geese**'s**

RULE 3:    Use an apostrophe alone to form the possessive of a plural noun that ends in *s*.

boys + **'** = boys**'**          Thompsons + **'** = Thompsons**'**

RULE 4:    Use an apostrophe and an *s* (*'s*) to form the possessive of an indefinite pronoun.

anybody + **'s** = anybody**'s**          someone + **'s** = someone**'s**

Do not use an apostrophe in a possessive pronoun.

That car is **ours**.          Is that cat **yours**?
The bird flapped **its** wings.          This cassette is **hers**.

RULE 5:    Use an apostrophe to replace letters that have been omitted in a contraction. A contraction is a word that is made by combining two words into one by leaving out one or more letters.

it + is = it**'s**          I + will = I**'ll**
we + are = we**'re**          is + not = isn**'t**

RULE 6:    Use an apostrophe to form the plurals of letters, figures, and words when they refer to themselves. Be sure to underline (italicize) these plurals correctly. Do not underline the *'s*.

three *b***'s**          five *4***'s**          *and***'s**, *if***'s**, and *but***'s**

## Exercise 10

**Using the Possessive Form**   Write the possessive form of each word or group of words below. Use an apostrophe and an *s ('s)* or an apostrophe alone (').

1. teacher
2. teachers
3. Ms. Sandoval
4. adults
5. deer
6. man
7. country
8. countries
9. dog
10. Celia
11. women
12. heroes

## Exercise 11

**Using Apostrophes**   Write each sentence. Use apostrophes where needed. Write *correct* if the sentence needs no changes.

1. The friends bicycles are ready for the long trip.
2. Ada has made sure shes prepared.
3. "Im ready to start,"Ada said.
4. "Were ready when you are," replied Jess and Kim.
5. "Is the bicycle with the basket yours?" asked Kim.
6. The friends stopped cycling to watch two soccer games.
7. "Why do all the shirts have *T*s on them?" asked Isamu.
8. "Its anyones guess," said Inez.
9. That shirt is hers.
10. A train went by with its horn blaring.

### *Writing Link*

What kind of bike would you take on a trip through the mountains? Write a paragraph describing your bike trip. Use some apostrophes in your paragraph.

## 20.8　Using Hyphens, Dashes, and Parentheses

**RULE 1:**　Use a hyphen to show the division of a word at the end of a line. Always divide the word between its syllables.

> Astronauts operate spacecraft and conduct engi-
> 　　neering, medical, and scientific experiments in space.

**RULE 2:**　Use a hyphen in compound numbers from twenty-one through ninety-nine.

> seventy-six books　　　　twenty-three flights

**RULE 3:**　Use a hyphen in a fraction that is used as a modifier. Do not use a hyphen in a fraction used as a noun.

> Some astronauts receive **one-half** pay upon retirement. [modifier]
> **One half** of all astronauts have a master's degree. [noun]

**RULE 4:**　Use a hyphen or hyphens in certain compound nouns. Check the dictionary to see which ones need hyphens.

> great-grandmother　　　vice-president　　　　attorney-at-law

**RULE 5:**　Use a hyphen in a compound modifier only when it precedes the word it modifies.

> She is a **well-trained** astronaut.　　She is **well trained**.

**RULE 6:**　Use a dash to show a sudden break or change in thought or speech. If the sentence continues, use a second dash to mark the end of the interruption.

> Dr. Owens—he lives nearby—teaches astronomy.

**RULE 7:**　Use parentheses to set off material that is not part of the main statement but that is, nevertheless, important to include.

> Flight training for the space program consists of training in simulators
> 　　(devices that reproduce the conditions of space flight) and in
> 　　other special equipment.

## Exercise 12

**Using Hyphens**   Use a hyphen or hyphens where needed in the items below. Write *correct* if an item needs no changes.

1. one half interest
2. great uncle
3. thirty five
4. Anglo Saxon
5. well liked leader
6. merry go round
7. thirty two missions
8. three fourths majority

## Exercise 13

**Using Hyphens, Dashes, and Parentheses**   Add hyphens, dashes, and parentheses where needed to the following sentences. Write *correct* if a sentence needs no changes.

1. Astronauts undergo a six month training course.
2. Astronauts must follow a low fat diet as part of their training.
3. The astronauts and cosmonauts in the Apollo Soyuz Test Project visited each other's countries.
4. The astronauts familiarized themselves with the equipment, with the flight plan, with but you know that.
5. The space travelers participated in joint rehearsals of the mission.
6. Dr. Ilych he is a fine teacher led the sessions.
7. As a scientist, Dr. Ilych is well regarded in Russia.
8. He trained two thirds of the participants.

### Writing Link

Imagine that you're an astronaut working with a cosmonaut. Write an entry in your journal relating your experience. Use hyphens, dashes, and parentheses.

## 20.9  Using Abbreviations

**RULE 1:**  Abbreviate a person's title and a professional or an academic degree that follows a name.

**Mr.** Carl Baird **Jr.**      Vivian Huang, **M.D**      Ana Elias, **Ph.D.**

**RULE 2:**  Abbreviate the names of certain organizations and government agencies, using capital letters and no periods.

North Atlantic Treaty Organization **NATO**

**RULE 3:**  Use the abbreviations *A.M.* and *P.M.* for time. For dates use *B.C.* (before Christ) and, sometimes, *A.D.* (after Christ).

8:45 **A.M.**          6:30 **P.M.**          30 **B.C.**          **A.D.** 476

**RULE 4:**  Abbreviate calendar items only in charts and lists.

**Tues.**      **Thurs.**      **Fri.**          **Feb.**      **Aug.**      **Oct.**

**RULE 5:**  In scientific writing abbreviate units of measure.

inch(es) **in.**      foot (feet) **ft.**      gram(s) **g**          liter(s) **l**

**RULE 6:**  In informal writing abbreviate street names.

Street **St.**          Avenue **Ave.**          Road **Rd.**          Court **Ct.**

**RULE 7:**  On envelopes use the Postal Service abbreviations.

### Postal Service Abbreviations

| | | | | | | | |
|---|---|---|---|---|---|---|---|
| | | District of | | Louisiana | LA | New Hampshire | NH | South Carolina | SC |
| | | Columbia | DC | Maine | ME | New Jersey | NJ | South Dakota | SD |
| | | Florida | FL | Maryland | MD | New Mexico | NM | Tennessee | TN |
| Alabama | AL | Georgia | GA | Massachusetts | MA | New York | NY | Texas | TX |
| Alaska | AK | Hawaii | HI | Michigan | MI | North Carolina | NC | Utah | UT |
| Arizona | AZ | Idaho | ID | Minnesota | MN | North Dakota | ND | Vermont | VT |
| Arkansas | AR | Illinois | IL | Mississippi | MS | Ohio | OH | Virginia | VA |
| California | CA | Indiana | IN | Missouri | MO | Oklahoma | OK | Washington | WA |
| Colorado | CO | Iowa | IA | Montana | MT | Oregon | OR | West Virginia | WV |
| Connecticut | CT | Kansas | KS | Nebraska | NE | Pennsylvania | PA | Wisconsin | WI |
| Delaware | DE | Kentucky | KY | Nevada | NV | Rhode Island | RI | Wyoming | WY |

**Using Abbreviations**   Write the correct abbreviation for each underlined item.

1. <u>after Christ</u> 1000
2. <u>Mister</u> Roosevelt
3. 76 Melrose <u>Avenue</u>
4. Don Newell <u>Junior</u>
5. <u>Wednesday</u>
6. one <u>quart</u>
7. Nashville, <u>Tennessee</u>
8. <u>April</u> 23
9. Tat Lam, <u>Medical Doctor</u>
10. <u>Internal Revenue Service</u>
11. 42 Bradford <u>Drive</u>
12. thirty-two <u>feet</u>
13. <u>November</u> 23
14. 1100 <u>before Christ</u>
15. fifteen <u>liters</u>

**Using Abbreviations**   Abbreviate each underlined item in the following sentences.

1. The letter was addressed to 14 Laurel <u>Street</u>.
2. The letter from <u>Representative</u> Gail R. Momaday contained information about the new proposal.
3. It stated that a meeting will be held from 11:30 <u>in the morning</u> until 4:45 <u>in the afternoon</u>.
4. The meeting will be held on <u>Monday, November</u> 17.
5. Scheduled speakers included <u>Doctor</u> Hilario Reyes.
6. <u>Governor</u> Carol McQuaid plans to speak.
7. Write to the <u>Environmental Protection Agency</u>.
8. The office is in Washington, <u>District of Columbia</u>.
9. That office is twenty <u>kilometers</u> from my house.

Astronauts N. Jan Davis, **Ph.D.**, and Mae C. Jemison, **Ph.D.**, experience zero gravity at **NASA's** Houston Training Facility.

### *Writing Link*

Write a letter inviting a friend to a party. Include all the necessary information. Use some of the abbreviations covered in this lesson.

## 20.10  Writing Numbers

In charts and tables you always write numbers as figures. However, in an ordinary sentence you sometimes spell out numbers and sometimes write them as numerals.

**RULE 1:**  Spell out numbers that you can write in one or two words.

In the early nineteenth century stagecoaches traveled at a speed of less than **twenty-five** miles per hour.

**RULE 2:**  Use numerals for numbers of more than two words.

The first coaches traveled a distance of **392** miles.

**RULE 3:**  Spell out any number that begins a sentence, or reword the sentence so that it does not begin with a number.

**Three thousand one hundred** coaches existed in England by 1836.

**RULE 4:**  Write a very large number as a numeral followed by the word *million* or *billion*.

Did these coaches carry more than **25 million** passengers?

**RULE 5:**  If related numbers appear in the same sentence, use all numerals.

For a trip of **390** miles drivers changed horses every **20** miles.

**RULE 6:**  Spell out ordinal numbers (first, second, and so forth).

In America, Wells, Fargo & Company ranked **first** in its coach service.

**RULE 7:**  Use words to express the time of day unless you are writing the exact time with the abbreviation A.M. or P.M.

The journey began at **six o'clock**. It ended at **9:15** P.M.

**RULE 8:**  Use numerals to express dates, house and street numbers, apartment and room numbers, telephone numbers, page numbers, amounts of money of more than two words, and percentages. Write out the word *percent*.

July **19, 1832**      **15** Summit Road      Apartment **6E**      **40 percent**

**Writing Numbers**  Use the correct form for writing numbers in the following sentences. Write *correct* if a sentence needs no changes.

1. The first stage line came into existence in England in about sixteen hundred seventy.
2. This stage covered a distance of six hundred and fifty-one kilometers.
3. Did coaches in England travel at least fifty-five million miles before the railways replaced them?
4. 200 years ago the United States Congress began mail service by stagecoach.
5. A trip of 360 miles meant drivers changed horses eighteen times.
6. Some trips from Philadelphia to Ohio began at six-thirty A.M.
7. The 1st stagecoach lines were established in colonial America in seventeen hundred fifty-six.
8. Horse-drawn coaches rode along at ten miles per hour.
9. Now Americans can fly to London in the Concorde jet at nearly fourteen hundred miles per hour.
10. Before eighteen hundred seventy-five the streetcar (or tram) had replaced the horse-drawn coach.
11. The 1st streetcars were called horsecars because horses pulled them.
12. By nineteen hundred and ten electric streetcars had replaced horsecars.

### Writing Link

Imagine that you're visiting Colorado and you take a stagecoach ride. Write a paragraph describing your ride. Use numbers in your sentences.

# *Mechanics* Workshop

## Punctuation

Time travel is one of Jack Finney's favorite subjects. "The presidents of the New York Central and the New York, New Haven and Hartford railroads will swear on a stack of timetables that there are only two," writes Finney in the story "The Third Level." However, Finney's narrator believes there are three levels at Grand Central Station, the monumental railroad station located in the heart of Manhattan. The passage has been annotated to show some of the rules of punctuation covered in this unit.

### *Literature Model*

#### *from* THE THIRD LEVEL

#### *by Jack Finney*

I turned into Grand Central from Vanderbilt Avenue, and went down the steps to the first level, where you take trains like the Twentieth Century . Then I walked down another flight to the second level, where the suburban trains leave from, ducked into an arched doorway heading for the subway—and got lost. That's easy to do. I've been in and out of Grand Central hundreds of times , but I'm always bumping into new doorways and stairs and corridors. Once I got into a tunnel about a mile long and came out in the lobby of the Roosevelt Hotel. Another time I came up in an office building on Forty - sixth Street, three blocks away.

Sometimes I think Grand Central is growing like a tree, pushing out new corridors and staircases like roots. There ' s probably a long tunnel that nobody knows about feeling its way under the city right now, on its way to Times Square, and maybe another to Central ➡

*Annotations (left margin):*

Period at the end of a declarative sentence

Comma before *but* that is joining main clauses

Hyphen in compound number

Apostrophe in a contraction

Park. And maybe — because for so many people through the years Grand Central *has* been an exit, a way of escape — maybe that's how the tunnel I got into . . . But I never told my psychiatrist friend about that idea.

Dashes to show an interruption in thought

## Mechanics Workshop Exercise 1

**Using End Punctuation**   Write each sentence, adding the correct end mark.

1. The narrator, a young man named Charley, claimed there were three levels at Grand Central Station
2. What a crazy idea
3. His friends didn't believe him
4. Would you believe him
5. Think of when your friends didn't believe you

## Mechanics Workshop Exercise 2

**Using Commas**   Write each sentence, adding commas where needed.

1. Having worked late Charley was in a hurry to get home.
2. He wanted to get home to Louisa his wife.
3. Because he was in a hurry he decided to take the subway rather than the bus.
4. He had been in Grand Central hundreds of times but he still got lost.
5. "That's easy to do" he said.

## Mechanics Workshop Exercise 3

**Using Punctuation Correctly**   Write each sentence, adding punctuation marks where needed. Use the punctuation marks indicated in parentheses. ➡

| SAMPLE | Thats easy to do. (apostrophe) |
|---|---|
| ANSWER | That's easy to do. |

1. I think Grand Central is growing like a tree, said Charley. (quotation marks)
2. Charley claimed he wasn't trying to escape he just wanted to get home. (semicolon)
3. He once ended up in an office building on Forty sixth Street. (hyphen)
4. Charleys wife must have wondered what happened to him. (apostrophe)
5. On the third level he found a newspaper called The World. (underlining for italics)

## Mechanics Workshop Exercise 4

**Proofreading**  The following passage is about Russian artist Simon Faibisovich, whose work appears on the next page. Rewrite the passage, correcting the errors in spelling, capitalization, punctuation, grammar, and usage. There are ten errors in all.

### Simon Faibisovich

[1] Simon Faigisovich is a russian painter who lives in Moscow. [2] Trained as an architect he taught hisself to paint. [3] His work was never shown publically before American gallery owner Phyllis Kind discovered him in 1987. [4] There have been several shows of his work in New York and chicago since then.

[5] Faibisovich paints large pictures of ordinary people doing ordinary things like stand at a bus stop or waiting in line for food. [6] His portraits are more than just snapshots. [7] The faces of the people he paints reflects a yearning for something else in their lifes. [8] Just as Charley views a train station as an opportunity to escape, the boy in the painting on the opposite page is clearly longing for something other then just another bus ride.

**Simon Faibisovich,** *Boy,* **1984**

# Punctuation

## End Marks and Other Punctuation

[pages 526–540]

Write each sentence. Add end marks, commas, semicolons, colons, quotation marks, italics, apostrophes, hyphens, dashes, and parentheses where needed.

1. Captain Jacques Cousteau developed a new means of transportation
2. Have you seen the television series The Undersea World of Jaques Cousteau
3. What a strange new boat that is
4. Please read about Cousteau's life
5. Helicopters are known as choppers eggbeaters or whirlybirds.
6. Igor Sikorsky an engineer flew the first single-rotor helicopter.
7. Today helicopters fly from Bethesda Maryland to Washington D.C.
8. The burro furnishes more than local color it provides the best means of transportation to some areas.
9. The Arctic is frozen land said Jamie.
10. People used dog sleds they had no other way to haul their belongings.

## Abbreviations

[pages 542–543]

Write each of the following sentences. Use the correct abbreviation for the underlined word or words that appear in each sentence.

11. <u>Mister</u> Tyler Jefferson is meeting me downtown.
12. We spent last summer at our house in Aspen, <u>Colorado</u>.
13. Pick up my friend Carmen at 429 Russell <u>Place</u>.
14. My new pool is four <u>feet</u> deep at its shallowest point.
15. The long-awaited letter from <u>Doctor</u> Langley has arrived.

## Numbers

[pages 544–545]

Write each sentence. Use the correct form for writing numbers in each sentence.

16. The ski lift closes at six fifteen P.M.
17. Modern skiing began about eighteen hundred fifty.
18. 90% of all skiers today ski for recreational purposes.
19. I always take 2 pairs of skis with me when I go skiing.
20. I'm 6th in line for the ski lift.

## Writing for Review

Would you rather be a snow skier or a water skier? Write a paragraph explaining your choice.

# Grammar Through Sentence Combining

Henri Matisse, *Beasts of the Sea*, 1950

## 21.1 Prepositional Phrases

Prepositional phrases are useful in sentence combining. Like adjectives and adverbs they enable you to give more information about nouns and verbs. Because prepositional phrases show relationships, they often express complex ideas effectively.

---

EXAMPLE
a. Latoya Hunter faithfully kept a diary.
b. Latoya's home was **New York City**. [from]
c. She wrote the diary **in seventh grade**.

Latoya Hunter **from New York City** faithfully kept a diary **in seventh grade**.

---

The new information in sentences *b* and *c* (in dark type) takes the form of prepositional phrases when added to sentence *a*. In the new sentence the phrase *from New York City* modifies the noun *Latoya Hunter*. The phrase *in seventh grade* modifies the verb *kept*. Prepositional phrases that modify nouns follow the nouns they modify. Prepositional phrases that modify verbs come before or after the verbs they modify. (For a list of common prepositions see page 430.)

A **prepositional phrase** is a group of words that begins with a preposition and ends with a noun or pronoun. Prepositional phrases modify nouns, pronouns, and verbs.

---

### Exercise 1

**Combining Sentences with Prepositional Phrases**
The following sentences are based on passages from *The Diary of Latoya Hunter,* which you can find on pages 30–34. Combine each group of sentences. Turn the new information into a prepositional phrase. In the first few items the new information is in dark type.

1. a. Latoya missed her old social life.
   b. She was **attending her new school**. [at] ➡

**2. a.** Latoya envied her diary.
   **b.** She envied the diary **for its detachment**.
**3. a.** Latoya's best friend had moved away.
   **b.** She moved **during the spring**.
**4. a.** Latoya's progress is revealed in her diary.
   **b.** Her progress was toward greater maturity.
**5. a.** Each new entry is like a snapshot.
   **b.** The entry is in her diary.
   **c.** The snapshot is of the writer's mind.
**6. a.** Latoya's diary traces her development.
   **b.** Her development was from an unhappy girl.
   **c.** Her development was into a self-confident young woman.

Exercise 2

**Combining Sentences**   Rewrite the paragraph below. Use prepositional phrases to combine sentences. Make any other changes in wording that you feel are necessary.

Latoya devoted one entry to a former teacher. The entry is in her diary. Her words create a wonderful picture. The words are about Mr. Pelka. The picture is of a warm and caring man. The class learned to empathize with other people. They learned this from Mr. Pelka. One day she learned the moving story of a Jewish girl. This girl lived in the time of the Holocaust. Mr. Pelka should go down in history. This is according to Latoya.

## *Invitation to Write*

Have you ever considered writing a diary of your own? What are some of the advantages of keeping a diary? Write a paragraph explaining whether the idea appeals to you and giving your reasons.

## 21.2 Appositives

You can use appositives to combine sentences in a compact and informative way. Appositives and appositive phrases identify or tell something new about a noun or a pronoun.

> EXAMPLE   **a.** Mars is too cold to support life.
> **b.** Mars is **Earth's neighbor**. [, + ,]
>
> Mars, **Earth's neighbor**, is too cold to support life.

The appositive phrase *Earth's neighbor* tells us more about the noun *Mars*. Note that the appositive phrase is set off with commas because it gives extra information about Mars. If an appositive supplies information that is essential for identifying a noun, it is not set off with commas. (For more information on appositives, see pages 350–351.)

An **appositive** is a noun placed next to another noun to identify it or give additional information about it. An **appositive phrase** includes an appositive and other words that describe it.

### Exercise 3

**Combining Sentences with Appositives**   The sentences below are based on an excerpt from *Living Treasure* by Laurence Pringle, which you can find on pages 238–242. Combine each group of sentences so that the new information is turned into an appositive or an appositive phrase. In the first few items the new information is in dark type, and the information in brackets indicates that you should add a comma or commas to the new sentence.

1.  **a.** Because of its climate our own planet is an oasis.
    **b.** The planet is **Earth**. [, + ,]
2.  **a.** According to the writer, scientists are astounded by the great diversity of life forms on earth.
    **b.** The writer is **Laurence Pringle**. ➡

3. **a.** The Swedish botanist developed the Linnaean system.
   **b.** The botanist was **Carl von Linné**.
   **c.** The Linnaean system is **the modern means of classifying plants and animals**. **[,]**
4. **a.** One threat to humanity is the loss of biodiversity.
   **b.** Biodiversity is the variety of life on earth.
5. **a.** The tropical rain forest is valuable to all of us.
   **b.** The rain forest is the heart of the earth's biodiversity.
   **c.** All of us are inhabitants of this planet.

**Exercise 4**

**Combining Sentences**   Rewrite the following paragraph. Use appositives and appositive phrases to combine sentences. Make any changes in wording that you feel are necessary.

   Funding for tropical research increased in the 1980s. This was a period of discovery of the rain forest. From one tree in Peru, for example, the entomologist collected many ants. The entomologist was Terry Erwin. His ants were examined by Edward O. Wilson. Wilson was a biologist at Harvard University. In that one tree Wilson discovered as many ant species as have been identified in all of Canada or Great Britain. These are areas far to the north of the rain forest. The biodiversity of the planet is probably unique in the solar system. The planet is Earth.

### Invitation to Write

   Choose one small living thing—an insect or a plant—and closely observe its physical appearance. Then write a paragraph describing your subject.

## 21.3 Adjective Clauses

Adjective clauses are useful in sentence combining. When two sentences share information, one of them can often be made into an adjective clause modifying a word or phrase in the other.

EXAMPLE
**a.** Dara and Jantu had both lost part of their families.
**b.** Dara and Jantu **were good friends**. [, who . . . ,]

Dara and Jantu, **who were good friends,** had both lost part of their families.

The new information in sentence *b* (in dark type) becomes an adjective clause modifying *Dara and Jantu* in sentence *a*. *Who* now connects the clauses. Notice the commas in the new sentence. Adjective clauses that add nonessential information require commas. Those that add essential information do not. (For more information see pages 452–453.)

An **adjective clause** is a subordinate clause that modifies a noun or pronoun in the main clause. The relative pronouns *who, whom, whose, which,* and *that* are used to tie the adjective clause to the main clause.

### Exercise 5

**Combining Sentences with Adjective Clauses**   The following sentences are based on an excerpt from *The Clay Marble* by Minfong Ho, which you can find on pages 88–92. Combine each numbered group of sentences so that the new information is turned into an adjective clause. In the first few items the new information is in dark type; the information in brackets indicates the relative pronoun to use and that a comma or commas are needed.

1. **a.** Jantu spent afternoons under the stone beam.
   **b.** She **loved to play with clay**. [, who . . . ,]
2. **a.** Palm fronds shaded one end of the beam.
   **b.** The beam **became a cavelike shelter**. [, which] ➡

3. **a.** Jantu made delicate figures from clay.
   **b. She had scooped** this clay **from a mud puddle. [that]**
4. **a.** Dara would watch Jantu.
   **b.** Dara **would hold Jantu's baby brother. [, who . . . ,]**
5. **a.** The girls talked of family members.
   **b. They had lost** family members. **[whom]**
6. **a.** Continuity in her life was important to Dara.
   **b.** Dara hated change.
7. **a.** The war had made many people suffer.
   **b.** The war had broken Jantu's family.
8. **a.** Jantu described a real family as a loving group.
   **b.** This group grows with new members all the time.

## Exercise 6

**Combining Sentences**   Rewrite the paragraph below.
Use adjective clauses to combine sentences. Make any
changes in wording and punctuation you feel necessary.

Jantu showed Dara some clay figures. Jantu wanted to
comfort her. The girls were interrupted by a rainfall. The
rainfall reminded Dara of long-lost rainy afternoons with
her family. Dara imagined her family as a soft blanket.
The blanket sheltered her. Jantu invited Dara to play
with the family of dolls. Jantu was remembering her own
lost family. In the clay figures Dara recognized her own
family members as well as members of Jantu's family.
Jantu had made their broken families whole again. Jantu
had the skill and the imagination of an artist.

### Invitation to Write

Think of a special friend with whom you can always
talk things over. Write a brief paragraph describing the
qualities that make your friend so special to you.

## 21.4 Adverb Clauses

You can use adverb clauses to combine sentences. They are especially effective when you wish to establish clear relationships between two or more actions. For example, adverb clauses can indicate that one action follows another or causes another.

EXAMPLE
**a.** Bel Kaufman read a great deal as a girl.
**b.** She was trying to master the English language. **[because]**

Bel Kaufman read a great deal as a girl **because she was trying to master the English language**.

In the new sentence the adverb clause *because she was trying to master the English language* modifies the verb *read.* The adverb clause tells why Bel Kaufman was reading so much. Note that the subordinating conjunction *because* makes this relationship very clear. An adverb clause may occupy several positions within a sentence. If it begins the sentence, it is followed by a comma. (For more information on adverb clauses, see pages 454–455.)

An **adverb clause** is a subordinate clause that modifies the verb in the main clause. Adverb clauses are introduced by subordinating conjunctions such as *after, although, because, before, since, when, whenever, if,* and *while.*

### Exercise 7

**Combining Sentences with Adverb Clauses** The following sentences are based on "The Liberry" by Bel Kaufman on pages 288–290. Use adverb clauses to combine each group of sentences. In the first few items the information in brackets signals the subordinating conjunction and the punctuation you should use.

1. **a.** Bel Kaufman came to New York City at the age of twelve. **[Before . . . ,]**
   **b.** She had lived in Russia. ➡

**2. a.** She never felt the need to use the library's card catalog.
  **b.** She went through the bookshelves alphabetically. **[because]**
**3. a.** She found a book with dogeared pages and many dates on its card. **[Whenever . . . ,]**
  **b.** She recognized a book that she would probably want to read.
**4. a.** Kaufman glanced through a book's pages. **[When . . . ,]**
  **b.** She enjoyed reading comments scribbled in the margins.
  **c.** She knew it was wrong to mark up a library book. **[although]**
**5. a.** One reader might write "How True!" in a book's margins.
  **b.** Another reader would write "This book stinks." **[, whereas]**
**6. a.** Kaufman always knew that the librarian was there for her.
  **b.** She needed help finding a book that she wanted to read.
**7. a.** Kaufman especially enjoyed reading books that were unassigned.
  **b.** She read those just for her own pleasure.
**8. a.** Kaufman wrote an essay about the importance of libraries.
  **b.** She was very concerned about cuts in funds for libraries.
**9. a.** People are increasingly troubled about children's reading skills.
  **b.** Public libraries are closing their doors.
**10. a.** People have less leisure time.
  **b.** They are less inclined to read.
**11. a.** In a library it is hard to avoid sitting down and reading a book.
  **b.** You are surrounded by large numbers of books and readers. ➡

**12.** **a.** It has a vast selection of reference works.
   **b.** They have to get information on a special assignment or project.
   **c.** The public library is also invaluable for many people.

Exercise 8

**Combining Sentences**   Rewrite the following paragraphs. Use adverb clauses to combine sentences. Make any other changes in punctuation or wording that you feel are necessary.

What needs do libraries fill? According to Bel Kaufman, libraries offer us a quiet refuge. We seek peace and privacy. Libraries also give people a chance to read. They have no other access to free books.

Bel Kaufman is very distressed about library closings. She remembers libraries so fondly. She taught high school English in New York City. She required her students to bring a library card to class. They actually had a card. They might go to the library. One student brought in his aunt's card. He did not have one of his own. Nevertheless, some of her students did use their cards. The cards were there. Some people still go to the library. The library is still there. According to Kaufman, the city will suffer. Everyone's neighborhood library is forced to close.

### Invitation to Write

Write about a valuable custom or institution that seems to be disappearing. Explain what gives it its value, why it is disappearing, and what might happen if it disappears.

# Part 3

# Resources and Skills

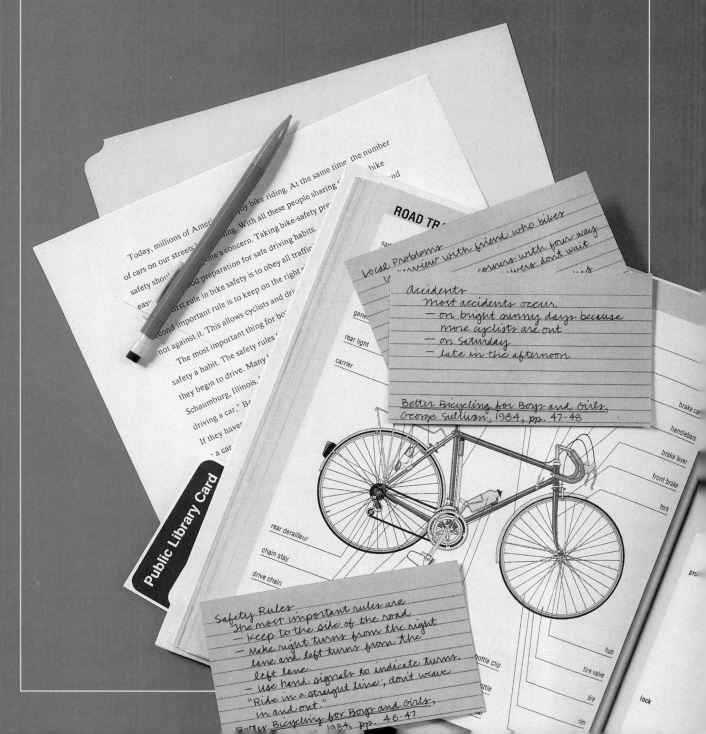

# Part 3 Resources and Skills

# Library and Reference Resources

## 22.1 The Arrangement of a Library

The library is a good place to satisfy your curiosity about anything from aardvarks to Zuñi Indians. It also offers a wealth of information you can use for school assignments and projects.

A trip to the library can be eye opening even when you don't have a purpose in mind. Just browsing, you might find a new magazine that's all about your favorite hobby. You might spot a video of a movie you've been wanting to see. Or you might find a book about a place you've always wanted to visit.

You can expect to make discoveries at a library. You can also expect most libraries to be arranged in roughly the same way. Turn the page to learn more about the arrangement of a library.

**Librarian** Call on the librarian whenever you need help. A librarian can show you how to locate the right resources and find the information you need.

**Young Adult and Children's Section** Books for younger readers, up to about age sixteen, are usually found in a separate area of the library.

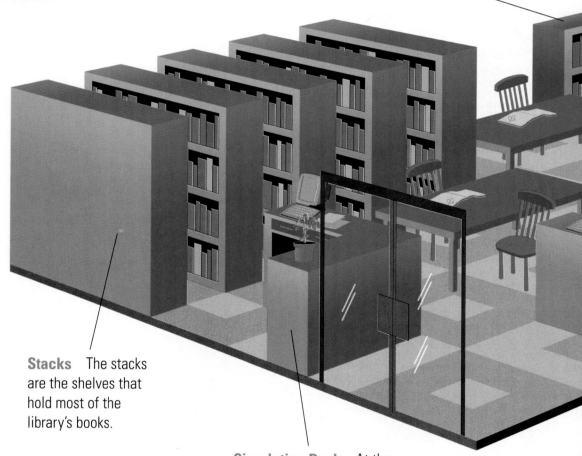

**Stacks** The stacks are the shelves that hold most of the library's books.

**Circulation Desk** At the circulation desk you check out the books you want to use outside the library.

**Reference** The reference section has dictionaries, encyclopedias, atlases, almanacs, and other reference works. Most reference materials can be used only in the library.

**Audio-Visual Materials** Videos, records, audiotapes, and compact discs are found in the audio-visual section. A librarian there can tell you which items you may check out.

**Newspapers and Magazines** Current issues of newspapers and periodicals are kept in a general reading area. A librarian can help you find older issues.

**Library Catalog** The library catalog contains information about each book in the library and gives the book's location. Most libraries have a card catalog. Many have a computer catalog as well.

---

### Exercise 1

In which section of the library might you find each of the following items?

1. A video of the film *Across Five Aprils*
2. *The Times Atlas of World Exploration*
3. This week's issue of *Sports Illustrated*
4. *Dictionary of the Middle Ages*
5. *A Wrinkle in Time* (a fantasy novel for young readers)

## 22.2　The Dewey Decimal System

Suppose a library had no system for organizing its books. You'd have to search every shelf to find a book you wanted. Many public libraries use the Dewey Decimal system to organize their books. This system groups books into ten broad categories of knowledge, as shown on the chart below.

| Dewey Decimal System | | | |
|---|---|---|---|
| Category Numbers | Major Category | Example of a Subcategory | Sample Book Title |
| 000–099 | General works | Encyclopedias | *World Book Encyclopedia* |
| 100–199 | Philosophy | The senses | *The Amazing Five Senses* |
| 200–299 | Religion | Mythology | *Greek Mythology* |
| 300–399 | Social sciences | Law | *We, the People* |
| 400–499 | Language | Chinese language | *Speaking Chinese* |
| 500–599 | Science | Astronomy | *The Night Sky Book* |
| 600–699 | Technology | Medicine | *Sports Medicine* |
| 700–799 | The arts | Dance | *Ballet Basics* |
| 800–899 | Literature | Plays | *Our Town* |
| 900–999 | History | Mexican history | *The Ancient Maya* |

Books in each major category are labeled with a similar number. For example, all books about science have a number in the 500s. Books about the arts—for example, painting, sculpture, photography, dance, theater—have numbers in the 700s.

Each major category is broken up into smaller categories. Each added digit, or single numeral, in the Dewey Decimal number narrows the category further. A book about photography would have a number in the 770s. Look at the Dewey Decimal number on the following page for *Mountains of Fire*. This book by Robert W. Decker is about volcanoes. Notice how each digit in the number further narrows down the topic.

| | | | |
|---|---|---|---|
| 500 | **Science** | A book about science is listed in the 500s. |
| 550 | **Earth Sciences** | This book is about a subcategory of science. |
| 551 | **Geology** | Geology is a subcategory of earth sciences. |
| 551.21 | **Volcanoes** | The numbers after the decimal narrow down the topic even further. |

Books are shelved in order according to the Dewey Decimal number and then alphabetically by author. For example, among all the books with number 551.21, a book by Robert W. Decker would come before a book by Margaret Poynter.

A fiction book is not usually given a Dewey Decimal number. Instead, the first line of the call number is either an *F* or *FIC*, for *fiction*. The second line almost always shows the first three letters of the author's name. Fiction books are arranged on the shelves by the author's last name. Books by the same author are further alphabetized by title.

### Exercise 2

Go to the nonfiction stacks in your school or neighborhood library. Find a book that looks interesting in each category listed below. Write down the book's Dewey Decimal number, author, title, and topic.

1. 000–099
2. 100–099
3. 300–399
4. 600–699
5. 700–799

How do you find the book you want in a library filled with books? The library catalog is the best place to start. Your library may have a card catalog, a computer catalog, or both. Either catalog can tell you which books the library owns.

## Using a Card Catalog

The card catalog, a cabinet of long, narrow drawers, holds cards describing each book in the library. The cards are arranged in alphabetical order.

Look at the examples below to see what kind of information is included on a card for a nonfiction book. The book's Dewey Decimal number, or call number, is usually printed in the upper-left corner of the card. This number also appears on the spine of the book.

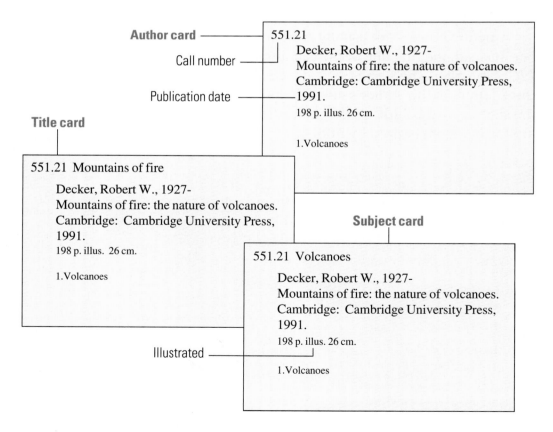

Author card — Call number — Publication date

551.21
Decker, Robert W., 1927-
Mountains of fire: the nature of volcanoes.
Cambridge: Cambridge University Press, 1991.
198 p. illus. 26 cm.

1.Volcanoes

Title card

551.21  Mountains of fire
Decker, Robert W., 1927-
Mountains of fire: the nature of volcanoes.
Cambridge:  Cambridge University Press, 1991.
198 p. illus.  26 cm.

1.Volcanoes

Subject card

551.21  Volcanoes
Decker, Robert W., 1927-
Mountains of fire: the nature of volcanoes.
Cambridge:  Cambridge University Press, 1991.
198 p. illus. 26 cm.

Illustrated

1.Volcanoes

Most fiction books have two cards: an author card and a title card. Nonfiction books usually have three catalog cards: an author card, a title card, and a subject card. In some libraries, subject cards are grouped separately from author and title cards.

You may also see cross-reference cards in the catalog. These cards direct you to other ways a subject is listed in the catalog.

## Using a Computer Catalog

Many libraries have a computer catalog in addition to a card catalog. You can use the computer catalog instead of the card catalog to search for authors, titles, and subjects. For example, suppose you are looking for books about volcanoes. Your computer search might proceed as follows:

1. Type in the subject, *volcanoes*.
2. The computer will show a list of all the books in the library on this subject. Each item is numbered.
3. Now, for more detailed information on an item, type in its number.
4. You will then see a screen, like the one shown here, with detailed information about the book.

The way the computer catalog works may differ slightly from library to library. Follow the on-screen directions to use any computer catalog. If you have trouble with your search, ask a librarian for help.

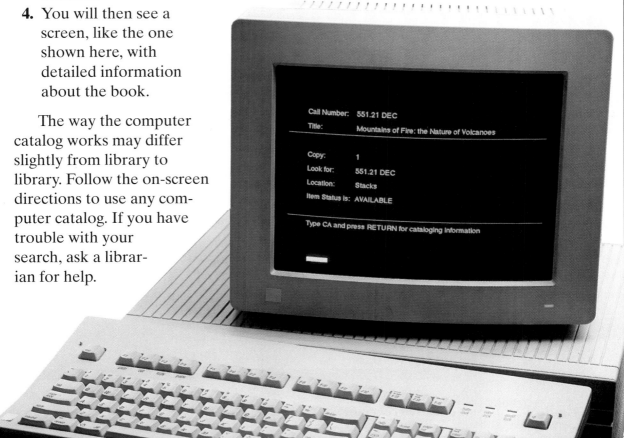

Call Number: 551.21 DEC
Title: Mountains of Fire: the Nature of Volcanoes

Copy: 1
Look for: 551.21 DEC
Location: Stacks
Item Status is: AVAILABLE

Type CA and press RETURN for cataloging information

# *Finding a Book*

When you have located a book you want in the catalog, write down its call number. In the stacks locate the shelf that holds books with numbers close to your call number. For example, if your number is 862.12, first find the 800s section. Then look for the 860s. If several books have the same call number, they will be shelved alphabetically by author.

**Identify** the book by the specific author, title, or subject.

**Look up** the book in the card catalog or the computer catalog.

**Find** the book in the stacks or in the reference section.

**Check out** the book at the circulation desk unless it must be used only in the library.

## Exercise 3

Use the card catalog or computer catalog to find a book for each of the following topics. List the author, title, and call number of each book you find.

1. Types of sailing ships
2. Rocks and minerals
3. Japan's economy
4. Castles
5. Egyptian mythology
6. Poems by Myra Cohn Livingston
7. Geometry
8. African masks
9. Guide dogs
10. Olmec civilization

## 22.4 Basic Reference Books

The next time you want to satisfy your curiosity about the world, try the library's reference section. The reference section contains many general information sources. These sources are useful when you are doing research or working on a class assignment. They're useful any time you need an answer to a question. The chart below gives some examples of the kinds of questions basic references can answer.

| Using Basic Reference Books to Answer Questions | | |
| --- | --- | --- |
| Question | Where to Look | Examples of Sources |
| When did Elizabeth I rule England? | **Encyclopedias** include general information on a variety of topics. | • World Book Encyclopedia<br>• Grolier Encyclopedia<br>• Encyclopedia Britannica |
| What is the average temperature in Lagos, Nigeria? | **Atlases** are collections of maps. They often include special maps on climate, population, and other topics. | • Hammond Contemporary World Atlas<br>• The Rand McNally Atlas of World Exploration |
| Who won the Nobel Prize for literature in 1992? | **Almanacs** provide lists, statistics, and detailed information on recent events. | • Information Please Almanac<br>• World Almanac and Book of Facts |

## *Encyclopedias*

You have probably used encyclopedias for research papers and class projects. These basic reference books may be contained in a single volume or in many volumes. General encyclopedias have articles on a wide variety of topics. Some examples are countries, animals, noteworthy people, historical events, and scientific ideas. Whatever you're looking for, you'll probably find something about it in an encyclopedia.

An encyclopedia is a good place to start a research project. An encyclopedia article will give you an overview of the topic. It may provide a list of books for further research.

In addition to general encyclopedias, most libraries have some specialized encyclopedias. These provide more detailed information on a specific subject. Two examples are the *Encyclopedia of Sports* and the *Encyclopedia of Science*.

Articles in an encyclopedia are arranged alphabetically. To find out if an encyclopedia has information on your topic, look up the topic in the index. The index may be contained in a separate volume. The index will tell you the volume and page numbers on which the information appears. Below is a sample encyclopedia page.

| | |
|---|---|
| *The guide word names the first complete entry.* | |

| | |
|---|---|
| *"See also" references lead you to other articles on the topic.* | |

| | |
|---|---|
| *A longer article may list books that contain additional information.* | |

| | |
|---|---|
| *Entries may be only a few sentences or several pages long.* | |

**196 · Dickey, James**

Recent criticism has demonstrated that Dickens can no longer be regarded only as an entertainer, though his ability to entertain is probably the major reason for his popularity. Whatever his other claims to greatness may be, Dickens ranks as a superbly inventive comic artist. His characters have been compared to those of Shakespeare in their variety, color, energy, and life. Dickens was aware of human evil, but he never lost his perspective. His art was sustained by an awareness and appreciation of the human comedy. K. K. Collins

See also *Dickens, Charles,* in the Research Guide/Index, Volume 22, for a *Reading and Study Guide.*

**Additional resources**

*The Charles Dickens Encyclopedia.* Comp. by John M. D. Hardwick and M. G. Hardwick. Scribner, 1973.
Frank, Lawrence. *Charles Dickens and the Romantic Self.* Univ. of Nebraska Press, 1984.
Johnson, Edgar. *Charles Dickens: His Tragedy and Triumph.* Rev. ed. Viking, 1977/Abridgment of original 1952 edition.
MacKenzie, Norman I. and J. D. *Dickens: A Life.* Oxford, 1979.
Page, Norman. *A Dickens Companion.* Schocken, 1983.
Wilson, Angus. *The World of Charles Dickens.* Academy Chicago, 1984. First published in 1970.

**Dickey, James** (1923- ), is an American poet and novelist. He is known chiefly for works that portray people testing their survival instincts against other people and nature. Some of his writings explore people's animal instincts, which include killing for enjoyment. Dickey writes in a clear, matter-of-fact style that shows people learning about the brutal side of human nature.

Dickey's novel *Deliverance* (1970) tells about a middle-class businessman who must struggle to survive in the wilderness. In his fight to survive, he has to kill another man. This experience teaches him that cruelty is part of people's nature. Many of Dickey's writings are based on episodes from his own life. Some of his works, particularly the poem "The Firebombing" (1964), reflect his experiences as a combat pilot. The pilot in this poem feels a sense of power at killing, but no sorrow.

Dickey was born in Atlanta, Ga. He won the National Book Award for poetry in 1966 for his collection *Buckdancer's Choice* (1965). His other collections include *Poems 1957-1967* (1967) and *The Strength of Fields* (1980). A number of his prose pieces were published in *Sorties: Journals and New Essays* (1971). Marcus Klein

**Dickinson, Anna Elizabeth** (1842-1932), was an orator of the Civil War period who spoke on abolitionism and women's rights. Woman orators were a novelty at that time, and Dickinson became known as the North's "Joan of Arc." She attracted large crowds with her emotional pleas to end slavery.

Dickinson was born in Philadelphia. She gave her first important speech in 1860, the year before the Civil War began, when she addressed the Pennsylvania Anti-Slavery Society. Dickinson was then only 18 years old. The next year,

*Dictionary of American Portraits*
**Anna E. Dickinson**

she spoke on the "Rights and Wrongs of Women." In 1864, she denounced the South in a speech to members of the U.S. Congress and President Abraham Lincoln.

After the Civil War, Dickinson frequently lectured on feminism and blacks' rights. She spoke for organizations called *lyceums,* which sponsored adult education programs. During some years, she earned as much as $20,000, a large income for anyone of her day.

Dickinson's speaking career declined in the early 1870's. She campaigned for the Democratic Party in 1872, and for the Republicans in 1888. She spent her last 40 years in seclusion. Nancy Spelman Woloch

**Dickinson, Emily** (1830-1886), was an American poet. Dickinson and Walt Whitman are considered the two most gifted poets in American literature. Like Whitman, she was influenced by the writings of American author Ralph Waldo Emerson. In her verses, Dickinson expressed Emerson's late pessimism. Many of her poems reflect the alienation of American intellectuals after the Civil War (1861-1865).

**Her life.** Emily Dickinson was born in Amherst, Mass., on Dec. 10, 1830. She was reclusive, and much about her is unknown. She never married, and after turning 30, seldom saw anyone other than her immediate family.

Dickinson's seclusion from society has fascinated her readers. Scholars believe that she chose to think and write in, as she wrote, "her own Society," rather than in the narrow-minded literary establishment of her time. This establishment expected female writers to confine themselves to domestic subjects and sentimental observations. Furthermore, there were few opportunities for the unmarried professional woman in America during the 1800's. Therefore, Dickinson chose to remain in her comfortable, upper-middle-class home. Although Dickinson's choice no longer seems so strange, people in her town viewed her as a curiosity and finally resented her unavailability.

*The Trustees of Amherst College, Amherst, Mass.*
**Emily Dickinson**

Dickinson always wrote as what she called the "supposed person." This person never tired of examining the unique facts of existence. Hidden away on the second story of her parents' home, she analyzed practically every aspect of nature in poems that she began to bind into small books that were called *fascicles.*

At about the age of 30, Dickinson began to look intensely at life itself, rather than looking for the normal expectations of life. While the Civil War raged, she produced the most and best of her poems. The poet continued to write in the 1870's but at a much slower pace. Probably one of her best poems, however, was written during this period of decline. Called "A Route of Evanescence," it describes the fluttering ascent of a hummingbird. For Dickinson, this erratic ascent was also the route of experience. Life was finally inscrutable, and its joy was to be found in studying its paradoxes.

**Her poems.** Dickinson wrote more than 1,700 poems, but scholars generally agree that she did not

## *Atlases*

An atlas is a collection of maps. Some atlases contain maps of all the countries in the world. The *Times Atlas of the World* is an example of a large general atlas. Other atlases may focus on one continent or one country. An atlas of the United States, for example, generally includes one or more maps of each state.

The maps in an atlas show various land and water areas—mountains, plateaus, oceans, lakes, and rivers. These are called natural, or physical, features. Maps also show cities, towns, roads, countries, and boundaries between places. These are called cultural features because they were made by people. Many atlases have special maps showing climate, population, natural resources, and other special information.

## Almanacs

Who first ran a mile in less than four minutes? What's the population of Bolivia? When is the next eclipse of the sun? What is the world's highest mountain? Largest ocean? Longest river? Deepest lake? Coldest place? The answers to these and thousands of other questions are in an almanac.

An almanac is a book of up-to-date general information. Almanacs are usually published once a year. They contain the most recent information for the preceding year. An almanac includes lists of important people and events and facts about governments, history, geography, and weather. It gives figures on population, industry, farm production, and much more.

Because an almanac presents a huge amount of information in very concise form, you can locate a specific fact very quickly. To look up a specific fact, use the index. An almanac's index is often placed at the front of the book rather than at the back.

## Exercise 4

Which would be the best resource to answer each of the following questions—an encyclopedia, an atlas, or an almanac?

1. Of what country is Maputo the capital?
2. Who was Victoria Woodhull?
3. Who was the Hero of Young America in 1989?
4. Is Thailand primarily forest or crop land?
5. What is a kookaburra, and where does it live?
6. What is the major cause of acid rain?
7. Who won the World Cup in soccer in 1990?
8. In what ocean are the Cook Islands located?
9. What countries border Lake Chad in Africa?
10. What film won the Academy Award for best picture in 1990?

## 22.5　Other Library Resources

When you think about a library's resources, you probably think of books. However, most modern libraries offer much more than books. Some libraries are now called resource centers to show that they include resources other than books.

### *Print Resources*

Newspapers and magazines, like books, are print resources. They offer up-to-date information on current events and issues. Most newspapers are published daily. Newspapers cover major national and world events as well as events of interest to the local community. Some newspapers, such as *U.S.A. Today* and the *Wall Street Journal*, are published nationwide. Most others are local newspapers.

Magazines, also called periodicals, are usually published weekly or monthly. Magazines that emphasize current events, such as *Time* and *Newsweek*, are called news magazines. Others, such as *Sports Illustrated* and *National Geographic World*, emphasize special interests. Whatever your personal interests are, you can find magazines devoted to them.

### *Nonprint Resources*

Nonprint resources can take many different forms. Micro-forms, audiotapes, compact discs, and videotapes are some of the nonprint resources you can find in libraries.

**Microforms**　Libraries often store old issues of magazines and newspapers on microforms. Microforms are reduced images on either rolls of film (micro*film*) or small film cards (micro-*fiche*). An entire issue of a magazine can be stored on a three-by-five-inch or four-by-six-inch microfiche. Microforms save space and are less likely to be damaged by use.

Special viewing machines enlarge the photographs for viewing. Some viewing machines can also produce copies of the enlarged image. Such machines are usually located in the newspaper and magazine section.

**Sound Recordings**   If you want to listen to music, a poetry reading, or a drama reading, try your library's collection of audiotapes and compact discs (CDs). The library may have players for each of these sound resources in the audio-visual section. You can check these recordings out to take home.

**Video Recordings**   Most libraries with audio-visual sections have a collection of videotapes. There you may find tapes of films, documentaries, how-to videos, and travelogues. Videos, like sound recordings, are usually listed in a special catalog in the audio-visual section and may be checked out.

| Nonprint Resources | | |
|---|---|---|
| **Resource** | **Information Available** | **Equipment Needed** |
| **Microforms** | Back issues of newspapers and magazines | Microform viewer or viewer-printer |
| **Audiotapes and Compact Discs** | Music, readings, dramas, sound effects | Audiocassette or CD player |
| **Videotapes** | Movies, documentaries, travel films | VCR and television set |

### Exercise 5

In what library resource would you expect to find each of the following? (Resources include magazine, newspaper, microform, audiotape, CD, and videotape.) More than one answer may be possible in some cases.

1. The results of a political poll taken just before the presidential election of 1988
2. The musical *Into the Woods* by Stephen Sondheim
3. An issue of *Sports Illustrated* describing an auto race held last month
4. An article about a new bridge now being built in your community
5. A recording by Janet Jackson

## 22.6    Using Magazines

Suppose you wanted to find information on the latest developments in computer technology. How would you find magazine articles on your topic? Your best bet would be to check the *Readers' Guide to Periodical Literature*. Magazines are called periodicals because they are published periodically. That is, they come out at regular intervals, such as weekly or monthly. The *Readers' Guide* is a useful source for finding magazine articles on almost any subject.

## *Using the* Readers' Guide

The *Readers' Guide* lists articles from more than 175 magazines. The articles are indexed by author and subject. Updated issues of the *Readers' Guide* appear regularly throughout the year. The following example from the *Readers' Guide* shows you how to read its information.

**ANIMALS IN ART** ——————————————— Subject heading
      *See also* Horses in art
Nature is my model [work of A. Manocchia]  il
    *The Conservationist* 46:28-33 Ja/F '92 ———— Magazine title
Rock solid art [animal likenesses created by artists
    Lin and Kira Wellford] il *National Geographic*
    *World* 199:9-12 Mr '92 ———————————— Volume number
**ANIMALS IN CAPTIVITY**  *See Zoos* ——————— Cross-reference
**ANIMATED CARTOONS**  *See* Cable television—
    Cartoons; Television broadcasting—Cartoons
**ANIMATED FILMS** *See* Motion pictures—
    Animated films; Videotapes—Animated films
**ANIMATION ART**
  **Collectors and collecting** —————————— Subheading
    Around it goes. R. Stark. il *Antiques & Collecting*
      *Hobbies* 97:48+ Mr '92
    Collecting animation art: focusing on a theme.
      J. Altyn. il *Antiques & Collecting Hobbies*
      97:44+ Mr '92
    Saturday morning magic [Filmation cels] H.S. ——— Article title
      Miller. *Antiques & Collecting Hobbies* 97:42-3 — Page numbers
      Mr '92 —————————————————— Issue date
    What's up (doc) in celluloid? S. Koenigsberg. —— Author of article
    *Antiques & Collecting Hobbies* 97:45+ Mr '92

# *Finding an Article in a Periodical*

You have found a listing for an article you want to investigate. Now what do you do? First, keep in mind that many libraries do not carry all of the magazines listed in the *Readers' Guide*. Check with a librarian to make sure the library has the one you want.

Write down the title of the magazine and the article, the date of the issue, and the article's page numbers. If the issue is recent, you will probably find it on the shelves. Older issues may be kept in hard-bound volumes containing as many as a full year's issues. Or they may be stored on microforms that can be viewed on a special machine.

## Exercise 6

Answer the following questions, using the excerpt from the *Readers' Guide* on page 577.

1. What other topic may list articles about animals in art?
2. Who is the author of the article "What's Up (doc) in Celluloid?" under "Animation Art"?
3. In what magazine and which issue (month and year) would you find an article about animal art made from rocks?
4. Under what heading would you look for an article about animals in captivity?
5. Under what headings in the *Readers' Guide* would you find articles about animated cartoons?

A dictionary and a thesaurus can help put more words on the tip of your tongue and at the tip of your pencil. Both references are essential tools for writers.

## *The Dictionary*

A dictionary contains entries in alphabetical order. An entry is a single term, or word, along with its pronunciation, definition, and other information. Some characteristics of three types of dictionaries are summarized below.

### Types of Dictionaries

| | Characteristics | Examples |
|---|---|---|
| **Unabridged Dictionaries** | • Detailed word histories<br>• Detailed definitions<br>• Found mostly in libraries | • *Random House Dictionary of the English Language*<br>• *Webster's Third New International Dictionary* |
| **College Dictionaries** | • Detailed enough to answer most questions on spelling or definition<br>• Widely used in schools, homes, and businesses<br>• 130,000–250,000 entries | • *Random House Dictionary*<br>• *The American Heritage Dictionary*<br>• *Webster's New World Dictionary* |
| **School Dictionaries** | • Definitions suitable for students' grade levels<br>• Emphasizes common words<br>• 90,000 or fewer entries | • *Macmillan Dictionary*<br>• *Webster's School Dictionary* |

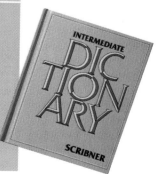

Each page of a dictionary has guide words along the top of the page. Guide words indicate the first and last entries on the page. Using the guide words will help you locate an entry much more quickly than browsing will.

Every page or every two-page spread has a pronunciation key at the bottom. The pronunciation key shows you how to use the special pronunciation symbols found in the dictionary.

Guide words

First entry on the page

Last entry on the page

Pronunciation key

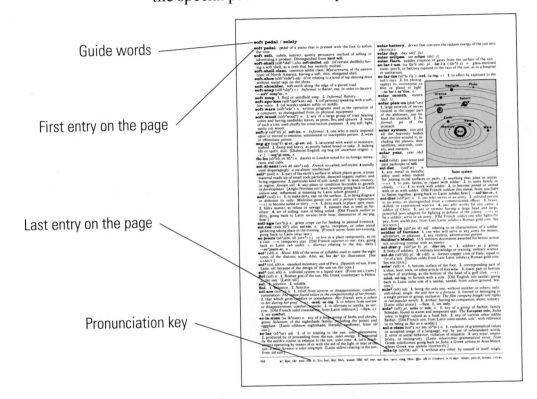

## *The Thesaurus*

A thesaurus is a special type of dictionary that lists only synonyms, or words with similar meanings. You probably most often use a dictionary to find the meaning of a particular word. When you use a thesaurus, you already know the meaning you want to convey. However, you need to find the word that best expresses that meaning. For example, you want to write that you were tired. But how tired were you? A thesaurus would give you *drained, exhausted, fatigued, tired, wearied, worn-out,* and more such words.

In a thesaurus entry each definition is followed by several synonyms. The entry may also include a cross-reference to one or more other major entries. If you look up a cross-reference entry, you will find more synonyms for the word listed. Following is an example of a thesaurus entry.

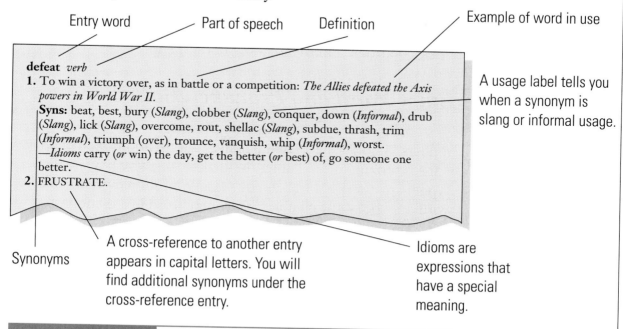

Entry word     Part of speech     Definition     Example of word in use

**defeat** *verb*
1. To win a victory over, as in battle or a competition: *The Allies defeated the Axis powers in World War II.*
**Syns:** beat, best, bury (*Slang*), clobber (*Slang*), conquer, down (*Informal*), drub (*Slang*), lick (*Slang*), overcome, rout, shellac (*Slang*), subdue, thrash, trim (*Informal*), triumph (over), trounce, vanquish, whip (*Informal*), worst.
—*Idioms* carry (*or* win) the day, get the better (*or* best) of, go someone one better.
2. FRUSTRATE.

A usage label tells you when a synonym is slang or informal usage.

Synonyms

A cross-reference to another entry appears in capital letters. You will find additional synonyms under the cross-reference entry.

Idioms are expressions that have a special meaning.

**Exercise 7**

Use a dictionary or a dictionary-style thesaurus to answer these questions.

1. What guide words are on the dictionary page that contains each of the following words?
   a. crackle     c. municipal
   b. groan      d. solarize
2. Other than at the bottoms of pages, where can you find a guide to pronunciation in a dictionary? Tell which dictionary you used to answer the question.
3. Does the word *deign* rhyme with *mine, mean,* or *main*?
4. What synonyms for *friendly* are listed in the thesaurus? Give at least three.
5. What are six synonyms for *sad*?

## 22.8 Using a Dictionary Entry

The dictionary offers much more than the definitions of words. In a dictionary you can find out how to divide a word into syllables. You can get information about a word's spelling and pronunciation, its part of speech, and its history. Many dictionaries have entries for places (like cities, countries, and rivers) and famous people.

### Entry Word and Pronunciation

A dictionary entry begins with the entry word. The word appears in bold type so that it stands out. In addition, the entry word is broken into syllables. In your writing you may need to hyphenate a word at the end of a line. You should break up a word only between syllables. The entry word in a dictionary will show you how to hyphenate a word.

The guide to a word's pronunciation follows the entry word. A special set of sound symbols shows how the word is pronounced. Simple words in the pronunciation key at the bottom of the page help you pronounce each symbol. Some of the vowel sounds would be shown in the pronunciation key something like this:

fat, āpe, cär; ten, ēven; is, bīte, gō, hôrn, fo͞ol, ūse

You also can find a complete pronunciation key at the front of the dictionary. Try using the sound symbols to pronounce the following word:

**in•noc•u•ous**   (i nok′ ū əs)

*Note that the last syllable has the schwa ( ə ) sound, which sounds like the a in ago.*

### Part of Speech

Dictionaries also indicate a word's part of speech. In the entry on the following page, for example, *partition* is first defined as a noun (*n.*) and then as a transitive verb (*v.t.*). You'll find a complete list of abbreviations used for the parts of speech at the front of the dictionary. The example shows the word's meanings for both parts of speech.

**par·ti·tion** (pär tish′ən) *n.* **1.** a dividing or being divided into shares or distinct parts; division or distribution of portions: *the partition of territory between rival states.* **2.** section or part into which a thing is divided. **3.** that which divides, as an interior wall separating parts of a room.–*v.t.* **1.** to divide into shares or distinct parts: *to partition land for sale, to partition office space into small cubicles.* **2.** to separate by a partition (with *off* ): *to partition off a space for storage.* [Latin *partitio* division.]

> *Note that* partition *as a noun means "a division." Partition as a verb means "to divide something into parts."*

> *The dictionary provides examples illustrating many of the word's definitions.*

## Definition

Many words have more than one meaning. Some words, in fact, have more than a dozen different meanings. Each definition in an entry is numbered, as shown above. In most school dictionaries, definitions are arranged from the most common to the least common.

## Word Origins

Most dictionaries indicate a word's origin and history at the beginning or end of an entry. This brief account tells how the word entered the English language. Sometimes the entry traces the word back through several stages. It shows how the word changed as it passed from language to language.

**bom·bard** (bom bärd′) *v.t.* **1.** to attack with artillery or bombs. **2.** to subject to a vigorous or persistent attack: *He bombarded her with questions.* **3.** Physics. to subject (atomic nuclei) to a stream of high-speed subatomic particles. [French *bombarder*, from *bombarde* cannon, from Medieval Latin *bombarda* weapon for hurling stones, from Latin *bombus* See BOMB.]

> *This word is traced back first to French, the language from which it was borrowed into English. Then the word is traced back to its Latin origin.*

Dictionaries often use abbreviations, such as *L.* for *Latin* or *Fr.* for *French,* to show a word's language of origin. You can find a list of these abbreviations at the front of the dictionary. The chart on the next page shows the origins of some English words.

| The Origins of Some English Words | | |
|---|---|---|
| **English Word** | **Origin** | **Word of Origin** |
| **cookie** | Dutch | *koeje*, meaning "small cake" |
| **gumbo** | Bantu | *gumbo*, referring to okra, the vegetable |
| **judo** | Japanese | *ju*, meaning "gentle" + *do*, meaning "way" |
| **thesaurus** | Greek | *thesauros*, meaning "treasure" or "storehouse" |

## Synonyms

A thesaurus is one place to look for synonyms. A dictionary may also offer a list of synonyms for some words. Some dictionaries give definitions to help you understand the differences in meaning among synonyms. Following is an example.

*An example sentence helps you understand the meaning of each synonym.*

**Syn. Excessive, immoderate, inordinate, intemperate, exorbitant** mean going beyond what is normal or proper. **Excessive** suggests an amount or quantity too great for what is required: *The summer rains were excessive and flooded the fields.* **Immoderate** implies going beyond bounds, esp. in emotional matters: *His speech was received by the opposition with immoderate laughter.* **Inordinate** suggests lack of judgment or regulation: *They asked an inordinate price for the house.* **Intemperate** implies lack of control: *His talk turned out to be an intemperate attack on bankers.* **Exorbitan**t suggests a rather sharp divergence from the normal: *The new job made exorbitant demands on his time.*

### Exercise 8

Use a dictionary to answer the following questions.

1. How is the word *peculiarity* divided into syllables?
2. From what language did the word *pecan* come?
3. What synonyms are given for *era?* List at least three.
4. What part of speech is the word *obstreperous?*

# Unit 23 Vocabulary and Spelling

## 23.1 Loan Words

How do languages grow and change? One way is through borrowing words from other languages. When people come into contact, they're likely to borrow some of one another's words. This can happen even when they speak different languages. This kind of word borrowing into English began when the language was still young.

## *Early Word Borrowings*

In the middle of the fifth century A.D., Germanic tribes from northwestern Europe settled in England. Today we refer to these people as Anglo-Saxons. Their language, now called Old English, was the earliest form of English.

In the late 500s, Christian missionaries came to England from Rome. They began to convert the Anglo-Saxons to Christianity. These missionaries brought to England not only their religion, but also their language—Latin. Many words still in use today were borrowed into Old English from Latin. Some examples are *candle, altar, temple,* and *school.*

Detail from Bayeux Tapestry, *William of Normandy's Ship Before Pevensey Shore,* c. 1066

A few hundred years later, in A.D. 1066, English came under another important influence. In that year the French-speaking Normans invaded England and conquered the Anglo-Saxons. Over the next few hundred years, many French words came into the English language. In fact, English has borrowed more words from French than from any other language. The chart on the following page shows some words borrowed from early French.

| English Borrowings from French | |
| --- | --- |
| Government and Law | city, authority, tax, prison, crime, suit, jury, bail |
| The Military | army, navy, soldier, sergeant, lieutenant, captain, assault |
| Dining and Food | dinner, table, fork, plate, roast, sausage, veal, pork |
| The Arts | music, art, beauty, color, design, theater, poem |
| Trades | barber, butcher, grocer, painter, tailor, carpenter |
| Religion | saint, grace, mercy, salvation, clergy, preach |

## *Words from Many Lands*

Not long after the Norman invasion, European traders began traveling regularly to the Middle East. Arab traders there sold them silk, spices, and other goods from Asia. Often, the Arabic words for these goods were passed on as well. Some English words that came from Arabic include *alcohol, cotton, mattress, orange, sugar,* and *syrup*.

In the late 1400s European traders and explorers began traveling even farther. They found new sea routes, explored new lands, and brought back new products—and new words. Portuguese sailors set up trade routes to Africa and Asia. Other Europeans—explorers, sailors, soldiers, missionaries, and colonists—traveled to the Americas. They brought back foods new to Europeans, such as chocolate, potatoes, turkeys, and maize (corn). The words for these foods were added to the English language.

The chart below shows some words that were borrowed from cultures around the world. A few of these words came directly into English. Most were borrowed by other European languages first and then borrowed into English. For example, *banana* began as an African word. The word was picked up in West Africa by traders from Portugal. Later, it was borrowed from Portuguese into Spanish. Then, after bananas were brought into England, the English started using the word. It became part of the English language.

| English Words Borrowed from Other Lands | |
| --- | --- |
| Africa | banana, chimpanzee, gorilla, okra, zebra |
| Australia & New Zealand | boomerang, kangaroo, kiwi, koala |
| India | bandanna, cot, ginger, jungle, loot, pepper, shampoo |
| Malaya & Polynesia | bamboo, ketchup, paddy, rattan, taboo, tattoo |
| Mexico & Caribbean Islands | canoe, chocolate, cocoa, coyote, hammock, tomato |
| Persia (now Iran) | caravan, musk, pajamas, scarlet, shawl |

## Exercise 1

Look up each of the following words in a dictionary. Tell what language each word was borrowed from.

1. boss
2. zinc
3. yak
4. bungalow
5. spaghetti
6. hurricane

## Exercise 2

Work with a partner or a small group. Do some research on European traders or explorers active between the 1100s and the 1800s. Find two new products they brought back to Europe. In a dictionary look up the words that name those products. Tell what language or languages each word came from.

# Family Resemblances

**P**erhaps you've been told that you have your grandmother's eyes, your father's voice, or your aunt's outgoingness. Similarities in appearance and personality often show up in families.

Languages belong to families, too. English is part of the language family called Indo-European. Most European languages plus many languages spoken in India belong to this family.

Words from different languages in the same family sometimes have family resemblances. These words, which look similar and often have the same meaning, are called cognates. But don't confuse them with borrowed words. Cognates are words that have descended from the same older language. For example, the English word *mother* has cognates in German (*mutter*), Latin (*mater*), Swedish and Danish (*moder*), French (*mère*), and Italian (*madre*).

Because they often began in very early languages, cognates usually refer to something basic about human relations or culture. Many cognates refer to body parts, family relationships, and plants and animals. The numbers one to ten in most Indo-European languages are cognates. For example, English *ten* has cognates in Latin (*decem*), Greek (*deka*), Spanish (*diez*), Welsh (*deg*), and Dutch (*tien*).

## CHALLENGE

*Can you figure out the English words for the cognates in this sentence?*

The vind blew snø against the Haus.

**FATHER**
Latin–Pater
Greek–Patér
Spanish–Padre
German–Vater
French–Père
Dutch–Vader

## Pick a Number

Following are the numbers one through five in different languages. Which word in each item is not a cognate?

1. en, uno, ichi, een
2. ni, dos, due, dva
3. tres, san, tri, tre
4. fire, vier, shi, four
5. cinq, cinco, cúig, go

## 23.2    Using Context Clues

Imagine this. You're reading a book and doing fine until you come across the word *exobiologist.* You have no idea what *exobiologist* means, and you don't have a dictionary handy. What do you do? One thing you could do is look for clues in the context. The context of a word is the words and the sentences that surround it.

## Context Clues

Writers often give clues to the meaning of an unfamiliar word. Sometimes they even tell you what the word means. In the paragraph above, for example, you are told what the word *context* means. The chart below shows some types of context clues.

| Interpreting Clue Words | | |
|---|---|---|
| **Type of Context Clue** | **Clue Words** | **Examples** |
| **Definition** The meaning of the word is given in the sentence. | that is in other words or which means | Janet put the wet clay pot in the *kiln,* **or** oven, to harden. |
| **Example** The unfamiliar word is explained through familiar examples. | like such as for example for instance | The new program has been *beneficial* for the school; **for example,** test scores are up and absences are down. |
| **Comparison** The unfamiliar word is compared to a familiar word or phrase. | too also likewise similarly resembling | Maria thought the dress was *gaudy.* Lisa, **too,** thought it was flashy. |
| **Contrast** The unfamiliar word is contrasted to a familiar word or phrase. | but on the other hand unlike however | Robins are *migratory* birds, **unlike** sparrows, which live in the same region all year round. |

## Using the General Context

You can tell from the sentence structure *that* exobiologist *is a noun that names a person.*

Sometimes you'll have to look for general clues in the context. The surrounding sentences may give you clues to the meaning of the unfamiliar word. Look at the passage below. Notice the clues in the general context that help you figure out the meaning of *exobiologist.*

> Maryann was determined to become an <u>exobiologist</u>. She knew that there was no proof that any <u>forms of life existed on other planets</u>. However, she knew it was possible that life *could* have developed beyond our planet. Maryann had been interested in <u>space exploration</u> ever since her childhood. She felt that the <u>study of exobiology</u> was an exciting new <u>field</u>, and she wanted to be part of it.

*These clues show that it has something to do with life on other planets.*

*These clues show that* exobiology, *a word related to* exobiologist, *is a field of study.*

You know from the other clues that the word has to do with life on other planets. You can figure out that an exobiologist studies life on other planets.

### Exercise 3

Use context clues to figure out the meaning of the italicized word in each passage. Write the meaning of the word. Then tell what context clue or clues you used.

1. Their pet dog, Topper, had been like a member of the family for more than ten years. It was no surprise, then, that Jeff's whole family *lamented* Topper's death.
2. Nikolai is *conscientious* about cleaning his room. Andrew, on the other hand, must be reminded again and again to clean up his room.
3. Julie, a straight-A student, is *exempt* from final exams. Carlos, another straight-A student, is also excused from taking the exams.
4. The film must be completely *immersed,* or covered with fluid.
5. The little boy was *naive.* For instance, he believed the stories older boys told him about space aliens.

# Does This Make ¢¢¢ 2 U?

H ave you ever played the picture game in which you draw a picture to represent a word? Your teammates must guess the word by looking at your drawing. The game is fun because not all words are easy to draw or guess.

What if you always had to use pictures when writing? You'd have something in common with people living about 5,500 years ago, when writing systems were first developing. Pictographic writing was one of the earliest forms of writing—before any alphabet was developed. In pictographic writing, a picture of a tree would mean "tree" and a picture of the sun would mean "sun." There are limitations to pictographic writing, though. Try creating a simple picture to mean "hungry" or "thinking" or "dizzy."

You'll soon find that a picture isn't always worth a thousand words.

As pictographic writing developed further, people used pictures to represent the sounds of words. For example, if you used pictographs today, a picture of the sun could mean "sun" or "son."

A picture could also be used in place of just one syllable of a word. Using a picture of a key to stand for the second part of *lucky* would be one example.

A picture that represents a sound is called a rebus. The use of rebuses was a big step toward the development of modern writing systems. The rebus is now popular in games and puzzles.

**CHALLENGE**

*Figure out the question in the rebus below.*

## Pictoplay

Using pictographs and rebuses, work with a partner to rewrite the note below. See how many syllables and words you can replace with pictures.

*Would you like to go to the store with me? I need to get some potatoes, corn, and beans for dinner tonight.*

## 23.3    Roots, Prefixes, and Suffixes

Like pieces of a puzzle, parts of words can be fitted together to make a whole word. Unlike a puzzle, however, the same word piece can be put together with many other pieces. Thus, a few word parts can make many different words.

The main part of a word is the root. Prefixes and suffixes are other pieces that can be attached to a root to change its meaning. The diagram below shows how prefixes, roots, and suffixes fit together to make new words.

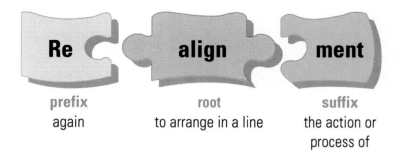

| prefix | root | suffix |
| --- | --- | --- |
| again | to arrange in a line | the action or process of |

## Roots

The root of a word carries the main meaning. Some roots, like the word *align*, above, can stand alone. Other roots must have other parts attached to make a complete word. For example, the root *ject* is useless by itself. But combined with a prefix it can become *reject, project,* or *inject.* Add a suffix and you get *rejection, projection,* or *injection.*

Knowing the meanings of common roots can help you figure out the meanings of unfamiliar words. The following chart shows two more helpful roots. Can you think of some other words that contain these roots?

| Roots | Words and Meanings | |
| --- | --- | --- |
| ***script*** means "writing" | *scripture* <br> *transcript* | sacred writing <br> a written record |
| ***phon*** means "sound" or "voice" | *telephone* <br> *phonics* | instrument for sending voices <br> the study or science of sounds |

# Prefixes

Prefixes can change, or even reverse, the meaning of a word. Two or more prefixes may have the same, or nearly the same, meaning. A single prefix may have more than one meaning. The chart below shows the meanings of some common prefixes. For example, *un-* (as in *unknown*) and *il-* (as in *illegal*) both can mean "not" or "the opposite of."

| Prefixes | | | |
|---|---|---|---|
| | **Prefixes** | **Words** | **Meanings** |
| **Prefixes that reverse meaning** | *un-* means "not" or "the opposite of" | unnatural<br>unhappy | not natural<br>not happy |
| | *il-* means "not" or "the opposite of" | illegal<br>illogical | not legal<br>not logical |
| **Prefixes that show relations** | *re-* means "again" | rebuild<br>reconsider | to build again<br>to consider again |
| | *super-* means "beyond, above, or more" | superfine<br>superhuman | extra fine<br>more than human |
| **Prefixes that show judgment** | *pro-* means "in favor of" or "on the side of" | progovernment | in favor of the government |
| | *anti-* means "against" or "opposite" | antiaircraft | against aircraft (as in "antiaircraft gun") |
| **Prefixes that show number** | *semi-* means "half" or "partial" | semiyearly<br>semisweet | twice a year<br>somewhat sweet |
| | *uni-* means "one" | unicycle<br>unilateral | one-wheeled vehicle<br>one-sided |
| | *bi-* means "two" | biweekly<br>bicycle | every two weeks<br>cycle with two wheels |
| | *tri-* means "three" | triangle<br>tripod | having three angles<br>three-legged stand |
| | *deci-* means "ten" | decade<br>decimal system | period of ten years<br>system based on tens |

# Suffixes

A suffix added to the end of a root word changes the meaning of the root. Many suffixes also change the part of speech of a root word. Learning the meanings and uses of suffixes can help you build your vocabulary. As with prefixes, two or more suffixes can have the same or a similar meaning.

*A single root or word can have a variety of suffixes added to it. Each one gives the word a slightly different meaning.*

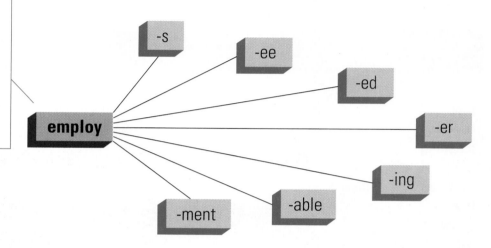

| Suffixes | | | |
|---|---|---|---|
| | **Suffix** | **Words** | **Meanings** |
| **Suffixes that show state of being** | *-ship* means "state or condition of" | leadership <br> friendship | state of being a leader <br> state of being a friend |
| | *-hood* means "state or condition of" | childhood <br> nationhood | condition of being a child <br> condition of being a nation |
| **Suffixes that mean "one who"** | *-ist* means "one who" | archaeologist <br> physicist | one who studies archaeology <br> one who studies physics |
| | *-ian* means "belonging to or characteristic of" | librarian <br> Bostonian | worker in a library <br> person who lives in Boston |
| **Suffixes that mean "related to"** | *-ish* means "relating to" or "like" | childish <br> boyish | like a child <br> like a boy |
| | *-al* means "relating to" | global <br> tropical | relating to the globe <br> relating to the tropics |

Notice that sometimes the spelling of a word is changed when a suffix is added to it. For example, the ending of *library* is changed to make the word *librarian*. Look at page 605 to learn more about spelling words with suffixes.

Words seldom have more than a single prefix added to them. However, more than one suffix can be added to the same word. Each added suffix can change the word's part of speech as well as its meaning. The following examples show how suffixes can change a single root word.

peace (noun)
peace + -ful = peaceful (adjective)
peace + -ful + -ly = peacefully (adverb)
peace + -able = peaceable (adjective)
peace + -able + -ness = peaceableness (noun)
peace + -able + -ly = peaceably (adverb)

## Exercise 4

Identify and write the meaning of the root in each of the following words. Then write the definition of each word. Use your dictionary for help if necessary.

1. prescription
2. objection
3. phonetic
4. manuscript
5. phonetician
6. microphone

## Exercise 5

Add a prefix, a suffix, or both to each of the following words. Use prefixes and suffixes from the charts in this lesson. Then write the definition of the new word. Use a dictionary to check your definitions.

1. legible
2. nature
3. form
4. war
5. done
6. highway
7. weekly
8. fresh
9. cycle
10. violin

# "Man Turns into Sea Monster"

The newspaper headline "Man eating lobster wrecks restaurant" probably wouldn't worry you. But "Man-eating lobster wrecks restaurant" might send you into a panic. The two phrases look similar, but their meanings are obviously very different. Why is that?

Like all other languages English has the capacity to grow, or add new words. One way to add words is through compounding, or joining words to make new words. The compound *man-eating* comes from joining *man* and *eating.*

Often the meanings of the words that make up a compound give a clue to its meaning. For example, *doghouse* means "a house for a dog." Sometimes, though, the meaning of the compound is more than the sum of its parts. The word *underdog,* for instance, doesn't refer to something under a dog but to a predicted loser in a competition.

Words that form compounds can be spelled closed (*troublemaker*), open (*high school*), or hyphenated (*man-eating*). Compounds can be made with most parts of speech—noun plus noun (*fire drill*), verb plus verb (*blow-dry*), adjective plus noun (*fast food*), and so on. The compounds themselves can be almost any part of speech, such as nouns (*role model*), verbs (*downsize*), or adjectives (*no-frills*).

## CHALLENGE

*Pronounce* black-board *and* black board. *Do you pronounce them differently? Try other similar compounds. How do we indicate compounds in speech?*

## Get It Together

See how many compounds you can form by joining words from opposite columns.

| | |
|---|---|
| bird | blue |
| over | house |
| light | dog |
| air | night |
| watch | flow |

As a writer, you want to present your ideas as clearly as possible. You also want your writing to be interesting and lively. A knowledge of synonyms and antonyms can improve your vocabulary and your writing.

## *Synonyms*

**The trouble began on a *sizzling* August day.**

Synonyms are words that have the same, or nearly the same, meaning. Synonyms can make your writing more colorful. When you describe something, you want to make your readers "see" what you describe. One way to do so is to avoid dull, overused words. For example, suppose you're describing a tired old dog walking across the street. You could simply write "The tired old dog walked across the street." Or you could write "The worn-out, ancient mutt hobbled across the street." Choosing the right synonyms for overused words can make your writing livelier.

A dictionary gives synonyms for some words. However, the best place to find synonyms is in a dictionary of synonyms. Such a book is also called a thesaurus. (See pages 580–581 for more information about using a thesaurus.) Remember that synonyms rarely mean exactly the same thing. For example, *weary, worn-out, drained,* and *exhausted* are all synonyms for *tired.* However, each word has a slightly different meaning. Check the meanings of synonyms to make sure the one you choose is the right one.

sizzling
blistering
scalding
sultry
torrid
scorching
red-hot
boiling

## *Antonyms*

Antonyms are words with opposite, or nearly opposite, meanings. *Up* and *down,* and *tall* and *short* are examples of antonyms. While many English words have synonyms, antonyms are less common.

Antonyms are often formed by adding a prefix meaning "not." *Un-*, *il-*, *dis-*, *in-*, and *non-* are all prefixes that can reverse meaning to form antonyms. For example, you can easily form antonyms for the words *happy, legal, comfort, complete,* and *fattening.* Just add the prefixes above in the order listed.

When adding a prefix to make an antonym, make sure you know the exact meaning of the new word. For example, you can add the prefix *dis-* to the word *ease.* However, the word formed, *disease,* is no longer an antonym for *ease,* as it was formerly.

## Exercise 6

In each of the following sentences, replace the underlined word with a synonym. Use a thesaurus if you wish. Hint: When checking a verb in the thesaurus, look for the present-tense form.

1. The horse <u>ran</u> around the track.
2. The flower was a <u>pretty</u> color.
3. Carla stood at the <u>top</u> of the mountain.
4. Jake waxed and <u>polished</u> his new car.
5. Rochelle <u>looked</u> out the window.
6. It was a <u>hard</u> test.
7. The meal was <u>tasty</u>.
8. We picked some of the <u>good</u> peaches.
9. Leon listened to the two men <u>talking</u>.
10. <u>Grab</u> the other end of the rope.

## Exercise 7

Think of an antonym for each of the following words. Then write a sentence, using the antonym. Underline the antonym in the sentence. Remember that many antonyms can be made by adding prefixes that reverse meaning.

1. cruel
2. friendly
3. dull
4. common
5. cheerful

# The Cat Wants His Pajamas Back

Those red sleepers are the cat's pajamas." Suppose a father said this to his young daughter about what she wanted to wear to bed one night. Should she try to scrounge up something else to wear so that she won't upset the cat? Or should she accept the compliment? It might help to know that in the 1920s *the cat's pajamas* meant "something good or desirable."

*The cat's pajamas* is an example of slang, the informal vocabulary of a group of people. It usually begins with a small group of people, who use it almost as a code for group identity. Over time more and more people may use it.

Slang goes in and out of style. Have you heard *rat fink,* meaning "someone who gives information behind another's back"? Does *swinging,* meaning "lively and up-to-date," ring a bell? These two phrases were popular in the 1950s and 1960s but aren't used now.

Some words begin as slang and later become accepted into the language. *Hot dog* and *fan* both began as slang. Other slang words simply remain so. Some current examples are *lip,* as in "Don't give me any lip," and *to knock off,* as in "Knock it off."

So you see, slang takes words and runs with them. Slang's "got it going on."

## CHALLENGE

*The passage below uses 1960s slang. What do the underlined slang words mean? What slang words would you use instead?*

Get with it, and go to the dance. It'll be a blast! I really dig school dances. They're boss.

## What's the Word?

Put your ears on "slang alert" for a day. Listen for examples of slang that you, your friends, or even characters on TV use. Create an American "Slanglish-English" dictionary. Write each word and its "translation," as in a foreign-language dictionary.

## 23.5　Homonyms

Did you ever play the *bass* or catch a *bass* in the lake? Did you ever shed a *tear* when you found a *tear* in your favorite shirt? Pairs (not *pears*) of words that sound alike or are spelled alike are called homonyms. Homonyms can be divided into two groups. One group contains words called homographs.

## Homographs

The word *homograph* is made up of two roots: *homo* (same) and *graph* (writing). Homographs are words that are spelled alike. However, the words have different meanings and may have different pronunciations. *Bass* (pronounced to rhyme with *face*) is a musical instrument or type of voice. (He sang in the *bass* section of the chorus.) *Bass* (pronounced to rhyme with *lass*) is a kind of fish. (I caught an eight-pound striped *bass*.) The chart shows some more examples of homographs.

| Homographs | | |
|---|---|---|
| **Word** | **Meaning** | **Example** |
| object (ob′ jekt) | a thing | What is that strange *object?* |
| object (əb jekt′) | to oppose | "I *object!*" the lawyer shouted. |
| sow (sō) | to plant | Farmers *sow* their crops. |
| sow (sou) | a female pig | The *sow* has five piglets. |
| lead (lēd) | to go in advance | Will you *lead* the way? |
| lead (led) | a kind of metal | This pipe is made of *lead.* |
| dove (duv) | a type of bird | The *dove* is a symbol of peace. |
| dove (dōv) | past tense of *dive* | He *dove* into the lake. |
| bow (bō) | a knot with two loops | The child learned to tie a *bow.* |
| bow (bou) | to bend at the waist | She refused to *bow* to the king. |
| wind (wind) | air that moves | Listen to the *wind* in the trees. |
| wind (wīnd) | to wrap around | Help me *wind* up this ball of string. |
| wound (wo͞ond) | an injury | Cover the *wound* with gauze. |
| wound (wound) | past tense of *wind* | He *wound* the gauze around his hand. |

# Homophones

Homophones are a second type of homonym. Homophones are words that sound alike. *Bass* (the instrument) sounds the same as *base* (as in *first base*). *Pair*, *pare*, and *pear* are another group of homophones.

Homophones sound alike but have different spellings and different meanings. That's why they're often confused. Always check a dictionary if you're unsure about which homophone to use. The chart below shows some common homophones. Can you think of any additional examples?

See

| Homophones |
|---|
| to, too, two |
| meat, meet |
| here, hear |
| there, their, they're |
| deer, dear |
| sail, sale |
| for, four |

Sea

## Exercise 8

In each sentence below, find as many words as you can that have homophones. Write each word you find. Then write its homophone or homophones.

1. Angela sat on the shore, waiting to see the sun come up over the horizon.
2. How much will the sail for the new boat cost?
3. I need to buy a necktie and a pair of shoes.
4. The boys will wait in here, and the girls will wait over there.
5. Would you like four more of those?

# Can You Pick a Flour?

**H**ow is bread made?"
   "*I know* that!" *Alice cried eagerly. "You take some flour—"*

   *"Where do you pick the flower?" the White Queen asked. "In a garden, or in the hedges?"*

   *"Well, it isn't* picked *at all," Alice explained: "it's* ground—"

   *"How many acres of ground?" said the White Queen.*

In this passage from *Through the Looking Glass,* Lewis Carroll plays with homophones, words having the same sounds but different meanings.

Most of today's homophones didn't always sound alike. *Bear* and *bare* began as English words with the same meanings as today—a *bear* was an animal, and *bare* meant "uncovered." However, hundreds of years ago *bear* and *bare* didn't sound the same at all. The word *bear,* spelled *bera,* had two syllables. The word *bare,* spelled *bær,* had the vowel sound of the *a* in *bat.* Gradually, the pronunciations grew closer until the words became homophones.

*Grate,* which was borrowed from French around 1440, meant what it means today, "a metal lattice to cover a window or fire." The English word *great,* which originally meant "thick" or "coarse," had two syllables. Later, the second syllable was lost, so that today we have another pair of homophones.

## CHALLENGE

*"Cinderella opened a photo shop and waited for her prints to come."* Think of another silly joke that depends upon homophones. Better yet, make one up.

## Homophun

Give the homophones for each pair of clues.

1. a story; what a dog wags
2. it stops your bike; a crack in a vase
3. bread before baking; female deer
4. a dark time; a medieval warrior
5. animal feet; a short rest

What would you think of a letter or an essay full of misspelled words? You might think that the writer was careless. You might even have trouble understanding the writer's ideas. Good writing includes careful attention to details such as spelling.

Do you have trouble with spelling? One reason for the problem may be that the spelling of English words doesn't always make sense. For example, pronounce the words *through, dough, ought, bough, cough,* and *rough.* Did you notice that the letters *ough* are pronounced differently in each word? Worse yet, the same sound can be spelled several ways. For example, pronounce *oh.* Some other ways to spell the same sound are *oe (doe), ou (soul), ew (sew),* and *oa (road).*

The best way to avoid spelling errors is to check your spelling against a dictionary. However, you won't always have a dictionary handy. Learning a few spelling rules will help you master the spelling of thousands of words.

## *Spelling* ie *and* ei

The letters *ie* and *ei* are contained in many English words. They often cause confusion. The following rhyme can help you remember how to spell words with these letter combinations. There are so few exceptions to this rule that you can easily memorize all the important ones.

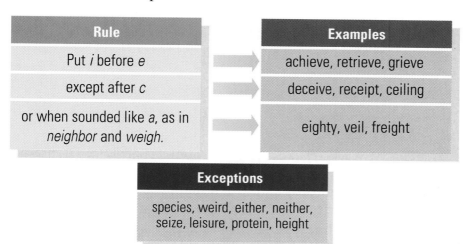

| Rule | Examples |
|---|---|
| Put *i* before *e* | achieve, retrieve, grieve |
| except after *c* | deceive, receipt, ceiling |
| or when sounded like *a*, as in *neighbor* and *weigh*. | eighty, veil, freight |

| Exceptions |
|---|
| species, weird, either, neither, seize, leisure, protein, height |

## Spelling Unstressed Vowels

English is full of words with an unstressed vowel sound. In dictionaries this sound is represented by a special symbol called a schwa ( ə ). Say the word *about* aloud, listening to the sound of the vowel in the first syllable. This unstressed vowel always *sounds* the same (*uh*), but it can be spelled *a, e, i, o, u,* or more than a dozen other ways. Listen for the sounds of the underlined letters in the words *canal, angel, pencil, person, circus, mountain,* and *sergeant.* All these words have the same unstressed vowel sound.

As you can see, words with this vowel sound can cause spelling problems. You can't just "spell it the way it sounds." Sometimes, however, you can get around the difficulty. Think of a related word in which the vowel is stressed. When the vowel is stressed, it may not be as great a spelling problem. For example, you may not be sure whether *legal* or *legel* is the correct spelling. However, you may know the related word *legality* (notice the stress). You can see that the vowel letter you want is *a.* The chart below shows some additional examples of how you can apply this process.

| Spelling Unstressed Vowels | | |
|---|---|---|
| **Unknown Letter** | **Related Word** | **Correct Spelling** |
| opp_site | oppose | opposite |
| rid_cule | ridiculous | ridicule |
| phot_graph | photography | photograph |
| observ_nt | observation | observant |
| inform_tive | information | informative |

## Suffixes and the Silent e

Many English words end with a silent letter *e.* When you add a suffix to words that end in a silent *e,* the *e* is often dropped. However, sometimes the silent *e* is kept. The following chart shows the rules for suffixes and the silent *e.*

| Adding Suffixes to Words That End with Silent *e* | |
|---|---|
| **Rule** | **Example** |
| When adding a suffix that begins with a consonant to a word that ends with a silent *e*, keep the *e*. | safe + -ly = safely<br>hope + -ful = hopeful<br><br>**Common exceptions**<br>awe + -ful = awful<br>judge + -ment = judgment |
| When adding -*ly* to a word that ends with an *l* plus a silent *e*, always drop the *e* and one *l*. | incredible + -ly = incredibly<br>laughable + -ly = laughably |
| When adding a suffix that begins with a vowel or *y* to a word that ends with a silent *e*, usually drop the *e*.<br><br>Sometimes the *e* is kept to avoid changing the sound of the original word. | shape + -ing = shaping<br>rose + -y = rosy<br>**Common exceptions**<br>dye + -ing = dyeing<br>mile + -age = mileage |
| When adding a suffix that begins with *a* or *o* to a word that ends with *ce* or *ge*, keep the *e* so that the word will keep the soft *c* or *g* sound. | trace + -able = traceable<br>change + -able = changeable |
| When adding a suffix that begins with a vowel to a word that ends in *ee* or *oe*, keep the *e*. | agree + -able = agreeable<br>canoe + -ing = canoeing |

# Suffixes and the Final y

Adding suffixes to words that end in *y* can often cause spelling problems. Follow these rules for adding suffixes to such words.

- When a word ends in a vowel + *y*, keep the *y*.
  play + -ful = playful          pray + -ing = praying
  enjoy + -ment = enjoyment

- When a word ends in a consonant + *y*, change the *y* to *i*.
  fry + -ed = fried              try + -ed = tried
  happy + -ness = happiness

- BUT if the suffix begins with an *i*, keep the *y* so that two *i*'s don't come together.
  fry + -ing = frying          carry + -ing = carrying

# Adding Prefixes

The addition of a prefix doesn't change the spelling of a word. This is a rule you can remember easily.

- When you add a prefix to a word, do not change the spelling of the word or the prefix.

| | |
|---|---|
| pre- + pay = prepay | re- + act = react |
| dis- + able = disable | im- + possible = impossible |
| un- + natural = unnatural | de- + odorize = deodorize |
| il- + legal = illegal | co- + operate = cooperate |

## Exercise 9

There is one misspelled word in each of the following sentences. Find the word, and write its correct spelling.

1. Luckily, our tickets were exchangable for a performance on another night.
2. Winning the trophy for the third straight year was a tremendous acheivement for our team.
3. The two friends were inseparible when they were children.
4. Attending the play was an agreable experience.
5. Jack tryed canoeing through white water, but he regretted it.

## Exercise 10

Look at each set of words below. Find the one misspelled word in each set, and write it correctly.

1. shoeing, changable, freeing
2. judgeing, safely, wholly
3. ilogical, immediate, correspond
4. relieve, deceive, hieght
5. grading, rosey, dyeing

# Leftover Letters

**E**nglish spelling can seem strange. Why, for example, is there a *w* in *two* and *answer*? What is *gh* doing in *thought* and *though*? Where did we get all those silent *e*'s?

The answers lie in the history of English. Like all languages English has changed over time, and one major change has occurred in its pronunciation. Until about five hundred years ago most of today's leftover letters stood for sounds.

Consider an old friend, silent *e*. Originally the final *e* in words like *bake* and *time* wasn't silent. It stood for an unstressed sound much like the final sound in *Rita.* The pronunciation changed, but not the spelling.

Silent *gh* is harder to explain since the sound it once stood for no longer exists in English. The letters *gh* spelled a rough, throat-clearing *k* sound. That sound is gone, but not the spelling.

You may wonder why all these left-over letters didn't disappear once pronunciations changed. The printing press, invented in 1440, was the main reason. By then pronunciation had begun to change, but spelling had not. Printers used the familiar spellings, which became standard as more and more people read books. Thus, printing helped to freeze many early spellings of English words.

## CHALLENGE

*Some people have wanted to simplify the English spelling system, changing* though *to* tho, *for example. What pro and con arguments can you think of for this proposal?*

## Can You Speak Old English?

Imitate early pronunciations of English words. Try to make each consonant letter stand for a sound.

1. folk
2. gnat
3. answer
4. two (long *o*)
5. light (short *i*)
6. knight (short *i*)

| | |
|---|---|
| sign | signal |
| bomb | bombard |
| hymn | hymnal |

## 23.7 Spelling Rules II

The rules in the last lesson and in this one will help you improve your spelling skills. You probably won't memorize all these rules right away. However, reviewing them from time to time should help you improve your spelling.

### *Doubling the Final Consonant*

Adding suffixes to words that end in a consonant can be confusing. In some cases you double the final consonant when adding the suffix. In other cases you don't double it. The following rules can help you avoid many spelling errors.

Double the final consonant when a word ends in a single consonant following one vowel and

- the word is one syllable
  run + -ing = running      ship + -ing = shipping
  mad + -er = madder      top + -ed = topped

- the word has an accent on the last syllable and the accent stays there after the suffix is added
  regret + -ed = regretted      prefer + -ed = preferred
  forget + -able = forgettable      commit + -ing = committing

Do not double the final consonant when

- the accent is not on the last syllable
  number + -ed = numbered      differ + -ed = differed

- the accent moves when the suffix is added
  prefer + -ence = preference      fatal + -ity = fatality

- the word ends in two consonants
  hang + -er = hanger      haunt + -ed = haunted

- the suffix begins with a consonant
  light + -ness = lightness      real + -ly = really

Special case: When a word ends in *ll,* and the suffix *-ly* is added, drop one *l.*

full + -ly = fully      dull + -ly = dully

# Forming Plurals

The usual way to form plurals in English is to add *-s* or *-es*. However, there are other ways to form plurals. The following chart shows the general rules for plurals.

| General Rules for Plurals | | |
| --- | --- | --- |
| **If the Noun Ends in** | **Then Generally** | **Example** |
| *s,* *sh,* *ch,* *x,* or *z* | add *-es* | bus → buses<br>rush → rushes<br>match → matches<br>tax → taxes<br>buzz → buzzes |
| a consonant + *y* | change *y* to *i* and add *-es* | buddy → buddies<br>candy → candies |
| a vowel + *y* | add *-s* | boy → boys<br>way → ways |
| a vowel + *o* | add *-s* | stereo → stereos<br>studio → studios |
| a consonant + *o* | generally add *-s*<br>**Common exceptions**<br>but sometimes add *-es* | solo → solos<br>photo → photos<br><br>cargo → cargoes<br>hero → heroes<br>tomato → tomatoes |
| *f* or *ff* | add *-s*<br>**Common exceptions**<br>change *f* to *v* and add *-es* | roof → roofs<br>cuff → cuffs<br><br>thief → thieves<br>hoof → hooves<br>wolf → wolves |
| *lf* | change *f* to *v* and add *-es* | shelf → shelves<br>calf → calves |
| *fe* | change *f* to *v* and add *-s* | wife → wives<br>knife → knives |

Some nouns don't follow the general rules in the chart on page 609. They form plurals in a special way. Most of these special rules are easy to remember. Some of them resemble the general rules. The following chart includes examples of each rule.

| Special Rules for Plurals | |
|---|---|
| **Special Case** | **Example** |
| To form the plurals of most proper names, add -s.<br><br>But add -es if the name ends in s, ch, sh, x, or z. | Troy → Troys<br>Smith → Smiths<br>James → Jameses<br>Thatch → Thatches<br>Rush → Rushes<br>Marx → Marxes<br>Jiminez → Jiminezes |
| To form the plural of one-word compound nouns, follow the general rules for plurals | pocketknife → pocketknives<br>gooseberry → gooseberries<br>pickax → pickaxes |
| To form the plural of hyphenated compound nouns or compound nouns of more than one word, make the most important word plural. | sister-in-law → sisters-in-law<br>school bag → school bags<br>head of state → heads of state<br>court martial → courts martial |
| Some nouns have irregular plural forms and do not follow any rules. You simply have to remember these plural forms. | goose → geese<br>mouse → mice<br>child → children<br>woman → women |
| Some nouns have the same singular and plural forms. | fish → fish<br>moose → moose<br>dozen → dozen<br>Sioux → Sioux |

## *Forming Compound Words*

The rule for spelling compound words is simple. Keep the original spelling of both words, no matter how the words begin or end.

surf + board = surfboard
green + house = greenhouse
easy + going = easygoing
side + walk = sidewalk

night + time = nighttime
inn + keeper = innkeeper
house + boat = houseboat
home + made = homemade

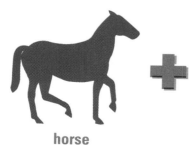  

horse          shoe          horseshoe

## Exercise 11

Find the one misspelled word in each of the following sentences, and write its correct spelling.

1. Mrs. Hart's grandaughter will perform two solos.
2. The calfs were injured when the barn ceiling collapsed.
3. The autumn leafs dropped slowly as gentle breezes shook the branches.
4. Two of the chief of staffs met with the president.
5. The truckload of noisy cattle frightened the gooses, which ran about the barnyard in a panic.

## Exercise 12

Look at each set of words below. Find the one misspelled word in each set, and write it correctly.

1. halves, puffs, elfs
2. fully, bookeeping, brothers-in-law
3. deer, mouses, children
4. permited, hopped, preferred
5. reelism, houseboat, observant

*Spelling Rules II* **611**

## 23.8　Spelling Problem Words

Do you often forget whether *tomorrow* has one *m* or two? Is the correct spelling *advertise* or *advertize?* Most people have trouble spelling certain words. But there are ways in which you can learn to spell even the most difficult words.

## *Improving Spelling Skills*

Here is a spelling method that will help you master the spelling of new or difficult words. As you write, notice words that you have trouble spelling. When reading, note unfamiliar words or words that look hard to spell. Keep a list of such words. Then use the following steps to learn to spell them.

| **Say It** | **Visualize It** | **Write It** | **Check It** |
|---|---|---|---|
| Look at the printed word, and say it out loud. Say it a second time, pronouncing each syllable clearly. | Without looking at the word, imagine seeing it printed or written. Try to picture the word spelled correctly. | Look at the printed word, and write it two or three times. Then write it without looking at the printed word. | Check what you have written against the printed word. Did you spell the word correctly? If not, try the process again. |

Remember also that your dictionary is an important tool for improving your spelling. If you don't know how to spell a word, check your dictionary. Don't say, "How can I look it up if I can't spell it?" You probably can spell enough of the word to find its entry. Does a word end in *-able* or *-ible?* Look up one spelling, and if you don't find the word, try another. Once you've located the word, use the four-step spelling method to learn it.

Another way to learn difficult words is to use memory devices, or tricks for remembering. Rhymes, such as *i before e except after c,* are good memory devices. You also can think up clues about how to spell a certain word. For example, if you have trouble remembering that *mathematics* has an *e,* remind yourself that there is *them* in *math<u>em</u>atics.*

Try to think of other tricks, sentences, or rhymes that help you remember how to spell the hard parts of troublesome words.

Keeping a personal word list of difficult words is another way to improve your spelling. You should keep your list up-to-date, adding new words as you come across them. Delete words from the list once you have mastered them. Study the words a few at a time, using the four-step spelling method.

## Easily Confused Words

Certain words sound alike or nearly alike but have different spellings and meanings. Look at the following example:

affect       "to bring a change in"
             *How does acid rain* affect *the forests?*

effect       "a result"
             *This test will have a bad* effect *on my final grade.*

If you don't know the difference between the two words, you're likely to use the wrong word and therefore the wrong spelling. Some of these easily confused words are listed below.

| Words Often Confused | |
|---|---|
| accept, except | loose, lose |
| affect, effect | than, then |
| all ready, already | their, there, they're |
| all together, altogether | to, too, two |
| choose, chose | whose, who's |
| its, it's | your, you're |

## Frequently Misspelled Words

The following words are often misspelled. Look for your "problem" words on this list. What other words would you add to the list?

## Words Often Misspelled

| | | | |
|---|---|---|---|
| absence | convenient | jewelry | receipt |
| accidentally | definite | laboratory | recognize |
| accommodate | disease | leisure | recommend |
| adviser | dissatisfied | library | restaurant |
| all right | embarrass | license | rhythm |
| analyze | environment | misspell | schedule |
| answer | essential | molasses | separate |
| beautiful | February | muscle | sincerely |
| beginning | foreign | necessary | succeed |
| blaze | forty | neighborhood | technology |
| business | funeral | niece | theory |
| cafeteria | genius | noticeable | tomorrow |
| canceled | government | nuisance | traffic |
| canoe | grammar | occasion | truly |
| cemetery | guarantee | original | usually |
| choir | height | parallel | vacuum |
| commercial | humorous | permanent | variety |
| colonel | immediate | physician | Wednesday |

## Exercise 13

On a separate piece of paper, write the word in the parentheses that correctly completes each sentence.

1. The team was (all together, altogether) satisfied with the outcome of the game.
2. Is this (your, you're) glove?
3. Do you think that Janet will (except, accept) the gift?
4. The car needs to have (its, it's) brakes replaced.
5. If it's not Kim's, then (whose, who's) is it?
6. How will this loss (effect, affect) the playoffs?
7. We can't afford to (lose, loose) the next game.
8. I think dogs are smarter (then, than) cats.
9. We (choose, chose) to see the movie last night.
10. The farmers harvested (their, there, they're) crops.

# Unit 24 Study Skills

## 24.1    The Parts of a Book

When doing research, you may find more books on your topic than you can read. How do you decide which books will be the most useful? How do you find out if a book has the information you need? Certain pages in the front and the back of a book can help you. These pages can give you clues about whether the information in the book is up-to-date and reliable.

## *In the Front of the Book*

The pages shown below are found in the front part of the book, before the main text. They can help you see whether the book contains what you need.

The **title page** gives the title of the book. It also names the book's author, authors, or editor.

The **contents** lists the names of the book's parts, chapters, sections, and so on. It tells you the page on which each one begins.

The date on the **copyright page** tells you when the book was published.

## In the Back of the Book

The glossary and the index are found in the back of a book. Glossaries are found especially in books that use many specialized or technical terms. You often find glossaries in books on science or technology and in some textbooks.

The **index** contains an alphabetical list of topics in the book, including important people, places, events, and terms. Page numbers are given for each entry.

The **glossary** is an alphabetical list of special or unfamiliar terms in the book. Each term is defined.

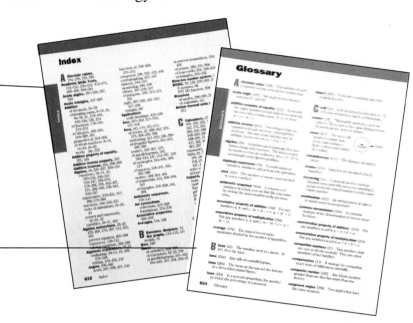

---

### Exercise 1

Use this textbook as needed to answer the questions. Tell where you found each answer.

1. On what page or pages are prefixes discussed in *Writer's Choice?*
2. What information besides the title can you find on the title page of *Writer's Choice?*
3. What unit in this book discusses capitalization?
4. Suppose you had a book called *An Introduction to Computers* and wanted to find a definition of *system disk.* Where would you look first to find it?
5. Where would you look to discover whether the book *An Introduction to Computers* was up-to-date?

Suppose you needed information about the structure of a plant cell or the events leading up to the Crusades. What would you do? Chances are you would read something. Reading is your most important tool for gaining information. However, there are different ways of reading. Knowing which way to use for your purpose can save you time.

## *Skimming*

When you skim a piece of writing, you glance over the text rapidly to find the main ideas. In skimming a textbook, for example, you might look at all the headings and illustrations and any words that are highlighted in bold type. You might also read the first sentence of each paragraph.

You can use skimming to preview material before beginning to read or to study for a test. You can also skim to find out if a book contains information you need.

## *Scanning*

When you scan, your eyes move over the text rapidly, looking for particular information. For example, you may be looking for a name, a date, a figure, or a definition. You might scan to review key terms or main ideas for a test. You often scan to see if a book has any information on a specific topic. Keeping your topic in mind, you would look for words that relate to it. While scanning, you're interested only in finding out if a topic is covered. You'll learn what the book or article actually says about the topic during your careful reading.

## *Careful Reading*

Careful reading means reading the text slowly and carefully to make sure you fully understand the information presented. You need to read carefully when learning material for the first time. Studying a new chapter in one of your textbooks would require careful reading.

When you do careful reading, you may sometimes need to read difficult passages more than once. For example, you need to read technical or scientific material very slowly and carefully to make sure you understand the ideas. If the material contains unfamiliar or technical terms, be sure to reread the passage until you thoroughly understand the ideas. If the book has no glossary, keep a dictionary handy to look up unfamiliar terms.

| Three Styles of Reading | | |
|---|---|---|
| **Style** | **Purpose** | **Examples of Purpose** |
| *Skimming* | Looking over a piece of writing fairly quickly to get an overall view of its content | Will I like this book of short stories? What is this article about? What are the main ideas of this chapter? How is this unit organized? What will I learn from this lesson? |
| *Scanning* | Looking rapidly over a piece of writing to find a particular piece or type of information | Does this book tell about the Trail of Tears? What are the characteristics of a sonnet? What key terms will I need to know to understand this chapter? Will I learn anything from this book about African Americans in the Civil War? |
| *Careful Reading* | Slowly and carefully reading a piece of writing in order to fully understand its content | What is the purpose of this article? What happens to the characters in this novel? What is this writer trying to say about changes in the English language? What can I learn about computers from this book? |

## Exercise 2

List some of the reading you have done, both for classes and for yourself, in the past several weeks. Next to each assignment write which of the three reading styles you would use, and tell why. Meet with a small group of your classmates to compare and discuss your lists.

## 24.3    Writing Summaries

Have you ever told a friend about a movie you saw or a book you read? Have you ever explained to a classmate what was covered in a class he or she missed? Summarizing—telling the main ideas of something—saves time. Imagine trying to tell someone every single detail about a movie. It could take longer than the movie itself.

Summarizing in your own words also helps you to organize and remember ideas. After preparing a written summary of something, you'll find that you understand it better.

## *When to Summarize*

Summarizing can help you almost anytime you need to understand and remember ideas or facts. The following chart shows some situations in which you might need to prepare a written summary of some sort.

| Summarizing | |
| --- | --- |
| **Situation** | **Kinds of Summaries** |
| Preparing a written or oral research report | Brief restatements of the important facts and ideas from the various sources you used |
| Listening to lectures, speeches, or discussions | Notes on the main ideas from the lecture, speech, or discussion. |
| Viewing a film or video documentary | Notes on the main ideas or techniques of the documentary |
| Reading textbook material | A restatement of the most important information in the textbook |

## *How to Summarize*

When you summarize a movie for a friend, you include all the important ideas or events. However, you leave out most of the details. In the same way, a good written summary includes only the main ideas. It leaves out examples and other supporting details.

When you write a summary, you should put the ideas in your own words. Using the author's words is quoting directly, not summarizing. Occasionally you may wish to quote a sentence or a phrase from the author. If you do so, be sure to use quotation marks around the author's words.

Compare the student summary below with the original text shown. Notice how the summary shortens the original but still includes the most important information.

Ferdinand Magellan (1480?–152   ...   mmanded
the first European voyage to sa
around the world, Magellan wa
his expedition was backed by t
monarch Charles I. What Ma
find for Spain was a westwar

The Spice Islands (the Mo
lured Magellan on his histo
thought he could reach the
sailing west across the Atl

The voyage began in 1
three years later in 1552.
crew members and one
the voyage and returned to Spain. Mag
himself was killed in the Philippines in April 1521.
Nevertheless, he is remembered as a great navigator and the first to command an around-the-
world voyage.

*Portuguese navigator Ferdinand Magellan commanded a 1519–1522 Spanish voyage to the Spice Islands. Magellan did not live to complete the voyage. However, he is remembered for being the first to show that it was possible to sail around the world.*

### Exercise 3

Find a short, interesting article in an encyclopedia or some other written source. If you wish, you can select about three or four paragraphs from a longer article. Write a brief summary of the selection you choose. Remember to use your own words.

Imagine having an hour or more each week to do what you want without losing study time. One way to gain extra free time is by learning efficient study habits. To get the most out of your study time, try making a study plan.

## *Setting Goals*

Music, art, or physical education classes might not require much work outside the classroom. On the other hand, you could have daily homework in math or many pages to read weekly in social studies. Begin by making a list of all your classes that require some study time. Next to each class, write any assignments you have received. Then set your goals for each class.

A goal is an objective you want to achieve. Learning to play the piano is a goal. Getting a passing grade on a test is another goal. Simply completing any school assignment, such as reading twenty pages of a textbook, can be a goal.

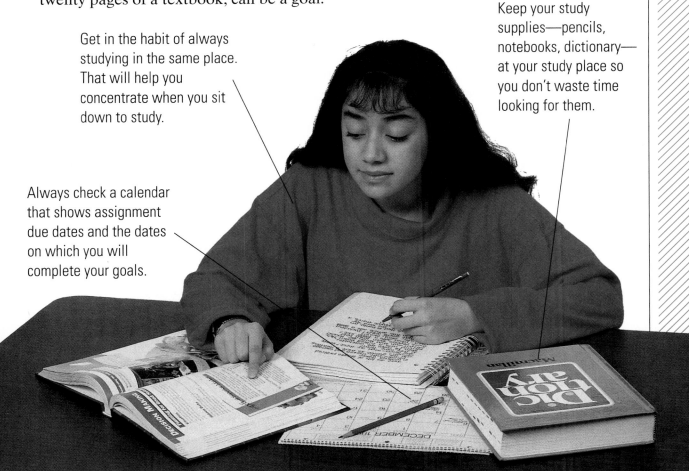

Keep your study supplies—pencils, notebooks, dictionary—at your study place so you don't waste time looking for them.

Get in the habit of always studying in the same place. That will help you concentrate when you sit down to study.

Always check a calendar that shows assignment due dates and the dates on which you will complete your goals.

Divide school assignments into short-term goals and long-term goals. Short-term goals are those that can be completed in one study session. Learning ten new spelling words or reading a few pages in a textbook are short-term goals. A long-term goal might be completing a research report, reading a novel, or preparing for a unit test.

Long-term goals can be broken down into smaller tasks. For example, studying for a unit test might require reviewing one chapter per study session. Completing a research report would include many short-term tasks. Looking for resources, gathering information, listing and outlining ideas, and writing a rough draft are some examples. Be realistic about what you can do in a study session of one or two hours. For instance, you probably can't read a novel or plan and write a report in one session.

## Scheduling Study Time

Setting goals is important, but just as important is setting deadlines to reach your goals. The tool that will help you reach your goals is a study-plan calendar. After you have listed your goals, write each one on your calendar. For long-term goals, first write the final due date. For example, if you have a unit test on the nineteenth, write that on your calendar. Then work backward from the final due date and write each short-term goal on the date that you will work on it. You might want to set goals of reviewing, say, one chapter each day for a week.

You may have a test in science and an oral report in English both due on Monday. If so, you need to carefully balance your study time for both so that you are not overwhelmed. Also, remember to write your goals on your study calendar as soon as you receive your assignments. You don't want to remember some night as you go to bed that you have an English test the following morning!

Be sure to write other important activities, such as sports, music lessons, or school club meetings, on your calendar as well. You probably wouldn't want to schedule writing a draft of a report on the same day that you have a band recital. The calendar on the next page shows a student's study calendar. You can use it as a model for one of your own.

## Monthly Planner

Month **October**

Top Priority List

| Sunday | Monday | Tuesday | Wednesday | Thursday | Friday | Saturday |
|--------|--------|---------|-----------|----------|--------|----------|
| | | | | 1 | 2 | 3 |
| 4 | 5 Study for social studies quiz | 6 Social studies quiz Read the story "To Build a Fire" | 7 Library research for science report | 8 Study new vocabulary words, English Complete exercise 12, math | 9 Do outline of science report English quiz on vocabulary words Hand in exercise 12, math | 10 |
| 11 | 12 start rough draft of science report | 13 write rough draft of science report | 14 Read chapter 26, social studies | 15 Revise rough draft, science report | 16 Learn new vocabulary words, English Complete exercise 13, math | 17 |
| 18 | 19 Type finished science report English quiz on vocabulary words Hand in exercise 13, math | 20 Proofread science report | 21 Hand in science report | 22 | 23 | 24 |
| 25 | 26 | 27 | 28 | 29 | 30 | 31 |

Important Phone Calls

Messages – Reminders

No. HT-1502 – Monthly

Visual Organizers, Inc. © 1987

## Exercise 4

Work with a classmate to make a list of your classes and the assignments due in each class. Discuss what special activities, such as sports or music lessons, you should include. Discuss with each other ways of breaking down long-term goals into several short-term goals. Discuss also what amount of time should be given to each goal. Then prepare an assignment calendar for one month, based on the list you develop.

## 24.5　Using the SQ3R Method

Some students spend hours every week studying but still have difficulty in their classes. Other students spend less time studying and seem to breeze through their schoolwork. One reason for the difference can be study habits. The SQ3R study method will make your study time more productive. The SQ3R method is based on five steps: **S**urvey, **Q**uestion, **R**ead, **R**ecord, **R**eview.

You can use the SQ3R method with any subject. Once you have learned the method and use it regularly, it will become a habit. Using the method, you will remember more of what you read and will understand it better. You will also be better prepared to participate in class.

You **survey** by skimming the text quickly. (See pages 617–618 for hints on skimming.) Remember, look for the main ideas in the material. Pay attention to any sentences or terms that are highlighted. Also look at all photographs, graphs, maps, and other illustrations. Think about how the graphic material is related to the main ideas.

The next step is to **question.** Write out a list of questions that you want to have answered when you read the material.

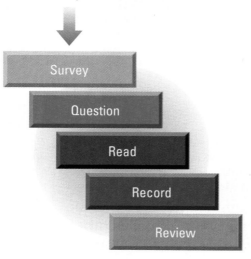

For example, suppose you are studying a section on Ferdinand Magellan in your social studies text. You might write such questions as, Who was Ferdinand Magellan? What was Magellan looking for on his voyage? Why was his voyage important? If you are studying a textbook that has its own review questions, add those to your list. Having a list of questions before you begin reading will help you focus on important ideas in the material.

**Read** through the material slowly and carefully. As you read, take notes about the main ideas and look for answers to your questions. Also, as you read, you may add questions to your list. Make sure you understand each paragraph or passage.

After you have carefully read the material, **record** the answers to your questions. Don't look in the book. Rely on your memory of what you have read to answer the questions. In this way you will test whether you have really learned the material. If you have to struggle to answer the questions, you may need to reread the material.

After answering the questions, check your answers against the material you have read. If you have missed any answers, **review** that section again. Following your review rephrase your questions, or write new ones that cover the same material. Continue rewriting questions and reviewing the material until you are able to correctly answer all questions. Keep your review questions and answers in your notebook. You can use this material later to study or to review for tests.

Choose from history a famous person who interests you. Read an encyclopedia article about that person, using the SQ3R method. Be sure you take notes, and prepare and answer your review questions carefully. After you have studied the material using the SQ3R method, answer the following questions. Try to do so without referring to your notes.

1. What was the full name of the person you read about?
2. What accomplishment is this person most noted for?
3. What inspired this person to achieve his or her accomplishments?
4. When did this person live, and when did this person make his or her most important achievement?
5. Where was this person born, or where did this person live most of his or her life?
6. Where did this person make his or her most important accomplishment?
7. Why is this person important in history?
8. How, if at all, is your life different because of this person?

Suppose someone asked you to go to the grocery store to pick up ten different items. What would you do to be sure you remembered all the items? Write them down, of course! Most people don't remember *everything* they read or hear, or even *most* of what they read or hear. That's why note taking is important.

## Taking Notes

As a student, you will need to remember many things. What was said in a classroom discussion? What are the main ideas in a video documentary shown in class? What important ideas did you find when researching a topic for a report?

**While Listening**    Taking notes during classroom lectures or discussions or while viewing films will help you remember what you hear. You can't write down every word that is said. Instead, listen for ideas the speaker emphasizes. Write the key words of those main ideas. Then write the key words for each supporting detail or example the speaker gives to support a main idea.

*Highlight or star major ideas or categories of information. Underline important ideas or examples.*

*Don't try to write notes in complete sentences. Use numbers, dashes, abbreviations, and symbols to save time.*

☆ Water pollution
  1. *oil spills*–tankers
  2. *chemical wastes*–industry
☆ Air pollution
  1. *exhaust fumes*–autos
  2. *carbon dioxide*–factories, forest fires
☆ Land pollution
  1. *garbage*–landfills
  2. *industrial waste*–dumping

**While Reading** Naturally, you don't want to copy down everything you read when doing research for a report. Have a specific topic or theme in mind when you begin your research. Take notes on just the information you think is important to your topic. Summarize that information in your own words, using as few words as possible.

Write your notes on 3 x 5 note cards. Use a new card for each source or each bit of information you read. At the top of the card write the name of your source, its author, and the page numbers where you found the information. You will need this information for your report. You may also need to go back to a source to look for further information.

Avoid copying long direct quotations. When using a quotation, make sure you copy the words exactly as they appear in the source. Enclose them in quotation marks, and include the name of the person being quoted.

*Always record the source of your information, that is, the title, author, and page numbers of the book or article.*

Michael Wyeth, The Story of Romulus and
Remus, pp.127–140.
    According to legend they were twin boys
brought up by a fe[...]
decided to build a n[...]
Tiber River. Romul[...]
argument. Then he [...]

Janet Harper, The City of Rome, pp. 23--25.
Rome has been an important city for more
than 2,000 years. According to legend it was
founded by twin brothers Romulus and
Remus, 753 B.C. Rome began as a small
village built on seven hills along the Tiber
River in Italy.

*Summarize the information in your own words. Write only the main ideas and important supporting details.*

# Outlining

After you finish your research, organize the information on your note cards. Examine the information on each card, and group cards with similar ideas together. Each group can be a main topic. Within each group, separate cards into subgroups. These will become subtopics in your outline.

You might try several ways of organizing your cards to see which works best. The order you use will depend on your topic. A history of early Rome would probably require chronological order, or the order in which events happened. A science paper on pollution could be ordered by cause and effect, showing how one thing causes another.

Following is an example of the start of an outline.

*Use Roman numerals to number your main topics. Main topics are the "big ideas."*

*Indent and use letters and numbers for subtopics and their divisions. If a main topic has subtopics, there must be at least two of them.*

*If you divide a subtopic, there must be at least two divisions.*

The Eternal City

I. The Founding of Rome
   A. The Myth of Romulus and Remus
      1. Twins cared for by wolf
      2. Romulus kills Remus and builds Rome
   B. Began as small village built on seven hills
II. Rome Becomes Powerful
   A. Romans defeat Etruscans
   B. Conquer neighbors in Italy

## Exercise 6

Work with a small group of classmates. Brainstorm to make a list of topics for a report. As a group, choose one of the topics. Then have group members read and take notes about the topic from a variety of resources. Look over the group's notes and decide on a method of organization for the material. Then, as a group, prepare an outline for a report on the topic.

## Understanding Graphic Information

Have you ever read so many facts at once that you had trouble grasping them? A paragraph containing many numbers, for example, could leave you wondering what the main point is. Tables, graphs, and other graphic aids often do a better job than text of organizing information for you.

## *Tables*

Tables organize information by putting it into categories arranged into columns and rows. You can read a table from top to bottom in columns or from left to right across rows. Look at the table below. Suppose you need information about immigration in the 1980s. Find the heading 1981–1989 at the top of the table and read down that column. To see how Asian immigration has changed since the 1950s, read across the row labeled Asia.

*The title tells you what kind of information the table contains.*

| Immigration to the United States by Region (numbers in 1,000s) | | | | |
|---|---|---|---|---|
| Regions | 1951–1960 | 1961–1970 | 1971–1980 | 1981–1989 |
| Europe | 1,492.2 | 1,238.6 | 801.3 | 593.2 |
| Asia | 157.1 | 445.3 | 1,633.8 | 2,478.8 |
| The Americas | 841.3 | 1,582.3 | 1,929.4 | 2,537.5 |
| Africa | 16.6 | 39.3 | 91.5 | 156.4 |
| All Other | 42.8 | 19.1 | 37.3 | 35.6 |

*Headings along the top and labels at the left side help you locate the information you need.*

*Note that numbers are given in 1,000s. The number 593.2, therefore, means 593,200 immigrants.*

## *Graphs*

Graphs are used to show groups of numbers. The numbers in a table, in fact, can often be turned into a graph. Two types of graphs you will see often in your schoolwork are bar graphs and circle graphs. Examples of both types of graphs are shown on the following page.

**Bar Graphs**    Each number in a bar graph is represented by a bar. The graph can have horizontal (left to right) or vertical (bottom to top) bars. The length or height of the bar indicates the size of the number. The bar graph below shows some of the same information that the table on page 629 shows. Notice how the heights of the bars allow you to compare the numbers easily.

*The scale at the left tells what the numbers mean. It also allows you to measure how much or how many of something each bar stands for.*

*You can quickly see how immigration has changed since 1951. From what region has the number of immigrants increased the most since the 1950s?*

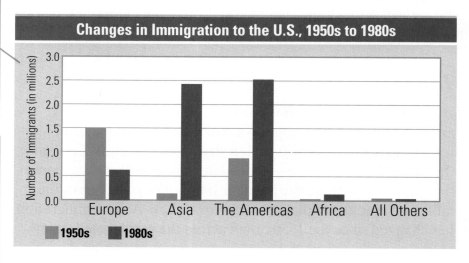

**Changes in Immigration to the U.S., 1950s to 1980s**

Number of Immigrants (in millions)

■ 1950s   ■ 1980s

**Circle Graphs**    In a circle graph, information is presented as slices of a "pie." (Circle graphs are sometimes called pie charts.) The graph begins with a circle that stands for the whole of something. For example, the whole circle could represent the world population. Each slice of the circle shows a part of the whole. If the whole circle is the world's population, each slice could show the population of one region.

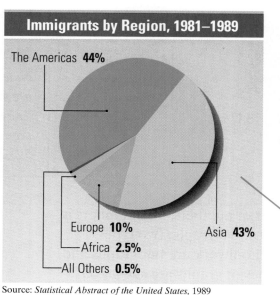

**Immigrants by Region, 1981–1989**

The Americas **44%**

Europe **10%**

Africa **2.5%**

All Others **0.5%**

Asia **43%**

Source: *Statistical Abstract of the United States*, 1989

*Notice how easy it is to compare the sizes of the slices. Which two regions come closest in numbers of immigrants?*

Since a circle graph shows parts of a whole, the slices are often marked as percentages. The whole circle is 100 percent— or *all*. The percentages of all the slices add up to 100 percent. The circle graph on the previous page shows information taken from the table on page 629.

## Maps

Maps show a portion of the earth's surface. Maps can show a variety of information. Physical maps show natural features of the earth's surface, such as rivers and mountains. Political maps show the boundaries of countries, states, and other political divisions, as well as cities. Physical and political features are often combined on a single map. Historical maps may show areas held by particular groups during a certain period in history. They may show changes in boundaries over time or other historical information.

*The title of the map tells what its subject is. The title of a historical map will tell what period of history the map shows.*

*Most maps have a key to explain the features they show. This map key explains how colors are used to show each period of growth of the Roman Empire.*

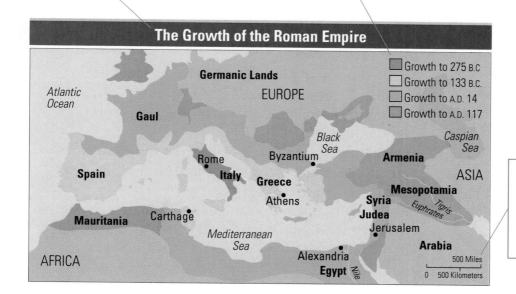

### The Growth of the Roman Empire

Growth to 275 B.C
Growth to 133 B.C.
Growth to A.D. 14
Growth to A.D. 117

Atlantic Ocean
Germanic Lands
EUROPE
Gaul
Black Sea
Caspian Sea
Rome
Byzantium
Armenia
ASIA
Spain
Italy
Greece
Mesopotamia
Athens
Syria
Euphrates
Tigris
Judea
Mauritania
Carthage
Jerusalem
Mediterranean Sea
Arabia
AFRICA
Alexandria
Egypt
Nile

*A map scale lets you measure distances on the map.*

500 Miles
0    500 Kilometers

# Diagrams

Has someone ever tried to describe an unfamiliar object or process to you? Perhaps you had trouble understanding it until he or she drew a picture. Being able to picture the parts of an object or to picture how the object works can help you understand it. That's why we use diagrams.

**Tooth**

— Crown

— Root

— Root canal

Diagrams are pictures that show a process or show relationships among parts of an object. In some diagrams each part of an object is labeled. A label may include an explanation of what that part does or how it relates to the whole. Diagrams help you understand an object much more easily than if you had a written or spoken description.

*Many diagrams are cutaways that show the inside of something you would not normally see.*

---

## Exercise 7

Answer the following questions about graphic information.

1. Which type of graphic aid would best show the areas controlled by Egypt in 1800 B.C.?
2. Which type of graphic aid would best show how the space shuttle works?
3. Which type of graphic aid would best show what portion of your total diet is made up of fruits and vegetables, protein foods, dairy products, grains, and other foods?
4. Which type of graphic aid would best show the amounts of oil imported by the five biggest oil-importing countries?
5. What region contributed the most immigrants to the United States in the period 1951–1960? Use a graphic aid in this lesson to answer.

## 24.8 Using Memory

Think of the trouble you'd have multiplying 1,634 x 391 if you didn't know the multiplication tables. (You may not always have a pocket calculator handy.) Memorizing certain information helps you in your schoolwork. It saves you the time of looking up the same facts over and over.

## How to Memorize

The most often-used memory technique is repetition—just repeating something over and over. Putting a group of items in some order can make them easier to remember. Alphabetical order, smallest to largest, and nearest to farthest are some possible ways of ordering items.

Writing out what you want to memorize is a good technique. Writing out poems, sayings, or long lists and saying them aloud as you write will help you memorize them.

## Tricks for Remembering

Another way of remembering material is by using tricks such as sayings or rhymes. The chart shows a few examples.

| Tricks for Remembering | |
|---|---|
| **Purpose** | **Memory Aid** |
| To remember the year Columbus sailed to the Americas | In fourteen hundred and ninety-two, Columbus sailed the ocean blue. |
| To remember that the order of the planets from the sun is Mercury, Venus, Earth, Mars, Jupiter, Saturn, Uranus, Neptune, and Pluto | My very excellent mother just served us nine pizzas. |
| To remember that the order of colors in a rainbow is red, orange, yellow, green, blue, indigo, and violet | Roy G. Biv |
| To remember that the person who runs a school is a principal, not a principle | The principal is my pal. |

The memory aids in the chart are just a few of the common ones. You can make up your own tricks to help you remember information. For example, you may need to memorize the scientific classifications of living things: kingdom, phylum, class, order, family, genus, and species. You could make up a sentence in which the first letter of each word is the same as the first letter of each category. Try to use the names of familiar people or places. Using familiar names will make it easier to remember your sentence.

Rhymes are especially effective memory tricks. Poetry is easier to remember than prose. Another effective trick is to see if the first letters of the items in a list spell a word or a name. For example, atoms contain protons, electrons, and a nucleus. Think of a pen to remember that fact. The name Roy G. Biv in the chart on page 633 is another example. It's even easier if the items do not have to be memorized in order.

Experiment with these techniques the next time you need to memorize information. Try tricks of your own as well. You may find just the right techniques for your own use.

## Exercise 8

Work with one or two classmates. Develop a memory trick to remember the names of the five Great Lakes from east to west: Ontario, Erie, Huron, Michigan, and Superior. Experiment with several of the techniques you learned in this lesson.

## Exercise 9

With one or two classmates brainstorm about some item of information that should be memorized, such as members of the animal kingdom or the names of important navigators during the Age of Exploration. Decide on the best technique for memorizing the information. Then develop a memory trick to remember it.

# Unit 25 Taking Tests

## 25.1    Test-taking Strategies

Your teacher has just announced you will have an English test in two weeks. How will you get ready for it? Learning the material to be covered is the most important step in preparing for a test. However, you can also get ready by learning how to take a test. Effective test taking involves budgeting your time wisely both before and during the test.

## *Preparing for a Test*

You can prepare for a test as soon as it is announced. First, note when the test will be given, and find out what it will cover. Then make a study plan that allows you to organize your time effectively. For suggestions on making a study plan, see pages 621–623.

Once you've decided how to budget your study time, start reviewing the material. Look over your textbook, class notes, homework assignments, and quizzes. Write a list of study questions as you review. If possible, get together with other students and work in a study group. Quiz one another with the questions each of you has prepared.

## *Taking a Test*

The day of the test has arrived. You've prepared wisely, and your hard work should pay off. Keep in mind, however, that tests usually last one class period or less. Since the time is limited, you will need to use your time efficiently during the test. The following page has some tips that will help you.

## Tips on Managing Your Time During a Test

1. Read the directions carefully before you begin. Understanding the directions will help you answer items correctly.

2. Answer all the items you are sure of first. Skipping hard items will give you time to answer all of the items you know.

3. After you have finished the easier items, go back and try the items you skipped. Give the best answers you can.

4. Allow time to check your answers before you turn in your test. This review will decrease your chances of making simple errors.

### Exercise 1

Choose the response that best completes each of the following statements:

1. A good way to prepare for a test is to make a _____ .
   **a.** class schedule      **c.** study plan
   **b.** study break         **d.** summary
2. It's a good idea to review your _____ .
   **a.** homework            **c.** quizzes
   **b.** textbook            **d.** all of the above
3. When a test is announced, one of the first things to find out is _____ .
   **a.** whether you will need a pencil or a pen
   **b.** what the test will cover
   **c.** the teacher's name
   **d.** how the test will be graded
4. When taking a test, it is a good idea to skip the _____ until you have completed the other items.
   **a.** first few items      **c.** easy items
   **b.** even-numbered items  **d.** difficult items
5. Allow time to _____ your answers before you turn in your test.
   **a.** remove              **c.** rearrange
   **b.** check               **d.** none of the above

Your teacher has just informed the class of an upcoming test. It will contain true-false, multiple-choice, matching, fill-in, and short-answer items. Even if you don't like dealing with these types of test items, don't panic. There are strategies you can learn that will help you answer them.

## True-False Items

A true-false item asks you to decide whether a statement is true or false. A single true-false statement may contain some information that is true and some that is false. However, the item should be marked true only if the *entire* statement is true. If *any* part of the statement is false, you should mark it false. Look at the following example.

> Columbus sailed westward from Spain in 1492 and landed at the site of present-day New York City on October 12.

*The first part of this sentence is true, but the second part is not. Columbus landed in what is now the Bahamas. The statement is false.*

## Multiple-Choice Items

Multiple-choice items are the kind you will encounter most often. Each item includes an incomplete sentence or a question and several responses. You must choose the response that best completes the sentence or answers the question. Read all of the responses before writing your answer. Eliminate those you know are incorrect. This method will help you zero in on the correct response.

Be careful about choosing responses that contain absolute words, such as *always, never, all,* or *none.* Since most statements have exceptions, absolute statements are often incorrect.

The following multiple-choice item might appear on an English test. As you read it, decide how you would select the correct answer.

Which statement concerning the book <u>Julie of the Wolves</u> is accurate?

a. It was written by Jean Craighead George.
b. It takes place in North America.
c. It is the story of a girl and wild animals.
d. all of the above

## Matching Items

In a matching activity you are given two lists of items. You must match items in the first list with items from the second list. Before you begin, notice whether each list contains the same number of items. Often the second column will contain more items than the first column. When that is so, some items in column 2 will not be used.

If each item is to be used only once, make a note of each item as you use it. (If you are permitted to write on the test, cross it out.) Complete the easy matches first. Then there will be fewer items to choose from when you try the more difficult matches.

Match each city with the name of its state.

___ 1. Chicago  a. Alaska
___ 2. Dallas   b. Florida
___ 3. Miami   c. Georgia
___ 4. Atlanta   d. Illinois
___ 5. Fairbanks  e. Texas
        f. Wisconsin

# Fill-in Items

Fill-in items usually consist of a sentence with one or more blanks for you to fill in. The number of blanks usually shows how many words will be needed for the response. Your answer should make the statement both true and grammatically correct. Check your choice by rereading the sentence with your answer included. Try answering the following fill-in item.

> The United States presidents carved on Mount Rushmore are _____, _____, _____, and _____.

*Notice that four names are needed. The correct fill-in answers are* George Washington, Thomas Jefferson, Abraham Lincoln, *and* Theodore Roosevelt.

# Short-Answer Items

Short-answer questions ask you for specific information. Always read the question carefully to be sure you understand what is being asked. Unless you are told not to, answer each question with a complete sentence. Look at the following question, which might appear on a social studies test.

> Why did the early colonists risk the dangerous voyage across the Atlantic Ocean to settle in America?

*First, think out your answer. You can compose the sentence in your head before you begin writing.*

*Be sure you understand the question before you begin your answer. In this case, you will need to give the reasons early colonists came to America.*

*Rephrase the question to answer with a complete sentence. For example:* The early colonists settled in America to gain religious and political freedom and economic opportunity.

Practice the test-taking skills you covered in this lesson. Read the passage below. Then answer the test items that follow the passage.

Although he never sailed himself, Prince Henry of Portugal (1394–1460) was an important influence on early exploration. Prince Henry's crews sailed the oceans more than five hundred years ago. They used their knowledge of water currents, winds, and the sun and stars to get them to their destinations.

These sailors also used instruments. Henry, often called the Navigator, set up a school of navigation in Portugal. He brought together experts who worked to improve the compass and the astrolabe. A compass shows directions. With an astrolabe, sailors can tell latitude, or distance from the equator. Led by Henry, the Portuguese developed a fast, maneuverable ship called a caravel. In addition, sailors kept careful records of all they saw. These records added to the information map makers needed and sailors used for later voyages.

1. True or False: Portuguese sailors depended on experience, not on instruments.
2. Why was Prince Henry called the Navigator?
   a. He sailed on many overseas voyages.
   b. He was the king of Portugal.
   c. He encouraged improvements in navigation.
   d. all of the above
3. Match each item with the correct description.
   1. astrolabe        a. indicates direction
   2. caravel          b. shows latitude
   3. compass          c. fast, maneuverable ship
4. Fill in the blanks: Map makers used information from _____ kept by Portuguese _____ .
5. Write a short answer: How did Portugal contribute to future world exploration by Europeans?

You are probably familiar with standardized tests, which are given to groups of students throughout the country. Does the thought of taking such tests frighten you? It shouldn't. You just need to familiarize yourself with the types of questions that could be asked. Knowing what to expect will help you relax and get good scores.

## *Reading Comprehension*

Reading-comprehension questions test how well you understand what you read. These items usually include a passage about a specific topic, followed by questions. The questions may ask you to identify main ideas or to recognize supporting details. The questions may also ask you to draw conclusions based on the passage. The following is an example of an item from a reading-comprehension test.

> Women artists have long been respected in Native American culture. Women in the Great Plains nations have created beautiful ceremonial robes and pottery. In traditional Navaho culture women artists wove magnificent rugs with bold designs and patterns. Cheyenne women developed the art of sewing porcupine and bird quills into elaborate symbols and designs. Some of these women even formed an organization called the Sacred Quillworker's Guild. Members of the organization teach the art to other Cheyenne women.
>
> What would be the best title for this passage?
> a. The Sacred Quillworker's Guild
> b. Basketry, Weaving, and Design
> c. Native American Women Artists
> d. Native American Artists

*The titles in* a *and* b *describe only supporting details. Item* d *is not specific enough. Item* c *focuses on the passage's specific topic and is the correct choice.*

# Vocabulary

Standardized tests often include vocabulary items. One type of vocabulary item asks you to complete a sentence with one of several multiple-choice items. To complete the sentence correctly, you need to know the meaning of a particular word.

Sometimes you can use your knowledge of word parts to identify a word's meaning. See if you can analyze the parts of *preface* to complete the item below.

*Notice that* preface *contains the prefix* pre-, *which means "before." You can use this knowledge to determine that the correct answer is* b.

1. A book's preface appears _____ .

   a. at the end of the book
   b. at the beginning of the book
   c. in the middle of the book
   d. just before the book's index

In another type of vocabulary item, you show that you understand a word's meaning by choosing a synonym for it. In the following example you must choose the word closest in meaning to the underlined word in the sentence.

*By trying each choice in the sentence, you can eliminate* worry, attack, *and probably* ignore. *The best synonym for* expunge *is* remove.

In delivering his speech, the senator decided to expunge the part that attacked the vice president.

a. ignore    b. remove    c. worry    d. attack

# Analogies

Analogy items test your understanding of relationships between things or ideas. For example, think about the relationship between *strong* and *weak*. The words are antonyms—words that have opposite meanings. A test item may begin with a pair, such as *strong* and *weak*. You must then choose another pair of words with a similar relationship. Since *strong* and *weak* are opposites, the second pair of words should also be opposites.

Strong is to weak as

a. big is to large          c. young is to old
b. picture is to frame      d. bowl is to spoon

Big *and* large *have the same meaning. A* picture *is contained in a* frame. *A* bowl *and a* spoon *are used together. Only* young *and* old, *choice* c, *are antonyms.*

Sometimes colons are used to shorten analogies. A single colon separates the words in each pair, and a double colon separates the two pairs. For example, "strong is to weak as young is to old" is shown as "strong : weak :: young : old." What is the relationship in the item below?

kitten : cat ::

a. book : play             c. horse : donkey
b. computer : calculator   d. calf : cow

*Remember, you read the single colon as though it said "is to" and the double colon as "as." This item begins "Kitten is to cat as . . ."*

If the relationship is unclear, try making up a sentence that describes the relationship between the first pair of words. For instance, in the example above you might say, "A kitten is a baby cat." Then try substituting each pair of words in that sentence. After trying each pair of words in the example above, you should find that *d* makes the most sense.

## Grammar, Usage, and Mechanics

Standardized tests often include sections that test your knowledge of grammar, usage, and mechanics. These items often present a sentence divided into several underlined sections. Each section is marked with a letter. You must tell which of the underlined sections contains an error. You can also indicate that there is no error.

Another type of item gives a sentence with only one section underlined. The sentence is followed by several possible corrections. One of the choices may be the same as the underlined part. Examples of both types are shown on the following page.

1. Each of the girls checked their own book
         a            b        c

   out of the library.  no error
         d           e

2. Aaron is the biggest of the two boys.

   a. the biggest       c. the more bigger
   b. the bigger        d. the most biggest

## Exercise 3

Use the test-taking strategies described in this lesson to complete the following items.

1. A transparent piece of glass is one that _____ .
   **a.** cannot be seen through   **c.** is easily broken
   **b.** is clear                **d.** is very thick
2. dentist : teeth :: _____
   **a.** mechanic : engines   **c.** dog : bone
   **b.** doctor : nurse        **d.** student : pencil
3. Choose the letter of the underlined section that needs to be corrected in the following sentence. Choose *e* if no correction is needed.

   The captain past the ball to another member of
         a       b               c
   the basketball team.  no error
            d        e
4. Decide whether the underlined section in the following sentence needs correction. Then choose the best correction from the choices listed.

   Meg has taken the dog out for a run in the park.
   **a.** has taken         **c.** has took
   **b.** take               **d.** taking

# Unit 26 Listening and Speaking

## 26.1 How to Listen

As you turn on the radio to listen to your favorite station, you run into a problem. You're ready to listen to music, but all you hear is static. When there's interference, it's difficult to enjoy or understand what you're listening to.

You may face forms of mental "interference" every day. Ignoring the static, though, will help you listen.

### *Listening in Class*

Does your mind ever wander during school? Maybe you can't stop thinking about your bad morning. Maybe the sun is shining, and you'd like to be outside. You have to get your thoughts back on track. You know you need to listen if you're going to learn. These tips will help you get started.

---

### Tips for Effective Listening

1. Sort out any interference, such as classroom noise or wandering thoughts. Focus your attention completely on the speaker.

2. Identify main ideas as you listen. Then write them down in your own words. These are the most important points to remember.

3. Put a star or check mark next to any ideas that your teacher tells you are especially important or that might appear on a test.

4. Review your notes after class. Do you have any questions? Clear them up right away to avoid confusion later.

---

**Interpreting Special Clues**   Gestures and tone of voice often indicate which information is important. Sometimes your teacher may speak certain words or phrases more loudly than others. Write those down. Hand and body movements also tell you to pay special attention to what's being said.

# Listening to Persuasive Speech

Television commercials, political speeches, and editorials on the evening news all have one thing in common. Each speaker wants to convince you that what you're hearing is the truth. Don't listen without thinking, though. You must decide if the speaker is saying something you can believe.

**Fact Versus Opinion**    Identifying the speaker's attitude is very important. Do you know when you're hearing facts and when you're hearing opinions? A fact is something that can be proven. An opinion is what someone *believes* to be true. In the following examples try to separate the facts from the opinions.

| Evaluating News Statements | |
| --- | --- |
| **Heard on the Evening News** | **Questions to Ask Yourself** |
| Today when both candidates met, Smith grudgingly shook hands with his opponent. | What one word tells me how the news reporter thinks the candidate feels? Is this necessarily true? |
| Twenty-seven boy scouts camped in the mountains last weekend. | Does this story introduction try to convince me of anything? |
| Last night a ferocious dog attacked a gas station attendant. | Would I feel differently if the dog were described as frightened rather than ferocious? |
| Local high school girls are taking a stand against their new band uniforms. | Does this statement try to persuade me of something, or does it just give me information? |

**Persuasive Speeches**    Speakers often try to sway you to their point of view. They use emotional words and actions to make you feel strongly about what they're saying. The emotional words they use are often adjectives and adverbs. Would you feel good about something described in such terms as *dreary, rotten, foul-smelling, eerie, dingy?* Probably not. Now think about these: *golden, shiny, energetic, wonderful, pure.* These words would probably make you feel good.

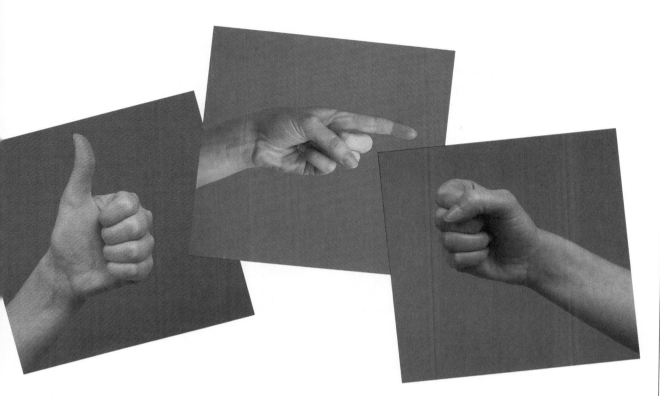

Speakers often use actions to accompany their emotional words. In these cases, you need to "listen" with your eyes. They might make eye contact with you and smile. They could nod their heads or move their arms or hands.

Emotional words and actions are good to use, but you need to think through what's being said. Speakers might be sincere, or they might be trying to force their messages on you. It's up to you to decide what their intentions are.

**Listening to Commercials** Commercials bombard us every day. Though they sometimes give information, their main function is to boost sales. They do this by delivering two messages—one is obvious, and the other is hidden. The obvious message is *what* you hear or see. The hidden message comes through in *how* the information is presented.

Have you ever heard a commercial declare that its product is new and improved? To know exactly what this means, you need to know what it was like before the improvement. If the product was poor to begin with, it may still be poor. Beware of words like *more, better, whiter, brighter, longer-lasting,* and so on.

Commercials also may give information that only *sounds* true. Your dog may eat the dog food advertised. But that doesn't mean that your dog will look as healthy as the dog in the commercial. That's what you're supposed to believe, though. Can you catch the faulty reasoning in the sample commercials in the chart below?

Rush right out, and pick up a tube of the new, improved Skinscrub. Those ugly skin blemishes will vanish in hours as the miracle ingredient X-34 goes to work.

| Advertising: Believe It or Not | |
|---|---|
| **Advertisement** | **Think It Through** |
| A girl wearing the advertiser's product sits among a group of friends, laughing and talking. | What is the hidden message here? If you wear this product, you will be as popular as the girl in the commercial. Is this true? |
| You are told that the bike advertised is the best in its class. | What class is the advertiser talking about? Maybe you do not need that kind of bike. Maybe it is not worth the money. |
| A famous actor tells you that the car in the television commercial is simply the best. | An actor may know about performing, but does that make him an expert on a car's performance? Should you believe him? |
| A group of athletes are shown celebrating a win while drinking a particular soft drink. | What idea are you being asked to accept? You are supposed to believe that if you drink the same soft drink, you will be a winner. |

**Evaluating What You Hear**   Faulty reasoning can exist in any form of persuasion. You may hear it in editorials on the news. You may hear it from your friends. At times you may even hear it from your own mouth. Look at the examples in the following chart. Do you recognize the faulty reasoning in each example? Where might you hear each form?

| Recognizing Forms of Faulty Thinking | |
|---|---|
| **Testimonial** | Fred Jackson, a famous water polo player, says, "After I get out of the pool, I dry my hair with an All Hot Air hair dryer." |
| **Bandwagon** | "Hot Fish Lips is the hottest band to come to town," the D.J. says. "The concert will be a sellout. Get your tickets now." |
| **Name Calling** | "The other candidate is a total loser. If he gets elected, it won't be long until he messes up our country." |
| **Faulty Cause and Effect** | "Mom didn't buy me new basketball shoes. I didn't make the team. I'd be a starter, though, if she'd bought me the shoes." |
| **Generalization** | "Six out of ten people chose Brighty Bright toothpaste over Brand X. Brighty Bright is the best toothpaste you can buy." |

## Exercise 1

Listen carefully to any radio or television advertising, television editorials, and conversations you hear this week. Try to determine what is really being said. Can you sort out the facts and opinions? Which ones use faulty reasoning to persuade the listener? Find at least two examples of the forms of faulty reasoning listed in the chart above. Share them with your class, and discuss why you believe or do not believe the messages.

Interviewing a person is a good way to get information. Information from an interview can add life to a paper or speech. It also makes research more fun. By talking with someone, you may find useful information that you wouldn't find in a book. If you improve your interviewing skills, you may never have trouble finding information again.

## *When to Interview*

Not every topic lends itself to interviewing. For example, let's say your oral report is on Christopher Columbus. Finding someone who sailed on the *Santa María* might be difficult. The library or museum is the place to go for that. Often, though, there are experts in the field you're researching, and they're right under your nose. You just have to look for them.

Let's say you're researching basketball rules. You might find information by asking the physical education teacher or the basketball coach. Or maybe you know someone who is a referee. When thinking about resources, don't overlook the people in your family, your school, or your community. Look at the chart below for examples of topics and possible sources of information about them.

| Subjects for Interviews | |
|---|---|
| **Topic** | **Resources** |
| The history of your town | Mayor's office; local historian; oldest resident |
| How ice cream is made | Ice cream shop owner; parents; restaurant manager |
| Fly-cast fishing | Family and friends; local bait-and-tackle store owner; fly-cast fisher |
| Laws about children | Lawyer or judge at juvenile court; law department professor at local university; social worker |
| Dog breeding | Local kennel; dog breeder; veterinarian |

When you interview someone, you become a reporter. Keep in mind the six favorite words of every good reporter: *who, what, where, when, why,* and *how.* These words are like the signs along a road. You need them if you want to get where you want to go. Otherwise you might get lost in your interview.

## *Preparing to Interview*

When you find someone to interview, write or call that person to request a meeting. Introduce yourself and your topic, and ask if there's a time you can meet. When you decide on a time, write it down and get ready.

Before you interview someone, find out all you can about your topic. Use encyclopedias, books, newspapers, and magazines to find basic background information. If you know some things about your topic before the interview, you can ask more in-depth questions.

Write out those questions. Then review them before you meet with your subject. You want to make sure you haven't left out anything important.

Some materials you may need for the interview include the following:

- a tape recorder (ask if it's OK to use it)
- a notebook (tape recorders don't always work)
- a couple of pens or pencils

651

The more prepared and professional you are in your interview, the better it will go.

For a helpful interview, you need to ask good questions. For example, if you interviewed a firefighter in your town, here are some questions you might ask.

| List of Sample Questions to Ask a Firefighter |
| --- |
| 1. What were you like as a child? Was it your childhood dream to be a firefighter? |
| 2. When did you decide to be a firefighter? |
| 3. Where did you attend school to learn to fight fires? What was the training like? |
| 4. What is the scariest thing about fighting fires? Have you ever been close to losing your life? |
| 5. What was the worst fire you ever fought? How long did it take to put it out? |
| 6. What tasks do you have to perform when you're not fighting fires? |

## Conducting an Interview

Check the questions from your notes, and take them to the interview. Then listen closely, take good notes, and ask follow-up questions. Also, be sure to relax. If you're at ease, chances are the person you're interviewing will be relaxed, too.

**Ask Open-ended Questions**   Open-ended questions can't be answered with a simple yes or no. The point of an interview is to get your subject to talk freely. Ask, "What's it like to ride a bronco?" rather than, "Is it frightening to ride a bronco?" The first question will encourage your subject to describe how bronco riding feels. You will get more information with questions like that. You'll also find more questions to ask as you go along.

**Avoid Saying Too Much**   Don't start a conversation with the person you're interviewing. You're there to listen. Don't get sidetracked into giving your own opinions about the topic. Just ask your questions, and then listen. Look at the following list of interviewing tips. Keep these in mind as you plan and conduct your interview.

## Interviewing Tips

1. Have a general idea of the information you want to gain from the interview. Review your questions. Make sure they flow in a logical order.

2. Start with the most important questions. Be friendly, but stick to business. Keep the interview going in the right direction. Remain in charge, and stay focused.

3. If you do not understand something, ask for clarification. If you want additional information about something that was said, ask a follow-up question.

4. Pay attention as you take notes. Jot down important points, but do not get overly involved in note-taking. Eye contact is a must. You can fill in the blanks later.

5. Thank the person when the interview is over. Ask whether you may phone if you think of additional questions. You may also want to send a thank-you note.

### Exercise 2

Make a family tree that goes back three generations. Find out the *who, what, where, when,* and *why* of each person on your tree.

Begin by writing down the names of people in your family who might provide information. Call them to see whether you could interview them. Then find as much background information as you can. Use the library or any family files for your research. Next, write out questions you can ask each person.

Conduct your interviews, using the guidelines in this lesson. Draw a family tree, and write out a short biography of each family member. Present your results to the class.

## 26.3　Speaking Informally

You engage in informal speaking many times every day. You talk with your friends in the lunchroom or at your locker. You speak to your parents or your neighbors. These are all examples of informal speech. The tone is casual, and everyone involved usually joins in. Here are some tips on speaking informally.

| Tips on Speaking Informally | | |
| --- | --- | --- |
| **Type** | **Description** | **Hint** |
| Conversation | This is the most informal type of speech. Each person is free to listen and speak spontaneously. | Courtesy is very important. Do not interrupt another speaker. Listen until he or she has finished. |
| Discussion | A discussion generally concerns one topic. One person may be chosen to act as discussion leader. The leader's job is to keep the group focused on the topic. | Letting each person speak in turn will help the group fully develop its ideas about the topic. |
| Announcement | Announcements are descriptions of upcoming events or activities. They should be brief but should provide all the important information. | After your announcement ask if there are questions. You want to be sure that everyone understands what you have announced. |
| Demonstration | The speaker explains how a process works or how something is made. | Demonstrate the steps of a process in the correct order. Number the steps so that your audience can follow the process. |
| Storytelling | Stories are usually meant to entertain, to teach a moral, or to make a point. You could tell a story about almost anything. | Let your enthusiasm for your story show in how you tell it. Act out the parts. Re-create the story. Draw your audience in. |

# *Making Introductions*

You'll have many opportunities to introduce people during your school life. Perhaps a new student will need to meet his or her new classmates. A new person might join your swim team. Whatever the occasion, the most important thing to remember is courtesy. Always treat the new person with kindness and consideration. You may be the new person yourself someday.

There are several important parts to an introduction. First, remember to use the full name of each person. You might say, "Evan, I'd like to introduce you to Miguel Hernandez. Miguel this is Evan Schmit." Notice that you introduce each person to the other. This helps each person feel equally important.

You might also think about what you know about each person. If they have something in common, mention it during the introduction. For example, suppose you know that Evan was the star first baseman on his former baseball team. You also know that Miguel loves baseball. This could be just the bit of information that will make their first conversation natural and comfortable. When introducing two adults or an adult and a younger person, you might be a little more formal. Read the following introduction:

SPEAKER:(turning to Ms. MacKelvey) Ms. MacKelvey, I'd like you to meet my mother, Mrs. Jennifer Chen. When she was young, my mother lived in San Francisco, very close to the area you're from. (turning to mother) Mother, I'd like you to meet Ms. Kathleen MacKelvey. She's going to be the new art teacher in our school.

*Mention something you think the two people might have in common.*

*Notice how the speaker turns from one person to another as the introduction takes place.*

*Be sure to use the first and last names of each person.*

# Participating in a Discussion

You probably take part in discussions of some kind every day. You may have them in classes, on sports teams, in choir, and so on. You probably also have discussions with your family or among friends.

Often in discussions groups try to make decisions. Discussion leaders are needed then, because people don't always agree. Leaders aren't the only people who help discussions run smoothly, though. It's the job of everyone involved. Here are some tips for taking part in an informal discussion.

## Tips for Participating in a Discussion

1. Let everyone take turns speaking. Do not interrupt when someone else is talking.

2. Pay attention to the discussion leader. If it is time to move on or quiet down, be cooperative.

3. Listen to what everyone says. Jot down notes on points you want to remember.

4. When it is your turn to talk, look at everyone around you. If you state an opinion, also state the reasons behind your thinking.

5. If something is unclear to you, ask a question.

6. Help the group stick to the topic under discussion. Make sure your comments relate directly to it.

# Explaining a Process

Building a model airplane and making blueberry muffins may not seem to have anything in common, but they do. Both are processes that require step-by-step directions.

When giving directions, explain the process in a simple and clear way, and in the correct order. If you don't give good directions, your blueberry muffins may end up tasting like the model airplane. On the next page you'll find step-by-step directions for explaining things.

Page is 1/2 line short

## How to Give Step-by-Step Directions

1. Determine your audience and the information they will need to understand the process.

2. Write out the process on a piece of paper. Make a diagram to use as a visual aid if you think that will help make the process clear.

3. Go back and fill in any steps you have forgotten.

4. Review the steps, and rearrange any that are out of order.

5. Reword each step so that it is simply and clearly stated.

# *Making Announcements*

If you had to make an announcement to your class about an upcoming event, would you know what to do? Making a good announcement requires you to consider three things. First of all, you must understand your audience. What do they need to hear? Second, consider the announcement itself. What are the facts? How can you make sure you state all the facts clearly and briefly? Finally, you need to decide how you can strengthen the persuasiveness of your announcement. How can you make people *want* to hear what you say?

## Tips for Making Announcements

1. Write down the most important points. The name of the event and the date, time, and place are necessary, so include them.

2. If you can, add a little life to what you have written. Think of your audience—what would make them want to attend the event?

3. Make sure everyone is quiet before you begin speaking. Look over your audience to get everyone's attention.

4. While speaking, look at your audience to convey your message.

5. Speak slowly and in a normal voice. Be sure that everyone has heard the entire message.

6. When you are done, ask if there are any questions.

## Exercise 3

Imagine that the following announcement came over your school's public address system. Meet with a small group to discuss the announcement. Have one group member read it aloud to judge its effectiveness. What is good about the announcement? What is not so good about it? Has anything been left out? Working as a group, rewrite the announcement so that it is as effective as you can make it.

*A dance will be held in the gym this Friday after the basketball game. If you attend the game, you get into the dance free. Our basketball team's record so far this season is 4–0. It's our school's best start in ten years. We're playing our biggest rival. Tip-off is at seven o'clock. The dance will follow immediately and go until midnight. The bleachers will be pushed back, and music will be played through the gym's sound system. If you want to come, you must have a permission slip filled out by a parent or guardian.*

## Exercise 4

Break into small groups to make a list of events that would require announcements. The events can be real or imaginary. Allow each member to choose one event and work independently. Make a list, including as much information about your event as you can. Don't actually write the announcement. Just list the information.

When your list is complete, fold your paper and put it into a container. Each group member should pick a list from the container and write a short announcement for it. Read the announcements aloud in your group, and discuss their effectiveness.

You may never speak to millions of people or even to your whole school. But at one time or another you'll probably give an oral report in front of your class. If you can master the oral report, who knows where you'll end up. You may give a speech one day as president of the United States.

There are many types of oral reports. You might be asked to explain something or to compare and contrast two topics. Perhaps you want to persuade the class to think the way you do about a topic. Oral reports are not long and involved speeches about a topic. Although there's often a time limit, it's surprising how much you can say in a few minutes.

Whatever the type of report, you can apply the same steps to prepare it. Preparation is the key to a successful presentation. That's where you have to start.

## *Preparing the Report*

You first need to think about your topic. Focus your topic, and break it down so that it's easier to research. If the topic is too broad, you'll get confused with too much information. If it's too narrow, you won't find enough information.

Next, focus on your audience. Who they are determines what you'll say. Suppose that you have to give an oral report both to your class and at a science fair. Your two reports will vary because of your two different audiences. The report to your class will be informal, filled with opinion and feeling. You'll be more formal at the science fair, though.

You also need to know why you're giving a report. Is it to inform or to persuade? Your purpose will determine what information you need and how you'll deliver it.

For example, imagine that your topic is "extending the school year." If you want to persuade, use emotion in your voice and in your hand gestures. Draw your audience in so that they can't help but believe you. If your purpose is to inform, though, don't overuse emotion. Just present the facts, and list both sides of the debate. Let your audience decide whether a longer school year would be good or bad.

As you prepare your oral report, use the diagram below to help you structure it. Notice the writing stages shown in the box between Prewriting and Presenting. You'll spend most of your time in the Drafting, Revising, and Practicing stages. Move back and forth among these until you're ready to present your report.

**Prewriting**
- Determine your purpose and audience.
- Decide on a topic, and narrow it.

**Drafting**
- Make an outline of the important points.
- Fill in the supporting details.
- Write out what you want to say.

**Revising**
- Review your report. Does it flow logically from one point to the next?
- Reword unclear statements.
- Write an outline on note cards to make practicing easier.

**Practicing**
- Practice your report out loud and alone, then again in front of a friend or family member.
- Ask for advice, and accept it to improve your report.
- Time the report if it needs to be a certain length.

**Presenting**
- Relax as you stand before your audience.
- Make eye contact with the audience at all times.
- Speak up, and speak clearly.

## *Practicing the Report*

It's good to first practice your report by yourself. Check your posture, and make sure your gestures are natural. Also, listen for places where your voice rises and falls. Are you emphasizing all your important points? If the main points aren't coming through clearly, try reworking your delivery.

Next, ask someone you know to listen to your report. After you finish, ask for comments and tips from your friendly audience. Often an audience spots mistakes that a speaker doesn't hear or see.

## *Presenting the Report*

As you see, effective speaking comes through good planning and much practice. After you finish writing and practicing your oral report, it's time to do the real thing.

Besides gestures, eye contact, and tone of voice, what else could you use to strengthen your report? How about using visual aids? These can add variety and interest to your report. They also help you show what you're saying. Seeing visual aids can help your audience remember more of what you say.

Have everything prepared and in place before you begin. Once you start, you don't want to stop for any reason. Showing visual aids should be as natural as any other part of your delivery.

### Exercise 5

Choose a topic from those listed below, or use one of your own ideas. Find something that the rest of your class might not know a great deal about. Narrow the topic if needed, and jot down some ideas about your audience. Think about what you would like to say in a two- to three-minute oral report.

- what's important about music
- the future with computers
- how sports teach a lot about life
- why I want to be president
- salamanders, the ancient amphibians
- why smoking is unhealthful

Develop your oral report, using the diagram on the previous page as a guide. After you research, write, and practice giving your speech, present it to the class.

## 26.5    Speaking Formally

Writing a formal speech is similar to writing a research paper, but it can be more satisfying. When you write a paper for a class, your teacher is probably the only one who reads it. But if you give a speech on the same topic, your whole class gets to hear it. Speeches are great opportunities to share with others what you've learned and what you believe in. You'll find that speeches are easy to give if you use the three steps of preparation, practice, and delivery. These steps all lead to a well-researched, well-organized, and successful presentation.

## *Preparing a Speech*

Preparation is the most important part of writing a speech. It's the foundation on which everything is built. A weak foundation almost always makes for a weak house. The same is true of speeches. Put a lot of time and effort into the preparation of your speech. Make it as strong as you can. If you do, you'll be able to write and deliver a strong speech.

**Prewriting**    You first need to consider the purpose of your speech. What are you attempting to do? Inform? Persuade? Then think of your audience. What do they already know about your topic? What don't they know?

Next, narrow the topic. A subject such as "Dogs of the World" is too broad. Maybe selecting one breed would be wise. You might further narrow the topic to either the characteristics or the history of the dog.

**Drafting**    Once you feel comfortable with your topic, audience, and purpose, it's time to move on. Write out your main point in one sentence. This is your thesis statement. It summarizes the entire speech. Your thesis statement might read, "Cocker spaniels are good pets for children." Everything in your speech should then support this statement.

With your thesis statement written, start drafting. Like a research paper, a formal speech usually contains three main parts. The introduction is first; it sets up the speech. Next comes the body, containing your main ideas and supporting details.

Last, the conclusion wraps up everything. There are two ways to compose your speech. You can write it out exactly as you'll say it, or you can use note cards. Outlining your main points and supporting details on note cards usually works better. You can refer to what you need to say without having to read your speech word for word.

Revising    At this point you want to take an X-ray of your speech. Look at its skeleton—the structure you've built out of words. Do your words support the ideas you want to get across? Does your speech flow logically from one idea to the next? Do all your ideas lead toward a conclusion? If you find areas where the structure breaks down, rework them. Don't be surprised if you go back and forth between drafting and revising. It takes time to fine-tune a speech.

Also, use strong transitions. You don't want to lose your audience when you move to the next thought. For example, you could begin another main point with, "*Another* way in which the cocker spaniel is a good pet . . ."

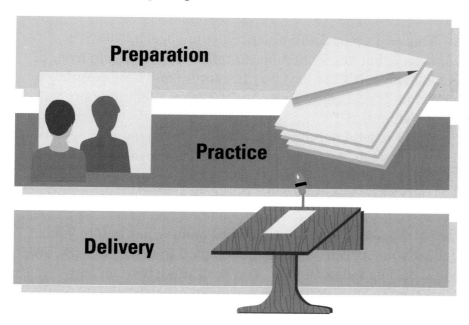

## *Practicing a Speech*

Once you write your speech, practice it as much as you can. If your speech is supposed to be a certain length, time yourself.

This will help you speed it up or slow it down. Also, practice delivering your speech in front of a mirror. Look for unnatural gestures or exaggerated movements. If you can, practice giving your speech into a tape recorder. Listen to your voice. Are you emphasizing important words and ideas? Are you speaking too slowly or too quickly? Are you pronouncing words clearly and distinctly?

Rehearse your speech in front of a few friends or relatives. Ask for comments on what is strong and what needs work. Don't be afraid of criticism. Consider the changes they suggest, and make the changes if you feel comfortable doing so.

If you can, practice your speech at the site where you'll later give it. That way, the surroundings will be familiar, and you'll feel comfortable when you deliver the speech.

Use your notes to remind yourself of the main points. Your note cards shouldn't serve as script, though. If you just read your speech, your audience may lose interest.

## *Delivering a Speech*

You've prepared and practiced your speech. Now it's important that you remember to relax. Be yourself in front of the audience. It's the best way to capture and hold people's attention. If you enjoy giving your speech, your audience will enjoy listening.

If you're a bit nervous, don't worry. Use that uneasiness to your advantage. Athletes, stage actors, and singers all know how to use "butterflies" to make their performance more energetic and full of life. You can do the same thing.

**Before the Speech**    At the last minute, just before you deliver your speech, you may be tempted to make changes. That could be a bad idea, though. You've drafted, revised, and rehearsed your speech. Changes might upset the careful preparation you've just completed. Change only what positively needs improvement in your speech.

Just before you speak, take a moment to look at your audience. You created your speech just for them. Keeping that in mind will help you deliver your speech confidently.

**During the Speech**　As you begin speaking, remember to make eye contact with your audience. Try talking to each person in turn. As you focus on each member of the audience, tell yourself that you're speaking directly to that person. Think about what you're saying and to whom you're saying it. When you take your mind off yourself, you become more relaxed.

Keep an eye out, too, for audience signals. No matter how well you plan, something unexpected can always occur. Think about what went wrong and how you can make it right. Above all, don't panic if something goes wrong. Below are some tips that will help you identify possible problems.

| Tips for Relating to Your Audience | | |
| --- | --- | --- |
| **Audience Signals** | **Interpretation** | **Speaker Response** |
| People in your audience are moving around in their chairs or staring off into space. | You may have lost their attention. | You may recapture their interest by raising and lowering your voice or adding gestures. Perhaps you need to speed up your delivery. |
| Your audience seems puzzled. Some are talking with a neighbor. | They may not have understood something you said. | You may need to back up and explain a portion of your speech again. Briefly review your main ideas before continuing. |
| You notice some people trying to get closer to you. A few are leaning forward in their chairs. | They may be unable to hear you. | Speak up. Maybe some other noises are preventing people from hearing. Ask the audience if you need to repeat anything. |
| Your audience is listening attentively and nodding. | You have their full attention. | You are doing well. Do not change a thing. Keep up the good work. |

Deliver your speech with all the gestures and voice variations you've practiced. You can also respond to your audience. If they smile, smile back. Whatever happens, though, don't allow yourself to be distracted. Use your note cards, and keep up the rhythm and flow of your speech. Stay focused on what you're saying, and you'll deliver a successful speech. Following are a few more tips for speaking effectively.

## Tips for Speaking Effectively

1. After you make an important point, pause a moment. A pause allows your audience to think about what you have said. It also creates a dramatic break that will capture people's attention.

2. Look around the room as you speak, making eye contact with each person in the audience. Think of your own experience. You probably dislike it when a speaker talks *at* you rather than *to* you.

3. Use your arms and hands while speaking. If you just stand there stiffly, your voice may also turn flat. Avoid going overboard. You do not want your gestures to be unnatural, but you do want them to strengthen your words.

4. To make sure you are speaking loudly enough, start out by speaking directly to someone in the last row of your audience.

## Exercise 6

Choose a partner to work with throughout this exercise. Together choose a topic for a formal speech. Pick one from the list below, or use another of your choice.

- the history of the trombone (or of another instrument)
- the extinct mammoth
- sign language: the language of the deaf
- the northern lights
- what you should know about cars
- the joy of computers

After you have narrowed and researched the topic together, you should each write and practice your own speech. Your speech can either inform or persuade. When you are finished, deliver them to each other. Discuss how your speeches are alike and different. What are the strong points and weak points? Make suggestions to each other for improving your speeches.

# Index

*Dragon of the Lost Sea* (Yep), 163
Drama, writing topics in, 125, 205

Prompts. *See* On Assignment;
    Writer's Choice activities;
    Writing Process in Action
    lessons
Pronoun-antecedent agreement,
    124, 386
Pronouns
    antecedents for, 124, 386
    definition of, 324
    Grammar Workshop for,
        398–401
    indefinite, 392, 482
    intensive, 394
    interrogative, 396
    object, 384, 388, 432
    as objects of prepositions, 432
    personal, 154, 384
    possessive, 390
    reflexive, 394
    relative, 452, 556
    subject, 384, 388
    Troubleshooter for,
        310–311
    using, 325
Pronunciation, 611
Proofreading, 82. *See also*
    Editing; Revising;
    Troubleshooter
    statistics, 266
    symbols for, 82
Proper adjectives, 406
    capitalization of, 406, 518
Proper nouns, 340, 514
    capitalization of, 340,
        514, 518
Publicity, writing, 276–282
Publishing. *See* Presenting
Punctuation. *See also*
    *specific marks*
    Mechanics Workshop for,
        546–549
Purpose, determining, for
    writing, 56–59

## Q

Question mark, 328, 526
Questions
    for interview, 224
    open-ended, 652

Quotation
    capitalization of first words
        of, 512
    direct, 512, 532, 536
    indirect, 512
Quotation marks
    for dialogue, 161, 162
    with direct quotations, 536
    with divided quotations, 536
    with title of short works, 536
    with other marks of
        punctuation, 536

## R

*Raise, rise,* 494
Rand, Judy, 188–192
*Readers' Guide to Periodical
    Literature,* 577
Readers Respond, 35, 93, 135,
    183, 247, 295
Reading
    methods of, 617–618
    note taking while, 627
Reading comprehension on
    standardized tests, 641
Real-world writing. *See* Case
    Study feature
Reason, as type of evidence, 265
Rebus, 591
Reference works
    almanacs, 573–574
    atlases, 572–573
    dictionary, 579–580, 582–583
    encyclopedias, 571–572
    thesaurus, 580–581, 584
Reflecting, 39, 97, 139, 185,
    247, 295
Reflexive pronouns, 394, 452
Relative pronouns, 452, 556
Reports, oral, 659–661
Research reports
    conducting interviews for,
        222–225
    drafting, 215, 226–229
    editing, 231
    in expository writing,
        214–232
    getting information for,
        218–221

outline for, 227
    parts of, 228
    presenting, 233
    prewriting, 218–226
    revising, 219, 230–232
Revising. *See also* Editing;
    Proofreading
    checklist for, 38, 69, 70, 96,
        138, 184, 246, 294
    considering audience in, 223
    creating variety in sentences,
        76–79
    in descriptive writing, 107,
        128, 138
    evaluating draft in, 68–71
    in expository writing, 219,
        230–232, 246–247
    making paragraphs more
        effective, 72–75
    in narrative writing, 146,
        170, 184
    in oral reports, 660
    in personal writing, 38
    in persuasive writing, 262, 294
    in research reports, 219,
        230–232
    in speeches, 663
    in writing process, 46, 50,
        68–79, 96
Rhymes, as memory aid, 634
*Rise, raise,* 494
"Robert Frost: Visit to a Poet"
    (Paz), 386
Role playing, 21
*Roll of Thunder, Hear My Cry*
    (Taylor), 120
Rooney, Andy, 260
Roots, 592
"Running Shoe," in *How
    Things Work,* 194
Run-on sentence, Trouble-
    shooter for, 302–303

## S

Salutation
    capitalization of, 512
    colon after, in business
        letter, 534
Saroyan, William, 520

# Acknowledgments *(continued from page iv)*

## Text

**22** From *Never Cry Wolf* by Farley Mowat. Copyright © 1979 by Farley Mowat. Published by Bantam Books, a division of Bantam Doubleday Dell Publishing Group, Inc. **26** From *Jacob Have I Loved* by Katherine Paterson. Copyright © 1980 by Katherine Paterson. Published by HarperCollins Children's Books, a division of HarperCollins Publishers. **28** From *Little by Little: A Writer's Education* by Jean Little. Copyright © 1987 by Jean Little. Published by Viking Kestrel. **30** From *The Diary of Latoya Hunter.* Copyright © 1992 by Latoya Hunter. Reprinted by permission of Crown Publishers, Inc. **72** From *The Names* by N. Scott Momaday. Copyright © 1976 by N. Scott Momaday. Published by Harper & Row Publishers. **88** From *The Clay Marble* by Minfong Ho. Copyright © 1991 by Minfong Ho. Published by Farrar Straus Giroux. **102** From *Song of the Gargoyle* by Zilph Keatley Snyder. Copyright © 1991 by Zilpha Keatley Snyder. Used by permission of Delacorte Press, a Division of Bantam Doubleday Dell Publishing Group, Inc. **106** From *Journey Outside* by Mary Q. Steele. Copyright © 1969 by Mary Q. Steele. Published by Puffin Books, a division of Penguin Books, Ltd. **111** From *My Ántonia* by Willa Cather. Copyright 1918, © renewed 1946 by Willa Sibert Cather. Reprinted by permission of Houghton Mifflin Co. **114** From *Over Sea, Under Stone* by Susan Cooper. Copyright © 1965 by Susan Cooper. Published by Harcourt, Brace, & World, Inc. **118** From *Island of the Blue Dolphins* by Scott O'Dell. Copyright © 1960 by Scott O'Dell. Reprinted by arrangement with Houghton Mifflin Company. **120** From *Roll of Thunder, Hear My Cry* by Mildred D. Taylor. Copyright © 1976 by Mildred D. Taylor. Published by Penguin Books. **123** From *The Joy Luck Club* by Amy Tan. Copyright © 1989 by Amy Tan. Published by G.P. Putnam's Sons. **126** From *Neighborhood Odes: Poems by Gary Soto.* Copyright © 1992 by Gary Soto. Published by Harcourt Brace Jovanovich, Inc. **130** From *The Gathering* by Virginia Hamilton. Copyright © 1981 by Virginia Hamilton. By permission of Greenwillow Books, a division of William Morrow & Co., Inc. **145** From "User Friendly" by T. Ernesto Bethancourt from *Connections: Short Stories by Outstanding Writers for Young Adults.* Copyright © 1989 by T. Ernesto Bethancourt. Published by Lerner Publications Co. **149** From *A Wind in the Door* by Madeleine L'Engle. Copyright © 1973 by Crosswicks, Ltd. Published by Farrar, Strauss, Giroux, Inc. **154** From *The Glad Man* by Gloria Gonzalez. Copyright © 1975 by Gloria Gonzalez. Published by Alfred A. Knopf, Inc. **158** "A Pot of Beans" from *Fat Man in a Fur Coat and Other Bear Stories* collected and retold by Alvin Schwartz. Copyright © 1984 by Alvin Schwartz. Reprinted by permission of Farrar, Straus & Giroux, Inc. **161** From "Mr. Mendelsohn" from *El Bronx Remembered: A Novella and Stories* by Nicholasa Mohr. Copyright © 1975. Published by Harper & Row, Publishers, Inc. **161** Reprinted with permission of Margaret K. McElderry Books, an imprint of Macmillan Publishing Company from *A String in the Harp* by Nancy Bond. Copyright © 1976 by Nancy Bond. **162** From *The Sun, He Dies* by Jamake Highwater. Copyright © 1980 by Jamake Highwater. Published by Lippincott & Corwell, Publishers, a division of Harper & Row, Publishers. **164** From *Dragon of the Lost Sea* by Laurence Yep. Copyright © 1982 by Laurence Yep. Published by Harper & Row, Publishers. **168** From "Marooned Off Vesta" from *Asimov's Mysteries* by Isaac Asimov. Copyright © 1968 by Isaac Asimov. Published by Granada Publishing Limited. **172** From "A Leg Full of Rubies" from *Not What You Expected* by Joan Aiken. Copyright © 1974 by Joan Aiken. Reprinted by permission from Brandt & Brandt Literary Agents, Inc. **176** "A Huge Black Umbrella" by Marjorie Agosin from *Where Angels Glide at Dawn: New Stories from Latin America.* Copyright © 1990 by Lori Carlson and Cynthia Ventura. Published by J.B. Lippincott Junior Books. **194** From *How Things Work* by David Macaulay. Copyright © 1990. Reprinted courtesy of Publications International, Ltd. **196** From *Eyewitness Books:*

*Rocks & Minerals* written by Dr. R.F. Symes and the staff of the Natural History Museum, London. Copyright © 1988 Dorling Kindersley Limited, London. Reprinted by permission of Alfred A. Knopf. **200** From *The World Book Encyclopedia, 1988 Edition.* Copyright © 1987 by World Book, Inc. **204** From *Merrill Life Science* by Lucy Daniel, Edward Paul Ortleb, and Alton Biggs. Copyright © 1993. Published by the Glencoe Division of Macmillan/McGraw-Hill Publishing Company. **210** From *Newsweek,* January 8, 1990. Copyright © 1990 Newsweek, Inc. Reprinted by permission. **234** From *The Cyclist's Sourcebook* by Peter Nye. Copyright © 1991 by Robert R. McCord, Inc. Published by The Putnam Publishing Group. **236** From *The Chocolate War* by Robert Cormier. Copyright © 1974 by Robert Cormier. Published by Dell Publishing Company by arrangement with Random House, Inc. **237** Reprinted with the permission of Atheneum Publishers, an imprint of Macmillan Publishing Company from *The Runner* by Cynthia Voigt. Copyright © 1985 Cynthia Voigt. **238** From *Living Treasure* by Lawrence Pringle. Copyright © 1991 by Laurence Pringle. By permission of Morrow Junior Books, a division of William Morrow & Co., Inc. **256** From "Diviner than the Dolphin . . ." by Dolphin Project. Copyright © July/August, 1992 by The Earth Island Institute. Published by Sierra. **260** From "Cats Are for the Birds" from *Not That You Asked* by Andrew A. Rooney. Copyright © 1989 by Essay Productions, Inc. Published by Random House, Inc. **268** Courtesy *Glamour.* Copyright © 1987 by The Condé Nast Publications Inc. **286** By permission of the publisher, Salem Press, Inc. *Magill's Survey of Cinema.* Copyright © 1980 by Frank N. Magill. **288** "The Liberry" by Bel Kaufman from *Reading Rooms.* Copyright © 1991 by Susan Allen Toth and John Coughlan. Published by Doubleday. **352** From "Morning—'The Bird Perched For Flight'" from *Earth Shine* by Anne Morrow Lindbergh. Copyright ©1966, 1969 by Anne Morrow Lindbergh. Published by Harcourt, Brace, Jovanovich, Inc. **378** From "The Sound of Summer Running" from *Dandelion Wine* by Ray Bradbury. Copyright © 1956 by Ray Bradbury. Published by Don Congdon Associates, Inc. **398** From "Phaethon" from *Mythology* by Edith Hamilton. Copyright © 1942 by Edith Hamilton. Copyright © renewed 1969 by Dorian Fielding Reid and Doris Fielding Reid. Reprinted by permission of Little, Brown and Company. **442** From "The Magical Horse" by Laurence Yep from *Teacher's Read Aloud Anthology* by Margaret H. Lippert. Copyright © 1993, Published by Macmillan/McGraw-Hill School Publishing Company. **486** From "Robert Frost: Visit to a Poet" from *On Poets and Others* by Octavio Paz. Copyright © 1986 by Octavio Paz. Published by Seaver Books. **496** From *The Clay Marble* by Minfong Ho. Copyright © 1991 by Minfong Ho. Published by Farrar, Strauss, & Giroux. **581** From *Roget's II: The New Thesaurus.* Copyright © 1984. Published by Houghton Mifflin Company. **583** From *Dictionary.* Copyright © 1987. Published by Macmillan Publishing Company.

## Photos

**AL**=Allan Landau; **AW**=Art Wise; **BET**=The Bettmann Archive, UPI/Bettmann; **RJB**= Ralph J. Brunke

**Cover:** Courtesy of the estate of Gabriele Hunter. Photo by Sharon Hoogstraten **3** Courtesy of Simone Bouyer. **4** AL **5** AW **6** Lester Lefkowitz/Tony Stone Worldwide(t); AL(b). **7** AL **8** Courtesy Ella Jenkins(l); AL(r). **9** ©Tony Freeman/PhotoEdit. **10** RJB **11** RJB(t)(b). **12** RJB **13** George Brecht, "Repository" 1961, mixed media, 40 3/8 x 10 1/2 x 3 1/8", Collection, The Museum of Modern Art, New York. **14** RJB **15** RJB **16** RJB **18** ©David Woo/Stock, Boston(t); RJB(b). **19** RJB **20** RJB **22** Tom Walker/Stock, Boston. **23** RJB **25** © Gilson Ribeiro. **26** Selection reprinted by permission of HarperCollins Publishers. Photo by RJB **28** RJB **29** Bridgeman/Art Resource, NY. **31** RJB **33** Giraudon/Art Resource, NY. **35** AW(t)(b). **36** ©Bob Daemmrich/The Image Works. **39** © Richard Hutchings/PhotoEdit. **41** © C. T. Chew, Seattle WA Collection of

Dr. and Mrs. Martin Haykin. **42** © William Jordan. **44** AW
**45** AW(l); William Archie/Detroit Free Press(r). **46** ©Bill Aron/
PhotoEdit(t); AL(bl)(br). **47** AL. **48** AL. **52** AL. **55** Picnic in
Washington Park, Pat Thomas, Milwaukee, WI, Acrylic over oil on
masonite. Dated 1975. 20 1/2 x 27 1/2". Collection of the Museum
of American Folk Art, New York City; Gift of Rose Winters
1980.23.1. **58** AL(l)(r). **60** AL **61** AL **63** Giraudon/Art Resource,
NY © 1992 Succession H. Matisse/ARS, New York. **64** AL **65** AL
**66** AL **67** National Museum of American Art, Washington
D.C./Art Resource, NY. **68** AL **71** British Museum Egyptian Tomb
Paintings C. 1400 B.C., Ht. 63.5 cm, Thebes, Tomb of scribe, Neba-
mun. **72** AL. **76** AL. **77** AL. **79** Hirshhorn Museum and Sculpture
Garden, Smithsonian Institution, Gift of the Joseph H. Hirshhorn
Foundation, 1974. Photograph by Lee Stalsworth. **80** AL **84** AL
**85** AL **90** © The Phillips Collection, Washington D.C. **92** Courtesy
Bernice Steinbaum Gallery. **93** AW (t)(b). **94** ©Tony
Freeman/PhotoEdit. **97** ©Bob Daemmrich/Stock, Boston. **99** Franz
Marc, German. 1880–1916, The Bewitched Mill, oil on canvas,
1913, 130.2 x 91.1 cm, Arthur Jerome Eddy Memorial Collection,
1931.522 photograph ©1992, The Art Institute of Chicago. All
Rights Reserved. **100** Marvin Kuret. **102-3** RJB **104** RJB
**105** Giraudon/Art Resource, NY. **106** ©Charles Seaborn/Odyssey
Productions/Chicago. **108** RJB **109** "Shalako and Aholas" by Mike
Kabotie. Photographed by Neil Koppes in Clara Lee Tanner's
"Southwest Indian Painting: A Changing Art," University of
Arizona Press, ©1973. **110** "Fruit of the Spirit," Martin Charlot
©1983. **114** ©John Elk III/Stock, Boston. **116** Robert Brenner/
PhotoEdit(l); Debby Davis/PhotoEdit(r). **118** ©1988 Pete
Saloutos/Photographic Resources. **120** Gayna Hoffman/Stock,
Boston. **121** Courtesy of the Artist and Deson Saunders Gallery,
Chicago. **122** Laura Derichs. **123** Laura Derichs(t); Ralph
Brunke(b). **124** Laura Derichs(t); Ralph Brunke(b). **125** Lilla
Cabot Perry (American, 1848-1933), "The Old Cobbler" (Portrait
of Luther N. Smith), 1928, oil on canvas. The National Museum of
Women in the Arts. Gift of The Honorable and Mrs. Cecil B.
Lyon. **126** RJB **127** RJB **131** Scala/Art Resource, NY. **132** Peter
Blume. "Light of the World," 1932. oil on composition board.
18 x 20 ¼ inches. (45.7 cm x 51.4cm). Collection of the Whitney
Museum of American Art. Purchase 33.5. **135** AW (t)(b). **136** Amy
Etra/PhotoEdit. **139** ©Larry Kolvoord/The Image Works.
**141** ©1992 ARS, New York/ ADAGP, Paris. **142** Tom Tondee(l);
Laura Derichs(r). **143** Laura Derichs. **145** Laura Derichs. **146** Tom
Tondee. **147** RJB **148** Photofest. **152** Florence H. J. Ward. **155**
Walters Art Gallery, Baltimore. **159** Courtesy of The Drabinsky
Gallery, Toronto. **160** From Alice's Adventures in Wonderland by
Lewis Carroll, illustration, S. Michelle Wiggins. Copyright © 1983
by Armand Eisen. Reprinted by permission of Alfred A. Knopf,
Inc. **164** Calvin and Hobbes © 1986 Watterson. Reprinted with
permission of Universal Press Syndicate. All rights reserved.
**168** NASA. **171** Boston Athenaeum. **172** RJB **173** Nathaniel Bruns.
**175** Asian Art Museum of San Francisco. The Avery Brundage
Collection. Accession B60 P2349. Photo copyright © 1992.
**179** Bridgeman/Art Resource, NY. **180** Art Resource, NY.
**181** AW (t)(b). **182** ©Tony Freeman/PhotoEdit. **185** ©Robert
Brenner/PhotoEdit. **187** Private Collection, Courtesy of the Curt
Marcus Gallery. © Mark Tansey, 1984. Photo Credit Bill Orcutt,
New York. **188** Courtesy Monterey Bay Aquarium. **189** AW.
**190** RJB. **191** © Charles Seaborn/Odyssey Productions/Chicago (t);
RJB (b). **192** ©Lawrence Migdale/Stock, Boston(l); AW(r). **193**
©Paul Conklin/PhotoEdit. **197** Courtesy of Carmen Lomas Garza.
**202** © Carl Roessler/Animals Animals (l); © Richard Kolar/Ani-
mals Animals(r). **205** Lilla Cabot Perry (1848–1933) The Visit, 1899
oil on canvas, 25 ⅜ x 31 ⅝in. Terra Foundation for the Arts. Daniel
J. Terra Collection, 1992.55. **206** Courtesy the Estate of Rube
Goldberg. **210** © 1990 Maresa Pryor/Earth Scenes. **213** Waldo
Pierce, Fire at East Orrington, Oil, 1940, Museum Purchase, 1950
William A. Farnsworth Library and Art Museum. **214** AL **216** AL
**217** Maxine Albro (1903–1966), California Agriculture, Fresco, left

panel, 10 x 21 feet Coit Tower, San Francisco, PWAP (Public
Works of Art Project), Photograph by Don Beatty ©1981. **220** AL
**222** Bob Daemmrich/Stock, Boston. **224** AL **226** AL **230** RJB **233**
Amidée T. Thibault, S. Albans, Vermont Wood, Columbia Bicycle,
1895, 84" x 66" x 36" deep. Collection of the Museum of American
Folk Art; New York City. Gift of David L. Davies, 1983.24.1. **235**
BET(l); Focus on Sports(r). **239** Courtesy of Patricia Gonzalez. **241**
Courtesy of Kathryn Stewart. **243** AW (t)(b). **244** ©Robert Bren-
ner/PhotoEdit. **247** ©Lawrence Migdale/Stock, Boston. **249** Cour-
tesy Kraushaar Galleries, NY. **250** Christine Armstrong. ©Review
& Herald. **251** AW. **252** Ralph Brunke(t); William DeKay/Detroit
Free Press(c). **253** RJB **254** RJB **255** AW **256** ©James D.
Watt/Animals Animals. **263** Scala/Art Resource, NY. **264** AL **267**
Courtesy John Weber Gallery. **268** AL **272** AL(l); AL(r). **279** Cir-
cus Parade, Kathy Jakobsen, New York, NY, oil on canvas, 1979,
24" x 36", Collection of the Museum of American Folk Art, New
York City; Gift of Robert Bishop 1979.11.1. **284** AL **291** AW
(t)(b). **292** ©Robert E. Daemmrich/Tony Stone Worldwide. **295**
©Richard Blake/Tony Stone Worldwide. **299** Courtesy of Kay
O'Rourke. **328** ©Mark Burnett/Stock, Boston(l); ©Greenlar/The
Image Works(lc); ©John Cancalosi/Natural Selection(rc); ©Neal
Mishler/Natural Selection(r). **337** © American Museum of Natural
History # 4587 (2). Photo by Lynton Gardiner. **339** Courtesy of
Holly Solomon Gallery, New York. **348** ©Bob Daemmrich. **355**
Courtesy of Robert McCall. **357** Howard Hodgkin, London. **358**
RJB **381** Courtesy R. H. Love Gallery. **383** ©Scala/Art Resource,
NY. **401** © Michael Holford. **403** Joseph Stella. The Brooklyn
Bridge: Variation on an Old Theme, 1939, oil on canvas. 70 x 42 in.
(177.8 cm x 106.7 cm). Collection of the Whitney Museum of
American Art, New York. Purchase 42.15. **416** Malcolm S.
Kirk/Peter Arnold, Inc. **427** © 1992 Charles Simonds, ARS, New
York. **429** Royal Collection, St. James' Palace. © H.M. Queen Eliz-
abeth II. **438** Robert Frerck/Tony Stone Worldwide. **440** SEF/Art
Resource. **445** © 1986, Helen Oji. Collection of Doris and Jack
Weintraub, New York, NY. **447** Fernand Léger, French,
1881–1955, Sketch for the Railway Crossing, oil on canvas, 1919,
64.8 x 72.4 cm, Joseph Winterbotham Collection, gift of Mrs.
Patrick Hill in memory of Rue Winterbotham Carpenter, 1953.341.
©1991 The Art Institute of Chicago, All Rights Reserved. **454**
Focus on Sports. **461** Courtesy Phyliss Kind Gallery, Chicago. **463**
Courtesy Robert Berman Gallery. **473** Courtesy Brooke
Alexander Gallery. **475** Herscovici/Art Resource, NY © 1992 C.
Herscovici/ARS, New York. **480** ©Bob Daemmrich(t); ©Tony
Freeman/PhotoEdit(b). **489** Giraudon/Art Resource, NY. **491**
Giraudon/Art Resource, NY. **499** Scala/Art Resource, NY. **501**
Giraudon/Art Resource, NY. **511** The Metropolitan Museum of
Art, Morris K. Jesup Fund, 1933.33.61. **516** ©Tony Freeman/Pho-
toEdit. **523** Courtesy Elaine Horwitch Galleries, Scottsdale, Ari-
zona. **526** Tony Freeman/PhotoEdit. **545** NASA. **549** Phyliss Kind
Gallery, New York and Chicago. **550** Claude Monet, French,
1840–1926, Saint-Lazare Train Station, the Normandy Train (La
Gare Saint-Lazare, le train de Normandie), oil on canvas, 1877,
59.6 x 80.2 cm, Mr. and Mrs. Martin A. Ryerson Collection,
1933.1158. **551** Henri Matisse, "Beasts of the Sea," Ailsa Mellon
Bruce Fund, ©1992 National Gallery of Art, Washington 1950, col-
lage, 2.955 x 1.540 (116 ⅜ x 60 ⅝). **563** Bill Bachman/Photographic
Resources. **564** Bob Daemmrich Photography. **569** AL **572** From
The World Book Encyclopedia. © 1992 World Book, Inc. By per-
mission of World Book, Inc. **573** AL, Atlas of the Living
World by David Attenborough. ©1989 by Marshall Editions Ltd.
Reprinted by permission of Houghton Mifflin Co. All rights
reserved. **574** RJB **578** AL **579** RJB **580** Courtesy of
Macmillan Publishing. **585** Giraudon/Art Resource, NY, With
Special Authorization of the City of Bayeux. **586** Art Resource,
NY. **597** ©Tony Stone Worldwide. **599** Tony Griff. **601** ©Willie L.
Hill, Jr./The Image Works(l); ©Thomas R. Fletcher/Stock,
Boston(r). **615** RJB **616** RJB **621** RJB **623** RJB **635** RJB **647**
RJB(l)(c)(r). **651** RJB